Lucie Podszun

Does Development Aid Affect Conflict Ripeness?

VS RESEARCH

Lucie Podszun

Does Development Aid Affect Conflict Ripeness?

The Theory of Ripeness and
Its Applicability in the Context
of Development Aid

VS RESEARCH

Bibliographic information published by the Deutsche Nationalbibliothek
The Deutsche Nationalbibliothek lists this publication in the Deutsche Nationalbibliografie;
detailed bibliographic data are available in the Internet at http://dnb.d-nb.de.

Dissertation Frankfurt University, 2011

D.30

1st Edition 2011

All rights reserved
© VS Verlag für Sozialwissenschaften | Springer Fachmedien Wiesbaden GmbH 2011

Editorial Office: Dorothee Koch | Anita Wilke

VS Verlag für Sozialwissenschaften is a brand of Springer Fachmedien.
Springer Fachmedien is part of Springer Science+Business Media.
www.vs-verlag.de

No part of this publication may be reproduced, stored in a retrieval system
or transmitted, in any form or by any means, electronic, mechanical, photo-
copying, recording, or otherwise, without the prior written permission of the
copyright holder.

Registered and/or industrial names, trade names, trade descriptions etc. cited in this publication
are part of the law for trade-mark protection and may not be used free in any form or by any
means even if this is not specifically marked.

Cover design: KünkelLopka Medienentwicklung, Heidelberg
Printed on acid-free paper
Printed in Germany

ISBN 978-3-531-18378-7

Meinen Eltern für ihre unendliche Liebe und Unterstützung

Acknowledgements

The work at hand was accepted as doctoral thesis by the Johann Wolfgang Goethe-Universität zu Frankfurt am Main in spring 2011. I am very grateful to my Doktorvater Professor Dr. Gunther Hellmann for his support and his detailed and open feedback, which was both helpful and inspiring at all times.

The entire project would not have been possible if not for the guidance by Professor I. William Zartman. He not only taught me the skills and knowledge needed, but also instilled in me the thirst for more academic research in the field of conflict management while I was his student in Washington D.C. He further encouraged me to face my research question and became my second supervisor and advisor throughout the last years. Thank you for your support.

I am indebted to Professor Alan J. Kuperman for opening my mind for conflict management.

My special thanks goes to my employer, Booz & Company, for enabling me to dedicate my time to this research project. Especially my formal and informal mentors, Dr. Klaus-Peter Gushurst, Dr. Wolfgang Zink, Dr. Rainer Bernnat, Marcus Bauer and Dr. Joachim Deinlein, supported me and welcomed me back into the working life after having finished the research. Thank you!

I would like to thank my friends for their individual support; especially Carrie Walter, Lisa Overbey, Katharina Ferl, Sean McBroom, Patrick Rohrmeier, Dr. Till Stenzel and Dr. Michael Wagner for challenging my work and dragging me out of my ivory tower when needed.

Finally and most importantly, I would like to thank my family and my partner, Jan Bakker, for their love and support.

Lucie Podszun

Table of Contents

Acknowledgements 7
Table of Contents 9
List of Figures 13
List of Tables 15
Acronyms 17

1 Introduction 21
   1.1 Research Objective 24
   1.2 Approach and Methodology 28
   1.3 Structural Overview 32

2 Development Aid and Ripeness in Context 35
   2.1 Socio Economic and Political Relevance 35
      2.1.1 Prevalence of Conflict in Developing Countries 36
      2.1.2 Effects of Conflict on Developing Countries 37
      2.1.3 The Need to Focus on Conflict Resolution Methods 39
   2.2 Aid and Conflict in the Academic Literature 40
      2.2.1 Overall Academic Relevance 40
      2.2.2 Academic Exigency of the Research – State of the Art 42
          2.2.2.1 General Contextualization in the Field of Conflict Management 43
          2.2.2.2 The Art of Conflict Resolution 48
          2.2.2.3 The Timing of Peace Efforts 51
          2.2.2.4 The Effect and Role of Development Aid in Conflicts 57
          2.2.2.5 The Intersection of Aid and Conflict Resolution Efforts 64
   2.3 Terminology and Definitions 65
      2.3.1 Conflict 65
          2.3.1.1 Type of Conflict 67
          2.3.1.2 Belligerents to Civil War 68
          2.3.1.3 Conflict Life-Cycle 69
          2.3.1.4 Mediation 71
          2.3.1.5 Third Party/Mediator 71
          2.3.1.6 Peace 72
      2.3.2 Development Aid 73
          2.3.2.1 Donors 74
          2.3.2.2 Increase in Development Aid 75
          2.3.2.3 Neutrality and Impartiality 77
          2.3.2.4 Unintentional Consequences 79

3 The Theory of Ripeness ... 81
3.1 Outline of the Theory of Ripeness ... 81
3.1.1 First Level Variables ... 83
3.1.1.1 Mutually Hurting Stalemate ... 83
3.1.1.2 Sense of a Way Out ... 85
3.1.2 Second Level Variables ... 86
3.1.2.1 Objective Elements ... 86
3.1.2.2 Persuasion ... 87
3.1.3 Mutually Enticing Opportunities ... 88
3.1.4 Ripeness ... 89
3.2 Wrong Timing ... 93
3.3 Academic Challenges to the Theory of Ripeness ... 94
3.3.1 Third Party Involvement ... 95
3.3.2 Four Essentials for Ripeness ... 96
3.3.3 Dependence on High Levels of Violence ... 98
3.4 The Theory of Ripeness Revisited ... 99
3.4.1 Independent Variables ... 99
3.4.1.1 Manipulable Variables ... 100
3.4.1.2 Non-Manipulable Variables ... 101
3.4.1.3 Summary ... 105
3.4.2 The Extended Theory of Ripeness ... 106
3.5 Hypotheses ... 107

4 Approach to the Case Studies ... 109
4.1 Objective, Design and Structure of the Case Studies ... 109
4.2 Variables to be Analyzed ... 111
4.2.1 Definition of Dependent Variable ... 112
4.2.2 Definition of Independent Variables ... 113
4.3 Case-Guiding Research Questions ... 115
4.4 Choice of Cases ... 116
4.4.1 Criteria for Relevance ... 116
4.4.2 Universe of Cases ... 118
4.4.3 Final Choice of Cases ... 124

5 Evidence from the Case Studies ... 129
5.1 Uganda ... 129
5.1.1 Background ... 130
5.1.1.1 History and Causes ... 132
5.1.1.2 Key Actors ... 138
5.1.2 Uganda Analysis ... 145
5.1.2.1 Conflict Ripeness ... 146

		5.1.2.2	Increase in Development Aid.. 164
		5.1.2.3	Effect of Increase in Development Aid on Ripeness 171
		5.1.2.4	Conclusion 179
	5.2	Burundi 181
		5.2.1 Background 182
		5.2.1.1	History and Causes 185
		5.2.1.2	Key Actors 191
		5.2.2 Burundi Analysis 197
		5.2.2.1	Conflict Ripeness 199
		5.2.2.2	Increase in Development Aid.. 216
		5.2.2.3	Effect of Increase in Development Aid on Ripeness 222
		5.2.2.4	Conclusion 228
	5.3	Cambodia.. 230
		5.3.1 Background 231
		5.3.1.1	History and Causes 232
		5.3.1.2	Key Actors 238
		5.3.2 Cambodia Analysis 240
		5.3.2.1	Conflict Ripeness 241
		5.3.2.2	Increase in Development Aid.. 259
		5.3.2.3	Effect of Increase in Development Aid on Ripeness 266
		5.3.2.4	Conclusion 279
	5.4	Synthesis of Findings... 281
		5.4.1 Comparative Findings 281
		5.4.1.1	Background to the Cases... 281
		5.4.1.2	Conflict Ripeness 283
		5.4.1.3	Increase in Development Aid.. 294
		5.4.1.4	Effect of Increase in Development Aid on Ripeness 298
		5.4.2 Contingent Generalizations.. 303
6	**Implications for the Theory of Ripeness** 305
	6.1	Comparison of Findings with Hypotheses 305
	6.2	Expansion of the Theoretical Model... 306
7	**Conclusions** 309
	7.1	Summary of Findings 309
	7.2	Lessons Learned and Implications for Policy-Making 311
	7.3	Critical Look at the Theory: Unresolved Issues/Valid Objections 314
Bibliography 319

List of Figures

Figure 1: World Map of Conflicts in 2008 37
Figure 2: Research Areas in Conflict Management 44
Figure 3: Economic Growth and its Impact on Conflict 57
Figure 4: Do No Harm Approach 61
Figure 5: Life-Cycle of Conflict 69
Figure 6: Theory of Ripeness 90
Figure 7: Function of Ripeness 92
Figure 8: Essentials of Ripeness according to Richard N. Haass 97
Figure 9: The Expanded Theory of Ripeness 107
Figure 10: Geographical Distribution of Potential Cases 127
Figure 11: Map of Uganda 131
Figure 12: Total ODA to Uganda, Net Disbursements in millions of US$ 166
Figure 13: %-Change in ODA in Uganda to Previous Year 173
Figure 14: Increase in Development Aid and Peace Initiatives in Uganda 174
Figure 15: Map of Burundi 184
Figure 16: Total ODA to Burundi, Net Disbursements in millions of US$ 217
Figure 17: Total ODA to Burundi in millions of US$ by Donor 218
Figure 18: %-Change in ODA in Burundi to Previous Year 219
Figure 19: Map of Cambodia 232
Figure 20: Total ODA to Cambodia in millions of US$ 264
Figure 21: Total ODA to Cambodia, Net Disbursements in millions of US$ ... 265
Figure 22: Expanded Theory of Ripeness with Normative Implications 308

List of Tables

Table 1: Types of IDA 77
Table 2: Overview of Independent Variables 105
Table 3: Overview of Variables to be Analyzed 114
Table 4: Case-Guiding Research Questions 115
Table 5: Universe of Cases 124
Table 6: Choice of Cases and Mediators 128
Table 7: Overview Phases of Conflict in Uganda 146
Table 8: Independent Variables Affecting Conflict Ripeness in Uganda 164
Table 9: Total ODA to Uganda, Net Disbursements in millions of US$ 166
Table 10: Case-Guiding Research Questions Uganda 181
Table 11: Overview Presidents of Burundi 1993-2006 194
Table 12: Overview Peace Initiatives in Burundi 199
Table 13: Overview Conflict Ripeness and IDA in Burundi 223
Table 14: Funds Requested by Consolidated Appeal in millions of US$ 225
Table 15: Case-Guiding Research Questions Burundi 229
Table 16: Independent Variables Affecting Ripeness in Cambodia 259
Table 17: Case-Guiding Research Questions Cambodia 279
Table 18: Case Studies and Phases Analyzed 284
Table 19: Comparison Mutually Hurting Stalemate 287
Table 20: Comparison Sense of a Way Out 290
Table 21: Summary: Effect of Independent Variables 292
Table 22: Summary Conflict Ripeness 294
Table 23: Summary Increase in Development Aid 298
Table 24: Summary Effect of IDA on Conflict Ripeness 301

Acronyms

ACF	Action Contre la Faim
AfDB	African Development Bank
AFRC	Armed Forces Revolutionary Council
AKUF	Arbeitsgemeinschaft Kriegsursachenforschung
ALF	Afar Liberation Front
AMIB	African Mission in Burundi
ANADDE	Alliance pour le Droit et le Développement Economique
ARDUF	Afar Revolutionary Democratic Unity Front
ASEAN	Association of Southeast Asian Nations
AU STF	African Union Special Task Force
AVSI	Associazione Volontari per il Servizio Internazionale
BINUB	United Nations Integrated Office in Burundi
BLDP	Buddhist Liberal Democratic Party
BMZ	Bundesministerium für wirtschaftliche Zusammenarbeit und Entwicklung
CGDK	Coalition Government of Democratic Kampuchea
CIA	Central Intelligence Agency
CNDD-FDD	Conseil national pour la defences de la democratie-Force pour la defense de la democratie
CNN	Cable News Network
COOPI	Cooperazione Internazionale
Cosimo	Conflict Simulation Model
COW	Correlates of War Project
CPA	Comprehensive Peace Agreement
CPN-M	Communist Party of Nepal-Maoist
CPP	Cambodian People's Party
CSMU	Military Committee for National Salvation
CSOPNU	Civil Society Organizations for Peace in Northern Uganda
DAC	Development Assistance Committee
DNS	Decision to Negotiate Sincerely
DRC	Democratic Republic of the Congo
EC	European Commission
ECOWAS	Economic Community of West African States
EU	European Union
FIS	Islamic Salvation Front
FMLN	Frente Farabundo Martí para la Liberación Nacional
FNL	Forces Nationales de Libération
FRODEBU	Front pour la démocratie au Burundi

FROLINAT	Front de Libération Nationale du Tchad
FUNCINPEC	Front Uni National pour un Cambodge Indépendant, Neutre, Pacifique, et Coopératif
GDI	German Development Institute
GDP	Gross Domestic Product
GNI	Gross National Income
GoSS	Government of South Sudan
GoU	Government of Uganda
HIIK	Heidelberger Institut für Internationale Konfliktforschung
HIPC	Highly Indebted Poor Countries
HSM	Holy Spirit Movement
ICC	International Criminal Court
ICG	International Crisis Group
ICRC	International Committee of the Red Cross
IDA	Increase in Development Aid
IDP	Internally Displaced Person
IGAD	Intergovernmental Authority on Development
IMF	International Monetary Fund
INPFL	Independent National Patriotic Front of Liberia
JIF	Juba Initiative Fund
JIM	Jakarta Informal Meetings
KM	Kacoke Madit
KPNLF	Khmer People's National Liberation Front
KPRP	Kampuchean People's Revolutionary Party
LRA/M	Lord's Resistance Army/Movement
LTTE	Liberation Tigers of Tamil Eelam
MEOs	Mutually Enticing Opportunities
MFDC	Mouvement des forces démocratiques de la Casamance
MHS	Mutually Hurting Stalemate
MILF	Moro Islamic Liberation Front
MNLF	Moro National Liberation Front
MSF	Médecins sans Frontières
NGO	Non-governmental organization
NPA	New People's Army
NPFL	National Patriotic Front of Liberia
NRA/M	National Resistance Army/Movement
NRC	Norwegian Refugee Council
OAU	Organisation of African Unity
ODA	Official Development Assistance
OECD	Organisation for Economic Co-operation and Development

ONUB	United Nations Operation in Burundi
OPM	Office of the Prime Minister
OSCE	Organization for Security and Co-operation in Europe
PALIPEHUTU	Parti pour la Libération du Peuple Hutu
PARENA	Parti pour le Redressement National
PCIA	Peace and Conflict Impact Assessment
PDK	Party of Democratic Kampuchea
PEAP	Poverty Eradication Action Plan
Perm Five	Permanent Five Members of the UN Security Council
PIP	Internal Partnership for Peace
PL	Parti Libéral
PP	Parti du Peuple
PRA	Popular Resistance Army
PRDP	Peace, Recovery and Development Plan for Northern Uganda
PRP	Parti pour la Réconciliation du Peuple
RENAMO	Resistência Nacional Moçambicana
RPB	Rassemblement pour le peuple du Burundi
RUF	Revolutionary United Front
SAPSD	South African Protection Service Detachment
SCIU	Save the Children in Uganda
SfCG	Search for Common Ground
SIPRI	Stockholm International Peace Research Institute
SNC	Supreme National Council
SPLA/M	Sudan People's Liberation Army/Movement
SWANU	South West Africa National Union
SWAPO	South West Africa People's Organization
SWATF	South West African Territorial Force
SWO	Sense of a Way Out
UCDP/PRIO	Uppsala Conflict Data Program/International Peace Research Institute
UK	United Kingdom
UN	United Nations
UN OCHA	United Nations Office for the Coordination of Humanitarian Affairs
UNAMIC	United Nations Advance Mission in Cambodia
UNDP	United Nations Development Program
UNHCR	United Nations High Commissioner for Refugees
UNITA	União Nacional para a Independência Total de Angola
UNOB	United Nations Office in Burundi
UNTAC	United Nations Transitional Authority in Cambodia

UPDA	Uganda People's Defense Army
UPDF	Uganda People's Defense Forces
UPRONA	Unité pour le Progrès National
URNG	Unidad Revolucionaria Nacional Guatemalteca
US	United States of America
USAID	United States Agency for International Development
USIP	United States Institute of Peace
USSR	Union of Soviet Socialist Republics
UTO	United Tajik Opposition
VENRO	Verband Entwicklungspolitik deutscher Nichtregierungsorganisationen
WDI	World Development Indicators
WHO	World Health Organization
ZANU	Zimbabwe African National Union
ZAPU	Zimbabwe African Peoples Union

1 Introduction

The analysis at hand is concerned with the improvement of strategies for the resolution of intra-state militarized conflicts by focusing on the effect of development aid.

In the political sciences, we observe a trend away from international wars to intra-state conflicts. In 2008, the UCDP/PRIO Armed Conflict Dataset accounted for 36 main conflicts throughout the world (cf. Gleditsch 2008a)[1]. Main conflict is defined in this context as "an incompatibility that concerns contested government and/or territory where the use of armed force between two parties, of which at least one is the government of a state, results in at least 25 battle-related deaths" (Gleditsch 2008b, p.1). Five of the 36 conflicts had a high intensity level, meaning that there were more than 1,000 battle-related deaths accounted for. Only one of the 36 conflicts was international while all others were either purely intra-state (30 conflicts) or internationalized (5 conflicts), which means that one or more of the domestic parties to the conflict received support by another state as a secondary party to the conflict[2].

Most of the observed conflicts take place in countries that can be called developing countries. A recent study observed that 90% of all wars and violent conflicts are located in developing countries (Klingebiel 2008, p.17), which

---

[1] Depending on the source, the number of conflicts differs slightly. For instance, the HIIK observed 39 conflicts in 2008 (cf. Heidelberger Institut für Internationale Konfliktforschung (2008): Conflict Barometer 2008: Crises - Wars - Coups d'État - Negotiations - Mediations - Peace Settlements, p.2).

[2] The trend away from international wars and to more intra-state conflicts has been outlined in many works; as for instance by Collier and Hoeffler (cf. Collier and Hoeffler (2004b): "Greed and Grievance in Civil War", *Oxford Economic Papers (U.K.)*, p.2); Alexis Heraclides (cf. Heraclides (1997): "The Ending of Unending Conflicts: Separatist Wars", *Millennium - Journal of International Studies*, p.679); the HIIK (cf. Heidelberger Institut für Internationale Konfliktforschung Conflict Barometer 2008: Crises - Wars - Coups d'État - Negotiations - Mediations - Peace Settlements, p.2); John Mueller (cf. Mueller (2004): The Remnants of War); SIPRI (cf. Stockholm International Peace Research Institute (2009): Armaments, Disarmament and International Security: SIPRI Yearbook 2009); or VENRO (cf. VENRO (2003): "Armutsbekämpfung und Krisenprävention: Wie lässt sich Armutsbekämpfung konfliktsensitiv gestalten?", *Verband Entwicklungspolitik Deutscher Nichtregierungsorganisationen e.V.*, p.10).

suggests that most countries at war have been or are receiving development aid. Taking into account that the average intra-state conflict lasts about seven years (cf. Collier, P. 2003, p.3 and Collier, P./Hoeffler 2004a, p.14) and thus can be defined as 'protracted' (cf. Carment, Samy and El Achkar in Bercovitch/Gartner 2009, p.217), we see a devastating picture for the developing world being trapped in a vicious circle of violent conflict and underdevelopment[3]. As Betty Bigombe, then consultant in the World Bank's Social Protection, Human Development and Post Conflict Units, put it in 2000 referring to the increase of conflict areas in developing countries: "As in any good business portfolio analysis, the World Bank must face the fact that a growing number of its clients live in countries affected by conflicts" (Bigombe in Wulf/Esser 2000, p.41).

As early as in 1980, Eckhard Hinzen and Robert Kappel edited a book called "Dependence, Underdevelopment and Persistent Conflict", in which they analyzed these three notions in the context of the political economy of Liberia (cf. Hinzen/Kappel 1980). This put scholarly inquiry into the connection between underdevelopment and conflict. The topic was taken up frequently in the subsequent decades. The much-cited notion that, "war results in poverty, poverty results in war" (VENRO 2003, p.8), describes the mutual effects the two notions of underdevelopment and war have on each other. Whether there is a direct causal relationship and if so in which direction it runs is highly debated (cf. Klingebiel 2008, p.17; Musto in Fahrenhorst 1999, pp.21-31; Tschirgi in Klingebiel 2006, p.42). What is apparent from empirical evidence is that most violent conflicts are fought in developing countries; or in many developing countries, civil war occurs as stated above (cf. Daase in Hellmann/Wolf, et al. 2003, p.176). Thus the two notions of poverty and conflict seem to be correlated or even directly causally connected (cf. Klingebiel 2008, pp.1-2).

Academia has begun to look more and more into the topic of intra-state conflict. With a rising number of academic institutes, schools and departments of universities dedicated to this topic[4], a substantial amount of academic writing has been produced lately examining different facets of conflict (cf. Gugel 2006, p.38, Muscat 2002, p.17). A solid account of the development in this field can be

---

[3] This is what Paul Collier calls a "conflict trap" (cf. Collier (2003): Breaking the Conflict Trap: Civil War and Development Policy, p.53).

[4] Throughout the last decades, many institutions have been established that focus on the topic of conflict management, some of which are for instance the Conflict Management Department at the School of Advanced International Studies/Johns Hopkins University; the Berghof Research Center for Constructive Conflict Management; the Peace Research Institute Frankfurt; the Austrian Study Center for Peace and Conflict Resolution; the Center for International Conflict Resolution at Columbia University; the International Crisis Group, among others.

found in Louis Kriesberg's chapter in "Turbulent Peace" (cf. Kriesberg in Crocker/Hampson, et al. 2001, pp. 407-426). Many authors have written about the sources of intra-state conflict (cf. for instance Arnson/Zartman 2005, Fearon/Laitin 2003b, Menck 2005, and entire sections in Bercovitch/Kremenyuk, et al. 2009 and Crocker/Hampson, et al. 2001, among others), the possibilities for the prevention of conflict (cf. for instance Brown, M.E./Rosecrance 1999, Davies/Gurr 1998, Hamburg 2002, Leatherman 1999, Lund 1996, and Carment/Schnabel 2004, among others) or the post-conflict consequences for a country and approaches to deal with them (cf. for instance Fukuyama 2004, Hampson 1996, Lederach 1997, Ottaway 2003, and an entire section in Crocker/Hampson, et al. 2001, among others).

"As such, conflict is normal, ubiquitous, and unavoidable. It is an inherent feature of human existence. It is even useful on occasion" (Bercovitch/Kremenyuk, et al. 2009, p.3). While conflict has to be accepted as a normal feature or even what has been called a "norm" in international affairs (cf. Haass 1992, p.1), the escalation of conflict into severe violence is not (cf. Haass 1992, p.1; Michael S. Lund in Hampson/Malone 2002, pp.159-184; Dean G. Pruitt in Zartman/Faure, et al. 2005, p.251).

The questions of how to stop violence and how to resolve a conflict have also been analyzed. Generally, there are three ways to approach such violence from an academic conflict management perspective: preventing violence altogether, finding ways to react after violence has occurred in order to prevent violence from re-occurring, and finally trying to identify ways to end violence through intervening into the ongoing conflict from outside. Here, the focus shall lie on the latter: conflict resolution strategies.

One such contribution was made by I. William Zartman outlining the Theory of Ripeness, which is concerned with the correct timing for the initiation of peace efforts (cf. Zartman in Stern/Druckman 2000). The theory states that a conflict has to be 'ripe' in order to have potential to be successfully resolved – other than through surrender and victory of the respective parties. It is argued that if conflict ripeness is not present at the initiation of peace talks, then the decision to negotiate sincerely was not taken honestly. In such a case, the initiation of peace talks might have a negative effect on the conflict in that the conflict is prolonged. It is feared that in these circumstances, parties only enter into negotiations for "short-term tactical advantage" (Stedman 1991, p.14). In order to avoid such dishonest intentions, it is thus crucial to establish ripeness for the potential resolution of conflicts. As Zartman put it, "if it is to succeed, a mediation initiative cannot be launched at just any time; the conflict must be ripe for the initiation of negotiation. Parties resolve their conflict only when they have to do so – when each party's efforts to achieve a unilaterally satisfactory result are blocked and the parties feel trapped in an uncomfortable and costly predicament" (Zartman/DeSoto 2010, p.5).

This analysis' focus lies on the effect of development aid on the resolution of conflicts, with the aim of critically testing a received wisdom about the impact of aid on poor and violent regions given at the time of attempted conflict resolution. Robert J. Muscat stated, "the presumption that economic development produces peace [...] has become a journalistic commonplace" (Muscat 2002, p.104). Economic development through development aid is often seen as a core principle to foster peace in developing countries. The question asked is whether this notion is always true: is development aid peace-enhancing in all circumstances?

1.1 Research Objective

Two areas of research will be linked and analyzed: conflict resolution strategies with a particular focus on the ripeness of the conflict to be resolved as well as the effect of development aid on ripeness. The research objective therefore is to find out whether development aid affects conflict ripeness and if so, with what quality.

From an academic perspective, a variety of different approaches exists, trying to improve international efforts by developing conflict resolution strategies. Debates concerning the best mediator, the most effective methods in mediation, the most applicable instruments to use and many other variables, approaches and methods are widely discussed in academia. Here, the focus lies on one specific challenge: the right timing for the initiation of peace efforts. The motivation to analyze this specific issue in-depth lies within a wider context: an escalated conflict does not only harm the people directly involved but also sets off a chain of extreme consequences for a much larger group: the whole country, the region, the continent and the entire world, given the status of globalization in our contemporary society. These consequences are magnified due to the fact that civil wars tend to protraction. Paul Collier outlines in his book "Breaking the Conflict Trap" that there are different components to why there is such a high global incidence of conflict; one of which he describes as, "if the typical conflict could be shortened, then the global incidence of conflict would decrease significantly" (Collier, P. 2003, p.7). It means that if it was possible to terminate conflicts, we could contribute significantly to a reduction of civil wars in the world. "Conflict management typically results in one of two outcomes: an agreement or continued fighting" (Scott Sigmund Gartner and Molly M. Melin in

Bercovitch/Kremenyuk, et al. 2009, p.564). So how can we ameliorate strategies that help reaching an agreement?

It leads to the question, why there are not more conflict management practitioners[5] in place or why, if there are any, they do not seem to work effectively – in any case: why aren't there more peace agreements instead of the prevalence of continued fighting? Richard Haass has found his answer: "The answers to these and similar questions lie in a single word: ripeness. The notion of ripeness is central to international affairs" (Haass 1992, p.6). Ripeness has to be seen as a twofold instrument. On the one hand, it serves as an analytic tool "to explain why agreements can be reached in certain situations", and on the other hand, it serves as a prescriptive tool "to help busy policymakers to identify disputes amenable to negotiation" (Haass 1992, p.7).

The quote expresses that academia and practice have to work together in order to achieve progress. Both fields should learn from each other and inform each other. The analysis attempts to provide practitioners in the field with more detailed information on how to handle internal militarized conflicts, answering Alexander L. George's request to "bridge the gap" between scholarship and practice in the field of conflict resolution (cf. George 1993, p.265).

The other point of focus in this analysis lies within the field of development studies. As was described above, most conflicts take place in developing countries. It is possible to identify a 'vicious circle' between under-development and conflict.

As a consequence, one important and significant influx of resources into developing countries is development aid. Aid comes in a variety of forms – monetary and non-monetary – as well as from a variety of donors – states, multilateral institutions, non-governmental and governmental organizations, private individuals and enterprises, among others. The architecture of aid is highly complex and has even been described as "over complex" (Burall/Maxwell, et al. 2006, p.3; Faust/Messner 2007, p.7; Muscat 2002, p.167). In a publication by the Oversees Development Institute, a list of examples makes clear the levels of complexity at which the aid community operates: for instance, the WHO is said to have about 4,600 separate agreements with donors and thus has to provide some 1,400 reports to donors each year; in Vietnam, 11 UN agencies provide between them only 2% of total development aid; and Uganda has over 40 donors delivering aid in-country – the government of Uganda's own

---

[5] The term 'practitioner' in this context refers to people working in practice on issues related to conflict management. In the following the same pattern applies: a 'practitioner' is someone who implements as also defined by Jonathan Goodhand (cf. Goodhand (2006): Aiding Peace? The Role of NGOs in Armed Conflict, p.5).

figures show that it had to deal with 684 different development cooperation instruments and associated agreements for aid coming into the central budget alone (cf. Burall/Maxwell, et al. 2006). This demonstrates that through the current aid structure, a form of competition for action among the involved organizations occurs (cf. Mehler/Ribaux 2000, p.13; Schlichte in Fahrenhorst 1999, p.48).

The mushrooming of NGOs is another sign of this development – an ever increasing number of organizations compete for funding and projects (cf. Debiel and Sticht in Brunnengräber/Klein, et al. 2005, p.133; Duffield 1997; Fischer, M. 2006; Galama/Tongeren 2002; Muscat 2002, p.246). For instance, USAID Administrator Andrew Natsios claims that, "in the immediate aftermath of the 1994 genocide, as many as one hundred NGOs claimed to have a presence [in Rwanda]" (Andrew Natsios in Zartman/Rasmussen 1997, p.344). This figure does not account for off-site aid or local institutions. One reason for the constant rise in numbers of NGOs is seen as originating from a series of Security Council resolutions, through which NGOs became entitled to deliver relief assistance even under war conditions (cf. Duffield 1997, p.530). This development facilitated the realization of a new business opportunity for NGOs in conflict settings.

Aid given during conflicts can have unintended consequences and do more harm than good (cf. Anderson 1999, p.1; BMZ 2005, p.20; Galama/Tongeren 2002, p.28; German Development Institute 2001, p.1; Klingebiel/Eberle, et al. 2000, p.1). What is clear is that if aid is given in conflict settings, the aid cannot remain entirely separated from the conflict (cf. Anderson 1999, p.1; Bush 1998, p.8; Galama/Tongeren 2002, p.11 and p.28): "When international assistance is given in the context of a violent conflict, it becomes part of that context and thus also of the conflict" (Anderson 1999, p.145) and "development projects in situations of socio-political tension or conflict can never be completely impartial" (Klingebiel/Eberle, et al. 2000, p.4).

As will be shown below, some literature and discussions exist about the idea that development aid is not always beneficial in the context of conflict. The original debate was primarily driven by Mary Anderson in her book, "Do No Harm: How Aid Can Support Peace – Or War". She outlines which dangers are hidden in delivering aid, specifically to countries at war (cf. Anderson 1999). But the debate never actually extended to the effect of development aid on peace efforts.

The debate on doing harm through development institutions and agencies appears emotional and loaded with moral accusations. Conflict managers accuse development practitioners of being short-sighted, focusing purely on saving lives in the very short run[6], and development workers accuse conflict managers of being too focused on ending the conflict and therefore losing sight of justice (cf. Stein in Stern/Druckman 2000, p.386; Natsios in Zartman/Rasmussen 1997, pp. 337-360). As for example Pamela Aall put it, "the focus in relief work is on saving lives, not managing conflict" (Aall in Crocker/Hampson, et al. 2001, p.369). This debate comes down to a discussion about peace and justice. What is more important?

It is acknowledged that there is a difference between peace and justice in this context, as has been pointed out by Harald Müller, who called for a separation of the terms due to their different meanings (cf. Müller in Hellmann/Wolf, et al. 2003, p.212). By no means shall there be an accusation against any institution trying to help people in good faith. It seems that a distanced and neutral analysis of the subject from an academic perspective is needed in this context because "it is a moral and logical fallacy to conclude that because aid can do harm, a decision *not* to give aid would do no harm. […] Our purpose is to improve aid" (Anderson 1999, pp.2-3).

So far, this chapter talked about the interplay between development aid and conflict. That is, it highlighted the idea that development aid given during conflicts might have consequences for the conflict, the people, and the country where the conflict is located – positive or negative. As will be seen below, this debate has already been led in various forms. What has not been done so far is to focus on one specific point of time, or phase, within the life cycle of conflicts: ripeness.

Basically, there are three observations that motivated me to investigate further into the topic and to formulate my research objective: firstly, there seem to be many internal militarized conflicts in the contemporary world that tend to be protracted and cannot be successfully solved even though peace efforts might have been made. Secondly, most – if not all – of these conflicts take place in developing countries. Thirdly, developing countries receive vast amounts of development aid.

It is crucial for the field of Conflict Management to invest into the research of the interplay between conflict resolution and development cooperation of a country. This is what is attempted in this analysis. The objective is thus to

---

[6] Mary Anderson called this approach "Mandate Blinders". It refers to people who "follow mandate with blinds on", in the sense that they simply fulfill their task of for instance feeding the population of a country without acknowledging the potential wider impact their mission could have (Anderson in Crocker/Hampson, et al. (2001): Turbulent Peace: The Challenges of Managing International Conflict, p.642).

combine the dynamics and observe to what extent the targeting of development aid and efforts to achieve peace can be improved. It should be noted at this point that it is impossible to create a blueprint for how to manage a conflict. The analysis follows the idea of the Dutch historian Jos Havermans: "There is no overall recipe for ending or preventing conflicts, because every conflict is unique. But there are general conclusions to be drawn, and communal lessons to be learned [...]. The 'lessons learned' may help the field, and the people working in it, move forward" (Havermans in Galama/Tongeren 2002, p.123). The analysis aims at assessing "what has worked in certain circumstances, why it has worked and what we can learn that can be applied or adapted elsewhere" (Goodhand 2006, p.5) as well as to analyze what has not worked, why it has not worked and how we can avoid such mistakes in the future.

1.2 Approach and Methodology

The study is conducted in different stages, using two methodological approaches: theory analysis and comparative case studies.

Before diving into the analysis, the analysis will demonstrate the socio-political and academic relevance of the topic as well as putting it into a broader context. Following George and Bennett, who stated that, "political scientists generally agree that research in their field should address important real-world problems" (George/Bennett 2005, p.263), it will be explained, why the specific focus of the effect of development aid on conflict ripeness was chosen as a research topic and to what extent this is a relatively tightly scoped topic in a larger context of political relevance.

The actual theory analysis will begin by focusing on the timing of peace efforts. In order to do so, the Theory of Ripeness will be presented and analyzed as a basis for the further research. The analytical instrument of theory-analysis consists of four steps. Firstly, the original theory is outlined and described. Secondly, the relevance of the theory is demonstrated. Thirdly, academic challenges to the theory are assessed before closing the theory-analysis by identifying open questions with respect to the analysis' research objective. The open questions will then be used as vehicles for the further analysis in the form of comparative case studies. It must be noted that this first analysis will be conducted on a purely abstract, theoretical level.

In the next step, the theory analysis serves as the basis for the comparative case studies. The comparative case studies will assess to what extent development aid affects the construct of the theory as outlined before. In order to do so, the increase in development aid will be considered as an independent variable to the Theory of Ripeness. In other words, it will be tested whether the independent variable of increase in development aid has an effect on the theory's dependent variable – does it magnify the outcome of the theory, does it destroy or decrease the outcome or is there no impact to be observed at all?

In order to be able to isolate the effect of development aid on conflict ripeness, the analysis will focus on an increase in development aid. The reason lies in the research design of comparative case studies. To identify what effect an independent variable has on the status quo of a given situation, the variable needs to be identifiable, measurable and traceable. Therefore, existing streams of development aid that remain unchanged would not be possible to isolate. A decrease of development aid would be another option to analyze. However, as the research objective asks what happens to the dynamics of a conflict once development aid comes into a country, the effect of an increase is of primary importance. Thus, the independent variable of interest will be defined as increase in development aid (IDA).

The methodology used is the approach to comparative cases as outlined by Stephen Van Evera (cf. Van Evera 1997) and Alexander L. George and Andrew Bennett (cf. George/Bennett 2005)[7], which the author believes is best-suited to do justice to the subject of study. This methodology includes three phases of analysis: firstly, a general definition of the case studies' objectives, design and structure of the research is formulated. Secondly, each case study is carried out individually in accordance with the formulated design. Thirdly, the analysis draws upon the findings of the case studies and assesses their contribution to achieve the research objective of the study. Such a qualitative method helps to test and further develop the theory to be assessed. It is aimed at analyzing the operationability of the Theory of Ripeness and concretizing it by evaluating the effect of an additional independent variable.

The case studies will be conducted by way of a structured focused comparison. From the theory analysis, certain hypotheses will be generated to be tested in the comparative case studies. These will help to design questions reflecting the research objective. The questions will be posed in each case and thus guide the approach in the cases without losing the ability to compare the individual findings so that generalizations might be drawn. The case studies are focused in the sense that they concentrate on certain aspects of the historical cases examined.

---

[7] As also explained and discussed in person: Personal Interview with Andrew Bennett on 05 May 2009 in Washington D.C.

A great challenge in this context is the choice of the universe of cases. It will be aimed at identifying cases which leave the research open, so that variance in the dependent variable is allowed for and can be neutrally examined. That means the approach is to select cases with no or limited variance in the independent variables and analyze the effect by way of process-tracing. With this in mind, both cross-case comparisons and within-case analyses will be conducted, so that the "risk of inferential errors that can arise from using either method alone" will be reduced (George/Bennett 2005, p.234). The goal is therefore to establish stable causal mechanisms that help yield useful generalizations. It is assumed that through the usage of this case study method, it is possible to leverage the four core strengths associated with it: firstly, the conceptual validity that can be explained by the specific contextualized comparison through small-n approaches; secondly, the possibility to derive new hypotheses; third, the mode of exploration of causal mechanisms; and fourth, the ability to model and assess complex causal relations (cf. George/Bennett 2005, pp.19-22). It is also acknowledged that the method of comparative case studies might carry certain risks for the research. George and Bennett list six such potential risks (cf. George/Bennett 2005, pp.22-34), which are selection bias, identifying scope conditions and 'necessity', the 'degrees of freedom problem' in case studies, the lack of representativeness, the dangers of single-case research designs, and the potential lack of independence of cases. I will not discuss each of these potential risks here, but will rather refer to them throughout the case studies in order to ensure that the risks are limited in their scope regarding their impact on the research findings. Generally, it is important to state that the process of selecting the cases as well as the way of approaching them is crucial. Therefore, the analysis follows a strict and transparent approach in identifying the universe of cases by outlining the necessary conditions in order to qualify for a class or subclass of the research.

The reason for using a small-n comparative case study-approach in the second part of the analysis lies in the nature of the research subject. Firstly, the research objective is highly focused. It analyzes whether the provision of development aid affects the concept of conflict ripeness and what kind of effect this might be. Specifically, it examines whether there exists a causal relationship between an increase in development aid and conflict ripeness. Thus, as will become clear in the explanation for the choice of cases, the relevant universe of cases narrows down to only a few, so that a large-n study would be impossible. Secondly, a small-n study is also better-suited to address this particular content. A qualitative case study allows the researcher to address the specifics in each individual case and to better monitor developments in the context of an entire situation rather than a single event. In quantitative studies – which also carry with them their own significant strengths as a method – it is crucial not only to reduce every event to one variable, but also to ensure that the variables can be applied equally to all cases, in order to be able to identify patterns. This does not allow for individual interpretative conclusions.

Given the context-specific nature of all conflicts, a large-n study does not seem helpful or manageable for the subject at hand. In each conflict, the belligerents differ in their type, power and style; it might not always be clear who the protagonists are; the third party plays a crucial role; and the overall picture is very complex (cf. Paffenholz 2001, p.4). Therefore, it seems more appropriate to look at all cases studied with great care and individual interpretative approaches. Only in this way is it possible to ensure that the results from the individual case studies can be compared and then to draw meaningful conclusions about the potential contingent generalization of findings and the building of a theory.

The idea to analyze, modify and test a specific theory in this context stems from the aim to contribute to theory-building in international relations' studies. While acknowledging the variety of potential approaches to this topic, this combination of a positivist and rather normative approach seems most applicable. As Stephen Van Evera expresses it, "theories are general statements that describe and explain the causes or effects of classes of phenomena" (Van Evera 1997, pp.7-8). In order to be able to analyze why certain peace efforts are not successful and then to take the next step of suggesting levers that might improve a given situation, conclusions and lessons learned will be drawn from the theory analysis, which then turns the analysis towards a prescriptive character. This is what Stern and Druckman describe when stating, "careful analysis of historical and other evidence, together with the development of clear diagnostic concepts and empirically tested theories of peace processes, can make a modest but significant contribution to practitioners' ability to understand and intervene to resolve conflicts" (Stern/Druckman 2000, p.83).

With the normative approach, it is aimed at developing an ideal construct describing interactions and causal relationships in the context. It should be noted that in such a construct, certain assumptions have to be made about the actors' behavioral patterns (cf. Bercovitch/Gartner 2009, p.2). A rational choice approach underlies the research in this respect. It is noted that the normative approach is not as congruent with reality as would ideally be wished for. However, it is assumed that by starting with an ideal construct, it is possible to draw certain prescriptive conclusions and thus to support policy-makers in decision-making processes with a useful tool. This is what has been referred to as generating useful generic knowledge from a scholarly point of view: "Practitioners need generic knowledge about the conditions that favor success of specific strategies they may employ" (George/Bennett 2005, p.272).

The reason for choosing the above outlined methodology lies with the author's aim to address the research objective appropriately. The Theory of Ripeness (understandably) suffers from allegations of tautology. It is arguably easy to explain a successful intervention by 'ripeness' and conversely to point out elements of 'unripeness' which had to lead to failure after the event. This analysis will go some way to answering this criticism, by assessing through theory analysis as well as by empirical analysis whether ripeness indeed carries potential as an instrument for conflict managers. It will test the operationability of the Theory of Ripeness, and in addition it is aimed at improving the Theory of Ripeness by concretizing it.

1.3 Structural Overview

In order to address the research question appropriately, the analysis is structured into seven chapters. After the introductory remarks including the research objective (Chapter 1.1), the approach and methodology (Chapter 1.2) as well as this structural overview (Chapter 1.3), the analysis' topic will then be put into context (Chapter 2), which consists of three dimensions: socio-economic and political relevance (Chapter 2.1), academic contextualization (Chapter 2.2), and an explanation of terminology and definitions (Chapter 2.3). The first dimension refers to the overall significance of the topic and its impact on the wider political sphere. In the second dimension, the state of the art regarding the academic exigency of the research in this field will be outlined in order to define the research gap this analysis sets out to fill. The academic overview in this area is also important in order to be able to contextualize the topic. The third dimension introduces basic concepts used in order to create a common under-standing of the terminology for the reader.

The third chapter is dedicated to the theoretical background of the dissertation regarding the conflict resolution strategy on timing. Firstly, there will be a detailed account of the Theory of Ripeness (Chapter 3.1). Secondly, the issue of wrong timing will be considered, thereby clarifying the relevance of 'right' timing (Chapter 3.2). Thirdly, academic challenges to the Theory of Ripeness will be outlined as covered in the academic literature (Chapter 3.3). Fourthly, the Theory of Ripeness will be revisited, including a definition of independent variables to the theory as well as the development of an extended form of the Theory of Ripeness that will serve as the basis for the subsequent analysis (Chapter 3.4). Finally, the focus will lie on the hypotheses resulting from the theory analysis, to be tested in the case studies (Chapter 3.5).

Chapter four outlines the approach to the case studies including the description of their objective, design and structure (Chapter 4.1). It will also present the variables to be analyzed (Chapter 4.2). Then, the case-guiding research questions to be asked throughout the analysis will be formulated (Chapter 4.3) and the choice of cases will be presented (Chapter 4.4). In this context, the universe of cases will be described before specifying why a particular choice of three cases was made.

In chapter five, the evidence from the case studies will be presented. The three cases will be examined individually including the background of each of them and the actual analysis of each case with regard to conflict ripeness, the increase in development aid, and the effect of an increase in development aid on conflict ripeness (Chapters 5.1, 5.2 and 5.3). The chapter closes with a synthesis of findings of the case studies (Chapter 5.4).

Chapter six deals with the implications that can be inferred from the evidence of the case studies in relation to the Theory of Ripeness. A comparison of the findings with the originally stated hypotheses will be made (Chapter 6.1) as well as an expansion of the theoretical model be conducted (Chapter 6.2).

The analysis closes in chapter seven with the conclusions. These will include three parts: firstly, a summary of findings will be presented (Chapter 7.1). Secondly, the lessons learned and potential implications for policy-making will be considered (Chapter 7.2). Lastly, the analysis will finish with a critical review in the context of the academic field. Valid objections and unresolved issues will be addressed (Chapter 7.3).

2 Development Aid and Ripeness in Context

In this chapter, the analysis' topic will be placed into context. Firstly, the socio-economic and political relevance of analyzing conflict ripeness and the impact of development aid will be presented (2.1). Secondly, the academic relevance will be outlined including the academic 'state of the art' and the conclusions drawn so far by researchers on this topic. This will lead to the open questions this research aims to answer (2.2). Lastly, the terminology and concepts used in this analysis will be defined (2.3).

2.1 Socio Economic and Political Relevance

Actors from the public and private sectors from the developed world make an ever increasing effort to invest into poor countries and regions as well as to provide aid on a large scale. "The West spent $2.3 trillion on foreign aid over the last five decades" (Easterly 2006, p.4). The development industry constantly grows. Not only the total amount of foreign aid, but also the number of institutions, particularly NGOs, involved, increases.

However, in many developing countries, no or only limited economic, social, political and security-related development can be observed. According to the World Bank's Global Monitoring Report 2008, more than 50% of the population in developing countries lives on less than $2 a day (Harmsen/Kireyev 2008, p.31). Such figures have sparked a vivid debate on the effectiveness of aid. Many academics and authors with a practical background have published their opinions, stating that development aid is ineffective in general such as William Easterly (cf. Easterly 2006), Dambisa Moyo (cf. Moyo 2009) or Volker Seitz (cf. Seitz 2009), or how it can be improved such as Abhijit V. Banerjee (cf. Banerjee 2007), Basil E. Cracknell (cf. Cracknell 2000) or Jeffrey D. Sachs (cf. Sachs 2005). Many criticize the evaluation processes of individual projects with the allegation that no consequences are drawn (cf. Kappel in Hansohm/Kappel 1993, p.113). Entire projects have been set up, bringing together scholars from the field analyzing how best to design evaluation-processes for measuring the effectiveness of development aid as for example the MIT sponsored Abdul Latif Jameel Poverty Action Lab[8].

In any case, it is beyond debate that many societies in our contemporary world are underdeveloped. The academic community discusses ways how to address such underdevelopment.

2.1.1 Prevalence of Conflict in Developing Countries

In the regions where poverty is most apparent, armed conflict, specifically intra-state armed conflict, prevails. In fact, most wars nowadays are civil wars and take place in developing countries (cf. Collier, P. 2003). Different institutions and global actors have examined the interrelation between civil war and development. The World Bank, for instance, concluded that, "it [civil war] is development in reverse"; they continue stating that, "... civil war thus reflects not just a problem *for* development, but a failure *of* development" (Collier, P. 2003, p.ix). Others emphasize the effect that such conflicts have on the overall development agenda, such as Siegmar Schmidt who states that such wars threaten to destroy all progress in development and potential for development (Schmidt in Hellmann/Schmidt, et al. 2007, p.542).

When looking at conflicts counted in 2008[9], it becomes clear that the prevalence of conflict is particularly significant in Sub-Saharan Africa and South Asia – regions where development and wealth are rare; regions where most of the contemporary development countries are situated; regions where poverty, hunger, and related problems are omnipresent. No conflict was observed in Europe. The dark shaded countries are those, where UCDP/PRIO observed a conflict in the year of 2008 that was either purely internal or internal-internationalized[10]. Excluded from the illustration are the US and Russia, which are also listed by UCDP/PRIO as conflict countries. The reason for excluding these two cases lies within their special character regarding their conflicts. They refer to the US involvement in Afghanistan fighting against al-Qaida and

---

[8] Cf. http://www.povertyactionlab.org.
[9] The data displayed in the graph below is taken from the UCDP/PRIO databank (cf. Gleditsch, "UCDP/PRIO Armed Conflict Dataset " (Uppsala Conflict Data Program (UCDP), www.ucdp.uu.se and Centre for the Study of Civil Wars, International Peace Research Institute, Oslo (PRIO), www.prio.no/cscw 2008a).). The conflicts shown are internal and internal-internationalized conflicts that were observed in the year of 2008.
[10] It is to be noted that this illustration solely mirrors the data from the 2008-findings of UCDP/PRIO and is aimed at demonstrating the prevalence of conflict in developing countries. It is by no means an indication for the subsequent development of the universe of cases.

Russian involvement in the Chechen conflict. The illustration shall solely serve the purpose of demonstrating the prevalence of conflict in developing countries.

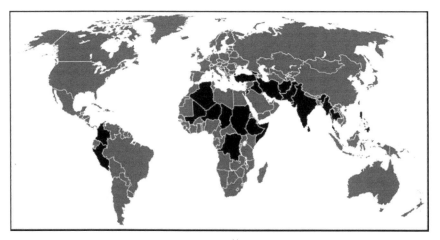

Figure 1: World Map of Conflicts in 2008[11]

Whether poverty increases the likeliness of violent conflict or whether violent conflict leads to sustained poverty, has not yet been resolved by academia. The fact that these two phenomena, poverty and conflict, seem to be intertwined also suggests that whenever conflict resolution efforts are initiated, they are placed in a country receiving development aid. That again explains the research interest of this analysis – what is the relationship between development aid and conflict resolution efforts?

2.1.2   Effects of Conflict on Developing Countries

Internal militarized conflict has disastrous effects on developing countries. Thanks to recent developments in the world of media, for instance the often quoted CNN-effect[12], the broad public knows about the impact such conflicts

---

[11] Source: Own illustration based on data from UCDP/PRIO (cf. Gleditsch (2009a): UCDP/PRIO Armed Conflict Dataset).
[12] The term "CNN effect" refers in this context to the broad coverage of world events through all sorts of media – be it television, journals, newspapers or the internet with social platforms such as

have on unstable societies. Terms such as refugee flows, displacement, forced migration, child soldiers, blood diamonds, genocide, and many more have been filled with pictures in our minds leaving us with terrible images of suffering and sorrow. In reality, it refers to a socio-political and economic instability of immense scale. As it is commonly acknowledged, in internal conflicts it is not the military personnel that are the main victims, but civilians (cf. Macrae/Zwi 1994, p.1). The SIPRI Yearbook 2009 identified the trend that internal conflicts increasingly lead to so-called one-sided violence. Parties to the conflict use violence against civilians as one of their military tools. As much as 99 percent of fatalities from one-sided violence occur in countries affected by armed conflict (cf. Stockholm International Peace Research Institute 2009, p.40). Furthermore, such conflicts also have a broad effect on the regional and global levels. Reduced incomes and raised mortality are as much consequences of conflict as are increases in the drug business, the spread of diseases and terrorism (cf. Collier, P. 2003, p.121). Internal and protracted militarized conflicts have disastrous long-term consequences for the people affected, the country they live in, the region surrounding the country at war and international affairs in general. This is also mirrored in the academic debate – specifically through a debate that was widely led in Germany triggered by the so-called Africa Memorandum from 2000 (as published in Engel/Jakobeit, et al. 2002). Here, the authors stressed the significance of structural stability as a central strategy for development (cf. Engel, Kappel, Klingebiel et. alia in Engel/Jakobeit, et al. 2002, pp.11-31). They suggest to focus on 'structural stability', i.e. to sustainably strengthen fragile and instable social and political institutions and norms (Engel, Kappel, Klingebiel, et alia in Engel/Jakobeit, et al. 2002, p.16).

The donor community plays a specific socio-economic and political role in this complex context of internal conflicts. The increased focus on development aid and the prevalence of civil war have led to a mushrooming of actors involved. Robert Picciotto states, "far from being a cartel, the aid industry has become ever more fragmented and competitive" (Picciotto 2006, p.19). New bilateral actors enter the stage. India, China, Slovenia and Thailand have recently started to become donors.

Twitter etc. It means that everyone can gain real-time information and pictures about developments from all over the world. This, however, is the customary use of the term. It was originally used to describe the impact of the 24-hour international television news channel, Cable News Network, that was said to have had great influence on the states' foreign policies during the period of the late Cold War due to its in-depth coverage of political events (cf. Gilboa in Bercovitch/Kremenyuk, et al. (2009): The SAGE Handbook of Conflict Resolution, p.455).

In the overall socio-economic and political context, it is unclear which role external actors to conflicts play in our contemporary state-systems. As the German Federal Government stated in one of its positioning papers in the context of conflict resolution and development, "external actors might impact the balance of power between peaceful and violent forms of conflict positively as well as negatively". They call this point "tipping the balance" (Bundesregierung 2004, p.9). It shows that the awareness for an ambivalent impact is given. To what extent do the donors act upon this?

Questions referring to issues of state sovereignty, legitimacy, and controlling and monitoring of projects come up (cf. Hampson in Crocker/Hampson, et al. 2001, pp.394-395). Gunther Hellmann stressed the dilemma for NGOs involved: "...and in the end, we should not ignore that also an NGO pursues an institutional self-interest, as for example the preservation of the inflow of charity donations and membership fees from their supporting realm. Thus, NGO representatives cannot just focus on the good of the commonality, but also on the good of their own organization" (Hellmann 2006, p.157). Andrew Natsios even goes further when claiming that NGOs' first goal has to be self-preservation as they are 'normal' institutions. This goal might contradict the notion of establishing peace in certain cases (cf. Natsios in Zartman/Rasmussen 1997, pp.337-360). It demonstrates the wider implications connected for actors involved in such complex situations. What function and role can they fulfill and what function and role should they fulfill? For the socio-economic and political context of the subject, the definition of their responsibilities is crucial as it determines the success or failure of peace efforts.

2.1.3   The Need to Focus on Conflict Resolution Methods

There is a need to invest in the analysis of the dynamics of conflicts in order to identify potential levers prolonging conflicts and/or hindering them from being resolved. Furthermore, there is also a need to research the effects of poverty on conflict. One such aspect is development aid. Development aid enters countries externally and is rarely accounted for. Thus, it is one component having an impact on the interplay between poverty and conflict. As the German Federal Ministry for Economic Co-operation and Development put it: "Achieving the Millennium Development Goals will fundamentally depend on whether conflicts can be stopped and peaceful living can be established. Development and peace entail each other mutually" (BMZ 2005, p.7). What exactly is the impact of development aid on the potential resolution or protraction of civil wars?

One lever the international community can draw upon to work against the prevalence of internal conflicts in developing countries is to invest more into the peaceful resolution of conflict. Conflict resolution is a subject that still requires considerable research in academia (cf. Stedman 1991, p.viii). Peaceful resolution in this context refers to a negotiated settlement – a peace agreement that ends violent conflict. Empirical studies show that with the involvement of a third party that mediates the crisis between the belligerents, turning negotiations into mediation, the probability to successfully solve the conflict rises significantly (cf. Wilkenfeld/Young, et al. 2005, p.55; Collier, P. 2003, p.121; Bercovitch/Gartner 2009). There is a need to analyze all aspects of mediation in order to improve this instrument.

The analysis therefore intends to contribute to the academic field of Conflict Management to shed more light on the complexity of seemingly intractable conflicts keeping countries deadlocked in disastrous situations and the effect of development aid on such conflicts at a specific phase of the conflict – the phase of ripeness.

2.2 Aid and Conflict in the Academic Literature

Having outlined why the analysis' topic is relevant in the socio-economic and political realm, it is also crucial to note why it is significant for academia. Before describing and analyzing the state of the art and academic exigency, the overall relevance of the topic for academia will be outlined.

2.2.1 Overall Academic Relevance

There has been a change in the overall perception of international politics as noted above. Due to the pressing issues observed in many developing countries as well as their 'mediazation' (cf. the CNN-effect), the overall international interest in internal conflicts grows consistently. Alongside the broad attention and urgent practical needs coming from internal conflicts, academia has turned towards further research of this topic. The academic field of conflict management has started to build a profound body of writing that should be expanded further. Christopher Daase wrote, "Until today, those perceptions have shaped socio-scientific theories assuming the state system to be the ultimate aggregate state of international politics and seeing war as an inter-state phenomenon. Yet, most militarized conflicts, which we colloquially call wars, do not comply with this pattern. They are mostly civil wars and have, if at all, but on one side a state-actor. The consequence is that the term and the (empiric) reality of wars increasingly diverge" (Daase in Hellmann/Wolf, et al. 2003, p.164). Daase's statement again emphasizes the relatively recent trend of an increasing number of internal conflicts and a decreasing prevalence of international wars. Academically, this new focus is slowly addressed with more and more scholars specializing in topics surrounding internal militarized conflicts. Most of these scholars aim at analyzing patterns of internal conflicts in order to be able to identify insights for practical use in policy-making. The analysis follows this positivist approach.

The methodological approach chosen involves theory testing, theory building and a causal-analytical framework. As Gunther Hellmann pointed out, it is not a question of which method is best for theory-building. It is rather a question of which approach is best suited for a specific research question (cf. Hellmann 1993, p.44). This opens the debate for which methodology should be used in this context. It has to be considered whether conflict resolution allows for general insights at all or whether knowledge in the field is always highly case-specific. Some argue from a normative perspective, others focus on rather reconstructive methods. This work might be criticized using an argument as put by Paul C. Stern and Daniel Druckman, "...because each international conflict situation is unique, scientific approaches that seek general laws cannot provide useful insights. In this view, useful knowledge is highly case specific". They continue stating that, "Neither of these extreme views [as described above] is satisfactory – and neither actually describes what competent scholars or practitioners do" (Stern and Druckman in Stern/Druckman 2000, p.39). The analysis uses neither of the extreme views, but finds a middle path that seems best suited to address the research topic adequately.

The chosen positivist approach is ideal to test whether development aid has an impact on conflict resolution efforts. The so-called "if-then" function is used in order to generalize patterns and ultimately be able to draw lessons for policy-advice.

Beyond the normative work, the analysis is written with a prescriptive character as used by Fisher and Ury (cf. Fisher, R./Ury 1981). It does not comprise a checklist for policy-makers on how to act. It rather asks to critically reflect potential challenges to policy practices before their implementation. Roger Fisher explains, "Machiavelli's Prince is a powerful book that is still read after almost five hundred years. This is so not because the prince for whom Machiavelli was writing followed his advice or even read the book. The book is powerful because Machiavelli asked a powerful question: What advice would you give a prince? [...] Generating advice – even if it is only hypothetical – is the best way to think rigorously about difficult problems" (Fisher, R./Kopelman, et al. 1994, p.6). It is fair to note that academic analysis may not serve as a blueprint for policy-makers. However, what is possible is to generalize on an abstract level, so that certain patterns can be identified. This at least helps policy-makers to assess the situation and take advice on what might work best. As said above, the theoretical analysis is based on behavioral theories such as rational choice approaches. A one-to-one implementation of all theoretical insights into reality will not be possible. Having stated this, the analysis aims at closing with a chapter of prescriptive character. This will be a chapter written solely on the basis of the subjective conclusions made by the author regarding possible lessons learned.

One specific theory is analyzed, the Theory of Ripeness; outlined, established and refined by I. William Zartman and others. Building on the theory, the analysis tries to address two notions: firstly, the operation-ability of the theory will be tested and secondly, an attempt in refining the theory in one specific aspect will be made. Zartman emphasized, "The Theory of Ripeness needs to be worked on, refined and detailed constantly. Only then, we can ensure that the theory actually receives the attention it deserves"[13]. The aim of this approach is to use the knowledge, expertise and insights from recon-structive research, analyze it, put it into causal-analytical frameworks and then turn the results into prescriptive guidelines. "Conflict Resolution is about ideas, theories, and methods that can improve our understanding of conflict and our collective practice of reduction in violence and enhancement of political processes for harmonizing interests" (Bercovitch/Kremenyuk, et al. 2009, p.1). This statement explains why academic research is of vital importance in the context of practical conflict resolution.

2.2.2 *Academic Exigency of the Research – State of the Art*

In the following, the topic is situated into the existing literature. The aim is to outline the academic exigency of the research. This will be conducted in five stages: firstly, a general contextualization in the conflict management field will be provided (2.2.2.1). Secondly, different theoretical concepts surrounding the art of conflict resolution will be presented (2.2.2.2). Thirdly, the timing of peace efforts will be looked at more specifically (2.2.2.3). Fourthly, research regarding the effect and the role of development aid in conflicts will be analyzed (2.2.2.4), before lastly, the chapter will close with an account of the state of the art

---

[13] Personal Interview with I. William Zartman on 07 May 2009 in Washington, D.C.

regarding the intersection of development aid and conflict resolution efforts (2.2.2.5).

2.2.2.1 General Contextualization in the Field of Conflict Management

The academic research in conflict management is not entirely new; it has been researched on as part of other academic fields. Relatively new is the focus on intra-state conflicts as an own academic discipline: "Although the systemic study of Conflict Resolution[14] is relatively new, conflicts and wars have long been the subject of research and teaching in such fields as diplomatic history, international relations, history, political science, law, and social psychology" (Bercovitch/ Kremenyuk, et al. 2009, p.1 and Reimann 2004, p.3). The new development of focusing on internal conflict management as an academic discipline stems from the trend of a constant decrease in the number of international wars and an increase in the number of internal conflicts. In line with the argument of the Democratic Peace Theory, John Mueller argues that, "the institution of war is in decline" (Mueller 2004, p.3) and accordingly called his book, "The Remnants of War" (Mueller 2004). He specifies this statement by adding that in his view, it is obvious that wars among developed countries, major wars, have disappeared. In parallel, a new type of warfare has emerged, which is violent conflict within states. Fearon and Laitin compared the two types of war and found that between 1945 and 1999, 25 interstate wars took place that killed at least 1,000 people each and lasted a median duration of about 3 months. Compared to that, in the same time period they counted 127 civil wars that also killed at least 1,000 people each with a median duration of 6 years, of which 25 were ongoing in 1999. They estimated that while there were about 3.33 million battle related deaths from the interstate wars, there were about 16.2 million battle related deaths in the civil wars (cf. Fearon/Laitin 2003b, p.75). These numbers show the pressing need to focus on internal conflicts.

The answer from academia to this development was the establishment of a conflict management science. Universities, institutes and schools have invested in distinguishing intra-state conflict from the general war-and-peace studies in order to be able to fully address this increasingly apparent phenomenon in international relations (cf. Gugel 2006, p.38 and Muscat 2002, p.17). One should note though that all academic challenges in the realm of conflict management do

---

[14] Conflict Resolution is meant here as what is defined in this analysis as conflict management (cf. below).

touch upon other disciplines such as international law, psychology, philosophy, economics, social anthropology, etc. pp. (cf. Reimann 2004, p.3).

The field of conflict management can be divided into three research areas: conflict prevention, which is situated pre-conflict; actual conflict management (while conflict resolution is considered to be part of the area conflict management)[15], which covers all subjects during a conflict; and post-conflict reconstruction, which deals with post-conflict challenges. The graph below visualizes the range of topics researched in the realm of conflict management studies, which can be filed under those three areas.

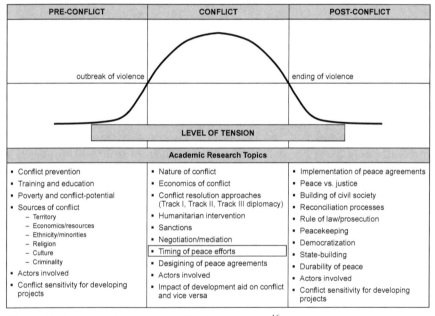

Figure 2: Research Areas in Conflict Management[16]

---

[15] For a detailed account on the evolution of the different meanings of conflict management, see the comprehensive account by Christoph Weller (Weller (2007): Zivile Konfliktbearbeitung. Aktuelle Forschungsergebnisse, pp.9-16).
[16] Source: Own illustration.

In the pre-conflict phase, the topics cover a broad range of issues, but are mainly focused on three areas: the prevention of large scale violence, the sources and nature of conflict, and the impact of development work on avoiding civil wars. To start with conflict prevention, the academic debate mainly focuses on how to resolve tensions within a country peacefully with sensitive communication, workshops and other integrative approaches, i.e. before violence breaks out (cf. Carment/Schnabel 2003; Carment/Schnabel 2004; Hamburg 2002; Leatherman 1999; Lund 1996; Meerts in Bercovitch/Kremenyuk, et al. 2009; Rosenberg 1999; Wallensteen 1998; or Zartman 2001b). Overlapping with this research topic, concepts of education and training with specific focus on pre-conflict phases are part of the debate. The general claim is to focus more on education and widespread training of civilians, so that an escalation of conflict into violence can be avoided (cf. Danesh 2006; Duffy 2000; or Walzer 1997). The essence of these debates deals with how to counter-act early signs of tension within societies. A specific role is attributed to the UN in this context as a third party that has the potential to foster conflict prevention. Scholars researching in this field point to the specific opportunities the UN offers (cf. Hampson/Malone 2002; Peck 1998; or Sriram/Wermester 2003).

The debate on the sources and nature of conflict embraces the idea of social movements as the outset for conflicts and the causes of conflict. The literature on social movements primarily deals with analyses on how social movements are formed initially and how they are organized over longer periods of time (cf. Coser 1967; Skocpol 1994; Stokes 1995; or Tarrow 1998). Scholars invested into analyzing social movements in order to trace the evolution from discontent to war. Specific debates surround topics such as the reasons and nature of protests (cf. Lipsky 1968 or Rubin/Pruitt, et al. 1994) and factors facilitating the outbreak of violence (cf. Gurr 1970 or McCarthy 1977).

Research on the sources of conflict is mainly driven by the question, which of the many potential factors is decisive (cf. Arnson/Zartman 2005; Crocker/ Hampson, et al. 1996; Menck 2005; or Rubin/Pruitt, et al. 1994): is it need, greed or creed as Arnson and Zartman summarized the debate (cf. Arnson/Zartman 2005)? While Collier and Hoeffler stress the significance of grievance and greed for the outbreak of violence (cf. Collier, P./Hoeffler 2004b), Fearon and Laitin put a special focus on identities and ethnicity as a cause of war (cf. Fearon/Laitin 2003b). Ted Robert Gurr gives this research another twist by analyzing to what extent minorities in general as opposed to only ethnic minorities are particularly at risk of triggering conflicts (cf. Gurr 2000). The topic of separatist movements overlaps in this context. The distinct needs of peoples striving for autonomy and potentially triggering civil war through that are researched on widely (cf. Heraclides 1997; or Neuberger 1986). Other motivations for civil wars are discussed such as religion (cf. Burke/Lapidus, et al. 1988 or Esposito 1983) and political ideologies (cf. Eckstein 1989).

Cordula Reimann categorizes the debate on sources of conflicts into subjective and objective causes. In her opinion, subjective causes refer to features such as identities, needs, and interests whereas objective causes represent structural features like the unequal distribution of resources (cf. Reimann 2004, p.4).

From the development studies perspective, the important intersection at this phase is the conflict sensitive design of development projects. This type of research is specifically concerned with the aim to analyze development projects and to assess whether they are conflict sensitive in the sense of counteracting potential intergroup tensions in a country. An in-depth analysis of the academic literature in this context will follow below.

The academic literature concerned with the post-conflict phase ranges from topics on the design of peace agreements, to reconstruction efforts, and the prevention of a re-outbreak of civil war. It is asked how to best draft and implement peace agreements and what is most important to include or to consider so that peace agreements are successful in the medium and long run (cf. Hampson 1996; Fortna 2004; or Stedman/Rothchild, et al. 2002). Connected to this field is the question of what challenges emerge from specific types of conflicts in the implementation of peace agreements. Samarasinghe and De Silva for example analyze this question with respect to ethnic conflict (cf. Samarasinghe/De Silva 1993).

The second area of research concerns state-building and what are the most efficient and effective ways in order to re-stabilize a country, including discussions about political systems (cf. Fukuyama 2004; Milliken 2003; Ottaway 2003; or Paine 2009) and issues of demobilization (cf. Andrew Rigby in Furley/ May 2006; Walter 1999; or Wulf/Esser 2000).

Connected to this is another debate on conflict prevention with regard to preventing a re-outbreak of violence (cf. Galama/Tongeren 2002; Hampson/ Malone 2002; Kurtenbach/Seifert 2010; Leatherman 1999; or Peck 1998). Further, post-conflict research also deals with notions of how to bring justice to a country that had suffered war. Here, debates surround war tribunals, reconciliation measures and general forms of prosecution (cf. Hayner 2002; Humphrey 2002; Lederach 1997 or Skaar/Gloppen, et al. 2005).

The intersection to development studies is similar to the pre-conflict phase. The aim is to research the effect of development projects on peace. The other point of analysis in this context is whether the post-conflict situation influences the practical implementation process of certain development projects or which development projects are especially needed in such a post-conflict reconstruction phase. Martina Fischer contributes to these questions by considering the role of the civil society throughout transformation processes towards peace (cf. Fischer, M. 2006). Kurtenbach and Seifert recently wrote an article summarizing the debates and challenges concerning 'development cooperation' and post-conflict situations. They point to the risks of backsliding into war, reconstruction and state building as well as individual donor strategies in this context (cf. Kurtenbach/Seifert 2010) by that producing a comprehensive overview of this topic.

What is of main interest for this analysis is the phase in between the pre- and the post-conflict phases – the actual conflict phase. The nature of intra-state conflicts is discussed – whether they are minor or major (cf. Sambanis 2004), whether they are affecting only one part of the country or larger regions (cf. Böge/Debiel 2003), or whether the actors involved are unorganized groups or military armies. Thorsten Bonacker contributed to the research by defining conflict as processes (cf. Bonacker 2005) instead of the previous description of conflicts as focused social constellations (cf. Wasmuht 1992).

Further, academics research on the levers that are decisive to the conflict. For instance the economics of conflict seem particularly appealing to many academics debating where finances come from and to what extent they are decisive factors for the continuation of the conflict (cf. Arnson/Zartman 2005; Berdal/Keen 1997; or Collier, P./Hoeffler 2004b). This includes research on capabilities and intentions in civil wars – do people fight primarily because they have the capabilities or because they are ideologically driven (cf. Fearon/Laitin 2003b; Gurr 2000; or King 2001)?

Additionally, there is research on the topic of the resolution of conflicts. This will be addressed separately in the following chapter.

Before moving on to the art of conflict resolution, three books should be mentioned that offer in a magnificent way a solid overview about conflict management debates. The first to mention is "Turbulent Peace: The Challenges of Managing International Conflict" (Crocker/Hampson, et al. 2001). This book is a collection of articles by many of the relevant authors from the conflict management field writing on the most pressing issues such as the sources and the changing global context of conflict, intervention strategies and their consequences, negotiation, mediation, and other political instruments, institutions and regimes of security and conflict management, and peace building. The second book worth paying attention to is called "International Conflict Resolution after the Cold War" (Stern/Druckman 2000). This compilation of articles focuses specifically on the challenges emerging in contemporary times after the bipolar superpower system had collapsed. The third and most recent of these publications is "The SAGE Handbook of Conflict Resolution" (Bercovitch/Kremenyuk, et al. 2009). Despite the fact that the title suggests a focus on resolution methods, the book rather defines conflict resolution in terms of conflict management and not solely on the termination of conflict as is often done in academic literature. This collection of articles gives an account on what has been published in the field of conflict management over the last years. In that, it covers the history and methods of study, issues and sources of conflict, methods of managing conflict, and finally current features and dilemmas in the study of conflict resolution. As the book combines content with an overview of the academic field, it truly functions as a good basis for conflict management studies.

2.2.2.2 The Art of Conflict Resolution

How do conflicts come to an end? Generally, two options seem possible, which are either victory by one party or a peace agreement by the belligerents. Destradi and Mehler see four potential endings to conflicts which are a military victory by one party, a peace agreement, the intervention of a third party, or a transformation of a violent conflict to lower intensity (cf. Destradi/Mehler 2010, p.1). It seems that the last two options are sub-categories of the formers ones. If a conflict transforms into lower intensity, it is hardly possible to speak of an end to the conflict; and if a third party intervenes, this external actor might have an impact on the conflict in the sense that it leads to either a victory of one side or a peace agreement. Therefore, the original two options seem appropriate.

The crucial question in the context of this work is what external parties can do to help terminating the violence (cf. Bercovitch/Diehl, et al. 1997). The resolution of violent intra-state wars can be pursued through three types of intervention: the interveners can use the instruments of military force, sanctions or peaceful diplomacy (cf. Frazier and Dixon in Bercovitch/Gartner 2009, p.46; Chester A. Crocker in Crocker/Hampson, et al. 2001, pp.233-234).

The use of military force is often labeled 'humanitarian intervention', referring to the idea that the military intervention in a different country helps the people, i.e. the civilians, and by that becomes an act of humanitarianism and justifiable in international world politics (cf. Bull 1984, p.2). Intervention is in those cases seen as coercive action by one or more states that involves the use of armed force on the territory of another state in order to prevent widespread suffering or death among the inhabitants (cf. Adams 2001, pp.3-51). This idea, however, is not un-debated. Some academics do argue that under certain conditions military intervention is legitimate for the protection of human rights (cf. Holzgrefe/Keohane 2003; Power 2003; Vincent 1974 or Wheeler 2000), while others question the effectiveness of humanitarian intervention and/or stress the norm of non-intervention and the concept of state-sovereignty (cf. Akehurst in Bull 1984; Bricmont 2006; Krasner in Lyons, G./Mastanduno 1995 or Thomas in Forbes/Hoffman 1993).

Further academic discussions on military intervention deal with the advantages and disadvantages of impartiality on part of the intervener (cf. Betts 1994), and strategies and logistics of interventions (cf. Bowden 1999; Fassin/Pandolfi 2010; Haass 1999; Kuperman 2001 or Seybolt/SIPRI 2007).

Sanctions can be unilateral (that is by one state), regional (that is by the states of one region) or multilateral (that is by a collectivity of states) and might take the form of commodity sanctions, meaning that they are restrictions on the economy of an entire country and by that affect the overall social situation, or the form of targeted sanctions, meaning that they are specific sanctions against individuals or individual groups such as financial sanctions regarding movements of money or assets of individuals or international travel sanctions. Academic research on sanctions focuses on the question whether sanctions pressure the relevant decision-makers into stopping violence or whether they are useless or even worsen the situation for the civilian population.

Strong opponents to the effectiveness of sanctions are Cortright and Lopez arguing that it is very unlikely that sanctions have the power to change politics (cf. Cortright/Lopez 2000). Daniel, Hayes, and De Jonge Oudraat argue that sanctions might work if they are part of a comprehensive coercive strategy (cf. Daniel/Hayes, et al. 1999). General accounts on the effectiveness of sanctions point to both the advantages and disadvantages of this instrument (cf. Haass/Council on Foreign Relations 1998; Hufbauer 2007; or Kern 2009).

The third type of intervention is peaceful diplomacy. This refers to the tool of mediation, meaning that a third party gets involved in a conflict between belligerents and tries to 'mediate' between them. It thus turns the dyadic constellation into a triadic relationship between the belligerents and the third party. Mediation is a broad field in the study of conflict management and embraces different research topics that can be divided into two categories: manipulable and non-manipulable factors. The manipulable category of research topics is concerned with questions about the design of mediations. Thus it is asked, what to do in order to guarantee success. There are three debates that are particularly significant: the choice of mediator, the type of mediation, and lastly the timing of mediation.

To start with the choice of mediator, it is asked which characteristics a mediator should possess to be most likely to succeed in the mediation process (cf. Bercovitch/Houston 1993). The debate in this context focuses on the type of actor and his or her individual advantages. Potential types are representatives of states, multilateral institutions, regional organizations or NGOs (cf. Bercovitch/Schneider 2000). One of the most pressing questions in this context concerning all actors is which individual advantage the mediator sees for himself; that is what is his or her self-interest to function as a mediator to the conflict (cf. Greig 2005). Good accounts on what individual states can contribute mostly provide for case studies and lessons learned (cf. Blaker/Giarra, et al. 2001; Cogan 2003; Slim in Bercovitch/Rubin 1992; or Touval in Bercovitch/Rubin 1992). The debate on multilateral institutions covers strengths and weaknesses that a multilateral actor can bring to the table (cf. Hampson 2003; Kleiboer 1996; or Peck 1996). Regional organizations as part of multilateral actors are said to bring specific values and problems, such as a deeper regional understanding of the culture and power systems, but might also be biased (cf. Jackson, R. 2000 or Peck 1998). Finally, the strengths and weaknesses of NGOs and religious groups are discussed emphasizing the vicinity to the grass-roots level, but also criticizing the potential bias, lack of high level connections as well as leverage (cf. Aall and Anderson in Crocker/Hampson, et al. 1996; Bartoli in Fisher, R.J. 2005; DeMars 2005; Fitzduff/Church 2004; or Natsios in Zartman 2007). Apart from the question of which type of institution is the best mediator, research also exists on whether the third party should be impartial. Reimann emphasizes the value of impartiality for actors without much leverage such as NGOs (cf. Reimann 2004, p.4). Others focus on the great potential that powerful mediators possess in terms of partiality as they might be able to better impact the dynamics (cf. Kleiboer 1996, p.372).

Second, the type of mediation is highly debated (cf. Bercovitch/Rubin 1992). Some authors praise the value of interactive problem-solving workshops such as Fisher (cf. Fisher, R.J. 1997; Fisher, R.J. 2001; or Fisher, R.J. 2005) or Kelman (cf. Kelman in Crocker/Hampson, et al. 1996), others the advantages of facilitated dialogues (cf. Bohm 2004 or Roberts 2002). Diamond and McDonald and Reiman suggest that a multi-track approach to diplomatic efforts might work best (cf. Diamond/McDonald 1996 and Reimann 2004).

Third, the best timing for the initiation of mediation is part of the academic discussion. A detailed account of this topic will be provided below.

The non-manipulable category includes factors that are structurally given, exogenous factors, and thus cannot be influenced by the third party. The individual debates in this context discuss to what extent such factors have an effect on mediation efforts of third parties. Examples here are the state of fragmentation of the belligerents' elites, arguing that there might not be one decision maker in any of the relevant belligerents, but that it is a group of people who might have opposing opinions (cf. Hampson 1996 or Iklé 1991). Connected to the fragmentation of elites is the debate on the loyalty of the people to the leadership teams and potential spoilers to peace efforts. The idea here is that even if elites decide and speak with one voice in mediation processes, this might not mean that the people follow the elites' decisions. Thus individual actors or groups of actors might spoil the mediation process (cf. Stedman 1997 or Walter 1999) or the stability and state of the government is at stake in general (cf. Fortna 2004). A further discussion surrounds the topic of the financial backing of belligerents and which impact such a financial situation has on the mediation's effectiveness (cf. Collier, P./Hoeffler 2004b).

A collection of articles on the topic of mediation was edited by Crocker, Hampson, Osler and Aall (cf. Crocker/Hampson, et al. 1999) and by I. William Zartman (cf. Zartman 1995) providing a good overview of critical issues in mediation processes.

Apart from the nature of the leadership and groups, more examples for non-manipulable factors are other structural aspects. These include for instance external support to one of the involved parties in form of diaspora money or a change to the overall structural constellation of conflicts as for example a transformation of the issue of conflict. Weighing the importance of these factors touches upon the structure agency debate in international relations with prominent proponents of the debate such as Martha Finnemore (cf. Finnemore 1996), Volker Rittberger and Michael Zürn (cf. for example in Rittberger 1990), and also Alexander Wendt and Anthony Giddens trying to overcome the dialectic debate by proposing a mutual influence of individualism and structuralism (cf. Wendt 1999 and Giddens 1984), among many others.

2.2.2.3 The Timing of Peace Efforts

Another debate in the academic literature on mediation processes is concerned with the timing for the initiation of peace efforts. In this context, it is argued that a specific point in time of the life-cycle of the conflict is of crucial importance: the moment of ripeness.

One of the first references to ripeness theory was made by Saadia Touval when covering the topic of the Arab Israeli conflict (cf. Touval 1982), stressing the importance of timing. I. William Zartman established and refined the concept of the Theory of Ripeness in a variety of publications (cf. Zartman 1985; Zartman 1989; Zartman in Stern/Druckman 2000; Zartman 2001c; Zartman 2007; and Zartman/DeSoto 2010; among others). The Theory of Ripeness follows the idea that specific variables have to be given, so that the conflict is 'ripe' for resolution. Only if conflict ripeness can be constituted, it makes sense to initiate peace talks since only then, the belligerents enter peace talks sincerely and do not use them opportunistically for other ends such as re-armament or restrengthening. The variables that have to be given are a mutually hurting stalemate

(MHS) and a sense of a way out (SWO). Zartman's approach was further developed by Richard N. Haass who stated that, "the absence of ripeness explains why diplomats fail" in the resolution of conflicts (Haass 1992, p.138).

Scholars tested the theory with different focal points as for instance Stephen John Stedman who confirmed the idea of ripeness by applying the concept to the conflict in Zimbabwe in the 1970s (cf. Stedman 1991) and Eamann O'Kane who applied the theory to the Irish conflict (cf. O'Kane 2006). Moorad Mooradian and Daniel Druckman tested ripeness in the case of the Nagorno-Karabakh conflict of 1990 to 1995, in which they identified ripeness (cf. Mooradian 1999). They especially emphasized one variable leaning on the work of Stedman regarding hardliners and softliners (cf. Stedman 1991). It refers to the idea that the leadership of the belligerents is particularly important for the successful usage of ripeness. It appears crucial whether the leadership is actually in a position to take and implement decisions such as the willingness to negotiate or whether their position is too weak within the construct of their group, so that when they enter negotiations, their troops will not follow their instructions, which would then be a kind of "involuntary defection" (cf. Iklé 1991, p.60; Fortna 2004, p.11 and p.18).

Other examples of identifying ripeness in specific cases were made by Alvaro DeSoto analyzing the Salvadorian conflict from 1989 (cf. DeSoto in Crocker/Hampson, et al. 1999), Chester A. Crocker who identified ripeness in the South West African conflict in 1988 (cf. Crocker 1992), and Alan J. Kuperman who tested the theory on Rwanda and Bosnia (cf. Kuperman in Khadiagala/Lyons 2001), among others. Bertram I. Spector concluded that ripeness as introduced by Zartman "has become a central conceptual framework employed by researchers to explain the onset of negotiation processes and by policy-makers to decide on those conflicts amenable to resolution and positive interventions" (Spector in Lyons, T./Khadiagala 2008, p.27).

Further research looked for ways to identify the elements of ripeness. Especially Thomas Ohlson et alia (cf. Ohlson/Stedman, et al. 1994), Timothy Sisk (cf. Sisk 1995), and Daniel Lieberfeld (cf. Lieberfeld 1999b) defined factors helping to pinpoint Zartman's two identified crucial variables of an MHS or an SWO. The most comprehensive overview of this effort has been published by Zartman together with Avaro DeSoto in "Timing Mediation Initiatives" (cf. Zartman/DeSoto 2010). Zartman and DeSoto developed a toolkit providing potential mediators with a checklist for the identification of ripeness. They suggest to take five steps to analyze a situation on whether ripeness exists, which consist of assessing the existence and the perception of a stalemate, assessing the existence and perception of a way out, inducing recognition of the stalemate and a way out, ripening the stalemate and a way out, and finally positioning oneself as a future mediator. These five steps prescribe what potential modes of actions can be taken if considering the initiation of peace efforts (cf. Zartman/DeSoto 2010).

The scholars Jeffrey Z. Rubin, Dean G. Pruitt and Sung Hee Kim shed a different light on the Theory of Ripeness by developing the so-called Readiness Theory (cf. Rubin/Pruitt, et al. 1994). Here, they basically focus on two aspects: the motivational ripeness that is defined as the motivation to achieve de-escalation and optimism about finding a mutually acceptable agreement. Pruitt further outlined the Readiness Theory in 1997 when applying it to the Israeli-Palestinian relations and the Oslo Talks. He describes how the Readiness Theory originally stems from the Theory of Ripeness, yet, "its structure comes from a psychological model of strategic choice, the author's goal/expectation theory of cooperation in the prisoner's dilemma" (Pruitt 1997, p.239)[17].

Others suggested refinements to the Theory of Ripeness focusing on individual variables of the theory. One such was generated from the above mentioned case study on Zimbabwe conducted by Stedman stating that only some, but not all parties have to perceive a hurting stalemate (cf. Stedman 1991). It depends on the degree of involvement of the respective parties and their individual leverage of counteracting a peace process whether their input is decisive.

Another refinement was suggested by Daniel Lieberfeld. He took up the notion that a mutually hurting stalemate can result from an impending catastrophe, i.e. a precipice, facing one or more of the belligerents. In the original theory, it was stated that such precipice is a consequence resulting from the dynamics of the conflict. Lieberfeld claims that an impending catastrophe must not always stem from a threat from the enemy, but might also come from domestic rivals to incumbent leadership (cf. Lieberfeld 1999b), i.e. from internal threats.

Alan J. Kuperman suggested refining the theory by stating that it implies a prescription for policy-makers regarding "ripening". In his view, it is possible for external parties to become pro-actively involved in the ripening process by way of manipulating the conflict in order to "make it ripe" (cf. Kuperman in Lyons, T./Khadiagala 2008). Kuperman draws three lessons from his empirical application of the Theory of Ripeness to the cases of Bosnia, Rwanda and Kosovo. He suggests firstly, that mediators "should propose peace terms that represent an actual compromise", so that the belligerents' vital interests are not threatened; secondly, that the notion should be included that "ripening is safer if the parties

---

[17] The Readiness Theory will be explained in more detail below.

lack a significant capability to escalate autonomously"; and thirdly, that "mediator threats and inducements must be sufficiently large and credible to persuade all sides that continued fighting or escalation is futile" (Kuperman in Lyons, T./Khadiagala 2008, p.18). The notion of ripening was taken up by others as for example by Zartman and DeSoto (cf. Zartman/DeSoto 2010) and Wilkenfeld, Young et alia (cf. Wilkenfeld/Young, et al. 2005, p.147). Kuperman further notes that the ripening-process has to be implemented carefully as it may backfire and thus escalate the conflict even further (cf. Kuperman in Lyons, T./Khadiagala 2008, pp.15-16).

Zartman himself further refined the theory by expanding it. He included mutually enticing opportunities (MEOs) as a variable into the theory in his work from 2006, "Ripeness Revisited: The Push and Pull of Conflict Management" (cf. Zartman in Hauswedell 2006). He outlines that once ripeness has been identified and taken up, the so-called pull factor comes into play, referring to the need to establish and maintain MEOs for the belligerents to keep the peace process alive and establish a durable peace. Some research is critical of the Theory of Ripeness, not offering refinements, but disapproving the concept. The main representatives of this school of thought are Marieke Kleiboer (cf. Kleiboer 1994) and Thanja Paffenholz (cf. Paffenholz 2001). They claim that ripeness is a tautology as it can usually only be analyzed in the aftermath of an event. Kleiboer claims that if the conflict was not ripe, there was no opportunity for a mediation to be successful anyways, rendering the theory useless (cf. Kleiboer 1994, p.109).

Paffenholz goes further and sees the Theory of Ripeness as a risk. She believes that potential interveners would wait for ripeness to occur. This implies the danger of inactivity. Paffenholz suggests to rather use a concept that she calls "window of opportunity" as windows can be "opened and closed". This refers to an event that can occur more often than only once (Paffenholz 2001, pp.9-10). This idea points to the notion of the correct acting on ripeness. It draws on the difficulty in identifying and then exploiting ripeness. Bruce W. Jentleson drew a comparison to crops in order to explain the phenomenon: "Natural processes do not work only in one direction; they can move toward ripening but also toward 'rotting'. The crops can be left in the fields too long as well as harvested in too early, but it also can deteriorate over time, grow worse, become too far gone" (Jentleson in Crocker/Hampson, et al. 2001, p.254). Jentleson's explanation thus highlights two potential risks, which are either waiting too long, so that ripeness passes, or acting too early, so that ripeness has not been fully established.

Another critique of ripeness in a milder form can be found in Fen Osler Hampson's work (cf. Hampson 1996). He acknowledges the importance of the concept of ripeness. However, Hampson states that ripeness might be a problematic notion due to its demanding character with respect to third parties (cf. Wilkenfeld/Young, et al. 2005, p.55; Collier, P. 2003, p.121). Ripeness is not seen as a self-perpetuating concept, but something that the third party has to work on for the sake of furthering the peace process. Hampson mentions the term "unripening" that could occur during the peace agreement implementation phase (Hampson 1996, p.16). He is concerned with the post-conflict implementation of peace agreements and thus sees ripeness as only one minor building block for it.

In different works on ripeness, those three objections have been answered to. The claim that the Theory of Ripeness is a mere tautology assumes that it is only possible to identify ripeness in "ad post"-analyses. If this statement was true, it is still possible to collect indications that hint towards ripeness in such a convincing amount that ripeness may be constituted. Just as in the discipline of law, indications are crucial factors to work with. These can qualify for *evidence* so that a policy action may be legitimized on the basis of the indications. The investigations for such evidence would undergo the exact same process as an "ad post"-analysis of a conflict. An actor in conflict resolution can only work on best options available – complete knowledge and security about the future course of events is an illusion. Thus, indications are the basis for the Theory of Ripeness, so that the theory can be used as a prescriptive theory for policy-makers and therefore does not fall under the classification of a tautological concept (cf. Kuperman in Lyons, T./Khadiagala 2008, p.9 and Zartman in Stern/Druckman 2000). The above-mentioned "checklist" by Zartman and DeSoto helping practitioners to identify ripeness during a conflict answers directly to the objection of tautology. In fact, with this publication, it is claimed that by using certain tools, it is possible to pinpoint ripeness through both objective and subjective indicators. Furthermore, the argument that it is only possible to identify ripeness once negotiations have started is also addressed. They state, "implementation of mediation depends first on recognition of the ripeness and then on exploitation of the moment" (Zartman/DeSoto 2010, p.6). This shows that situations are accounted for in which ripeness was identified, but negotiations did not take place. This logic in itself makes the accusation of tautology invalid. A last aspect Zartman and DeSoto bring up in this context is the objection that not all negotiations are a result of ripeness. However, in "Timing Mediation Initiatives", they quote Iklé saying that, "negotiation may be a tactical interlude, a breather for rest and rearmament, a sop to external pressure, without any intent of opening a sincere search for a joint outcome". Zartman's way to address this is to add "sincere" or "serious" to the goal of negotiations (cf. Zartman/DeSoto 2010, p.47). This notion also answers Jentleson's fear that a mediator could act too early or too late, so that ripeness is not at the height of its intensity. It shows that through certain tools, it actually is possible to determine whether ripeness exists or not and how intense such ripeness might be.

Second, the risks for policy-makers were mentioned as criticism of the Theory of Ripeness in terms of inactivity. It is assumed that policy-makers might just wait for the moment to be ripe and therefore do not act. This critique was taken up by several academics (cf. Khadiagala 2007, p.4; Kuperman in Lyons, T./Khadiagala 2008; Zartman in Stern/Druckman 2000; Zartman/DeSoto 2010, pp.35-42). According to these proponents of the theory, a third party can pro-actively influence a situation, so that they further ripeness at a given moment. This can be done through the above quoted general instruments of mediators, which contain threatening the use of force, the use of force, sanctions, inducements, or peaceful diplomacy. Accordingly, "the absence of ripeness is not a valid reason for inaction. Prospective mediators (and the parties themselves) can develop a policy of ripening, cultivating both objective and subjective elements of ripeness if these elements do not appear on their own" (Zartman/DeSoto 2010, pp.6-7).

The last criticism concerned the idea that one should rather use the expression of "windows of opportunity" as they can actually be opened and closed repeatedly (cf. Paffenholz 2001). Zartman believes that this criticism does not contradict the Theory of Ripeness (personal interview with author in June 2009[18]). The theory does not state that ripeness is a one-moment opportunity in a conflict. Quite the opposite, moments of ripeness might come often, or might come never if not pushed: "Ripeness is dynamic; it can emerge as easily as it can disappear" (Haass 1992, p.145). In this context, it is worth mentioning that in much of the related academic literature, the authors use the term ripe moment to describe ripeness. This has repeatedly led to confusion in debates on the Theory of Ripeness. Ripeness is better explained as a phase than a moment. Therefore, the author will – where appropriate – use the term 'ripe phase' in order to express the idea that ripeness is not a single occasion that is apparent for an hour or one day. It rather reflects that ripeness is a phase in the dynamics of a conflict. It can occur never, once or several times throughout a conflict. The length and intensity of ripeness might also differ from time to time.

---

[18] Personal Interview with I. William Zartman on 18 June 2009 in Munich, Germany.

2.2.2.4 The Effect and Role of Development Aid in Conflicts

Regarding the schools of thought and research about conflict and development, two aspects are specifically interesting: firstly, the debate about the relationship between economic development and conflict; and secondly, the debate about development projects and conflict. The two cover different topics. While the first debate analyzes the origins of conflict, the second looks at the effect of development projects on the course of the conflict or the effect a conflict takes on the implementation of development projects. The first debate entails three relevant schools of thought (cf. Esman in Montville 1991, pp.477-490). The first school of thought states that through economic development and growth, tensions between groups are minimized as economic expansions make a positive-sum game possible. The second school of thought states the opposite. Here, it is assumed that economic growth raises expectations and discontents, and sharpens the resentments of the relatively disadvantaged. It describes a situation that can be called a zero-sum game. The third school of thought does not believe that economic growth has any impact at all on the sources of conflict as it is assumed that those originate from other, rather political causes. It is an independent approach to development.

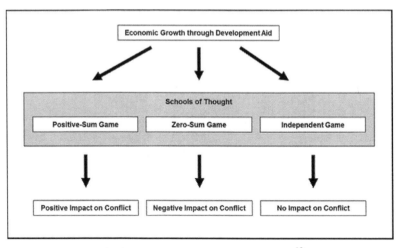

Figure 3: Economic Growth and its Impact on Conflict[19]

---

[19] Source: Own illustration.

Representatives of the Positive-Sum Game school of thought are James Fearon and David Laitin. They assume that the primary source of conflict is poverty. Thus, if a country experiences overall economic growth, they believe that in parallel an overall decrease of poverty will occur, leading to less tensions and conflict (cf. Fearon/Laitin 2003b). This line of thought is also supported by Paul Collier and Anke Hoeffler through their econometric model predicting the outbreak of civil war. They state that what matters most is need. If people have nothing to lose, they will take up arms and fight. However, if a country is blessed with economic growth, the need felt before is reduced and thus the costs for conflict rise. Therefore, war is less likely to break out (cf. Collier, P. 2003, p.8; Collier, P./Hoeffler 2004b). Another supporter of this argument is Philippe Le Billon. He stresses the idea that growth reduces the risk of conflict; yet, he also points to the risk of economic shocks in the process of economic growth, which then potentially creates greater vulnerability to conflict (cf. Le Billon in Bercovitch/Kremenyuk, et al. 2009).

The Zero-Sum Game school of thought is reflected in the works of Jeffrey Rubin, among others. He outlines that what matters most in terms of increasing tensions is the so-called perceived relative deprivation (cf. Rubin/Pruitt, et al. 1994), which means that some people from the community feel that they are disadvantaged relative to others. This feeling can be intensified by an increase in the overall economic wealth because the crucial point in this context is the perception relative to others as opposed to the absolute suffering of people. Thus, this school of thought is based on the idea of the predominance of grievance or greed when it comes to the causes of conflict.

The Independent Game school of thought expresses the idea that conflict and economic growth are neither having a positive nor a negative effect on each other. It is assumed that the causes for tensions and conflict lie within political issues and ideologies. Thus it is a form of creed that matters most. Representatives for this school of thought are academics focusing on non-economic matters. John A. Vasquez and Brandon Valeriano emphasize the importance of territorial disputes for civil wars (Vasquez and Valeriano in Bercovitch/ Kremenyuk, et al. 2009) and Ted Robert Gurr stresses the significance of minority issues from a political perspective rather than an economic one (Gurr in Crocker/Hampson, et al. 2001).

The three schools of thought are also mirrored in the book "Rethinking the Economics of War: the Intersection of Need, Creed, and Greed" (Arnson/ Zartman 2005). The book's authors mostly come to the conclusion that none of the three notions is mutually exclusive and solely responsible for the generation of tensions or conflict. It is rather the combination of all that feeds into it. It is assumed that in every case there is always more than one consequence from a certain development. Thus, economic growth might have a positive impact on one group, it might have a negative one on the other and finally there might be a third group that is not affected by this at all. Need, creed and greed are helpful categories to analyze the sources of conflict.

The second debate about development and conflict concerns the impact of development projects on conflict and vice versa. While the notion that conflicts have a negative impact on the implementation of individual development projects and the overall development progress of a country is trivial[20] or as Robert Kappel put it, "no one can avoid realizing that the continent [Africa] is still marked by civil wars, political instability and also wars, which of course destroys any potential for development" (Kappel 1999, p.3), the other direction of the relationship is not as un-debated.

The debate on the effect that development aid takes on conflicts can be structured into two categories. One considers the indirect consequences of projects on the conflict's status. The other covers the research on development projects that are dedicated to peace building. The latter will be discussed in the next sub-chapter below.

The former category of research concerns the question of what impact aid-projects (indirectly) have on the course of conflicts. Andreas Mehler and Claude Ribaux consider this in their work from 2000 (cf. Mehler/Ribaux 2000) and discuss how it is possible to prevent unintentional exacerbations of conflict through technical cooperation. They claim that this debate was triggered through the disastrous events in Rwanda (Mehler/Ribaux 2000, p.12). As part of their argument, they take up the notion of most agencies claiming they are 'apolitical' actors; yet Mehler and Ribaux state, that "this philosophy is an obstacle to conflict management, because technical cooperation is per se of political nature" (Mehler/Ribaux 2000, p.18). They claim that conflicts constitute very complex constellations of events. Especially due to the involvement of countless actors such as development agencies, peace building organizations, diplomatic repre-sentatives, the government, the donors and many others, it seems impossible to

---

[20] Those readers interested in a detailed account on the effects of conflict on development projects, can find an in-depth account in the work of Karl Wolfgang Menck (cf. Menck (2005): Gewaltsame Konflikte in Entwicklungsländern: Ursachen und Maßnahmen zur Vermeidung, pp. 7-14). Additionally, a list of problems/challenges and proposals for solution on the impact of conflict on humanitarian projects is provided in a study published by the Stiftung Entwicklung und Frieden (Debiel/Fischer, et al. (1999): "Effektive Krisenprävention: Herausforderungen für die deutsche Außen- und Entwicklungspolitik", *Stiftung Entwicklung und Frieden*) and in a study by Stephan Klingebiel and Katja Roehder (Klingebiel and Roehder (2004): "Development-Military Interfaces: New Challenges in Crises and Post-conflict Situations", *German Development Institute, GDI, Reports and Working Papers*).

control the impact that development projects have on the course of the conflict. Thus, they suggest to follow the approach of "Do No Harm" (cf. Mehler/Ribaux 2000, p.15).

A similar argument was made by Peter Uvin. He analyzed the impact of development aid on the outbreak of violence in the case of Rwanda. He further addressed the question of why it was not possible for the development institutions that were present in Rwanda to prevent the escalation into a genocide or at least function as 'early warners' to the international community. Uvin's conclusions are mainly focused on stressing the issue of a lack of coordination among the large number of different donors present in the country (cf. Uvin 1998). Also other scholars made the demand for better coordination among the actors in the so-called development society in conflict situations (cf. Belgrad/ Nachmias 1997; Breslauer/Kreisler, et al. 1991; Burall/Maxwell, et al. 2006; Cracknell 2000; or Faust/Messner 2007) and more reflection with respect to their impact on the conflict situations (cf. Atmar/Goodhand 2002; various authors in Klein/Roth 2007; or Klingebiel 1999).

A further dimension of the do-no-harm debate concerns unintentional consequences from the delivery of development aid due to logistics. Daniel P.L. Chong summarizes this fear by stating, "humanitarian aid often plays into the framework of the parallel economy by delivering resources through the hands of combatants" (Chong in Milliken 2003, p.203). What is meant in this context is the notion that "despite the best intentions of aid workers, and at times because of them, they become logisticians in the war efforts of warlords, fundamentalists, gangsters, and ethnic cleansers" (Rieff 1998, p.30).

A range of frameworks has been developed that take up the challenge of designing development work in a conflict sensitive way: Mary Anderson's "Do No Harm" is one of the most cited and referred to approaches in this academic field. In her book "Do No Harm – How Aid Can Support Peace – or War", she outlines the approach (Anderson 1999). The findings are based on experiences from the Local Capacities for Peace Project, which was conducted by interviewing aid workers. Anderson concludes that aid projects cannot be conducted independently from the conflict situation in the country they are acting in. The aim of the project was to improve the processes of aid delivery, so that doing harm can be avoided. Anderson believes there are five ways in which aid affects conflict: theft of the aid resources by warriors, an affection of the markets by reinforcing either the war or peace economy, distributional impacts concerning intergroup relationships by feeding tensions or reinforcing connections, substitution of local resources required to meet civilian needs, freeing them to support the war, and finally the legitimization of people, their actions or agendas (Anderson 1999, p.39). Anderson's vision is to transform negative impact of aid projects into positive impact. Three action points are proposed: a change of the attitude of the aid workers, an awareness for lifestyle issues of the aid workers, and an awareness for the safety of the aid workers (Anderson 1999, pp.60-63). Thus, Do No Harm actually sees the aid workers in the field as the main lever to change the impact. Anderson's approach can be visualized as demonstrated below.

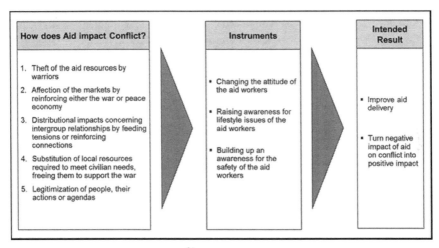

Figure 4: Do No Harm Approach[21]

Acknowledging the notion that development projects might have unintended negative consequences for the further course of the conflict, many authors refer to Do No Harm as the minimum requirement: Mark Hoffmann states that there is a need to further develop an understanding of the contexts, conditions and circumstances when operating in a conflict region (cf. Hoffman 2004). Robert Muscat thinks that all agencies involved in aid work should at least "adopt the Hippocratic Oath of Do No Harm" (cf. Muscat 2002, p.124). Jörn Grävingholt mentions Do No Harm as an important principle for crisis prevention efforts (cf. Grävingholt 2004), and Martina Fischer recognizes the principle as one that most agencies have committed themselves to (cf. Fischer, M. 2006).

---

[21] Source: Own illustration on basis of Mary Anderson's approach (cf. Anderson (1999): Do No Harm: How Aid Can Support Peace - Or War).

A similar approach has been established by Kenneth Bush a little earlier. He called his approach the "Peace and Conflict Impact Assessment (PCIA)" (Bush 1998). Bush identified five areas of potential peace and conflict impact, which are the institutional capacity to manage violent conflict and to promote tolerance and build peace, military and human security, political structures and processes, economic structures and processes, and finally social reconstruction and empowerment. In his opinion, those are the five areas, where development projects might have a negative impact on the course of the conflict. In the further definition of those five areas, it becomes clear that content-wise they are relatively close to Anderson's definitions. Bush suggests analyzing projects along those five areas in order to avoid unintended consequences. Mark Hoffman further outlined the PCIA by challenging it through issues and problems connected (cf. Hoffman 2004). For example, he suggested that the practitioners needs to develop a "far more sophisticated sense of the linkages and interconnections" between different types and levels of evaluations (Hoffman 2004, p.17). It shows that the PCIA was taken up and further developed in the field.

'Conflict Sensitivity' is another approach, developed by Maria Lange and Mick Quinn. It demands from development projects to continuously analyze the situation they are working in to measure the impact their work has on the project. The approach demands that the people in charge of development projects in conflict situations should undergo a threefold analysis. Firstly, they should understand the (conflict) context in which they operate. Secondly, they should understand the interaction between their intervention and the (conflict) context and thirdly, they should act upon the understanding of this interaction in order to avoid negative impacts and maximize positive impacts on the (conflict) context and the intervention (Lange/Quinn 2003, p.5).

Also other authors have addressed the challenges arising from conducting development projects in conflict situations. Stephan Klingebiel advised the German development cooperation on how to implement projects (cf. Klingebiel 1999 and Klingebiel/Eberle, et al. 2000). He recognized the risk of negative implications regarding the conflict through development projects. Klingebiel suggested to strategically collect experiences, so that consequences can be monitored. He also stressed the need for better donor coordination among the governments and institutions on an international level[22]. Klingebiel believes that

---

[22] The demand for better donor coordination comes up in a lot of research in this field. Examples are Spelten/Hausmann, et al. (2006): State and Non-State Cooperation for Crisis Prevention and Peace-Building Policy; Picciotto (2006): Development Effectiveness at the Country Level; or regarding mediation: Crocker/Hampson, et al. (1999): Herding Cats: Multiparty Mediation in a Complex World, pp.57-59.

mainstreaming conflict sensitivity in all development work is necessary and even developed a specific instrument, the Tension and Conflict Impact Analysis, which outlines six steps to be taken in order to design projects in a conflict sensitive way (cf. Klingebiel/Eberle, et al. 2000, pp.II-III). This idea is reflected in much of the work of researchers at the German Development Institute. They consistently point out that more coordination among actors involved in the field is important and even crucial so that a negative impact on conflict through development projects can be minimized (cf. German Development Institute 2001, German Development Institute 2002, and German Development Institute 2004).

Klaus Schlichte points to another dimension of how development aid can negatively affect conflict (Schlichte in Fahrenhorst 1999). He stated that the aid-donors unintentionally take a legitimizing role. Belligerents gain political legitimacy by close contacts to donors. This especially appeals to non-state actors. With this argument, Schlichte took up the fifth aspect of Anderson regarding the impact of aid on conflicts. Schlichte expanded this aspect in that he also mentioned the longer period-dimension, which goes beyond the time of the conflict and considers the establishment of the group in the international arena in the long run.

Regionald Moreels demanded a culture of conflict prevention as a basis for every development project (cf. Moreels in Wulf/Esser 2000). David R. Smock suggested a plan of eight steps that NGOs can take to minimize the negative impact of humanitarian aid including improved planning and providing aid having the longest term benefit to particular targeted groups (cf. Smock 1996, p.v). Others focused on addressing specific agencies and asking them to operate accordingly (cf. Betty Bigombe addressing the World Bank and Reinhart Helmke addressing the UN in Wulf/Esser 2000).

Ben Barber wrote an article with the title "Feeding Refugees, Or War?" (Barber 1997). In this article, Barber empirically analyzed the issue and tried to identify the potential consequences that emerge from providing aid to countries at civil war. Barber points out that humanitarian aid can be twisted, so that it rather fuels the conflict instead of helping the civilians. His case studies mainly surround the topic of refugees and how rebel groups can re-strengthen themselves through receiving food and shelter from relief organizations. One example he mentions concerns the impact aid can have in the context of refugee camps: "the packed camps, protected international sympathy and international law, provide excellent cover for guerrillas and serve as bases from which they [the rebels] can launch attacks" (cf. Barber 1997, p.8).

The debates on aid and conflict have been taken up in a conference in the Netherlands in 2001 with the title "International Conference Towards Better

Peacebuilding Practice". In the summary, it becomes clear that most actors involved do acknowledge the existence of an interrelationship between aid and conflict and the possibility of negative consequences. Their answer to this challenge is to focus on training the people in the field, so that they personally approach projects with greater care in terms of conflict sensitivity (cf. Galama/Tongeren 2002).

A slightly different opinion is outlined in a study by the Stiftung Wissenschaft und Politik, which is concerned with "unintended consequences of humanitarian assistance" in the case of Sudan (Loane/Moyroud 2001). Due to the fact that the authors' focus is purely on humanitarian aid and thus does not assess longer run development projects, they cover only part of what is referred to by other authors mentioned above. However, it is claimed that assistance is in fact delivered in respect of the principles of humanity and impartiality and that it cannot be proven that relief exacerbated conflict. They argue counterfactually when stating that, "there was almost no aid to the South [of Darfur] during the first civil war and very little during the first seven years of the current war" (Loane/Moyroud 2001, p.39) and by that arguing that conflict prevailed nevertheless and must therefore have been exacerbated by other factors. Thus the conclusion is that if relief was stopped, war would not end.

All viewpoints in the debate on conflict and aid show a common and broad acceptance in the wider academic community that development projects do affect the course of the conflict. This effect might be positive or negative, intended or unintended.

2.2.2.5 The Intersection of Aid and Conflict Resolution Efforts

When looking at the intersection of aid and conflict resolution, two categories of impact are of importance. The first concerns conflict resolution efforts made by actors from the development aid providers. The second refers to (indirect) consequences of development aid on conflict resolution efforts.
To start with the former, different approaches exist analyzing the effectiveness of specific conflict prevention efforts by development agencies (cf. Galama/ Tongeren 2002, p.16 and p.160; Klingebiel/Eberle, et al. 2000, p.I). This refers to NGOs and other development agencies specialized on easing tensions or reconciliation of divided groups (cf. Aall in Crocker/Hampson, et al. 2001, pp.365-383). It is what is called Track II and III diplomacy. Bigdon and Korf provide an account on the advantages of such diplomacy emphasizing that development agencies are valuable for initiating peace efforts due to their vicinity to the grass-roots level (cf. Bigdon/Korf 2004). Fitzduff and Church

make the argument that the influence of NGOs in this field constantly rises given their increasing budget (cf. Fitzduff/Church 2004). The idea of development organizations to take on a proactive role in peace building is mirrored in the maximalist school of thought. While this school of thought argues that one should leverage the potential of development organizations in additional areas than solely pure development work, its opponent, the minimalist school of thought, believes that NGOs and other development agencies do more harm than good in such areas and thus should only focus on 'core' developmental work (cf. Goodhand 2006). Robert Picciotto is a strong proponent for the maximalist school of thought stating that conflict management should be one of the core tasks of development agencies (cf. Picciotto 2006).

The second category of research in this context concerns the (indirect) consequences of development aid on conflict resolution efforts. While we have seen that quite a substantial body of literature exists considering the facets of impact of development aid on conflict in general, no direct reference was found regarding the question to what extent it has an effect on conflict resolution efforts, specifically, on conflict ripeness. This is where the analysis steps in and tries to contribute to the academic body of literature through theory and empirical analysis: does development aid affect conflict ripeness?

2.3 Terminology and Definitions

Before starting the actual analysis, this sub-chapter provides an overview of the terminology used. It is structured into the two areas of *conflict* (3.3.1) and *aid* (3.3.2). Individual terms will be defined, as well as concepts. The reason lies within the sometimes varying definitions of certain terminology, which is apparent in the complex topic "reflecting distinct moral discourses and political positions" (Goodhand 2006, p.9); or as Ropers coined it, the "non-uniform terminology" in the field (Ropers 1997, p.5). The aim is to create a basis of definitions for the further analysis.

2.3.1 Conflict

The Latin root of the word conflict is 'confligere', which means 'to bang together', 'to clash'. In political sciences, the term has not been properly defined in one single sense. *Conflict* can refer to a range of meanings and varies depending on each author (cf. Muscat 2002, p.107). In its purest sense, conflict is a social process (cf. Bercovitch/Fretter 2004, p.3), meaning nothing more than a perceived divergence of interest of two or more people (cf. Rubin/Pruitt, et al. 1994, pp.7-8; Heidelberger Institut für Internationale Konfliktforschung 2008, p.i; Bercovitch/Kremenyuk, et al. 2009, p.3; among others). This in itself does not say anything about the type of parties involved or about the intensity of the conflict. Conflict is prevalent in any situation or constellation of people – in families as well as among friends, conflict is a common notion. Thorsten Bonacker points to the fact that in certain situations, a divergence of interests can even have a pacifying effect (cf. Bonacker 2005, p.16; Bercovitch/Fretter 2004, p.3). Thus conflict does not always have a negative notion. Interests in the context of conflict are defined as a form of aspiration, which are "a behavioral representation of the things that Party strives for or believes it must exceed" (Rubin/Pruitt, et al. 1994, p.12).

On the political level, the meaning of conflict differs depending on its intensity. As stated above, conflict is a norm in international relations (cf. Bercovitch/Kremenyuk, et al. 2009, p.10). The type of conflict that the analysis is concerned with displays a level of intensity, at which the social process has escalated into violence. The parties to the conflict use violent means in order to pursue their respective interests. This follows Carl von Clausewitz's definition of war as outlined in his famous treatise "On War", published in 1832: "War is an act of violence intended to compel our opponent to fulfill our will" (Clausewitz/Graham, et al. 1968, p.101). Von Clausewitz also outlines that war can never consist of a single event. It is rather an ongoing sequence of events. This is what differentiates war or in this context civil wars from terrorist attacks. The terms militarized conflict and civil war are used synonymously in this analysis.

It is important to distinguish international war and internal militarized conflict. International war refers to military actions between two or more parties, in which the primary belligerents are state-actors. Internal, intra-state or civil war, instead, refers to a conflict within a state. Unlike international war, it is fought on its territory and does not follow any structure of rules (cf. Collier, P. 2003, p.11). Structure of rules in this context refers to a phenomenon from international war. Here, we have witnessed the establishment of certain laws of war (cf. Cohen and Deng in Stockholm International Peace Research Institute 2009, p.21). But these seem not to be applicable in internal conflicts. Even though some authors claim that the distinction between international and internal conflicts becomes increasingly blurred (cf. Goodhand 2006, p.10), this analysis follows a definition related to the nature of the primary actors. International wars' primary actors on both belligerent sides are state-actors, whereas in internal conflicts only one of the belligerents constitutes a state-actor (if at all).

2.3.1.1 Type of Conflict

Tetzlaff and Jakobeit define five types of war. They differentiate between firstly, anti-colonial national wars of independence, secondly, inter-state wars about borders, resources or humans, thirdly, secession wars within ethnic-cultural heterogeneous states, fourthly, anti-regime wars or internal wars, and fifthly, the so-called new wars that are characterized as regional wars, which cannot be defined with the commonly used categories of war and peace (Tetzlaff/Jakobeit 2005, p.106). In this analysis, the types of interest are the third, fourth and fifth ones. Neither anti-colonial nor inter-state wars will be covered.

Furthermore, the adjectives accompanying the terms "conflict" or "war" describing the violent character such as "armed", "militarized" or simply "violent" do not differ in their meaning as for this analysis. If used, they refer to the high level of intensity of the conflict described. A *major* conflict or war and a *minor* conflict or war are to be distinguished at this point. When using *major*, I refer to Paul Collier's and Anke Hoeffler's definition of civil war of at least 1,000 combat-related deaths per year (cf. Collier, P./Hoeffler 2004b, p.5; Collier, P./Hoeffler 2004b, p.5)[23]. *Minor* describes a conflict in which there are between 25 and 999 combat-related deaths per year. Both those terms have in common that they refer to a situation in which there are at least 5% fatalities on each side of the belligerents in order to distinguish the conflict from one-sided massacres.

A last notion regarding the type of conflict refers to the internal character. As Tetzlaff and Jakobeit point out, it seems that most civil wars do not necessarily stay completely internal (cf. Tetzlaff/Jakobeit 2005, p.108). Rather, there seems to be more and more of a spillover-effect, observed in countries such as Chad, Congo, among others. Böge and Debiel identified at least three of those effects which go beyond borders of states. Firstly, they refer to refugees entering neighboring countries on large scale; secondly, the usage of refugee camps that are located close to borders as possibilities for rebels to re-strengthen and recruit; and thirdly, the tendency that more and more governments fight rebels even beyond borders without paying attention to the norm of sovereignty (Böge/ Debiel 2003, p.313).

These observations are important when characterizing the developments and types of conflicts. Therefore, it is significant to keep in mind that some conflicts tend to go beyond borders and thus are not purely internally led. However, the

---

[23] The reference of 1,000 combat-related deaths per year is often made in academia in order to define civil wars. The author does acknowledge that there are plenty of problems related to this categorization, particularly the fact that this absolute number is not weighed against population numbers. However, it seems a helpful category in order to at least use some kind of definition-barrier.

main issue of the conflict remains internal and as appropriate, I will continue calling those conflicts internal in the following despite spillover-effects.

2.3.1.2   Belligerents to Civil War

In the case of internal conflict, only one of the belligerents – if at all – is a state-actor. The other party(ies) is (are) a non-state-actor (cf. Stott 2007, p.2). It is important to distinguish between a non-state actor in an internal war and actors from communal violence (cf. Collier, P. 2003, p.11). For the purpose of this analysis, a non-state-actor as a belligerent to civil war is defined as a party to the conflict as consisting of a group of people that is (a) organized, (b) militarized and (c) in possession of an agenda. Those three characteristics are important in order to be able to distinguish a civil war from a crisis or a rebellion (cf. Collier, P. 2003, p.67).

The two latter types of conflict (crisis and rebellion) are referred to as unorganized spontaneous acts against the state, whereas a belligerent of a civil war must fulfill more criteria: being organized (a) means that it has to be possible to identify a certain hierarchical structure in a critical mass of followers. There has to be someone like a leader to the group who is responsible for his subordinates. The leader or leadership team has to also be in official charge to speak for the group. They have to be in charge of ensuring the sustainability of the group. This refers primarily to the financing of such an organization. Members have to receive shelter, food and arms in order to be able to survive. Militarized (b) refers to the notion that the group has to identify itself as soldiers using force as an instrument in order to pursue their interests. This is done by for example openly wearing weapons or uniforms. The third characteristic is to be in possession of an agenda (c). It differentiates a party to a civil war from criminals – having an agenda means that the group has identified and formulated a specific set of interests. They are pursuing those interests and have outlined them to their combatants. Since the combatant disagrees, the group uses force in order to achieve its goals. This mirrors the initial definition of conflict: a divergence of interests. Therefore, such a group is a political organization with regard to their agenda (c). It is a military organization with regard to their militarized character (b). And it is further a kind of consolidated organization as it has to ensure the financing and control over its group. This is what was called before the organized character of the group (a).

2.3.1.3 Conflict Life-Cycle

A conflict as defined above is often described as having a specific life-cycle (cf. Bercovitch/Rubin 1992, p.253; Rubin/Pruitt, et al. 1994). The analogy helps to contextualize the subject of the analysis. The typical life-cycle of a conflict includes five stages, which are durable peace, stable peace in which first tensions are arising, unstable peace in which confrontations occur, crisis when there is an outbreak of violence and war. The same five stages are mirrored in the de-escalating phase from war when a ceasefire is agreed on, to crisis when a settlement is negotiated, to unstable peace when there is a phase of rapprochement, to stable peace with reconciliation and finally durable peace. The five stages of escalation and de-escalation are also connected to a certain room for maneuver for external parties. External parties in this context are third parties entering the conflict in order to impact it. The potential actions for third parties range from diplomatic efforts, via peacemaking, enforcement to post-conflict peace building.

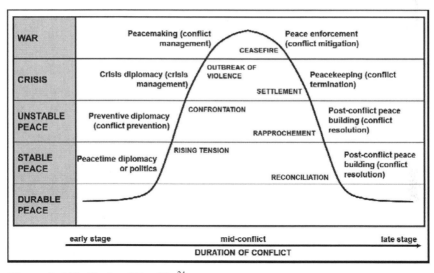

Figure 5: Life-Cycle of Conflict[24]

---

[24] Source: Own illustration after Michael S. Lund in Bercovitch/Kremenyuk, et al. The SAGE Handbook of Conflict Resolution, p.290.

The life-cycle as illustrated in the figure above follows the general framework of how Michael S. Lund describes the cycle. Regarding the life-cycle of conflict, it is to be noted that conflict follows the course of dynamics. Conflict is not a static notion but rather a process (cf. Bercovitch/Fretter 2004, p.4). This means that probably no single conflict has actually ever followed the line drawn above in a strict sense. And no course of conflict is equal to another. It rather goes through what Goodhand calls individual "micro cycles" (Goodhand 2006, p.70). The life-cycle of conflict describes the general stages that each conflict will go through – earlier or later in the time, overlapping at times (cf. Kurtenbach/Seifert 2010, p.10). What is possible though is to identify patterns that are repeated in the individual cycles. The challenges emerging from this complexity of conflict-cycles are particularly mirrored in the practical world of conflict management and development cooperation. As Kirsten Garacochea from the BMZ pointed out, the usage of conflict stages is often impossible due to the blurring of the individual phases and overlapping dynamics[25]. However, assuming that conflict is a social process, it means that it is possible to have an impact on the course of conflict – to manage conflict. It means, it is possible to "move from an incipient, latent stage to maturity and termination" (Bercovitch/Fretter 2004, p.13).

In much of the conflict-related academic literature, terms such as conflict management, conflict resolution, conflict prevention, conflict transformation, peacemaking, peace building, peacekeeping and others are used interchangeably (cf. Reimann 2004, p.2). For the purpose of this analysis, the term conflict resolution will be used in a specific way[26]. Conflict resolution will refer to the actual effort of trying to *resolve* a conflict, i.e. implying a display of peace efforts that lead to a settlement of the conflict as opposed to simply disable one or more of the parties involved from being able to use violent means (cf. Mehler/Ribaux 2000, p.32). The term is defined to only be applicable when an external third party acts in order to bring peace to the conflict that is to terminate the conflict.

Peace agreement in this context is defined as having one of three potential meanings: "formal agreements (treaty, armistice, ceasefire), semi-formal agreements (letter, oral declaration), or tacit understandings (mutual understandings by adversaries, neither stated or written)" (Wilkenfeld/Young, et al. 2005, p.55).

---

[25] Cf. Personal Interview with Kirsten Garacochea on 20 July 2010 in Berlin, Germany.
[26] In some academic literature, conflict management is defined as reaching a political settlement and conflict resolution as resolving all outstanding issues in conflict (cf. Bercovitch and Gartner (2009): International Conflict Mediation: New Approaches and Findings, p.4). However, this seems a confusing approach given that for example humanitarian intervention could be understood as methods of conflict management as well.

2.3.1.4 Mediation

Mediation is defined as a negotiation between belligerents with the support of a third party. It is a subset of negotiation in the sense that it is "an activity made necessary by the inability of the conflicting parties to overcome their conflict and produce a joint agreement on their own. [...] Mediation turns the dyadic relation between the parties into a triad" (Zartman in Bercovitch/Kremenyuk, et al. 2009, p.325; also cf. Bercovitch/Diehl, et al. 1997, p.759; Kleiboer 1996, p.360; and Touval and Zartman in Crocker/Hampson, et al. 2001, p.436; among others). Negotiation is "the process of combining conflicting positions into a joint agreement" (Zartman in Bercovitch/Kremenyuk, et al. 2009, p.322).

Thus, "mediation is essentially a pacific, non-coercive and non-binding approach to conflict management that is entered into freely by the concerned parties, who at the same time maintain control over the substance of the agreement" (Fisher, R.J. 2001, p.4). A mediator is an entity or a person facilitating negotiations. Richard H. Solomon refers to the potential challenges associated to "official" mediation. He states, "the desire of different mediators to assume leading positions, and to take credit for any successes, fosters a competitive and self-interested aspect to the diplomacy of peacemaking that can undermine the coherence of efforts needed to achieve success" (Solomon in Crocker/Hampson, et al. 1999, p.299). Thus, an "official" mediator has to be the one mediator who actually does take the leading role. It may become dangerous if too many third parties try to act as mediators in parallel and by that compete against each other.

2.3.1.5 Third Party/Mediator

The third party may be any actor or form of actor, displaying peace-initiation efforts (cf. Bercovitch/Gartner 2009, p.4). This means, the actor might be a single private person, a government official or an organization: "The list of potential mediators in international conflicts and crises is extensive: single states, groups of states, international governmental organizations, regional governmental organizations, private transnational organizations, private individuals, or a combination of any of these" (Wilkenfeld/Young, et al. 2005, pp.5-6). Mediators might be traditional Track I-, Track II- or Track III-actors as defined by Thanja Paffenholz[27] and also use all these modes for mediation. The third

---

[27] Thanja Paffenholz describes Track I-actors as „usually UN agencies, UN missions, and regional organizations such as the Organisation for Security and Cooperation in Europe (OSCE) or individual

party needs to perceive itself as an external party to the conflict trying to bring the belligerents together with the intention to reach a peace agreement. The third party acts as a mediator. Johannes Vüllers and Sandra Destradi recently published an article covering the topic of the increasingly diverse body of potential types of mediators and the impact thereof. They categorize mediators in four types, which is a useful approach: multilateral institutions, specifically the UN, the Great Powers, regional organizations and neighboring states, and finally specialized NGOs (cf. Vüllers/Destradi 2010).

An external party that intervenes militarily in order to destroy one of the parties and helps one party to victory will not be covered in the research. An external third party must not be biased to the extent that it pursues an end to the conflict by the extreme option of victory and surrender (cf. Kleiboer 1996, p.360). It is neither assumed that a third party mediator has to be entirely neutral (cf. Bercovitch/Rubin 1992, p.6). It depends on the context to which extent the mediator is biased towards one of the parties. This includes the debate on ideal characteristics a mediator should possess. The question whether the mediator should be "insider-partial" or "outsider-neutral" is particularly interesting. It covers the idea that both models might have advantages as well as disadvantages. An "insider-partial" might have a better understanding of the context and might also own greater trust by the belligerents. An "outsider-neutral", might display the needed distance to both parties in order to make credible threats (cf. Assefa 1992, p.105; Khadiagala 2007, pp.5-6; and Wehr/Lederach 1991, p.87).

2.3.1.6 Peace

Different definitions of peace prevail in the academic literature – commonly differentiated as the theory-oriented debate versus the policy-oriented approach; or as termed by Kurtenbach and Seifert as a broader concept versus a non-war conception of peace (Kurtenbach/Seifert 2010, p.11).

In this analysis, when talking about ending a conflict, this refers to bringing peace to the country. Peace will be defined as the absence of violence and thus follows Harald Müller's notion that, "a narrow definition of the term *peace*, which concentrates on the absence of physical violence […], offers practical advantages for the research and is normatively legitimate" (Müller in Hellmann/

---

states". Track II- and Track III-actors "are usually international peace organizations as well as development NGOs, action-oriented research institutes or church-based organizations" (Paffenholz (2001): "Designing Transformation and Intervention Processes", *Berghof Handbook for Conflict Transformation*, p.8).

Wolf, et al. 2003, p.241). This does not imply a judgment of any sort about the justice or fairness of the peace. In fact, in order to establish peace, it may sometimes be necessary to involve actors that committed severe crimes against humanity – an approach hardly compatible with justice (cf. Albin in Bercovitch/ Kremenyuk, et al. 2009, p.581). What is defined as just and fair is often a subjective notion and dependent on the individual perspective (cf. Musto in Fahrenhorst 1999, p.21). The establishment of a fair and just government lies within the field of post-conflict reconstruction and state-building and is not of primary concern to this analysis.

2.3.2   Development Aid

Turning to the other field of research, development aid, there are also terms to be defined. Aid can consist of external monetary and non-monetary influx. External influx refers to any payment, investment, material or personnel that enters into a country and which is financed by external sources. Influx itself can take different forms (also other than development aid) such as diaspora money, private investments, state loans, grants, development projects, or charity.

The external sources providing development aid can be of any kind – governmental or non-governmental; public or private. Development aid can be declared emergency or humanitarian aid; it can be charity-based or systematic aid.

Relief – used synonymously to emergency and humanitarian aid in this analysis – is defined as a subset of development aid that is applied in emergency and humanitarian cases. As Pamela Aall defines it, "Relief is characterized by short-term, emergency service in the face of a disaster, whether natural or man-made. These operations include airlifting food, clean water, and sanitation equipment to distressed populations; establishing shelter for homeless victims; repairing salvageable structures; and preventing, containing, and treating life-threatening diseases" (Aall in Crocker/Hampson, et al. 2001, p.369). The idea is that relief and development cannot be clearly separated anymore. Especially in situations of longer man-made disasters, the line between relief and actual development work is blurred (cf. Bigdon/Korf 2004, p.4; Duffield 1997, p.530; Götze 2004, p.216).

Others see humanitarian aid as completely distinct from development aid as for example Stephan Klingebiel and Katja Roehder. For them, it is not only the immediate character of relief work that is distinct, but also the surrounding context. They assume that for relief work, there is no consent of the partner country needed due to international law provisions (cf. Klingebiel/Roehder 2004, p.33). However, as Pamela Aall suggests, the distinction between the two approaches diminishes (cf. Aall in Crocker/Hampson, et al. 2001, p.368). The borders are not clear-cut and it is not properly defined, at what point humanitarian aid turns into development aid. For that reason, relief will be considered as a subset of development aid; acknowledging that there are specific challenges to relief work in conflict settings that are distinct from longer-term development projects. It is important to note though that the only kind of humanitarian aid considered is aid that follows as a response to manmade disasters as opposed to natural disasters. Manmade disasters are defined as stemming from conflicts. Thus only aid that is provided in the context of a conflict will be of interest.

The analysis follows the definition of development aid as outlined by Dambisa Moyo in her publication on "Dead Aid": "Broadly speaking there exist three types of aid: humanitarian and emergency aid, which is mobilized and dispensed to catastrophes and calamities [...]; charity-based aid, which is disbursed by charitable organizations to institutions or people on the ground; and systematic aid – that is, aid payments made directly to governments either through government-to-government transfers (in which case it is termed bilateral aid) or transferred via institutions such as the World Bank (known as multilateral aid)" (Moyo 2009, p.7).

2.3.2.1 Donors

The provider of aid can be any institution from the so-called development society. Development society refers to any donor and implementing agency involved in development, i.e. governments that give bilateral aid, multilateral institutions that channel aid, private institutions, companies or private individuals giving aid and NGOs of any kind involved in developing work. NGOs in this context are defined as not-for-profit institutions that are private and self-governed. They are generally dedicated to further civil society, end human suffering and promote human needs[28]. Jonathan Goodhand identifies four areas of work: the provision of humanitarian relief in emergencies, the promotion of long-term social and economic development, the promulgation, protection and

---

[28] Dirk Hansohm refers to the problematic implications associated with the term NGO. He provides a range of different definitions by scholars and institutions, stressing that NGOs can take different forms and especially intentions/tasks. The definition used in this context must therefore be seen as not complete and only pragmatic for the sake of this analysis' research. For the outline of definitions, see Hansohm and Kappel (1993): Schwarz-weisse Mythen: Afrika und der entwicklungspoli-tische Diskurs, pp.184-186.

monitoring of human rights, and the pursuit of peace through support for conflict resolution (Goodhand 2006, p.15). It is important to note that some NGOs may solely focus on one of the four areas and others may cover all four areas.

When mentioning NGOs, this refers to organizations that are involved in any type of development work in countries in conflict. The kind of the work must not primarily be connected to peace building activities. This means it also refers to work such as promoting health institutions, education, human rights, environment or economic development as well as work in the fields of good governance, civil society and answering basic human needs. Thus, the analysis follows Martina Fischer in her definition: "Non-governmental organizations (NGOs) are usually referred to as non-state, non-profit orientated groups who pursue purposes of public interest, excluding the private sector" (Fischer, M. 2006, p.3).

2.3.2.2 Increase in Development Aid

In this analysis, a new variable is introduced into the academic writing on conflict and development, which is increase in development aid (IDA). This variable deserves some clarification. While development aid in itself has been explained above, the new variable concerns an increase. The reason mainly lies in the pragmatic approach towards research in the sense that it is only possible to identify the impact of a variable if the variable is isolated and traceable (cf. Van Evera 1997). An ongoing development project that is set in a country of interest cannot be examined if no change occurs. However, if a new project starts, it is possible to isolate the effects of such new event in the context of the surrounding situation.

Increase in this context possesses two dimensions. It refers on the one hand to an actual increase in value of an ongoing effort. That is, if a development project's budget is increased significantly or if the number of a development project's personnel is raised, then we can identify IDA. This is also true for financial assistance in the sense that financial support to one of the belligerents might be increased. The second dimension refers to the initiation of entirely new efforts. Thus, if a new development project is started or if new financial assistance is provided, IDA is also given.

Now, the question arises of what counts when referring to IDA with respect to other development efforts. Let us imagine a situation in which new financial assistance is provided by one donor with another donor cutting his assistance – is it the absolute value of aid that counts or the relative? The answer is simple: the assessment has to be based on what is new or increased and whether the effect is not offset by other happenings. The reason for this approach lies within the significance of the concept of perception in the Theory of Ripeness. It is always the perception of the actors involved that is decisive (cf. Destradi/Mehler 2010, p.2). Therefore, if IDA occurs, it depends on whether the receiver perceives it as an increase for it to function. It is therefore crucial that at least one of the belligerent parties to the conflict perceives an increase. Whether this might be a significant amount of monetary support or the technical support for a borehole is only crucial with respect to the relevant actor's assessment. If the decision-maker of one of the belligerents feels that the additional borehole might strengthen his group significantly, then the technical support for one borehole has to count as IDA. This, of course, might be exaggerated to the readers' eyes but it illustrates the general rule of how to identify IDA. It is not the absolute amount of value in development that comes into a country that counts, but it is the relative perception of the individual relevant actors that is significant.

For the purpose of the further analysis, development is split into three dimensions as generally also referred to in the development aid community and formulized by the DAC (Development Assistance Committee)[29]: financial assistance, technical assistance and personnel dedicated to development work. IDA in those three dimensions can be defined as three types: *Type I Increase in financial aid:* As noted by Kurtenbach and Seifert it is mostly the recipient's government that is the receiver of financial aid (cf. Kurtenbach/Seifert 2010, p.23). The form of financial aid can be manifold. It might be in the form of grants, loans, or bilateral official development assistance (ODA). It is defined as an increase if a new stream of financial aid is opened or existent streams are increased in volume. *Type II Increase in technical aid:* The second type of aid, technical aid, refers to non-monetary support; i.e. development support in the form of material goods. The channels through which this support is delivered are direct bilateral aid streams (from government to government), through NGOs (as in operational, international or community-based organizations; cf. Fischer, M. 2006, p.3), or other donors, going directly to the civilian population in need. Technical aid also includes humanitarian help. It is again then an increase in technical aid, if new projects are initiated providing for more goods or existing projects receive significantly more support in the form of material assistance. *Type III Increase in personnel dedicated to development work:* Aid in the form of type three refers to international staff that implements development projects. The donor in this case might be either governmental or non-governmental depending on whether the projects are conducted bilaterally, multilaterally or

---

[29] Cf. http://www.oecd.org/glossary/0,2586,en_2649_33721_1965693_1_1_1_1,00.html.

whether they are non-governmental projects. The receiver might be the government or the people in need directly. An increase here exists if more people are sent to work in development projects in the country of relevance.

	Type I	**Type II**	**Type III**
Description	Increase in financial aid	Increase in technical aid	Increase in personnel dedicated to development work
Donor	State-actors, multilaterals	State-actors, multilaterals, NGOs	State-actors, multilaterals, NGOs
Receiver	Government of developing country	People in need directly and/or government of developing country as distributor	Government of developing country and/or people in need directly

Table 1: Types of IDA[30]

2.3.2.3 Neutrality and Impartiality

One further feature of most organizations involved in development aid should be explained. Actors from the development society often call their projects neutral and impartial when working in conflict or post-conflict situations (cf. Loane/Moyroud 2001, p.54; Janice Gross Stein in Stern/Druckman 2000, pp. 386). Some even list neutrality and impartiality as principles in their core values (cf. Klingebiel/Roehder 2004, p.10). As Jeanette Schade put it, "neutrality has been considered as one of the core premises for the assignment of humanitarian organizations in conflict and post-conflict situations since the beginnings of humanitarian international law (1864) and the foundation of the International Committee of the Red Cross (ICRC) 1863" (Schade in Klein/Roth 2007, p.179).

What is meant by neutrality and impartiality in this context? The original idea is that those organizations have the aim to provide humanitarian aid to the people independent of their political affiliation or their role in the conflict (cf. Klingebiel/Roehder 2004, p.39). Thus in its purest sense, it stresses the actual humanitarian character of the aid work as opposed to any political meaning. This

---

[30] Source: Own illustration.

definition is what can be generally understood under the term impartiality. Neutrality, however, should be understood in a more distinct way. While the organizations using this term to describe their work refer to neutrality as meaning that they do not want to affect the conflict in any direction, this analysis interprets it differently to a certain extent. When claiming that the aid delivered is *impartial*[31], i.e. feeding and sheltering everyone independent of their ideology, position or history, *neutrality* might not be possible (cf. Debiel/Fischer 2000, p.5; Schlichte in Fahrenhorst 1999, p.51). By providing aid impartially, specific groups of the population are supported. Only by this simple fact, any organization involved affects the conflict and by that – per definition – cannot work neutrally. When NGOs assume they are acting impartially and neutrally and even make this their claim, this might narrow their view for the complexity of the situation and thus avert that they become conflict sensitive in their individual actions.

The actual situation appears very complex. Aspects such as discrimination, feeding soldiers, corruption, etc. have to be taken into account in conflict situations, which all necessarily add to the fact that aid organizations cannot work neutrally. As Jörn Grävingholt put it, "any attempt to 'work around conflicts' in crisis regions, putting on as it were a mien of neutrality, is as a rule bound to fail. Proceeding on the principle that in acute or potential conflict situations every form of external aid is conflict-relevant, a conflict-sensitive development cooperation would thus be restricted to the first two options" (Grävingholt 2004, p.33). The analysis assumes that while the development society might try to act under the principle of impartiality, organizations providing aid in conflict and post-conflict situations will always affect the situation and thus cannot be bound by the principle of neutrality: "Humanitarians must acknowledge that their actions in a complex emergency can have profound political consequences. [...] I, and others, allege that the context of relief assistance has changed so radically that apolitical neutrality is a useful fiction but no longer a viable option" (Stein in Stern/Druckman 2000, p.401).

---

[31] Klingebiel and Roehder outline the different understandings of impartiality, stating that as opposed to humanitarian aid organizations, UN actors define impartiality as ruling out any toleration of serious human rights violations (cf. Klingebiel and Roehder "Development-Military Interfaces: New Challenges in Crises and Post-conflict Situations", p.39).

2.3.2.4 Unintentional Consequences

The last term to be explained is unintentional consequences. As mentioned above, it is assumed that the development society in its collectivity has 'good intentions' when providing aid. The aim is to 'make the world a better place' and to help the people affected by humanitarian disasters, poverty and conflict. Thus a certain good faith is acknowledged in the organizations' aims when providing money, personnel or resources. As outlined above, such honorable intentions are not necessarily mirrored in reality. As the NGO Saferworld put it, "to a casual observer, it might appear that all development programs make a positive impact. Unfortunately, peaceful aims do not always guarantee peaceful outcomes and some well-meaning development programs actually end up in fuelling the conflict" (Saferworld 2008, p.1). Often, projects are not conflict sensitive or do rather harm or even do more harm than good. In such cases, it will be referred to unintentional consequences assuming that the intention was to do good, when the actual result was a negative impact on the overall conflict context. This is not to be confused with the terms *misuse* or *abuse* of aid. Misused and abused aid refers to intended negative consequences of aid delivery.

3 The Theory of Ripeness

The theory to be analyzed is called the Theory of Ripeness. The Theory of Ripeness has been researched on and discussed for about three decades. As outlined above, it was Saadia Touval who was one of the first academics writing on ripeness (cf. Touval 1982). It has also been stated in the academic overview (Chapter 2.2) that the Theory of Ripeness was applied in different case studies by a range of authors who criticized and refined it in different ways. Therefore, it is important to note that this analysis refers to the Theory of Ripeness as outlined by I. William Zartman (cf. Zartman in Stern/Druckman 2000).

In this chapter, the theory will first be outlined and explained (3.1). Secondly, a theoretical conceptualization of the Theory of Ripeness will be provided. This demonstrates counterfactually why the concept of ripeness is of major importance in the overall mediation process (3.2). Thirdly, academic challenges to the theory will be presented, spurring open questions with regard to its operationability as well as the applicability of the Theory of Ripeness. In part, these challenges to the theory are aspects that should be researched on in further studies on ripeness. However, they do not challenge the theory in the sense that they would make the theory untenable. Therefore, it is important to hint towards these open questions, yet, it does not seem necessary to answer them in a full academic context (3.3). Fourthly, the Theory of Ripeness will be revisited, incorporating findings from the relevant academic literature into the theory, so that with the inclusion of a range of further independent variables, it is possible to create an extended version of the Theory of Ripeness that can serve as the basis for the subsequent empirical analysis (3.4). Lastly, hypotheses will be extrapolated from the theory analysis guiding the subsequent case studies (3.5).

3.1 Outline of the Theory of Ripeness

The origins of the Theory of Ripeness go as far back as to 1974, when Henry Kissinger while being US Secretary of State commented in the New York Times that, "a stalemate is the most propitious condition for settlement"[32]. Stalemate is one of the components of the Theory of Ripeness. When Kissinger made this statement, he referred to the idea that in a conflict situation, a certain kind of stalemate should be given in order to be able to reach a settlement between the belligerents.

The notion was taken up by a range of academics, specifically I. William Zartman who started publishing on the topic in 1978 in his book "The Negotiation Process: Theories and Applications" (Zartman 1978) and who eventually established the Theory of Ripeness in academia through multiple refinements. The essence of the theory is best summarized by Zartman himself when he stated that, "parties consider positively the notion of conflict resolution through direct or mediated negotiation when they perceive the conditions of *ripeness*" (Bercovitch/Kremenyuk, et al. 2009, p.329). So what exactly does *ripeness* mean? Many conflict management scholars have written on the process of peace negotiations and the different modes to end violent conflict. The Theory of Ripeness concentrates on one specific point in this context; it deals with the right timing of the initiation of peace talks during an armed conflict. As Haass summarized it, "What is meant by ripeness is the existence of the prerequisites for diplomatic progress, that is, circumstances conducive for negotiated progress or even solution" (Haass 1992, p.6).

In Zartman's opinion the moment to seize an opportunity for peace talks by an external third party bringing the belligerents to a negotiating table has to be ripe for the negotiations to be sincere. This does not mean though that if there was a ripe phase, this guarantees a successful outcome to the peace talks. Ripeness is thus defined as "a necessary, but not a sufficient condition" (Zartman in Stern/Druckman 2000, p.227) for the successful resolution of violent conflicts. Without ripeness, a successful outcome of the peace efforts is impossible; however with ripeness, success is not a given but rests under the further influence of additional conditional variables.

For the sake of illustration, one might draw upon the example of a fruit. Let's picture an avocado. For an avocado to be enjoyable, the avocado has to be ripe. If an avocado is harvested too early, it is not enjoyable. If the avocado is harvested too late, it is rotten. There is, however, a phase, in which the avocado is ripe to be harvested. This is what is meant by explaining that a situation has to

---

[32] Cf. *New York Times*, Kissinger, Henry: 12 October 1974.

be ripe, so that peace negotiations have a potential to be successful. If peace negotiations are started too early or too late, they will not be successful[33].

3.1.1 First Level Variables

The Theory of Ripeness as described in existing literature consists of two levels of variables for the definition of *ripeness*. First level variables are a mutually hurting stalemate (MHS) and a sense of a way out (SWO). Second level variables are objective elements and persuasion. This means that if an MHS exists in an intra-state conflict and further this is connected to an SWO by the individual parties to the conflict, then ripeness is given and it is possible for the actors to decide to negotiate sincerely in order to potentially end violence.

3.1.1.1 Mutually Hurting Stalemate

The term MHS characterizes a situation in which the belligerents are locked in a conflict, in which it does not seem possible to achieve victory for either side. This is what is referred to as a stalemate in a conflict. No progression can be achieved anymore; a deadlock between the belligerents exists.

The deadlocked situation has to be painful to both sides of the conflict, i.e. hurting. A hypothetical cost-benefit analysis of each party would come to the conclusion that the conflict is hurting more than benefiting the individual parties to the conflict and that there is no hope of turning the dynamics of the conflict around, so that victory might be possible after all; or as Touval and Zartman expressed it, "the most obvious motive [to accept mediation as a belligerent] is the expectation that mediation will gain an outcome more favorable than the outcome by continued conflict" (Touval and Zartman in Crocker/Hampson, et al. 2001, p.432). It has to be clear to the belligerents that the current situation is not sustainable and does more harm than good to its own people, own troops, or own elites. Important for the concept of ripeness is the notion that the hurting stalemate has to be mutual, which means it must be perceived by all belligerents. None of the belligerents must feel it can still win the conflict by victory and the cost of maintaining the current situation has to be too high to afford (cf. Fortna

---

[33] The analogy to a fruit in this context, however, should not be taken too far. An example for this is the fact that an avocado can only be ripe once. Yet, a ripe phase in a conflict might occur never, once, or more often – dependent on the conflict setting.

2004, p.13). It is important to note, that mutual in this context does not refer to a symmetric perception. The intensity of the perception can vary between the belligerents (cf. Zartman/DeSoto 2010, p.13).

A stalemate can take different forms. Zartman contrasts two images about the stalemate. The first image is a 'plateau'. Zartman describes this as "a flat and unending terrain without relief" (Zartman in Stern/Druckman 2000, p.228). I.e. the respective relevant actors in the conflict see no end to the violence, the crisis, the situation. They just see an infinite continuation of the current deadlocked state – which is the stalemate. If no potential victory is in sight, the motivation to fight and continue the struggle loses its attractiveness.

The second image Zartman refers to is a 'precipice', which is the exact opposite of a plateau. A precipice "constitutes a point that signifies a sudden and significant worsening of the situation" (Zartman in Stern/Druckman 2000, p.228). A precipice can emerge from within the conflict, which would mean that structural changes occur; or external actors can create the precipice by using the means of power politics. An example for the former precipice emerging from within the conflict is for instance the sudden death of the leader of a group (cf. the example of leadership change as outlined in the literature review). If we picture a belligerent group that is led by a very strong individual, it is possible to discern that the sudden death of such a leader would strongly impact the morale of the troops. The potential consequence could be a perceived hurting stalemate. The second kind of precipice is created by an external actor. This could be a mediator with the intention to manipulate the situation. He or she could for instance threaten military action against one of the actors in order to change the balance of the current state of affairs. In both cases, the belligerent actor has lost the hope for victory. As Touval and Zartman clarified, "plateau and precipice are precise but perceptional conditions, and they have governed the timing of successful mediation in most cases. They are not self-implementing: they must be seen and seized" (as quoted in Crocker/Hampson, et al. 2001, p.435). It is to be noted that both the plateau and the precipice describe states of hurting. For an MHS to be existent, both belligerents have to perceive hurting in one form or the other, so that the hurting is 'mutual'.

An MHS is not sufficient for the establishment of ripeness. A second variable is of crucial importance, the SWO. The reason lies in the notion that a cost-benefit analysis does not account for the security dilemma; because even "when the cost of war outweighs the incentives to attack, uncertainty about the opponent's intentions can undermine cooperation" (Fortna 2004, p.15). Therefore, the MHS is a necessary variable; but it is not sufficient for the explanation of ripeness.

3.1.1.2 Sense of a Way Out

An SWO signifies that the belligerents discern that a negotiated solution to the conflict can potentially be found. Among the conflicting parties, the perception has to prevail that a bargained settlement could satisfy the underlying needs of each and that such a settlement could be achieved. This requirement has twofold implications. The first implication is that each party to the conflict has to have a consensus among itself. As often pointed out in academia, it is hardly possible to find an actor in such a conflict that has one opinion. Normally, each group is fragmented in for example hardliners and softliners or the fighters and the intellectual heads, etc. Thus, most groups display rather heterogeneous structures. Thus, the crucial point is that the dominant deciding group is of the opinion that there might be a way out of the conflict that makes sense and is beneficial to the group. It does not help if this opinion prevails among a small group that is insignificant when it comes to decisions. Such notion can only succeed if the predominant individuals of the actor display an SWO and believe they can also *sell* the way out to its other members.

In this context, two academic debates are relevant. First, the debate spurred by Stephen John Stedman on spoilers in peace processes where he outlines that there might be individuals in a movement who agree to peace initiations, however, are not really convinced of the benefits of a peace agreement (cf. Stedman 1997). The control over those individuals is crucial for the leadership of a party to the conflict, so that their decisions are followed and supported by the whole group and not destroyed by individuals. The second debate relevant to the concept of SWO is Michael Brown's and Fred Charles Iklé's discussion on the relevance of the leaders of belligerents (cf. Brown in Crocker/Hampson, et al. 2001 and Iklé 1991). The question is which type of actor can "better" start peace talks – a dove or a hawk? Iklé argues that the better "seller" of compromises might be the former hawk as in the case of Nixon who was able to open up China being a strong representative for anti-communist movements in the US administration (cf. Iklé 1991, pp.59-83). In any case, an SWO needs to be felt by the relevant leadership of a group and be perceived as implementable as well, without having to confront stark opposition from its own faction.

Further, the second implication is that the two parties to the conflict must not only find a consensus among themselves, but they also have to perceive that the opposing belligerent might see the way out as well. If a relevant actor decides whether he or she assumes it possible that there is a way out, he or she has to also perceive that the opponent is ready for such a step. An SWO is thus dependent on the perception of all actors to the conflict and on their feeling about whether there might be an option to negotiate sincerely and eventually conclude a peace agreement.

Those two first level variables, the existence of an MHS and an SWO on both sides to the conflict are primarily determining whether ripeness exists at a specific point in the conflict, so that it would make sense to initiate peace talks since negotiations at this point would have the potential to be led sincerely by the belligerents. This would mean that the belligerents are not abusing the proposal for peace talks, using the chance to re-strengthen themselves, but actually believe in the potential for a peace agreement. Thus in a situation, in which an MHS and an SWO exist, the conditions for ripeness are fulfilled.

3.1.2   Second Level Variables

Further, the Theory of Ripeness accounts for second level variables, which are 'objective elements' and 'persuasion'. These second level variables impact the first level variables.

3.1.2.1   Objective Elements

Objective elements refer to quantifiable and measurable proof that defines whether a belligerent objectively still has the possibility to win the war by victory. Examples for this are the number of soldiers, of weapons, the financial resources available or the state of nutrition of the troops.

Especially with respect to objective elements, the mediator can play a crucial role. A mediator can identify objective elements and disclose them to the belligerents. According to Zartman and DeSoto, the identification can occur through four notions: they can analyze the costs that produce pain, they can recognize that losses are a sign of pain, they can evaluate changes in leadership, and they can assess changes in allies (cf. Zartman/DeSoto 2010, pp.13-18). Once a mediator has identified objective elements speaking for a hurting stalemate, he can use this knowledge for his mediating – or in this case rather – ripening effort (cf. through the instrument of the other second level variable, persuasion). This refers back to the academic discussion on both tools for mediators as well as challenges to the Theory of Ripeness. Acknowledging that a mediator can 'ripen' a conflict means that a mediator may use his leverage to create objective elements if they don't exist. One could picture a case in which a mediator uses force in order to weaken one of the belligerent parties, so that they feel an MHS. The second potential task for a mediator could then be to 'persuade' the belligerent of the MHS. Because even though all objective factors speak for a hurting stalemate, the parties involved might not perceive it.

Objective elements have to be seen as the measurable and quantifiable facts about a conflict situation. Given that the Theory of Ripeness builds on the perception of the relevant actors, objective elements are not decisive (and therefore no first level variables) but they might magnify the perception of an MHS. As Zartman and DeSoto explained recently, "while ripeness is a matter of perception, that perception is usually related to objective elements" (Zartman/DeSoto 2010, p.6).

Coming back to the avocado example, objective elements are what can be measured with regard to the ripeness of the avocado. Thus, it is for instance the avocado's firmness, i.e. something testable. Therefore objective elements are a second level variable since they might support or weaken the actual perception of an MHS, however, they do not constitute one. The reason lies in the importance of the subjective evaluation of the relevant actors.

3.1.2.2 Persuasion

This is where the other second level variable, persuasion, comes in. Persuasion appeals to the perception of the belligerents and can thus be seen as a diplomatic tool for conflict managers (cf. Aggestam in Zartman/Faure, et al. 2005, pp.280-281). Ripeness depends on the perception of the actors involved. Even if all objective elements speak against a potential victory of one of the actors, the perception of such actors might differ. They might still be convinced of their potential to win and thus are not able to feel an MHS or perceive an SWO. In such a case, ripeness cannot exist. But with the help of persuasion, a third actor has the potential to influence the perception of the belligerents and by that impact the magnitude of the importance of the first level variables: "another thing that mediators might do is help Party and Other to understand that the time to act is now. It is usually not sufficient for Party alone to perceive that a conflict has reached the point of stalemate. Other must also see the conflict this way, or efforts to move to de-escalation will probably fail. Mediators can help, since they may be able to approach a reluctant Other and *persuade* it that Party's readiness makes the time right for movement" (Rubin/Pruitt, et al. 1994, p.163). This notion refers back to the importance of a competent and capable mediator since the role of the mediator in this case would be to help a situation to ripen.

While according to the existing literature objective elements only influence the first level variable of an MHS, persuasion antecedes both first level variables. Regarding the MHS, the mediator can persuade belligerents by disclosing the objective facts of a situation. He can make clear that the hurting is too intense to be sustainable or that victory has moved out of sight given the capabilities of the relevant actor. Regarding the SWO, the mediator can offer diplomatic solutions that might not reveal themselves to the belligerents without external support.

3.1.3 Mutually Enticing Opportunities

Furthermore, Zartman expanded his own theory by including mutually enticing opportunities (MEOs) as a potential substitute for an MHS. The idea behind MEOs is that "positive incentives, not only negative incentives, can motivate conflict transformation" (Spector in Lyons, T./Khadiagala 2008, p.28). The basis for MEOs is, as Zartman expressed it, that the issue of the conflict becomes depassé, no longer justifying bad relations with the other party or the mediator that it imposed; or the attraction lies in the possibility of winning more cheaply than by conflict or else a possibility of sharing power that did not exist before (cf. Zartman in Stern/Druckman 2000, p.241). MEOs thus constitute a form of positive inducements, which can range from expansion of power to economic gains or political achievements (cf. Gartner and Melin in Bercovitch/Kremenyuk, et al. 2009, p.568). MEOs are a possibility to enlarge the pie of gains and by that to turn a zero-sum solution into a win-win situation for the belligerents. Jeffrey Z. Rubin illustrated this way of thinking when explaining integrative solutions to conflicts (cf. Rubin/Pruitt, et al. 1994, pp.193-213).

It is possible to explain this addition to the theory by drawing upon the example of an orange: the issue of the conflict is an orange that both parties to the conflict want to have in their possession. In order to turn the issue of the conflict away from a zero-sum solution to a win-win situation, alternative ways of solving the conflict have to be found that are acceptable to both parties. There are three possibilities to do so: firstly, one could reach out for a side-payment by a third party, which would mean that a third party buys another orange, so that both parties can have one. Secondly, the way of compensation could be made non-specific. This option also includes a side-payment by a third party that compensates one of the parties to the conflict for the loss of the orange by paying for it. Thirdly, one could use the method of bridging. This means that we try to find out, what really is at stake for each of the parties to the conflict through for example track-two diplomacy (workshops) and then prioritize. Regarding the example of the orange, this means that for example the result of such effort could be that one party actually strives for the peal of the orange while the other for the inside. Through problem-solving workshops, one could find out these differences in priorities and eventually find acceptable solutions to the conflict for all actors involved (cf. Rubin/Pruitt, et al. 1994, p.169; D'Estrée in Bercovitch/Kremenyuk, et al. 2009, p.143).

Thus MEOs support an alternative to continued fighting: "an enticing opportunity is a positive outcome of de-escalation, an improvement in the status quo that is only available if the conflict can be ended and hence is capable of encouraging a motive to de-escalate. When there is an enticing opportunity, conflict carries opportunity costs (rather than real costs, as in the case of a hurting stalemate), which motivate a desire to end it" (Pruitt 1997, p. 241). The focus of the Theory of Ripeness has shifted through the inclusion of MEOs as a first level variable from the only perception of the belligerents of "having had enough" to including the option that the cost-benefit analysis is decisive since positive incentives could outweigh the costs of the war. To be added is the notion that in this case, a rather powerful third party with respect to resources or leverage might be better. This is what Daniel Lieberfeld refers to as, "parties with more resources may provide security guarantees or economic rewards for cooperation" (Lieberfeld 1999a, p. 79), which brings up the question of the best criteria for an ideal mediator.

An 'ideal' mediator in this context would be characterized as a third party that has the leverage to facilitate the inclusion of MEOs. This has twofold implication for the mediator, comparable to the MHS: firstly, the mediator can use objective elements in the sense of creating MEOs and offering them to one or more of the belligerents in the form of inducements. Secondly, the mediator can use the tool of persuasion in order to disclose such opportunities to the belligerents if needed. Therefore, the second level variables of objective elements and persuasion function equally in the case of MEOs as they do for an MHS. Before focusing solely on MEOs instead of the MHS, one should mention though that the likeliness to be successful if there is an MHS is judged as higher by some academics. For example Dean G. Pruitt says that the problem with MEOs is that, "they involve the expectation of gain, which has been shown to be less motivating than the expectation of loss" (Pruitt 1997, p.242).

To sum up, if an MHS is not apparent in a given situation, it might be the case that MEOs function as an alternative instead and take the place as the crucial ingredient to ripeness. They are then part of the dependent variable.

3.1.4   Ripeness

Two levels of variables have been described: the first level variables, MHS/MEOs and SWO, and the second level variables, objective elements and persuasion. For the core definition of ripeness, only the first level variables are decisive. If an MHS/MEOs and an SWO exist, ripeness is established. These are – as mentioned above – the necessary but not sufficient conditions for the successful resolution of conflict. The second level variables merely function as intensifiers of the first level variables. This constellation translated into the terminology of comparative case studies means that ripeness constitutes the dependent variable, consisting of the two ingredients or conditions MHS/MEOs and SWO. The second level variables, persuasion and objective elements constitute independent variables to the theory. The graph below visualizes the described theory:

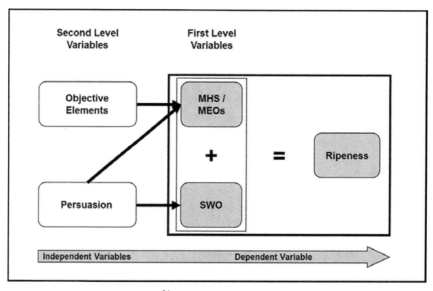

Figure 6: Theory of Ripeness[34]

The graph above illustrates the Theory of Ripeness as outlined in the existing literature. The dependent variable is ripeness. Ripeness consists of two conditions, which are MHS/MEOs and SWO. Both these conditions, also called first level variables, have to be apparent, so that ripeness can be constituted. This is visualized by the plus-sign between the two first level variables. This means, a

---

[34] Source: Own illustration.

situation of conflict can be described as ripe if an MHS/MEOs and an SWO can be identified. In that sense, the ripeness and MHS/MEOs + SWO express the same meaning from a different perspective. While MHS/MEOs + SWO is translated from the perspective of the acting agent, ripeness is the description for a situation from an analytic perspective. That is, ripeness is the result of an assessment of the situation.

The second level variables serve as independent variables to the dependent variable. These two variables, objective elements and persuasion affect the first level variables and by that affect the level of intensity of ripeness. However, they do not constitute ripeness. It shows again the importance of perception in the Theory of Ripeness. Objective elements are not decisive, but rather the actors' perception is what counts in order to reach ripeness. Bertram I. Spector describes perception in this context as the consideration of "how aware the parties are of their conflict status" (cf. Lyons, T./Khadiagala 2008, p.27). It refers back to the notion of the importance of a mediator. Other actors, i.e. third parties, have the power to influence the objective situation as well as the belligerents' perception of the situation. The perception can significantly be affected or even fundamentally shaped by an outside-actor such as a mediator through persuasion, but also through other means. This is true for both conditions for ripeness, the MHS/MEOs and the SWO. It is to be asked in how far exactly and by what means third parties can affect the first level variables through the instrument of the second level variables according to Zartman's theory. One such measure is for instance 'muscular mediation'[35], meaning pressuring or forcing actors into making compromises as mentioned above in the context of power politics and the creation of a precipice by an external actor. It is what Khadiagala describes as, "where power distribution inhibits meaningful negotiation, the mediator's role in creating stalemates becomes one of intricate empowerment of the weak against the strong party" (Khadiagala 2007, p.4).

Now the question arises of what ripeness stands for? What exactly is the definition of ripeness? Ripeness is the phase in a conflict cycle, in which it is possible to initiate peace efforts, meaning acting upon ripeness, as only in the ripe phase, peace efforts have the potential to be successful. Only when it is initiated during this phase, then a decision to negotiate sincerely (DNS) can truly be made. In that context, success is defined as DNS. If negotiations are initiated during a conflict phase which is not ripe, then the peace effort has no chance for success, but instead is determined to fail (i.e. no DNS). The reason lies within the belligerents' intentions when entering peace negotiations. If they do not perceive

---

[35] Cf. *The Wall Street Journal*, Kuperman, Alan J.: Rambouillet Requiem: Why the Talks Failed.

an MHS/MEOs and an SWO, then they enter the negotiations under false premises and use the negotiations in order to gain a tactical or strategic advantage in their advancement of the conflict, i.e. their motivation to enter the negotiations is not 'sincere', as outlined by Stedman (cf. Stedman 1991, p.14).

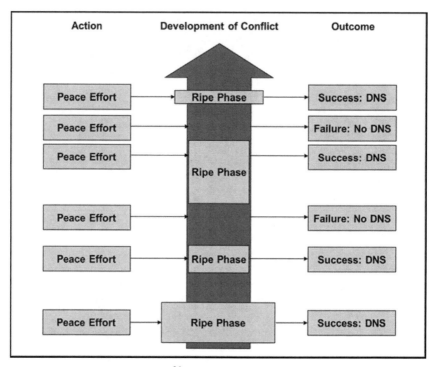

Figure 7: Function of Ripeness[36]

The graph illustrates the function of ripeness. The development of a conflict might entail several ripe phases as illustrated through the four boxes in the middle of the graph. It is to be noted that depending on the case, a conflict might have plenty of ripe phases or none, answering Thanja Paffenholz' objection in terms of 'windows of opportunity' as outlined in chapter 3.2.2.3. Whether or not

---

[36] Source: Own illustration.

the DNS subsequently leads to actual negotiations and a potential peace agreement is not a function of ripeness anymore. The further success of the peace process is thus dependent on a range of additional variables.

Furthermore, it is important to note that apart from the fact that ripe phases can occur various times throughout a conflict, they can also vary in their looks (expressed in the graph through the varying sizes of the ripe phases' boxes). Ripeness might be more or less intense in the value of the two conditions (cf. the width of the boxes) and the phase might last longer or shorter (cf. the height of the boxes). It might be intentionally created by external parties or emerged naturally from the course of the conflict. Ripeness might be very visible to the actors involved or a hidden perception. In any case, the effect of ripeness on the further course regarding the DNS is equal. However, the difference in the character of the ripe phase is crucial with respect to the effect of independent variables on ripeness. The shape of the ripe phase determines to what extent ripeness can be intensified, to what extent ripeness is not affected by external impacts, or to what extent ripeness can be destroyed.

Concluding, it should be noted that the Theory of Ripeness is firmly grounded in behavioral theories such as the public choice notions of rationality, the public choice studies of negotiation, and game theory (cf. Zartman in Stern/Druckman 2000p.229). It is the idea that the decision-making actors in a given constellation weigh alternatives and take rational decisions for the theory to hold. Especially as the Theory of Ripeness builds on the idea of a cost-benefit analysis, one has to assume that the causal relationships are dependent on the rationality of the actors – at least within their scope of information, knowledge, and perception.

3.2 Wrong Timing

Why is the right timing important for the initiation of peace talks? If the peace efforts are initiated at a wrong time during the conflict when the conditions for ripeness are not given, those efforts are wasted. It means that if a third party comes in and invests resources, energy and ideas on the initiation of peace talks, these are lost without any gain. This does no harm yet. Harm might be done if one or more of the belligerents signifies interest in peace talks but is not sincere about it as explained above. Then, the belligerents might use the time of mediated negotiations in order to re-strengthen their troops. Further, they could also use it as a military strategy in order to make the opponent believe something that is not mirroring reality. An example would be that a rebel group signals the state actor that its resources are diminished; and thus the state becomes less attentive. This way, the rebel group could launch an attack against the state that is not prepared.

Wrong timing implies that either no gain and no harm is done except for the loss of resources, energy and ideas of the mediator, or harm is indeed done by indirectly helping one of the parties to regain control over the situation. A further consequence could be increased tensions between the belligerents and thus a more determined ideological will to continue fighting, which counteracts the idea of resolving a conflict. Such increased emotional tensions might also lead to a more intense level of violence, so that instead of stopping the violence, the mediator unintentionally contributes to worsening the situation.

Another aspect that is affected if the timing is not right for mediation is the durability of an eventual peace agreement. If the entire process of peace talks and mediated negotiations works well and the parties to the conflict sign an agreement, it still might be the case that the durability of the agreement is limited if the conditions for ripeness had not been given in the first place. This constellation would entail that the parties to the conflict had not displayed their honest intentions, but rather played along and used the peace efforts for their advantage. This has been referred to by Scott S. Gartner and Molly M. Melin, who stated that, "the nature of the conflict management process affects the durability of agreements" (Gartner and Melin in Bercovitch/Kremenyuk, et al. 2009, p.567). If the nature of the process is characterized by dishonesty of the parties, the agreement cannot be assessed as a step towards peace.

Concluding, it means that if the conditions for ripeness are not given at the point of the initiation of peace talks, i.e. if an MHS/MEOs and/or an SWO are lacking, the efforts for conflict resolution are bound to fail as the risks are high that tensions between the belligerents exacerbate and the situation escalates further.

3.3 Academic Challenges to the Theory of Ripeness

As mentioned above in the chapter on the academic state of the topic (cf. chapter 2.2.2), different authors have written about the Theory of Ripeness and suggested refinements to the theory. Others have identified a lack of explanatory power to certain aspects. Before the variable of IDA is addressed in the subsequent chapters, the challenges to the theory brought up by others will be critically reviewed.

3.3.1 Third Party Involvement

One part of academic challenges concentrates on the role of the third party regarding the Theory of Ripeness. Key discussions focus on the intervener's motivation as well as the intervener's tasks[37].

Why do mediators come in as third parties to a conflict, with what interest and at what time do they do so? A range of motivating factors for mediators can be thought of – a mediator might want to intervene into a civil war because of pure power reasons. He or she might see an advantage through the intervention – be it because of the regional (in)stability, resource interests in the target country, or the usage of the civil war for a so-called proxy conflict. Other reasons might be international responsibility in the face of humanitarian catastrophes provoked through a protracted, ongoing civil war. A third motivating factor might simply be that the mediator feels he could be needed and successful. However, independent of what the initial motivation is to intervene, what is of interest in this context is to how to motivate the mediator to pay attention to ripeness. What is the line of argument to convince potential mediator to be sensitive to the concept of ripeness?

In the ideal case, mediators decide to come in at a phase of ripeness. But as Touval and Zartman acknowledged themselves, "since mediators are motivated by self-interest, they will not intervene automatically, but only when they believe a conflict threatens their interests or when they perceive an opportunity to advance their interests" (Touval and Zartman in Crocker/Hampson, et al. 2001, p.434). Thus, how is it possible to connect the mediator's incentives to ripeness? There is a relatively simple answer to this question. It is crucial for policy-makers as potential mediators that the efforts are wasted and perhaps even do harm, if the intervention is conducted at the wrong timing. The answer is rather superficial and more research should be invested into this normative challenge. Nevertheless should it be in the fundamental interest of the mediator to identify the actual point of ripeness so that efforts are not wasted.

With regard to the tasks of mediators Harold H. Saunders poses the question, "why and how do they [the belligerents] arrive at the conclusion that some kind of joint effort with other involved parties is both necessary and possible?". He also asks what enables the parties to realize that "they have had enough" and "why and how can parties reach out to the other side?" (cf.

---

[37] When using the term "intervention" in this context, it is referred to the peaceful intervention of a third party in the form of diplomacy with the aim to initiate peace talks as opposed to the rather common use of the term "intervention" in the context of military and/or humanitarian intervention.

Saunders in Crocker/Hampson, et al. 2001, pp.483-484). Saunders' questions are directed towards the perceptions of the belligerents. He asks what influences the perceptions and how they can be changed.

For the success of peace efforts, and thus for the Theory of Ripeness, the third party is crucial (cf. Samarasinghe/De Silva 1993, p.188; Walter 1997, p.335; and Zartman in Zartman 1995, p.341). It is important to note again that the Theory of Ripeness does not describe processes of negotiations between parties themselves, but it describes the process of conflict resolution efforts by a third party – which is the central actor in this respect. It is thus the mediation process that is of interest. A third party has the crucial role in this context to make belligerents realize and perceive certain situations. This explains why the notion of perception is constantly stressed.

Furthermore, it is also the mediator who takes on the facilitating role so that the belligerents can actually reach out to one another. The third party is key in this process and will also play a role in the further analysis, conclusions and particularly solutions of this analysis' research analysis. In this context it is crucial to further investigate the question to what extent a perception has to be established, by whom, and what exactly constitutes such perception for the analysis of ripeness[38].

3.3.2 Four Essentials for Ripeness

Richard N. Haass concludes that the structure of first and second level variables is not explanatory for the Theory of Ripeness and suggests to instead use a different approach and define four *essentials* for ripeness (Haass 1992, pp.27-28).

---

[38] With regards to the current research topic in this analysis such discourse on perception would go beyond the manageable amount here. Therefore, the analysis uses – as stated above – indications from primary and secondary sources in order to identify indicators towards perceptions, so that ripeness can eventually be identified.

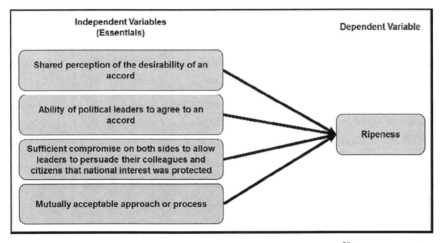

Figure 8: Essentials of Ripeness according to Richard N. Haass[39]

Haass defines the four essentials as independent variables determining the dependent variable of ripeness. The four essentials are shared perception of the desirability of an accord; the ability of political leaders to agree to an accord; sufficient compromise on both sides to allow leaders to persuade their colleagues and citizens that national interest was protected; and finally, a mutually acceptable approach or process.

Haass's four essentials do mirror important aspects, but they do not necessarily qualify as independent variables defining ripeness as the dependent variable or cannot be clearly differentiated from the original notions as outlined above. The first essential, *shared perception of the desirability of an accord*, refers to the idea that both parties "have had enough". This is what Zartman calls an MHS in combination with a desire for a peace agreement, which in a way mirrors the idea of an SWO. Thus the first essential does not actually contribute additional insights to the theory. The second essential, the *ability of political leaders to agree to an accord*, refers to the internal strength and leverage of the respective groups' leaders. However, this aspect is not an essential for ripeness as it stands independent from the concept of ripeness. It is a variable crucial for the design of the peace agreement and the subsequent course of events, as is the third essential, *sufficient compromise on both sides to allow leaders to persuade*

---

[39] Source: Own illustration.

their colleagues and citizens that national interest was protected. Both aspects function independent from ripeness; chronologically at a later stage in the mediation process. The same is true for the fourth essential, the *mutually acceptable approach or process*. Also this aspect refers to a rather functional factor that defines the actual peace agreement process.

It is thus important to clarify that the Theory of Ripeness sets in at an earlier stage than the actual design process of a peace agreement. The Theory of Ripeness sets in at the point when a third party decides whether it should go in and initiate peace efforts. This can mean that the third party either is able to identify ripeness that is already given in the relevant situation or that it sees itself in the position to be able to *ripen* the situation; that is to use means of force or persuasion to make the belligerents perceive that the phase is ripe. Chester A. Crocker, Fen Osler Hampson and Pamela Aall have summed up this argument in a very convincing way when stating that, "when third parties engage in peacemaking – helping parties to recalculate the costs and benefits of continuing the fight, assisting parties to reframe the issues, nurturing a state of ripeness, developing friends of the process to help in implementation, working in the larger society to develop a vision of an alternative future, or bringing a forgotten conflict to the world's attention – they are putting pressure directly on the sources of intractability: the deeply ingrained attitudes and modes of behavior of the parties and the conditions that have allowed the conflict to continue unchecked" (Crocker, Hampson and Aall in Bercovitch/Kremenyuk, et al. 2009, p. 504).

3.3.3   Dependence on High Levels of Violence

A rather moral challenge to the Theory of Ripeness derives from the idea that due to the concept of an MHS, "timing for conflict settlement depends on raising the level of conflict until a stalemate is reached and then begins to hurt. This is a sobering conclusion. It suggests that the settlement depends more on the 'push' of a hurting stalemate than on the 'pull' of an anticipated attractive outcome" (Mooradian 1999, p.726). This purely negative picture of the implications of the Theory of Ripeness does not hold.

With the inclusion of MEOs, it is believed that the positive incentives display similar power as the negative hurting aspect. Furthermore, it is to be noted again that the theory is based on the idea of perception. It is not the objective elements that are the dominant decisive factors, but the perceptions about the MHS, the MEOs, and the SWO. Assuming that the belligerents' leaders are rational thinkers, one can conclude that the hurting does not have to be realized, but that the threat of the hurting, the loss of perspective, and the loss of hope for victory are sufficient for the perception that underlies ripeness. Even though the implication that timing for conflict settlement depends on the level of the escalation of the conflict is per se not wrong, it is not a prerequisite for the establishment of ripeness. Zartman commented on this moral challenge by stating, "practitioners and students of conflict management would like to think that there could be a more positive prelude to negotiation, without the push of a mutually hurting stalemate but through the pull of an attractive outcome; or, in other words, the replacement of a Hurting Stalemate by the Enticing Opportunity and hence the distinction between two types of ripeness, one 'negative' and one 'positive'" (Zartman in Hauswedell 2006, p.178).

Nevertheless, the 'dependence on high levels of violence' cannot be rejected altogether. Through the analysis, it became clear that objective elements function as an intensifier with respect to the perception of an MHS. Thus, if the situation deteriorates significantly, i.e. if the levels of violence, suffering, and misery rise, the perception of an MHS is much more likely. This poses a challenge to the theoretical analysis in terms of policy-making advice.

3.4 The Theory of Ripeness Revisited

Having outlined the Theory of Ripeness in its pre-existing form, having considered the consequences of wrong timing, and having addressed academic challenges to the theory, the Theory of Ripeness will now be 'revisited'. In the following, the Theory of Ripeness will be adopted to the form that will serve as the basis for the subsequent analysis with respect to the effect of IDA on ripeness.

3.4.1 Independent Variables

As seen above, the academic literature has highlighted several variables that might affect ripeness – either in a positive way in that they intensify ripeness or negatively by destroying ripeness[40]. Ripeness is seen as a status that implies that certain conditions are stable. With additional variables touching upon this status, the characteristics of the status might change. Therefore, it is important to be

---

[40] The variables looked at in this context impact ripeness once ripeness is established. That is, the variables might increase or decrease the level of ripeness. However, they do not create ripeness.

aware of those variables as a mediator, so that the opportunities and risks resulting from them can either be leveraged or avoided.

The variables analyzed in this context are extensions of the originally outlined second level variables, that is the independent variables. IDA will be analyzed as an independent variable. For the analysis, it is essential to be able to clearly measure and trace the individual effects the independent variables might have on the dependent variable of ripeness. Only then, it is possible to isolate the variable of IDA to observe to what extent it affects conflict ripeness. For that end, the two independent variables of objective elements and persuasion will be included into a broader framework of variables that explain the potential causal mechanisms in more detail.

As outlined in Chapter 2.2.2.2 'The Art of Conflict Resolution' under the section on 'Peaceful Diplomacy', in the realm of mediation, there are two categories of factors: manipulable and non-manipulable factors. According to the academic literature, these seem to be the core factors that the mediator has to pay attention to when deciding to mediate in a conflict. As the work analyzes to what extent one specific independent variable affects conflict ripeness, these categorizations seem to be a helpful structure for looking at further independent variables. The underlying question with relevance for policy-making is what variables affect conflict ripeness in what way, so that a mediator can carefully analyze the situation and leverage the potential and avoid risks associated to this. Thus, to the mediator it is on the one hand important to know about the potential effects that manipulable variables can take and leverage them. On the other hand, the mediator should also know about the non-manipulable variables and their potential effects in order to place them into their larger framework of the mediation effort, so that the conflict resolution process is not endangered by their effects. When referring to non-manipulable variables in this context, this means that the mediator generally has no direct access to the variable, i.e. it is a variable of which the mediator is not in charge; it is initiated, controlled, or governed by another actor or simply through structural adjustments.

3.4.1.1   Manipulable Variables

Three manipulable variables emerge from the academic literature that seem crucial in potentially affecting conflict ripeness. These are variables that can be used by the mediator as tools in order to affect conflict ripeness. They are thus variables that originate from actor-based decisions as opposed to structural changes to the situation. However, they might imply structural adjustments as a consequence. The first variable to mention is persuasion. In this context, persuasion serves as a tool to the mediator. By means of communication and diplomatic efforts, the mediator can persuade one or more of the belligerents and by that affect the situation and thus the dependent variable of conflict ripeness. Persuasion must be understood as outlined in detail above (cf. Chapter 3.1.2.2).

The second manipulable independent variable is an extension of persuasion by material means. This refers to inducements. While persuasion only concerns communication, inducements refer to the mediator persuading one or more of the belligerents by offering inducements. This implies a certain leverage of the mediator so that he can actually offer inducements. Inducements thus refer to a positive offer to the belligerents. It affects the conflict ripeness in that it enlarges the potential 'pie of gains'. In that sense, inducements must be seen in relation to MEOs. However, the two concepts are distinct from each other. While MEOs function to establish ripeness in the first place – as an alternative to an MHS -, inducements as an independent variable are offered once conflict ripeness is established. Thus, inducements do not create ripeness, but they manifest ripeness at best. They affect a given ripe situation.

The third manipulable independent variable is pressure by the mediator. While the two previous variables were concerned with positive incentives to the belligerents, pressure serves as a variable with which the mediator can pressure the conflicting parties into certain situation. In that sense, it is a variable that affects conflict ripeness and thus has the potential to intensify the level of ripeness. The pressure might take the form of sanctions or of the use or threat of use of military power. In that sense it refers to the above mentioned notion of muscular mediation (cf. The Wall Street Journal 1999). The Theory of Ripeness in its original form referred to objective elements as one of the variables impacting ripeness. Objective elements can be seen as one part of the mediator's pressure. If the mediator can change the status quo by putting pressure on the individual conflicting parties, he is able to possibly also change what has been called objective elements (that is for instance the objective strength of troops). However, in line with the significance of perception, it is the intersubjectivity of this variable that is decisive. It is not the objective situation that counts, but its interplay with the subjective perception thereof on part of the belligerents. Therefore, the term pressure better expresses the value of this independent variable.

3.4.1.2   Non-Manipulable Variables

Equally, there are independent variables that might affect conflict ripeness that are not directly manipulable by the mediator. These cover variables that are driven by other actors such as the belligerents, another external entity or structural changes. Four such non-manipulable variables are discernable.

With respect to the belligerents, variables to be considered are twofold. The first one to mention is a change in leadership. If there is a change in leadership in one of the belligerent groups, this might affect the situation. The leader, or rather leadership, functions as the decision-maker in a conflict situation. If a new leadership comes into office, the intentions or perceptions can change – for the worse or the better. They might perceive ripeness more intensely or they might instill a new hope for victory and thus fighting (cf. Iklé 1991, Mooradian 1999). The way of causation is one of the three following options. If there is a change of leaders, there might be no change to the overall situation as the actual character of the leadership is not changed (option 1). If the character of the leadership changes, it depends on the situation whether this has a positive (option 2) or a negative (option 3) impact on ripeness. Potential effects on the MHS could be that either the new leadership feels stronger or displays more hope. This would lead to a destruction of the stalemate. Although it could also mean that the new leadership perceives the hurting of the stalemate even more intensely. Then, the level of ripeness is intensified. Similarly, the change in leadership might have two effects as well regarding the SWO. The new leadership might feel that there is no potential or there is increased potential for a benefitting agreement. This way of categorizing the effect of leadership or rather a change in leadership on a given situation is based in the ideas of Max Weber referring to three types of leadership, which are traditional, charismatic and rational (cf. Weber/ Winckelmann 1976, p.124). Each type has a different style and by that differs in their impact on a given situation. Therefore, dependent on what type of leader was exchanged into what new type of leader, the outcome varies.

The second variable concerning the belligerents is also concerned with leadership. Instead of focusing on a change in leadership, it refers to the character of leadership: the assertiveness of leadership. In the situation of ripeness, the two constituting variables seem to be highly dependent on to what extent the leadership can implement their ideas and decisions. This refers to the situation in which the leadership perceives an MHS/MEOs and/or an SWO. Again, different causal mechanisms seem possible. If the leadership, and therefore the decision-makers, are assertive and can promote their ideas and perceptions to their followers, then the level of ripeness will be intensified. The more firm they can stand behind the perception of an MHS/MEOs and the SWO, the stronger the intensity. On the other hand, if decision-makers cannot stand firm to their decisions and not implement them, ripeness might be negatively affected or even destroyed (cf. Stedman/Rothchild, et al. 2002) by way of hurting the MHS/MEOs and/or the SWO. It is then a demonstration of weakness on part of the leadership and therefore has the effect that the leadership – even though feeling the ripeness – cannot translate its thoughts towards the own followers as well as towards the belligerent and the mediator. Therefore, the decisions made by the leadership will not be met with credibility by the receiver. This variable also includes of what has been described as 'involuntary defections' or spoilers in the relevant academic literature as explained above. This factor is important if the belligerent parties have already made direct or indirect (through a mediator) agreements as signs for the willingness to negotiate. Such agreements range from offering meetings to ceasefires. If such agreements cannot be held because of exogenous reasons (involuntary defections), the belligerent might think that the other party's sincerity is questionable and thus at least one of the two first level variables, MHS/MEOs or SWO is negatively affected (cf. Fortna 2004). Then, the level of intensity of ripeness is reduced as both first level variables are negatively affected.

The second category of non-manipulable independent variables is dependent on other actors than the belligerents or the mediator. The first variable to mention here is external support to the belligerents. Thinkable is a situation, in which a belligerent receives resources from an external party to the conflict. This might include assistance by other states or institutions to either the state-actor as belligerent or the non-state-actor in form of diaspora money, state assistance or private support. The support might be of political or financial character. If one or both of the belligerents experiences a change in the backing of their cause, this will affect the situation of ripeness by impacting both the level of perceived hurting (i.e. the MHS) and the sense for a way out. The way of causal mechanism in this respect follows a direct pattern. If a belligerent receives more support, he might feel stronger and thus the MHS and the SWO are reduced. If the belligerent receives less support, the perception of hurting and the sense for a way out are increased in their intensity. In that sense, this variable can be formulated as external support that can either ameliorate or deteriorate the belligerents' situations.

The last independent non-manipulable variable to be mentioned is IDA. Intuitively, it might be surprising to perceive IDA as an independent variable in this context. However, as mentioned above, two phenomena seem to go hand in hand, which are conflict and underdevelopment. Also stated above was that development aid is a substantial influx into a country at war. The research objective is therefore to find out whether IDA affects conflict ripeness and thus is categorized correctly as an independent variable in this context and if so, of what quality the effect is. The question is what happens when development aid – an increase in development aid – occurs at a ripe phase? To what extent does

IDA function as an independent variable affecting ripeness? Does IDA have a positive, negative or no effect altogether on the level of ripeness?

The potential effect and quality of impact of IDA on conflict ripeness will be addressed in the subsequent chapters through comparative case studies. All potential independent variables will be analyzed carefully in order to be able to isolate the effect IDA might take on conflict ripeness.

In order to be able to test IDA as a potential independent variable, the importance of counterfactual analysis becomes apparent. Only if it is possible to carefully weigh the potential effects of all the individual independent variables on the dependent variable, generalizations on the impact of IDA can be drawn. It is a very helpful tool in order to understand the topic and context fully as a researcher. As Zartman put it, "counterfactual analysis is a minefield. Yet every decision actually taken is a selection among alternatives, so that the course of history is made up of an unending chain of choices. Any choice can be examined in the context of its alternatives. [...] Counterfactual policy analysis needs to examine why the policy proposed was not adopted at the time" (Zartman 2001a).

Before closing this chapter, I would like to refer to the potential inclusion of structural adjustments constituting non-manipulable variables as opposed to the agency approach outlined above. The structure-agency debate has been led widely throughout the academic discipline of international relations as mentioned above. The author takes the stance in this context that any change or transformations to a given situation – here the phase of ripeness – must be initiated by an actor. Even a transformation that at first sight seems intuitively to be of a structural nature, has been initiated in one way or the other by an actor in form of one of the above described methods. For example, a change of a conflict constellation from being a conflict motivated by creed into being a conflict motivated by greed, is believed to be agency-driven. In such a case, it is thinkable that an external actor finances a part of the war and as a consequence, the conflict transforms. In and by itself, structure by itself seems not to have an impact on a given conflict situation that is at a ripe phase[41].

---

[41] The author acknowledges diverging opinions on this topic in the realm of social constructivism. Given the scope of the analysis, a detailed account on the diverging opinions does not seem purposeful. In the context of the analysis of a ripe phase, it seems appropriate to follow the approach of focusing on actors' based initiatives.

3.4.1.3 Summary

The analysis has shown that there is a range of independent variables to the dependent variable of conflict ripeness. These independent variables carry the potential to affect the dependent variable in different ways. They might intensify or reduce the level of ripeness by changing the nature of the conditions for ripeness, being the MHS/MEOs and the SWO. The independent variables can be categorized into two types from the perspective of the mediator: manipulable and non-manipulable variables. The first type, manipulable independent variables, is directly connected to the mediator, as the mediator is the owner of these variables. The mediator can initiate and use them as tools and by that directly affect the intensity of the level of ripeness and by that has the chance to manipulate the dependent variable (cf. Bercovitch/Houston 1993; Bercovitch/Schneider 2000; and Greig 2005). The second type of variables is owned by other actors than the mediator. Either the belligerents or other external parties to the conflict are in charge of these. The following table gives an overview of the variables identified.

Independent Variables	Type of Variable	Initiator
Persuasion	Manipulable	Mediator
Inducements	Manipulable	Mediator
Pressure	Manipulable	Mediator
Change in leadership	Non-manipulable	Belligerents' leadership
Assertiveness of leadership	Non-manipulable	Belligerents' leadership
External support to belligerents	Non-manipulable	External party
Increase in development aid	Non-manipulable	External party

Table 2: Overview of Independent Variables[42]

The table provides for seven independent variables that are differentiated in their individual type: either manipulable or non-manipulable variables. This categorization must be perceived as given from the perspective of the mediator. When

---

[42] Source: Own illustration.

testing the effect of each of these independent variables on the conflict ripeness in the case studies, three objects of initiative must be assessed. The manipulable variables (persuasion, inducements and pressure) all refer to changes in the theoretical concept that are initiated by the mediator. The change in leadership and assertiveness of leadership are non-manipulable from the perspective of the mediator. These two variables depend on the initiative of the leadership of the respective belligerent. Lastly, external support to the belligerents and the increase in development aid are variables that are not manipulable by the mediator. They are initiated by external parties to the conflict. The analysis will show to what extent IDA serves as an independent variable to conflict ripeness with a significant effect and of what quality such effect is.

3.4.2 The Extended Theory of Ripeness

The Theory of Ripeness as outlined by Zartman and others (cf. Zartman in Stern/Druckman 2000) serves as the basis for the analysis in this book. Given the research interest of focusing on the effect of one additional independent variable to the theory, IDA, the theory has been extended and concretized in order to be able to clearly isolate the research variable.

The graph below visualizes the Theory of Ripeness by presenting the independent variables and the dependent variable. While the independent variables are categorized into the respective initiator of the variables being either the mediator, the belligerents' leadership or an external party and provides for seven variables including the research variable of IDA, the dependent variable, ripeness, is presented as consisting of two ingredients, which are the MHS/ MEOs and the SWO. When those two ingredients are given in a conflict situation, ripeness exists. The two ingredients can be affected by the independent variables and by that change the level of the intensity of ripeness. Some variables intensify the perceived ripeness; some reduce the level of ripeness. The question is whether IDA is correctly categorized as an independent variable and under what conditions IDA functions as an intensifier or a reducer of the level of ripeness.

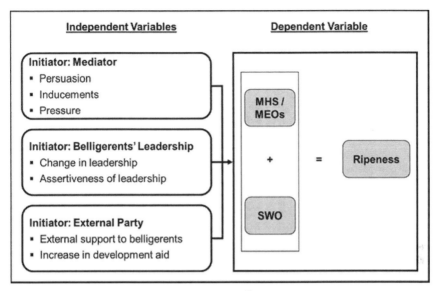

Figure 9: The Expanded Theory of Ripeness[43]

3.5 Hypotheses

A range of hypotheses can be drawn from the contextualization and analysis of the Theory of Ripeness as well as the introduction of the additional independent variable of IDA. The analysis has so far moved on a purely theoretical and abstract level. Thus, before applying the analyses to real-case, empirical examples, hypotheses resulting from such abstract analysis should be formulated in order to be able to subsequently make comparisons and draw conclusions to the previous theory analysis.

Recalling the Theory of Ripeness including the challenges and variables affecting ripeness, there is one (or more) phase(s) in the dynamics of a conflict that might be described as *ripe*. However, it seems that even if ripeness can be established in some cases, the following process to initiate sincere peace talks often fails – the moment of ripeness is destroyed. This analysis' overall research objective is to find out whether the independent variable of IDA affects conflict ripeness and if so, in what way: positively or negatively? What are the conditions

---

[43] Source: Own illustration.

for such pattern? The subsequent hypotheses help in putting the additional independent variable of IDA into the context of the theory analysis and by that in relation to the other independent as well as the dependent variable.

The theoretical analysis provided for the assumption that conflict ripeness is the dependent variable. If conflict ripeness consisting of the ingredients of an MHS/MEOs and an SWO is the dependent variable, this would also mean that there are independent variables that carry the potential to affect the level of intensity of conflict ripeness. In order to be able to target the research objective and to analyze whether and to what extent IDA has an effect on conflict ripeness, it is crucial to further dive into the causal relationships between the independent variables and the dependent variable. Therefore, the three types of initiator of the independent variables have to be analyzed and weighed carefully in their effect. Then, it is possible to isolate IDA and trace the chain of events in this regard. From this analysis, the following four hypotheses can be drawn[44]:

H_1: *If a mediator consciously uses his instruments of persuasion, inducements and pressure, then he is able to positively affect conflict ripeness. Thus, through leveraging the manipulable independent variables, the intensity of the dependent variable, conflict ripeness, is increased.*

H_2: *If changes to the conflict situation occur that are not manipulable or controllable by the mediator, they carry the potential to negatively affect conflict ripeness. Thus, because of non-manipulable independent variables, the intensity of the dependent variable, conflict ripeness, might be reduced or destroyed.*

H_3: *If an increase in development aid occurs at a ripe phase and the mediator is not in charge of this influx into the country of interest, then the intensity of the dependent variable, conflict ripeness, is generally reduced or even destroyed.*

H_4: *Only if the mediator becomes the initiator of an increase in development aid and by that transforms IDA into a mediator's tool, then he can leverage the influx and thus positively affect conflict ripeness, strengthening the intensity of the independent variable.*

The subsequent analysis will focus on the above outlined research question. As a result of the analysis, it will be possible to compare the findings with these four hypotheses and thus come to a conclusion.

---

[44] In the following, H_1 stands for hypothesis 1, etc.

4 Approach to the Case Studies

After the theory analysis, including the contextualization of the topic and the formulation of the hypotheses, it is now crucial to test and affirm or discard the above stated hypotheses with the help of empirical cases. With the usage of the method of comparative case studies, it is possible to shed more light onto the subject. In this chapter, four steps will be taken before the actual cases will be analyzed and the hypotheses tested. Firstly, the objective, design and structure of the case studies will be introduced (4.1). Secondly, the variables to be analyzed will be identified and described (4.2). Thirdly, the case-guiding research questions will be formulated (4.3). Fourthly, the approach to the choice of cases will be explained and the actual cases be presented (4.4).

4.1 Objective, Design and Structure of the Case Studies

As indicated above, the case studies are conducted as comparative case studies. The method follows the approach outlined by Alexander George and Andrew Bennett in their work, "Case Studies and Theory Development in the Social Sciences" (cf. George/Bennett 2005).

The objective of the analysis is twofold. The first one is to test an existing theory, the Theory of Ripeness as established by I. William Zartman (cf. Zartman in Stern/Druckman 2000) and refined and further developed by others as outlined above. The aim is to apply the theory in its original form to the cases selected and observe whether or not and if so, to what extent the Theory of Ripeness can actually explain the course of events in each individual case.

The second objective is to further develop the theory into a more extensive version, so that the power of applicability can be increased. It is thus aimed at operationalizing and concretizing the Theory of Ripeness. The case studies shall serve as an instrument for theory development. The case studies test the Theory of Ripeness deductively and through that suggest to incorporate a new variable (as suggested in George/Bennett 2005, p.111).

The design of the case studies follows the needs from the theory analysis in order to reach the overall research objective. The method of causal interpretation is applied. Specific case-guiding research questions are generated from the outlined hypotheses, which will be examined individually in the following. This will be done with the help of defined variables in order to ensure control over the case studies and findings. The congruence procedure will be applied. The theory, here the original Theory of Ripeness, predicts certain outcomes on the basis of specific initial conditions (cf. George/Bennett 2005, p.179). By this, the value of independent and dependent variables will be established generally and then filled with specific findings in each case individually. However, the values have to be comparable in all cases. The value and variance of the dependent variable will be compared in all settings with the predictions/hypotheses made beforehand. "If the outcome of the dependent variable is consistent with the theory's prediction, then the possibility of a causal relationship is strengthened" (George/Bennett 2005, p.179).

It is important for the design of the case studies that the comparability of the cases is ensured (cf. Collier, D./Mahoney 1996). Therefore, a controlled comparison is conducted. The controlled comparison aims at a high degree of similarity between the cases in the value of the variables. Only if this is given, a small-n analysis has potential to display explanatory power from the causal interpretation.

The instrument of counterfactual analysis will thus also be included in the design. For the interpretation in individual cases, counterfactual analysis will help to identify and measure the effect of individual independent variables (cf. Stern/Druckman 2000, p.83). This is crucial in small-n analyses since the main challenge is to find the actual causal mechanism – to conduct a clear process-tracing. By applying such method, the risk of spurious correlation can be reduced. A clear process-tracing is needed to identify the correct causal path between the independent variable(s) and the outcome of the dependent variable. It is important to pay attention to three aspects as outlined by George and Bennett: firstly, to specify the predicted contributing and counteracting effects of each potential causal factor, secondly, to identify where underlying causal arguments are complementary and competing, and thirdly, to guard against the bias of what has been termed explanatory over-determination (cf. George/Bennett 2005, p.188). Besides these three aspects, it is also crucial to avoid of what David Hackett Fischer had called "historians' fallacies" (cf. Fischer, D.H. 1971), referring to the significance of correct historical analysis when conducting empirical case studies, so that one does not step into the trap of the logic of thought, which might contradict the actual trace of happenings.

The analysis follows the method of structured and focused comparison in order to comply with the challenges of comparative case studies. The approach aims at 'structuring' the analysis into a generalized design that is applied in each case individually before brought together in an overall synthesis of findings. The focused aspect refers to the emphasis on the actual research objective. That is, the cases to be analyzed will not deal with the overall context and course of events in general, but be focused on the relevant chain of events. Therefore, also within-case analyses will be included into the research.

The case studies' structure thus follows logically from the previous analysis. Firstly, the variables to be analyzed will be outlined and defined in detail, so that the expected outcomes from the analysis become clear (4.2). Secondly, the formulation of case-guiding research questions will follow that are extrapolated from the theory analysis, the outline of the hypotheses and the different variables (4.3). The research questions are held on a theoretical level, so that they can be applied equally to all cases, independent from the content in each case. Thirdly, the choice of cases will be presented including the reasoning for the choice (4.4). Finally, the actual case studies follow in the next chapter (5).

The case studies are structured into several steps. Each case will be dealt with individually. In order to give a general context to each case, a brief background will be provided beforehand comprising of a historical overview as well as the introduction of the key actors. The Theory of Ripeness will be applied to each case and the individual variables analyzed in order to examine whether conflict ripeness was given. Then, the independent variables will be analyzed with respect to the potential effect on conflict ripeness as the dependent variable. This will include a special focus on the research variable of IDA. Finally, the relationship between conflict ripeness and IDA will be assessed in-depth with respect to a potential causal pattern. The individual circumstances under which IDA had different effects will be identified and outlined. Following the individual analyses, the findings will be brought together in a synthesis of the case studies in order to be able to compare the findings and potentially derive at contingent generalizations that can in a translated form serve as lessons learned for policy-making.

4.2 Variables to be Analyzed

Different types of variables are being analyzed as part of the comparative case studies. In this section, the individual variables will be defined in detail including a provision of what the boundaries and values of the variables are. Firstly, the dependent variable (4.2.1) and secondly the independent variables will be detailed (4.2.2)

4.2.1   Definition of Dependent Variable

As outlined above, the dependent variable to be analyzed is conflict ripeness. Conflict ripeness is the sum of two ingredients, which are an MHS/MEOs and an SWO. If these two ingredients are both apparent in a conflict situation, then conflict ripeness is given. Now, the question arises how it is possible to pinpoint and identify ripeness in the case studies. What exactly does ripeness entail – when does a ripe phase begin and when does it end? What is the difference between a ripe phase and a phase that is not ripe? In order to answer these questions, it is helpful to define a kind of threshold that serves as a boundary to 'ripeness', which functions as a plausibility benchmark when assessing whether or not a situation is ripe in the course of the case studies. For the threshold to be crossed either an MHS or MEOs must be perceived from both belligerents and a way out of the current deadlocked situation in form of a negotiated settlement must be sensed by the affected conflict parties. It is important to note that the two belligerents must both perceive the SWO and the MHS/MEOs, meaning that it must be of a 'mutual' character. What is decisive for the existence of ripeness is thus that the protagonists have to perceive that they find themselves in a mutual hurting situation, which is characterized by a deadlock in form of either a precipice- and/or a plateau-situation as explained above in Chapter 3.1.1.1. The protagonists in this context are the leadership of the individual belligerents. If they do not both perceive an MHS, they have to perceive the option for MEOs. The MEOs have to be significant enough, so that they offer more than the belligerents can gain from continued fighting. This means that the MEOs, in order to be able to function as a core ingredient to ripeness, have to have the potential to fulfill the interests and aspirations of the conflicting parties that are the core reasons for the conflict. However, the one ingredient of either MHS or MEOs is not sufficient. It is as described above a necessary but not sufficient condition for ripeness. In order for ripeness to exist, also an SWO must be perceived by both belligerents. Again, the crucial aspect is the perception of the main actors. Only if it can be established that the 'deciders' of the respective parties perceive that there is a way out of the violent conflict, the variable is satisfyingly fulfilled.

When defining the dependent variable in this context, conflict ripeness, it is, however, not sufficient to hint towards the ingredients. As frequently mentioned, the perception of the decision-makers is decisive here. However, given that this is an empirical case studies that will be conducted, it is not possible to exactly know and therefore accurately trace the decision-making process when it comes to conflict ripeness. That is why a small-n study was chosen as the best approach towards this research subject. With careful interpretative analysis, the decision-making process will be followed by focusing on indices that constitute a threshold for conflict ripeness.

The threshold consists of five notions. Firstly, either an MHS or MEOs must be identifiable. Secondly, an SWO must be identifiable. Thirdly, an MHS is judged as being identifiable if both belligerents find themselves in situations in which continued fighting appears impossible. Such impossibility is marked by two alternatives. Either they face a situation in which continued fighting would most probably lead to a total disaster and a complete destruction of their own group. This would mark a precipice-situation. Or the situation does not offer any potential for victory or even betterment on a minimum level, which constitutes a plateau-situation. The author will carefully analyze evidence and indices from different sources in order to be able to assess whether or not such threshold had been passed. Fourthly, MEOs will be accepted as given, if the opportunities present themselves to the belligerents that fulfill the core demands of the individual groups. The opportunities might be offered by another actor (for instance the mediator) or they might be offered through a change in circumstances of the situation. Decisive for the assessment is whether such opportunities seem to exist and whether they have been disclosed to the belligerents. Fifthly, an SWO is accepted as given as ingredient to ripeness if both belligerents seem to acknowledge that the alternative to continued fighting might work in their interest. The SWO again might be offered to the belligerents by a third party or it might present itself through a change in the situation. Important for the assessment is whether there are enough signs on part of the belligerents that indicate their willingness to consider a way out of the current situation. Thus, the dependent variable of conflict ripeness will be defined as given if the two ingredients of MHS/MEOs and SWO can be identified by the author. Then, however, it is also possible to describe the level of intensity of ripeness. The ripeness might be weak or very strong, a long or a short phase. Important is that the minimum requirements as outlined above can be identified.

4.2.2   Definition of Independent Variables

The in-depth description of the intensity of the level of ripeness is crucial when analyzing the independent variables. The independent variables are seen as effects on conflict ripeness, meaning that they can change the quality of the dependent variable. The independent variables thus have the power to increase or reduce the level of intensity of ripeness. Reducing the level of intensity might even lead to the destruction of the ripe phase, if it reduces the intensity so much that it goes below the defined threshold line. Seven independent variables will be analyzed as part of the comparative case studies, while the seventh is the actual research variable, IDA. Here, it will be assessed to what extent IDA serves as a significant independent variable to conflict ripeness and what conditions lead to which effects on the dependent variable. The other six independent variables are persuasion of the belligerents by the mediator, inducements offered by the mediator to the belligerents, pressure put on the belligerents by the mediator, a potential change in leadership on part of one or more of the belligerents, the assertiveness of the leadership, and the status of external support to the conflicting parties. These variables will be analyzed individually and weighed in their significance of effect on the dependent variable. Only if all of these are considered carefully, it is possible to trace the effect of the research variable, IDA, on conflict ripeness. In the analysis of each of these variables it will be assessed whether the respective variable was apparent in the individual case analyzed, and if apparent to what extent it changed the status quo. Specifically, it will be assessed to what extent the inde-pendent variables were initiated by the respective initiator of these variables: the mediator, the belligerents' leadership and/or another external party. The way of analysis is interpretative in form of process tracing. The following table summarizes the variables to be analyzed.

Type of Variable	Name of Variable
Dependent variable	Ripeness (MHS, MEOs, SWO)
Independent variable (initiator mediator)	Persuasion
Independent variable (initiator mediator)	Inducements
Independent variable (initiator mediator	Pressure
Independent variable (initiator belligerents' leadership)	Change in leadership
Independent variable (initiator belligerents' leadership)	Assertiveness of leadership
Independent variable (initiator external party)	External support to belligerents
Independent variable and research variable (initiator external party)	Increase in development aid

Table 3: Overview of Variables to be Analyzed[45]

---

[45] Source: Own illustration.

4.3 Case-Guiding Research Questions

As indicated above, the case studies will be conducted with the help of a range of case-guiding research questions. The questions mirror the previous analysis of the Theory of Ripeness, the individual hypotheses and the outlined variables to be analyzed. The following table presents the research questions guiding the analyses in all case studies individually. In each case, each question will be asked. It is then possible to compare the results and thus arrive at contingent generalizations. It is to be noted that these questions only function as guiders through the individual case studies. As said above, it is essential to individually interpret and analyze the cases including their circumstances and developments, so that a process tracing method in the empirical approach is possible. The questions thus simply serve as a framework that helps in being able to accumulate the findings of the individual case studies and generalize afterwards.

#	Case-Guiding Research Questions
1	Is it possible to identify an MHS?
2	If not, is it possible to identify MEOs?
3	Is it possible to identify an SWO?
4	Can conflict ripeness be affirmed?
5	To what extent does persuasion affect conflict ripeness?
6	To what extent do inducements affect conflict ripeness?
7	To what extent does pressure affect conflict ripeness?
8	To what extent does a change in leadership affect conflict ripeness?
9	To what extent does the assertiveness of the leadership affect conflict ripeness?
10	To what extent does external support to the belligerents affect conflict ripeness?
11	Can IDA be observed?
12	Is it possible to identify an effect of IDA on ripeness?
13	Does IDA affect ripeness positively?
14	Does IDA affect ripeness negatively?
15	Under which conditions does IDA affect conflict ripeness positively and under which conditions does IDA affect conflict ripeness negatively?

Table 4: Case-Guiding Research Questions[46]

---

[46] Source: Own illustration.

4.4 Choice of Cases

The cases must fulfill a range of criteria to be applicable for the analysis of this work. It is aimed at selecting a choice of cases that allows comparing the impact of individual variables in the interplay of all variables. Specifically, the variance in the dependent variable is of interest. Therefore, the 'frame of comparison' issue has to be taken into account (cf. Collier, D./Mahoney 1996, pp.71-72). The choice has to ensure that the type of intervention is defined: the effect of IDA.

The choice of cases is narrowed down in different steps. Firstly, the criteria for relevance will be outlined. These are the criteria that have to be fulfilled, so that cases qualify for the universe of cases (4.4.1). Secondly, all potential cases will be screened and filtered according to the criteria as outlined in the first step. In order to find all potential cases, the most prominent datasets for conflicts will be compared and a list of applicable cases created, which constitutes the universe of cases (4.4.2). Thirdly, the final choice from the universe of cases will be made and introduced on the basis of additional research, relevance and expertise criteria (4.4.3).

4.4.1 Criteria for Relevance

In order to define the universe of cases, seven criteria will be identified that serve as conditions so that a case can qualify for the universe of cases. In that sense, the seven criteria serve as categorization tools for individual sub-classes that together constitute the universe of cases. The universe of cases displays all cases that are potentially interesting and valid for the further analysis in this work. Seven criteria have been identified that are decisive for the universe of cases.

First, each case has to display a major conflict in the country of interest. This means the analysis follows the common approach in this context defining *wars* as conflicts with at least 1,000 battle-related deaths (cf. Gleditsch 2008b, p.1). In this context, it is important to mention that most datasets observe each year individually. Some conflicts, however, display phases in which violence varies in its intensity. This is important throughout the case selection process so that it can be ensured that only major conflicts are analyzed. Yet, in the analysis, years with low intensity in between more violent phases will still be taken into consideration as a conflict must always be apprehended in its entirety. Therefore, the exact definition is that there has to be more than 1,000 battle-related deaths accumulated over the entire period of the conflict; however, there must be at least one year surmounting this. Further, there have to be at least 100 battle-related deaths on each side of the conflict in order to exclude so-called one-sided violence and massacres.

Second, extra-systemic and colonial wars are excluded due to their specific nature and characteristics. It is not clear whether such wars must be defined as internal or international due to the issue of conflict being the struggle for independence. Furthermore, one party to those conflicts is the colonist state, which is normally a state that cannot be described as a developing country. Due to this specific constellation, those wars are excluded from the potential cases to be analyzed.

Third, the case must be an internal conflict, meaning that only on one side of the conflict can be a state-actor. This applies only to the primary party to the conflict. It aims for excluding all international conflicts. It does not exclude so-called internationalized conflicts where one (or more) of the belligerents receives support from other states.

Fourth, the conflict of interest must take place in a developing country since only in those countries it is possible to observe streams and impacts of development aid. In order to determine whether the country of interest is a developing country, data from the World Development Indicators (WDI) will be used, displaying whether a country received official development assistance and official aid (cf. Organization for Economic Cooperation and Development 2010).

Fifth, the universe of cases is limited to conflicts with an onset between 1960 and 2000. The reasoning for such limitation lies within striving to achieve the best explanatory results for the research objective. Given that the tracking of WDI data started in 1960, it makes sense to concentrate on the period thereafter. Furthermore, the research covers protracted conflicts. Data on such conflicts is best covered if the war-onset does not lie in the recent history, i.e. after 2000, since then, the complexities surrounding a conflict are often only poorly analyzed in terms of changing perceptions and individual actors.

Sixth, as outlined above, a protracted civil war is defined by Collier and others as a conflict that lasts at least six years. Protraction is an interesting feature of some civil wars given that it leads to a situation in which war becomes a normal feature of life; where children do not experience a life in peace; where development aid cannot be delivered under the label of emergency aid anymore. Therefore, the work specifically analyzes protracted conflicts. It does not imply necessarily that the findings are exclusive to protraction. Indeed, it would be interesting to further investigate on the effects in the context of non-protracted conflicts. However here, the focus shall lie on protracted situations. Therefore, only cases of protracted conflicts, lasting at least six years, will be considered.

Seventh, the research objective is concerned with strategies for conflict resolution. Therefore, the primary target audience are third parties considering efforts in mediation. Therefore, the seventh criterion is that there is an official and identifiable mediator. This means, that an entity (be it a person, a country, or an organization) must have somehow officially declared that he/they intend to function as a third party to the conflict by promoting peaceful diplomacy. The way of declaring this, can be of any kind, but a willingness to pacify the conflict must be displayed and communicated. Thus, the seventh criterion is the involvement of a third party. In summary, the following seven criteria must be fulfilled in each case to qualify for the universe of cases:

- Major conflict
- Exclusion of extra-systemic and colonial conflicts
- Internal conflict
- Conflict located in a developing country
- Onset of the conflict after 1960, but no later than 2000
- Protracted conflict (six years or longer)
- Identifiable mediator in place

4.4.2   Universe of Cases

In order to screen for potential cases, relevant conflict datasets were assessed and compared[47]. The following datasets were taken into account: AKUF[48], COW intrastate war[49], Fearon and Laitin 2003[50], COSIMO[51], Sambanis[52], and UCDP/ PRIO[53]. These six datasets were assessed individually, compared and then adjusted to one database, answering the needs for this specific research objective. The way of doing so was to take each dataset individually and filter it with respect to the criteria for the universe of cases as outlined above.

AKUF accounts for all wars and armed conflicts since 1945 separated by continents. Latin America was seen as having had 30, Europe 16, Africa 64, Middle East 60 (including Western Sahara, Morocco, Algeria, Tunis, Libya, and Egypt), and Asia 68 conflicts. This makes a total of 238 conflicts listed by

---

[47] A comprehensive introduction to conflict datasets is provided in Eck (2005): "A Beginner's Guide to Conflict Data: Finding and Using the Right Dataset", *UCDP Papers (Uppsala Conflict Data Program, Department of Peace and Conflict Research)*.
[48] Cf. http://www.akuf.de.
[49] Cf. http://www.correlatesofwar.org.
[50] Cf. Fearon and Laitin (2003a): "Additional Tables for 'Ethnicity, Insurgency, and Civil War'", *http://www.stanford.edu/group/ethnic*.
[51] Cf. http://hiik.de/en/kosimo/index.html.
[52] Cf. http://pantheon.yale.edu/~ns237/index/research.html#.
[53] Cf. http://www.prio.no/CSCW/Datasets/Armed-Conflict.

AKUF. The time range monitored by AKUF presently finishes in 2007. What is displayed about the conflicts is the country where the conflict is set, the description of the conflict (belligerents and if appropriate the conflict name), and the years in which the conflict took place. It is, however, not entirely clear, which definition is used by AKUF as a threshold to qualify as war. The number of required casualties for example is not given. AKUF's definition of war holds that three notions must be fulfilled. Firstly, there must be at least two armed conflict parties of which at least one must be of a government. Secondly, on both belligerent sides, there must be a basic centrally organized military leading. Third, the armed acts must be somehow continuous and not only incidental and spontaneous clashes[54].

The second dataset analyzed is the COW intrastate war. As the name implies, only intrastate wars are tracked in this specific set. It is a very extensive coding of the conflicts with respect to the individual categories including detailed start and end dates, the victorious side, outside intervention, total battle deaths of state participants as well as of all participants and the type of war, among others. The timeframe is also very extensive dating from 1816 to 1997. Unfortunately, no conflicts after 1997 were accounted for. COW has a violence threshold of 1,000 battle-related fatalities per year; military and civilian deaths are counted, although the victims of massacres are excluded[55].

Fearon and Laitin developed a dataset of civil wars (Fearon/Laitin 2003a) for their article "Ethnicity, Insurgency, and Civil War", published in the American Political Science Review (cf. Fearon/Laitin 2003b). This dataset is particular as the two scholars used data from other scholars and accumulated the input in order to create their own dataset for their research. They counted all civil wars between 1945 and 1999 on countries with a population of more than 500,000 inhabitants in 1990. It led to 161 countries analyzed. In total they account for 127 civil wars. Their violence threshold is 1,000 battle related casualties with 100 dead on each side at least. The definition of civil conflict is, "fighting between agents of (or claimants to) a state and organized, nonstate groups who sought either to take control of a government, to take power in a region, or to use violence to change government policies" (Fearon/Laitin 2003b, p.76). What is different about the list of Fearon and Laitin compared to the other accounts is the inclusion of anti-colonial wars, of which they count 13.

The COSIMO dataset accounts for more than 500 conflicts since 1945, including over 2,500 phases of conflicts. COSIMO is a databank established and

---

[54] Cf. http://www.sozialwiss.uni-hamburg.de/publish/Ipw/Akuf/kriege_aktuell.htm#Def.
[55] Cf. http://www.correlatesofwar.org.

led by the Heidelberg Institute for International Conflict Research (HIIK). It tracks a great variance of variables in the conflicts including political systems of the belligerents, issues of conflict, modalities of conflict resolution, and what is of particular interest, the mediator. COSIMO's definition of political conflict is the clashing of overlapping interests on national values and issues. Conflict has to be of some duration and magnitude by at least two parties determined to pursue their interests and win their case. At least one party is an organized state[56]. COSIMO also counts conflicts that are non-violent in their intensity. The definition COSIMO uses for a mediator states, "mediators are actors that intervene in the conflict and take over a mediating or facilitating role for negotiations. A mediator, however, must not have any own interests with regard to targeted support at one of the direct actors to the conflict"[57].

The civil war dataset by Nicholas Sambanis presents the data slightly differently than the previous datasets in that Sambanis uses a country-year format. That means each country and each year are displayed and then coded with regard to their conflict level. The coding and use of the dataset is explained in his article, "What Is Civil War?" (Sambanis 2004). In this article, Sambanis outlines that he believes in pluralism of civil war lists in order to refine and re-question coding mechanisms. The differences between the individual lists, he thinks, stem from the definition of the threshold of violence, the challenge of determining the beginning and the end year of a civil war, and the question of how to determine whether a conflict is intra-, inter- or an extra-state war (cf. Sambanis 2004, p.815). Sambanis' coding involves the following eleven criteria for an armed conflict to be classified as a civil war: firstly, the location of the war is in a state that is member of the international system with a population of at least 500,000; secondly, the parties are politically and militarily organized and have publicly stated objectives; thirdly, the government must be a principal combatant; fourthly, the main insurgent must be locally represented and recruit locally; fifthly, the start year of the war is the first year that the conflict causes at least 500 deaths; sixthly, throughout the duration, the conflict must be characterized by sustained violence; seventhly, throughout the war, the weaker party must be able to mount effective resistance; eighthly, a peace treaty that produces at least 6 months of peace marks an end to the war; ninthly, a decisive military victory by the rebels that produces a new regime should mark the end of the war; tenthly, a cease-fire, truce, or simply an end to fighting can also mark the end of a civil war if they result in at least 2 years of peace; and eleventh, if new parties

---

[56] Cf. http://hiik.de/en/kosimo/index.html.
[57] Cf. Personal Interview by Email with Natalie Hoffmann, HIIK, 14 September 2010.

enter the war over new issues, a new war onset should be coded (Sambanis 2004, pp.829-831). Sambanis explains the individual criteria in much more detail than reproduced here. In general it is a very concise and comprehensive definition that requires detailed empirical research in order to be able to classify conflicts. In total, Sambanis coded 145 civil war onsets.

The last dataset considered was the UCDP/PRIO armed conflict dataset, Version 4-2009[58]. As part of a larger program on conflict data, this dataset accounts for 260 conflicts monitored since 1946. The definition of armed conflict is "a contested incompatibility that concerns government and/or territory where the use of armed force between two parties, of which at least one is the government of a state, results in at least 25 battle-related deaths" (Gleditsch 2009b, p.1). The dataset also includes low intensity conflicts as well as international and extra-systemic conflicts. Mediation is not covered.

All of the six datasets were analyzed carefully, filtered with regard to the criteria as defined for the relevant universe of cases, re-coded and compared. It became clear throughout the process that the individual datasets – as outlined above – use at times very different coding methods as well as definitions. Therefore, the comparison of the individual cases accounted for is not always straight forward and had to be complemented extensively by empirical research. The universe of cases includes conflicts that are major, not extra-systemic or colonial, internal and located in a developing country. Further the onset must have taken place in or after 1960. They must be protracted in the sense of lasting at least six years and a third party must have displayed its intention to function as a mediator. Especially the last criterion, third party, is crucial in this context. An example like the conflict between Bangladesh and the Shanti from 1974 and 1997 was excluded as there was no official external party being in charge of mediating. The Chittagong Hill Tract Peace Accord that concluded the protracted conflict in 1997 was driven by the Bangladeshi government, in this case initiated in 1996 by the newly elected Bangladeshi prime-minister Sheikh Hasina Wajed. Therefore, it was a true negotiation that took place as opposed to mediation. As the research objective is to assist external parties in their conflict resolution efforts, such case is excluded from the universe of cases.

Also the other criteria are not undebated. As indicated above, the beginning and ending years of conflicts are often highly discussed. Further, the type of war is often discussed, too.

From this definition a list of 31 conflicts could be extracted that are part of the universe of cases. The table below presents the conflicts including their location

---

[58] Cf. http://www.prio.no/CSCW/Datasets/Armed-Conflict.

or party I, their conflict name or party II, the year in which the conflict started, the year in which it ended, and a selection of mediators involved in the conflict. The list of conflicts is sorted by the location where it takes place, followed by the year of the onset of the conflict, the ending year of the conflict and the mediator(s) involved. It is to be noted that the universe of cases as outlined below is a combination of reflected comparisons between the individual datasets analyzed as outlined above and further empirical analyses of the individual cases.

ID	Location or Party I	Conflict Name or Party II	Year Beginning	Year Ending	Mediator
1	Afghanistan	Mujahideen	1978	1992	Saudi Arabia, UN, USSR
2	Algeria	FIS	1992	1999	UN
3	Angola	UNITA	1975	2002	Portugal, US, USSR, Zaire
4	Burundi	Hutu and Tutsi groups	1993	2006	UN, Tanzania, South Africa
5	Cambodia	Khmer Rouge, FUNCINPEC, etc.	1978	1998	ASEAN, Australia, France, UN, Indonesia, Perm Five
6	Chad	FROLINAT, various	1965	Ongoing	Nigeria, OAU
7	El Salvador	FMLN	1981	1992	Catholic Church, UN
8	Ethiopia	Ogaden / Tigray / Oromo / ALF	1975	Ongoing	OAU, UN, Tanzania
9	Guatemala	URNG, various	1978	1994	UN
10	India	Kashmir	1989	Ongoing	International Olympic Committee, UN, US

ID	Location or Party I	Conflict Name or Party II	Year Beginning	Year Ending	Mediator
11	Indonesia	Aceh	1990	2005	ASEAN, Crisis Management Initiative, EU, Finland
12	Lebanon	Various militias	1975	1990	Arab League, Syrian Arab Rep., UN, US
13	Liberia	NPFL, INPFL	1989	1996	Côte d'Ivoire, ECOWAS, Ghana, UN
14	Morocco	Polisario	1975	1988	Arab League, OAU, UN
15	Mozambique	RENAMO	1975	1992	Catholic Church, Italy
16	Namibia	SWAPO, SWANU, SWATF	1973	1989	UN
17	Nepal	CPN-M	1997	2006	UN
18	Nicaragua	Contras	1981	1990	Contadora Group, Ben Wisch
19	Papua-Neuguinea	Bougainville	1988	1998	New Zealand, Peter Wallensteen
20	Philippines	MNLF / MILF	1968	On-going	Indonesia
21	Philippines	NPA	1972	On-going	Norway, US
22	Senegal	MFDC (Basse-Casamance)	1989	1999	Guinea-Bissau
23	Sierra Leone	RUF, AFRC, etc.	1991	2002	UK, UN
24	Somalia	post-Barré war	1991	On-going	Arab League, UN, Ethiopia, Italy, OAU

ID	Location or Party I	Conflict Name or Party II	Year Beginning	Year Ending	Mediator
25	Sri Lanka	LTTE	1983	2009	India, UN, Norway, UK
26	Sudan	Anya Nya	1963	1972	Ethiopia, World Council of Churches
27	Sudan	SPLA	1983	2003	J. Carter, Egypt, US, Ethiopia, IGAD, Kenya, Nigeria, T. Rowland
28	Tajikistan	UTO	1992	1998	Afghanistan, Iran, Pakistan, Russia, UN
29	Uganda	LRA	1986	Ongoing	B. Bigombe, GoSS, and others
30	Yemen	Royalists	1962	1969	Arab League, Iraq, Morocco, Sudan, UN
31	Zimbabwe	ZANU, ZAPU	1972	1979	UK, US

Table 5: Universe of Cases[59]

4.4.3 Final Choice of Cases

The final choice of cases must fulfill all seven criteria as outlined above. Therefore, the final choice of cases must be part of the universe of cases. The universe of cases comprises 31 conflicts. Taking into account that some conflicts might also provide more than one potential phase to analyze, the number of potential case studies goes beyond the scope of this analysis since the comparative case studies are a method of small-n. Therefore, a careful analysis is

---

[59] Source: Own illustration.

needed which demands a selection out of the universe of cases that represents the other cases adequately and that thus serves as exemplary with respect to identifying causal mechanisms. At the same time, it is not useful to only focus on one case. A single case study might offer interesting findings about the specific case, but cannot serve as a basis for potential generalizations. In order to determine the final choice of cases several more steps were undertaken in the analysis of the cases. First, the 31 cases were assessed with respect to their type of conflict. All conflicts were categorized into two general types: autonomy/ secessionist or anti-regime wars. This classification – also used by AKUF – helps in understanding and interpreting certain patterns of a conflict. The above mentioned underlying aspirations in the two types of conflict differ greatly. While an anti-regime war aims at changing the structures within a country, the autonomy/secessionist war is marked by the struggle of one group in the state to become independent. The process of resolving such conflict might differ greatly. While it is not argued that the analysis cannot be applied to any one of the types, for the comparative analysis it is useful to concentrate on one type of cases in order to rely on certain similarities in the setup of the cases. This fulfills the request of controlled comparison as outlined above. Given that an autonomy/ secessionist war is often set in a larger context of a region than focused truly on one state, the analysis will only cover anti-regime wars. In line with this argument, eleven conflicts were excluded from the potential choice of cases.

The eleven concerned cases that were classified as autonomy/secessionist wars were Ethiopia 1975-ongoing given the strive of the Ogaden to separate from the country; India 1989-ongoing due to the Kashmir separatist movement; Indonesia 1990-2005 with the strive of the separatist movement of Gerakan Aceh Merdeka to become an independent state; Morocco 1975-1988 in the conflict with Polisario given their establishment of a government in exile; Namibia 1973-1989 in its strive for independence from South Africa; Papua-Neuguinea 1988-1998 facing the demand of the Bougainville Revolutionary Army for independence; Philippines 1986-ongoing due to the Muslim struggle for autonomy; Senegal 1989-1999 with its conflict over the region of Casamance where the people of Diola strove for autonomy; Sri Lanka 1983-2009 with the autonomy struggle by the Tamils; and the two conflicts in Sudan 1963-1972 and 1983-2003 in which South Sudan fought for independence. Having excluded these eleven cases from the list of the potential cases to be analyzed, twenty cases remain. All these twenty cases carry the potential to be analyzed in the following with respect to their potential conflict ripeness and the effect of potential increases in development aid on the status of conflict ripeness and are thus interchangeable regarding the choice of cases. As the analysis of twenty cases would still significantly surmount the scope of this work, three cases were selected to be analyzed that represent the other cases as well. For this final selection, three additional aspects were looked at that mirror the criterion of representativeness for the universe of cases. Firstly, the final choice should at least cover two continents or regions. This aspect is important in order to avoid false results of the analysis that were predetermined due to the geopolitical or geographical situation. By analyzing cases from at least two different continents, it can be assured that the location of the conflict has no impact on the course of events and thus on the generalization of findings. However, at the same time, at least two cases should be set on the same continent and preferably also in the same geographic region in order to again be able to interpret causal mechanisms in line with the requirement of controlled comparison. Thus, ideally, the choice of cases includes cases from two different continents and two cases from the same region. Secondly, the motivation for the anti-regime conflicts should vary. They should not all be of a certain sub-type such as only territorial, only ethnic, or only ideological disputes. The potential range of motivations for conflicts is large – it includes topics such as religion, ethnicity, power, grievance, among others. Thus, at least three conflicts should be identified that display different motivations in their conflict issues. Thirdly, the involved third party as mediator should vary in its character in order to avoid that predetermined results are identified due to this aspect. This means that the cases analyzed should have different types of mediators such as NGOs, multilateral institutions, states and/or individuals. Again, if different types are covered in the case studies, it is possible to avoid that the type of mediator impacts the outcome of the dependent variable. Ideally, it is possible to identify at least one case that provides for a within case comparison with different mediators. Then, the effect of the mediator can be clearly isolated and taken into account with respect to further interpretative results.

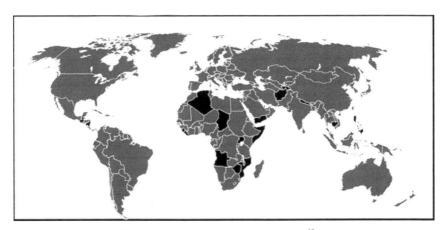

Figure 10: Geographical Distribution of Potential Cases[60]

The graph above shows that the potential cases are distributed in the following order: Three cases are located in Latin America, two in the Middle East, ten in Africa and five in Asia. For reasons of plausibility, at least two cases should thus be placed in Africa and one in Asia so that the findings represent most of the other cases adequately. When identifying the two cases in Africa that should lie in one geographic region, it is plausible to choose Uganda and Burundi as adequate cases. In the case of Uganda, we can observe a conflict that fulfills the criteria for the universe of cases (cf. case number 29 in the universe of cases). It further is an anti-regime war set in the northern region of Uganda between the rebel army, the Lord's Resistance Army (LRA) and the Government of Uganda (GoU). The phase of analysis would cover a rather long period of time, in which several efforts of mediation were undertaken (between 1986 when the current President came into power and today). Two mediators stick up from the analysis who pursued very promising peace initiatives, which were Betty Bigombe as an individual and the Government of South Sudan (GoSS) as a state-actor. Further, the motivation for the conflict stems from an old grievance issue separating the society of Uganda. In that sense, the Ugandan case is suited for representing the universe of cases in the analysis part of the work. The second case from Africa would consequently be Burundi (cf. case number 4 in the universe of cases). The Burundian case also fulfills all outlined criteria to qualify for the universe of cases and is an example of an anti-regime war. Burundi is situated in the same

---

[60] Source: Own illustration.

geographic region as Uganda and thus the focused comparison can be ensured when looking at these two cases. While the conflict in Burundi also touches upon the grievance issue, it is not a conflict between two areas but between ethnicities. Burundi further offers the possibility for a within-case analysis as the specific phases to be analyzed would be threefold: firstly, the phase between 1993 and 1995, in which the Special Representative of the UN Secretary-General, Ahmedou Ould-Abdallah, made a peace effort; secondly, the phase between 1996 and 2000, which was characterized by a peace initiative under the auspices of Julius Nyerere, followed up by Nelson Mandela; thirdly the phase between 2000 and 2006, which was characterized by efforts under the leadership of South Africa, specifically Jacob Zuma. Thus, also this case offers the possibility to look at the impact of different types of mediators and their individual impact. Having identified two cases for the analysis, it is then important to include a further case into the choice that covers a different continent or region. Given that one quarter of the potential cases are located in Asia, an Asian case would complement the choice of cases to a satisfactory extent. When examining the potential five Asian cases, one particularly seems appropriate for the analysis. It is a protracted internal war that was mediated by an international organization. Given that the two previously selected cases were mostly mediated by individuals or states, it would now be helpful to include a case in which an international organization takes on the mediating role. Further the case should be clearly definable with respect to the belligerents and the motivations of fighting. The case particularly appropriate in this respect is the Cambodian case (cf. number 5 in the universe of cases). The case concerns the conflict between four conflicting Cambodian factions: the FUNCINPEC (Nation-al Front for an Independent, Neutral, Prosperous and Cooperative Cambodia), the KPNLF (People's National Liberation Front), the Khmer Rouge, and the Phnom Penh Government. The phase to be analyzed is the mediation process leading up to the signing of the Paris Peace Agreements in 1991 and the subsequent two years until late 1993 under the auspices of the UN.

Conflict	Time of Interest	Third Party
Uganda	1986 onwards	B. Bigombe, GoSS, and others
Burundi	1993 – 2006	UN, Tanzania, South Africa
Cambodia	1990 – 1993	UN, Perm Five

Table 6: Choice of Cases and Mediators[61]

---

[61] Source: Own illustration.

5 Evidence from the Case Studies

Turning to the actual evidence from the case studies, each of the three cases will be examined individually: Uganda, Burundi and Cambodia.

5.1 Uganda

The first case study is set on the African continent, specifically East Africa. The country of interest is Uganda. What is analyzed in the context of Uganda's history is not a single phase or moment of ripeness as in the example of Cambodia. Instead, it is a chain of events – a range of phases of interest over a longer period of time. We look at the conflict in Northern Uganda between the Government of Uganda (GoU) and the rebel group, the Lord's Resistance Army (LRA), which displays a long history. Concretely, the time between 1986 and today is considered, given that the conflict is still unresolved. The objective is to assess whether ripeness existed at any point in time and it will be evaluated whether independent variables affected such potential ripeness. It will be assessed whether it is possible to identify IDA as an independent variable entering the country and whether such IDA affected conflict ripeness. If such a correlation can be identified, the quality of the causation will be analyzed accordingly as well as the conditions outlined that led to the respective causal path(s).

The case study is structured in three parts: firstly, in order to contextualize the case study properly, a background to the conflict is provided (5.1.1) including the history and causes (5.1.1.1) as well as an outline of the actors involved (5.1.1.2). Secondly, the actual analysis will be conducted (5.1.2). Here, three aspects are covered: the question of whether ripeness existed at any point throughout the course of events and whether independent variables affected such ripeness (5.1.2.1); then, whether IDA can be identified at potential phases of ripeness (5.1.2.2), and finally, whether IDA – if identified – had an effect on ripeness, of what quality it was and which conditions accompanied the potential effect (5.1.2.3). Thirdly, the case study closes with a conclusion reflecting the findings with respect to the theory analysis (5.1.3).

5.1.1 Background

Uganda, located in the Great Lakes region of Sub-Saharan Africa, currently has about 32 million inhabitants, living in 80 different districts[62]. It is neighboring Sudan in the North, Kenya in the East, the Democratic Republic of the Congo (DRC) in the West, and Rwanda and Tanzania in the South. Uganda is a republic with a multiparty system that was legalized in 2005. President Yoweri Kaguta Museveni is head and chief of state and rules together with Prime Minister Apolo Nsibambi in Kampala, the capital of Uganda. Museveni came into power in 1986 and since then, serves the third term of his presidency. Nsibambi was appointed Prime Minister in 1999. About 50% of the total population is younger than 15 years and about 35% of the total population lives below the poverty line (est. 2001)[63]. Northern Uganda, the main regional focus of the case study, has an estimated population of 3.2 million with an annual growth rate of 3.61% in 2005 (cf. Government of Uganda 2007, p.xii). While life expectancy at birth lies at 52.72 years on average for the whole of Uganda, Northern Uganda has a life expectancy of 44.3 years (cf. Government of Uganda 2007, p.xii). In 2005, the Government of Uganda (GoU) estimated that about 2.6 million people were internally displaced in Northern Uganda, living in so-called internally displaced persons (IDP)-camps (cf. Government of Uganda 2007, p.xii).

---

[62] Cf. https://www.cia.gov/library/publications/the-world-factbook.
[63] Cf. https://www.cia.gov/library/publications/the-world-factbook.

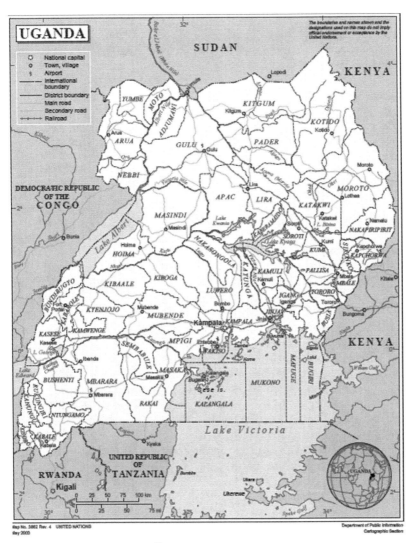

Figure 11: Map of Uganda[64]

---

[64] Source: United Nations, "Uganda, no. 3862 Rev.4 May 2003, United Nations," (2003a). Published with the courtesy and approval of the United Nations.

5.1.1.1 History and Causes

The history and causes to the conflict in Uganda will be presented in three parts. Firstly, the pre-Museveni era will be described. Secondly, the era Museveni will be outlined, and thirdly, special emphasis will be placed on the development of the conflict with the Lord's Resistance Army.

Since 1894, Uganda was a British protectorate. It gained independence in 1962, which spurred competition for central state power amongst rival tribes. Uganda is scarred with a North-South divide that stems from the pre-colonial and colonial eras, when ethnic stereotypes were manifested through the favoring of individual ethnic groups at the expense of others. Northerners had traditionally been recruited for the military whereas Southerners staffed the political administration. Uganda's first President, A. Milton Obote, coming from the North, stacked the national army with Northerners (Acholi and Langi). Obote's playing of ethnic favorites and military-dominated rule angered many Southerners and increased their hostility against the Langi and Acholi.

In a military coup, Major General Idi Amin seized power in January 1971 and by that overthrew the government of President Milton Obote who fled into exile to Tanzania. Initially greeted by the Ugandan people as a 'liberator', Idi Amin soon established a military dictatorship and abolished basic civil rights that had been enshrined in the Constitution (cf. Europa Publications. 1978, p.1026)[65]. Amin's reign is often referred to as *Amin's Slaughterhouse*, due to the fact that Uganda suffered from most terrible crimes against humanity during the subsequent eight years. Amin ordered massacres of the tribes that had supported Obote – the Langi and Acholi tribes (cf. Kasozi/Musisi, et al. 1994, p.111). Besides, Amin expelled all Israeli and Asian inhabitants (about 60,000 people), particularly Indians, from the country in order to give their businesses to Ugandans, which seriously cracked the Ugandan economy. It is estimated that about 300,000 people were murdered by the regime (Bercovitch/Fretter 2004, p.86). Foreign support diminished during the years and left Uganda eventually nearly isolated[66]. Uganda's economy was basically destroyed. Idi Amin was toppled in 1979 when Tanzanian troops invaded Uganda (cf. Umozurike 1982,

---

[65] In March 1971, Amin suspended the Political Activities Decree (freedom from arbitrary arrest, of expression, assembly, association, and movement), the Armed Forces Decree, and the Detention Decree etc., among others.

[66] Trade relations were cut off by the US in 1977/78; Soviet support was terminated in 1978; and except for Libya, no Arab state supported Amin militarily in 1979.

p.303)[67]. As opposed to the previous and subsequent leaders of Uganda, Amin's power base was in the North-West of the country (Allen 2006, p.28).

Amin's dictatorship was followed by another round of killings that even further intensified the North-South tensions: Milton Obote – backed by Tanzania – returned to power once again in 1980 after short leaderships by Yusufu Lule and Godfrey Binaisa and was responsible for the so-called Luwero Triangle massacres of about 300,000 mostly Baganda in the early 1980s. Obote had restored the dominance of the Northern tribes, the Acholi and Langi (cf. Human Rights Watch 1997, p.63 and Furley/May 2006, p.118). In the summer of 1985, Bazilio Tito Okello, the commander of Uganda's army's Northern region, led a coup against Obote and successfully installed a military government. Okello initiated negotiations soon after, which led to the signing of a power-sharing agreement inked in Kenya's capital Nairobi in December 1985. It was to be the end of the long civil war. However, Yoweri Museveni, one of the signatories to the agreement, was not satisfied with the agreement and restarted fighting within the same month. On 26 January 1986, Museveni took the capital Kampala and was sworn in President (cf. Bercovitch/Fretter 2004, p.86). He established a no-party state under the leadership of the National Resistance Movement (NRM) in Kampala (cf. Nyeko and Lucima in Accord 2002, p.20)[68]. It is estimated that until Museveni's Presidency, about 800,000 or 1,000,000 Ugandans had been killed in "state terror, civil strife, and ethnically motivated assaults" since independence (Deininger/Bank. 2003, p.9).

Museveni, a Southerner, has been President of Uganda ever since 1986 and achieved in developing the country to higher living standards. His initial form of government was a socialist-inspired no-party system that only opened up in 2005 with legalizing a multi-party system (cf. Buckley-Zistel 2008, p.70).

Uganda has often been praised both in history and in contemporary times. Winston Churchill was impressed by its beauty and called it "the pearl of Africa"[69]. With Museveni as president, Uganda has become *the* African success story and role model, as declared by the World Bank, the UN, and the US,

---

[67] For instance, the production of cotton fell from 400,000 bales in 1970 to 100,000 in 1979. A similar decline could be witnessed in the production of tea, sugar cane, coffee, and tobacco.

[68] For detailed and thorough overviews of Uganda's history until 1986, see Amaza (1998): Museveni's Long March: From Guerrilla to Statesman, Kasozi/Musisi, et al. (1994): The Social Origins of Violence in Uganda, 1964-1985, Kutesa (2006): Uganda's Revolution, 1979-1986: How I saw it, Museveni/Kanyogonya, et al. (1997): Sowing the Mustard Seed: The Struggle for Freedom and Democracy in Uganda, Mutibwa (1992): Uganda Since Independence: A Story of Unfulfilled Hopes, or Omara-Otunnu (1987): Politics and the Military in Uganda, 1890-1985.

[69] Note by Winston Churchill in his diary "My African Journey" during his visit to Uganda in 1907. He proclaimed it due to Uganda's magnificence in its variety of landscape, wildlife and culture.

among others for its incredible development[70]. Uganda is one of the few countries in Sub-Saharan Africa that managed to reduce the HIV/AIDS prevalence to a rate below 5% of the population, it kept a life expectancy at birth of over 50 years in average, and as mentioned above only 35% of its population lives below the poverty line, which indicates a big success compared to the figures of 1986 when more than 55% of the population lived below the poverty line[71]. As early as in 2001, Uganda was praised by the World Bank as being "among the top economic performers in Africa" (Datta-Mitra/Dept. 2001, p.xiii). Part of Museveni's success was to focus on the restoration of a sound economic system. For instance, he returned the property to the Indian people who had been expelled by Amin before[72]. Other strategies included a government's development agenda[73], which led to great results throughout the 1990s. The number of Ugandans who are unable to meet basic needs fell from 56% in 1992 to 38% in 2003. Also sectors like health, education and water and sanitation profited highly from the development agenda as illustrated by the government (Government of Uganda 2007, p.vi). In 1997, the GoU introduced the Poverty Eradication Action Plan (PEAP), and was thus the first country to prepare such a "comprehensive and participatory national development strategy"[74].

Despite the economic success of the government, the GoU had to fight many rebel movements[75]. In 1986, Museveni's army, the National Resistance Army (NRA) mainly faced two rebel groups. One group was the Uganda People's Defence Army (UPDA). In March 1988, NRA commander Major Salim Saleh reached an agreement with the UPDA commanders, which resulted in the Gulu Peace Accord signed on 3 June 1988 (cf. Nyeko and Lucima in Accord 2002, p. 21). The UPDA became integrated into the NRA and the national army was renamed into the Uganda People's Defence Forces (UPDF). The other rebel group that was fought was founded as a reaction to Museveni's taking power by Alice Auma in the North of Uganda in Acholiland: the Holy Spirit Movement

---

[70] Cf. for example: http://www.un.org/ecosocdev/geninfo/afrec/vol14no2/uganda.htm.; http://www.un.org/ecosocdev/geninfo/afrec/vol14no4/htm/uganda_box.htm.;http://www.avert.org/aidsuganda.htm.; http://www.undp.org.ug/hivaids.htm.; among others.

[71] Cf. https://www.cia.gov/library/publications/the-world-factbook.

[72] Cf. *Der Spiegel*, "Uganda: Nach Hause", 2/1994.

[73] For instance, the GoU implemented a far-reaching Economic Recovery Program (ERP) to bring about internal financial stability (cf. Kapoor (1995): Restructuring Uganda's Debt: The Commercial Debt Buy-Back Operation, p.3).

[74] Cf. http://web.worldbank.org/WBSITE/EXTERNAL/COUNTRIES/AFRICAEXT/UGANDAEXTN/0,,menuPK:374947~pagePK:141132~piPK:141107~theSitePK:374864,00.html.

[75] The Refugee Law Project counted 14 insurgencies until 2004 (Lomo/Hovil, et al. (2004): Behind the Violence: Causes, Consequences, and the Search for Solutions to the War in Northern Uganda, p.4).

(HSM). Alice Auma called herself 'Lakwena', which means 'the messenger' and was built on a mystic belief of spirits guiding her movement (cf. Prunier 2009, p.81). Lakwena's group had three major goals. It wanted to establish a political and military opposition to Museveni, followed the mission to cleanse the Acholi themselves of the sins committed in earlier wars and wanted to deliver elements of Christianity and traditional belief. Lakwena received popular support in the North as Museveni comes from the South being a Munyankole, which made him suspicious to the Northerners fearing reprisals for earlier controversies between the North and the South (cf. Finnström 2008, p.97). The UPDF defeated the movement in 1987 after the rebels had tried to reach Uganda's capital, Kampala. A short distance before Kampala, in Jinja district, the HSM had to surrender.

Yet, the movement was not completely destroyed. After Lakwena was defeated, her uncle Severino Lukoya took over, but was arrested soon. Lakwena's alleged nephew, Joseph Kony[76], established a new rebel group, the Lord's Resistance Army (LRA)[77] and declared himself the military and spiritual leader of the movement (cf. Human Rights Watch 1997, p.69). Kony absorbed the remnants of both the HSM and the UPDA willing to continue fighting (cf. Nyeko and Lucima in Accord 2002, p.18). Ever since then, the UPDF are fighting the LRA in the North of Uganda, but have not been able to achieve victory. The causes for the conflict and the reasons of why the LRA are fighting are highly debated (see the detailed account below).

More or less common agreement was found regarding the underlying factors causing the conflict. The GoU summarized these in its Peace, Recovery and Development Plan for Northern Uganda in 2007 (PRDP). They stated that there are political and historical causes of the conflict as well as socio-economic ones. The former include poor representation of Northerners in the government, marginalization from central institutions, regional divide between North and South, divisive colonial policies, and corruption of leadership. The socio-economic causes include imbalances in public investments and fiscal transfers, underdevelopment, weak social service provision, competition over scarce resources, land disputes, political and economic gains of some individuals and

---

[76] The actual status of relationship between Lakwena and Kony remains disputed. Sometimes it is suggested that he is her cousin, other times that they are not connected at all. Kony himself claimed to be her nephew (cf. Allen (2006): Trial Justice: The International Criminal Court and the Lord's Resistance Army, p.37).

[77] The name of the movement changed several times. Initially, it was called the United Holy Salvation Army. It changed into United Democratic Christian Army, to Lord's Salvation Army and later into Lord's Resistance Army. For reasons of clarity, the later name LRA is being used throughout the case study.

the marginalization of pastoral communities. Further the GoU refers to security causes of the conflict including impunity, human rights abuse, criminalization, proliferation of small arms, and weak border controls (Government of Uganda 2007, p.24). In total, this represents a rather reflective approach to the underlying causes to the conflict in 2007. Especially the North-South divide in the country is a recurrent theme in all accounts of the country's history and given as the main reason for the insurgency (cf. Furley/May 2006, p.115, Haarhaus 2009, p.2 and Lomo/Hovil, et al. 2004, pp.7-12).

In the early years of the insurgency, Kony established a rather small guerrilla group, operating solely in the North close to the Sudanese border; mainly in the districts of Kitgum, Pader and Gulu (cf. Prunier 2009, p.81). In the 1990s, the LRA became more active and larger, and they started shifting their tactics (cf. Gingyera-Pinycwa 1992 and Human Rights Watch 1997, p.69). In those times, the LRA began developing their instrument of using the population as the main victims of their insurgency to hurt the government. As Chris Dolan observed, "1991 saw the beginning of LRA mutilations and maiming reminiscent of those RENAMO in Mozambique, including the cutting of lips and noses and the use of padlocks on the mouths of people they thought might report them to the authorities" (Dolan 2009, p.45).

The conflict was further intensified through the involvement of South Sudan. Allegedly, the GoU supported the SPLA in the South of Sudan fighting the government of Sudan as a rebel group. In return, Sudan supported the LRA by supplying weapons, ammunition, food, and a basis for the rebels to backtrack, re-organize and re-strengthen themselves in South Sudan (cf. Prunier 2009, pp.81-82). Later in the course of the conflict during the year 2006, the LRA started spreading even further and also opened up bases in the DRC and the Central African Republic (cf. Prendergast/Spiegel 2008, p.2).

In that context, the conflict can be described as displaying four main characteristics. Firstly, it is a conflict between the GoU and the LRA. Secondly, it is a conflict between the predominantly Acholi LRA and the wider Acholi population as the main victims in the insurgency. Thirdly, the conflict is fuelled by the animosity between Uganda and Sudan who are – or at least were – supporting the respective rebellions on each other's territory; and fourthly, the conflict continues a historically developed North-South divide (cf. International Crisis Group 2004a, p.1).

The actual length of the conflict is judged differently by different sources in the academic literature depending on their individual definitions of conflict. Most of the above mentioned conflict databases start counting the conflict as a civil war from the mid-1990s with the shift of strategy and intensified fighting by the LRA. However, given the actual taking of power of Museveni in 1986 and the immediate resistance of the HSM, from which the LRA was mainly born, I count the beginning of the civil war in 1986.

While Museveni has frequently been praised by the international community as a model for good guidance of a country and has even been called 'donor's darling'[78], he was not able to bring the 24-year old civil war in the North to an end. This had disastrous effects for Northern Uganda with regard to development. The great achievements regarding poverty reduction in Uganda are not reflected in the North. As the GoU itself formulated it in 2007, "the welfare indices for Northern Uganda have not improved at the same pace as the rest of the country" (Government of Uganda 2007, p.vi).

When going on a ten hours' bus ride up north from Uganda's capital city Kampala, one reaches Gulu, a district capital with some 40,000 inhabitants, the main center of the insurgency. There, one can witness the effects of the 24-year old conflict between the GoU and the LRA. Thousands of children commute into town every night. Their motivation to sleep within the town's borders rather than in their rural villages is reasoned in the fear of abduction or rape by the LRA. This is the main instrument of the LRA – they abduct the children and use them as child soldiers or sex slaves (cf. United Nations 2006e, p.1). Asking Samuele Tognetti, the administrator of St. Mary's Lacor Hospital in Gulu in 2005, about how the status is at the moment in Northern Uganda, he answered, "quiet – there were only about 4,000 children commuting to my hospital to sleep each night during the past weeks. This is an indicator for how close the rebels are. 4,000 means they are far away. At times, we have up to 15,000 children sleeping everywhere in this hospital – under the trees, on the balconies, and on the streets. Then we know it is really dangerous out there"[79].

These images illustrate that Uganda does not completely fit into the purported success story because the country is plagued by an internal protracted and disastrous conflict in the North. The LRA has achieved to survive for about 24 years now. The conflict has emerged to be one of the most violent and brutal rebellions existing in the world today. According to the Justice and Peace Committee in Kitgum, the rebels had abducted more than 20,000 children by 2001 (cf. Leggett 2001, p.31). Millions of people have been internally displaced, living under the most terrifying conditions for as long as 20 years[80] and the GoU as well as the UN estimate about 100,000 deaths due to the conflict (Government

---

[78] For example by the German Federal Ministry for Economic Cooperation and Development: http://www.bmz.de/de/was_wir_machen/laender_regionen/subsahara/uganda/index.html.
[79] Personal Interview with Samuele Tognetti (Administrator of St. Mary's Lacor Hospital) in August 2005 in Gulu Town, Uganda.
[80] The numbers are officially indicated by the GoU: http://www.statehouse.go.ug.

of Uganda 2007, p.25 and United Nations 2006d, p.1). Further, in 2007, the GoU counted some 218 IDP-camps with populations ranging from 10,000 to up to 60,000 people per camp. In total, 84% of the population in Northern Uganda are dependent on external food aid (Government of Uganda 2007, p.25). This reflects what UN Under-Secretary-General for Humanitarian Affairs, Jan Egeland, expressed about the situation in Northern Uganda as being "among the worst humanitarian disasters in the world" (International Crisis Group 2004a, p.i)[81]. In 2007, Oliver Furley observed that Uganda had the third largest IDP population in the world after Sudan and the DRC (Furley in Furley/May 2006, p.118) and in 2010, the organization Internal Displacement Monitoring Centre still counted at least 437,000 people being internally displaced in Northern Uganda[82].

5.1.1.2 Key Actors

The Ugandan conflict displays different actors. The principal domestic players are the GoU and the rebel group LRA. Furthermore, there are a range of international actors involved, which include individual states, mediators and donors. These actors will be introduced individually including contextualizing them in the case.

One of the two belligerents is the Government of Uganda (GoU), being the state-actor in the conflict in Northern Uganda. The current GoU came to power in January 1986 and has been ruling Uganda ever since. Central is the head and chief of state, President Yoweri Kaguta Museveni. Museveni is also the chief of the national armed forces, the Uganda People's Defence Force (UPDF), that are fighting the rebel group.

President Museveni, born in 1944 in Kyamate, Ankole District, comes from South-Western Uganda. He studied economic and political sciences at the University College Dar es Salaam in Tanzania and after that worked as a researcher for President Obote's office from 1961 until 1971. Museveni joined Obote's group in exile in Tanzania during Amin's reign. He was appointed Minister of Defence in Obote's second regime. In 1980, Museveni founded the Uganda Patriotic Movement (UPM) and run as candidate in the elections in

---

[81] Jan Egeland's visit and his comments were widely published. He called the conflict "the biggest neglected humanitarian emergency in the world", a "human tragedy", and "a moral outrage" (cf. Atkinson (2009): From Uganda to the Congo and Beyond: Pursuing the Lord's Resistance Army, p.4; or *The Guardian*, http://www.guardian.co.uk/world/2004/oct/22/2.).
[82] Cf. http://www.internal-displacement.org.

December 1980, but did not win a seat in Parliament. As a response, he started a guerrilla insurgency against Obote with his Popular Resistance Army (PRA), which lasted until 1986, when he took Kampala and was sworn in President (Nyeko and Lucima in Accord 2002, pp.16-17).

As mentioned above, Museveni's government has been very successful in restoring peace in most parts of Uganda and in developing the economy. Nevertheless, Museveni also faces critique in at least two respects. The first area of critique is his slow opening for democracy and his general style of governance in Uganda. This includes accusations of corruption in the government as well as critique regarding the treatment of opposition. In 2005, Museveni amended the Constitution, removing presidential term limits, so that he could run a third time for President even though he had previously fought for a limitation of presidential terms and introducing the multi-party political system. Protests arose in Kampala when Museveni detained the opposition leader, Kizza Besigye, four months before national elections on charges of treason and rape[83]. However, the protests did not escalate; nor did Museveni change his politics.

The second area of critique deals with the conflict in the North. Museveni's army was accused to have contributed to the brutality and violent excesses in the North. For example the German journal Der Spiegel publicized an account of how members of the NRA had massacred civilians in 1987[84]. Further, the strategy of forcing the population into camps was perceived skeptically by some. Being a protracted conflict, the population has been living in these camps for up to 20 years. The living conditions in the camps are mostly disastrous with lack of food, diseases, and overcrowding paired with poor infrastructure[85]. Besides the behavior of the UPDF and the camp-strategy, Museveni is sometimes accused of 'not wanting to end the conflict in the North' (cf. Allen 2006, p.48). Some people suggest that Museveni topples any effort to bring peace to the country because of an interest to keep the war going. On the other hand, Museveni supported several peace initiatives[86].

The other belligerent in the conflict is the Lord's Resistance Army (LRA), a rebel group, consisting of mostly Acholi Ugandans fighting the GoU. The goals

---

[83] Cf. *Der Spiegel*, "Uganda: Schlappe für den Autokraten", 6/2006.
[84] Cf. *Der Spiegel*, "Uganda: Land ohne Hoffnung", Nr. 16/1987.
[85] A comprehensive account on the situation in IDP-camps in Northern Uganda is provided by IDMC and the NRC from 2009: Internal Displacement Monitoring Centre and Norwegian Refugee Council (2009a): "Peace, Recovery and Development: Challenges in Northern Uganda", *Internal Displacement Monitoring Centre (IDMC) and the Norwegian Refugee Council (NRC)*.
[86] A detailed account on the peace initiatives and individual motives in the process will be discussed below.

and strategy of the LRA are not entirely clear and they are often characterized as an irrational actor with no clear political objective (cf. Allen 2006, p.25; International Crisis Group 2004c, p.1; and International Crisis Group 2005b, p.7). The LRA is based on a Christian motion, namely the Biblical Ten Commandments and aims at overthrowing President Museveni in order to establish a regime in accordance with the Ten Commandments (cf. Bercovitch/ Fretter 2004, p.106). The LRA has approximately a size of 3,000 people, although it is difficult to determine the exact size of the group due to its usage of child soldiers (cf. Allen 2006, p.40; International Crisis Group 2005b, p.3). It is estimated that the number of soldiers varies greatly[87]. Only the top commanders are known. The leader is Joseph Kony who is also the founder of the LRA and has been in charge ever since then. Second-in-command used to be Sam Kolo, who defected in February 2005. Vincent Otti took over his position and was responsible for negotiations with the government. Otti was killed by the LRA in 2007 on charges of betrayal (cf. Atkinson 2009, p.12). Since then, Dr. David Nyekorach Matsanga was in charge of leading the LRA delegation during negotiations (cf. Accord 2010, p.7).

The LRA is organized in a similar pattern as a regular infantry army. It comprises five brigades called Stocree, Sinia, Gilva, Shila and Control Altar. The chain of command follows a strict hierarchy. Kony receives orders from the 'spirits'[88] and passes them on to the command where the orders are translated into operational actions. From there, they are given on to the divisions, brigades and subordinate units (cf. Nyeko and Lucima in Accord 2002, p.19).

The LRA comes from the Acholiland, operating in a region where the people are rather skeptical towards the government due to the traditional North-South divide of the country. The population is thus rather prone to support the rebel group. Looking at the tactics and strategies of the LRA, an interesting ambivalence arises though. The main targets of the LRA are defenseless civilians from the region – the Acholi. Thus, the LRA targets its own tribal group. The reasoning behind this approach lies in the desire to discredit Museveni in his position as president. The LRA moves in small groups of up to ten fighters. These groups attack IDP-camps and villages both during night and over the day. They massacre, mutilate (with the intention to cleanse the population from sins), and abduct children. These tactics make it hard for the UPDF to fight the rebels,

---

[87] Tim Allen suggests that the actual size of the LRA is highly speculative (cf. Allen Trial Justice: The International Criminal Court and the Lord's Resistance Army, p.40).

[88] Apparently, there are four holy spirits guiding Kony, which are 'Juma Oris', 'Silindy Makay', 'Who are You?', and 'Divo' (cf. Dolan (2009): Social Torture: The Case of Northern Uganda, 1986-2006, p.301).

which in return is perceived by the population as if the government is unable or unwilling for that matter to protect the people in the North, contributing to the rebel group's strength (cf. Haarhaus 2009, p.3).

Thus, the main victims are the Acholi people, suffering most from the LRA's violence (cf. Dolan 2009, p.1). As mentioned above, it is the LRA's instrument to abduct children. It is estimated that the LRA has kidnapped about 60,000 Ugandan children, which translates into one in three male and one in six female adolescents in Northern Uganda (cf. Carlson/Mazurana 2008, p.4). The rebels terrorize, kill, rape and mutilate the people and burn down entire villages leading to large scale insecurity in the region. The government's reaction was the 'drain-the-lake-to-catch-the-fish'-strategy by forcing most of the population to move to so-called 'protected villages', which are commonly known as IDP-camps (cf. Dolan 2009, pp.110-111). The reasoning was twofold. The GoU wanted to created so-called safe zones where the population is protected and the strategy is part of a counter-insurgency plan to destroy the source for resources for the LRA in the Northern Ugandan Hinterland (cf. Haarhaus 2009, p.3 and Schlichte in Bakonyi/Hensell, et al. 2006, p.158). Given that the Northern region was traditionally mainly dependent on agriculture (mostly animal rearing and food crops), the displacement has destroyed the principal source of income for the population (cf. Banfield 2008, p.14). Additionally, the situation has brought up another unique phenomenon, which is night commuting. The uncountable numbers of children commuting into town at night in order to hide from the rebels are called night commuters[89]. Due to the increased difficulty for the LRA to target the population and to subsist in the region, they expanded the territory where it operated. First, it spread into South Sudan and later also into the DRC and the Central African Republic. Prendergast and Spiegel even stated, "Kony has successfully morphed from a rebel/predator in Northern Uganda into a genuine regional warlord" (Prendergast/Spiegel 2008, p.2). However, this seems to exaggerate the actual strength of the group. Even though the LRA is operating in other countries in the region, the conflict remains to be an inherent Northern Ugandan issue. To retreat into other countries' territory is rather a tool used by the LRA to re-strengthen and re-arm themselves and not an expression of a genuinely regional movement.

The LRA's strength is mainly based on spiritual leadership to which Joseph Kony is central (cf. Allen 2006, p.42; Human Rights Watch 1997, p.74; and

---

[89] For a detailed account on the impact of the conflict on individual children's lives, see the insightful book "Wanderer der Nacht" by the Polish journalist Wojciech Jagielski (Jagielski (2010): Wanderer der Nacht. Eine literarische Reportage).

Lomo/Hovil, et al. 2004, p.19). He claimed to have inherited his 'aunt' Alice Auma Lakwena's spirits, who speak through him and give orders to his followers. The Acholi and thus also Kony's fighters are very susceptible to such system of belief given a strong traditional culture of spiritual belief in Northern Uganda (cf. Lomo/Hovil, et al. 2004, p.14). Not very much is known about Kony as he prefers to avoid the public, or as Lomo and Hovel express it, "Kony himself is shrouded in a veil of secrecy" (Lomo/Hovil, et al. 2004, p.13). Only few pictures exist of Joseph Kony. He is said to be about 50 years old (born in 1961), stemming from the Acholi village Odek in Omoro Country of Gulu District (cf. Nyeko and Lucima in Accord 2002, p.17). He did not finish school, but instead trained as an 'ajwaka', a kind of spiritual healer, as it had been the tradition in his family (cf. Allen 2006, p.38). Reports from abducted children that had been freed suggest that Joseph Kony has about 50 wives and plenty of children. Nevertheless, Kony emphasizes discipline within the LRA: alcohol and drugs are strictly forbidden, but sexual intercourse or the giving of wives is used as an instrument to reward combatants (cf. Allen 2006, p.43).

Kony has gained international publicity after Museveni had referred the case of the LRA to the International Criminal Court (ICC) in 2003 (cf. Bayne 2007, p.7). The LRA was the first case for the ICC. Luis Moreno Ocampo, first Prosecutor of the ICC, issued arrest warrants against five members of the LRA in 2005: Joseph Kony, Vincent Otti, Okot Odhiambo, Dominic Ongwen and Raska Lukwiya. Only two of them are still alive (Kony and Ongwen)[90].

Kony and his group are often described as madmen and/or irrational actors who are simply brutally and violently massacring people without a clear agenda or objective. However, the protraction of the conflict and individual statements, developments and events suggest that this would be too fast a judgment[91], or as HRW suggests, "a misleading oversimplification" (Human Rights Watch 1997, p.62; cf. also Allen 2006, p.44). In 1997, the Kacoke Madit (KM) was held in London. Translated as "the big meeting of Acholi", the KM involved mainly Acholi living in the diaspora as well as representatives from the civil society, traditional Acholi and religious leaders, and representatives from the GoU. It was part of a peace initiative driven by civil society actors, mainly the Catholic organization Community of Sant'Egidio. At this conference it was the first time that the Lord's Resistance Movement (LRM), the so-called political wing of the

---

[90] Raska Lukwiya was killed by the UPDF in August 2006, Vincent Otti and Okot Odhiambo were killed by the LRA in 2007 (cf. Internal Displacement Monitoring Centre and Norwegian Refugee Council (2009b): Uganda: Returns Outpace Recovery Planning, 39).

[91] Details regarding the LRA's negotiation pattern as well as the mentioned developments and events will be discussed below.

LRA, formulated their objectives and ideas. Specifically, the LRM stated their goals were "to remove dictatorship and stop the oppression of our people, to fight for the immediate restoration of competitive multi-party democracy in Uganda, to see an end to gross violation of human rights and dignity of Ugandans, to ensure the restoration of peace and security in Uganda, to ensure unity, sovereignty and economic prosperity beneficial to all Ugandans, and to bring an end to the repressive policy of deliberate marginalization of groups of people who may not agree with the NRA ideology" (Government of Uganda 1997, pp.5-6). This was a very clear and pragmatic statement. But it is still doubted whether the LRM was actually acting as official representatives of Joseph Kony.

Another actor that is noteworthy in this context is Sudan. Sudan is the only known external supporter of the LRA. This stems from an old-dated disagreement between Uganda and Sudan. While Museveni supported Sudan's rebel group, the Sudanese People's Liberation Movement (SPLM), against the Khartoum government[92], the Sudan government supported the LRA. The LRA used to receive training, weapons and the provision of safe havens in South Sudan (cf. Bayne 2007, p.6). As the ICG has pointed out in their Africa Briefing from June 2005, "Sudan bears major responsibility for the duration of the Northern Uganda conflict because it has played a central role in revitalizing and sustaining the LRA during the last decade" (International Crisis Group 2005c, p.4). After the change in government in Sudan, the power constellation changed. In December 1999, after long negotiations and substantial international pressure on President Bashir's government in Sudan, a peace treaty was signed by the GoU and the government of Sudan in Nairobi, the Nairobi Peace Agreement (cf. Allen 2006, p.50). The agreement provided for an end to the support of the rebel groups on both sides. In 2002, Sudan even allowed the UPDF to enter its territory to chase the LRA fighters.

Currently, it is believed that the LRA does not receive support anymore from Sudan. However, it is very likely that the LRA still keeps hidden bases in South Sudan. Further, the LRA has obtained munitions from Sudan for its weapons even after the signing of the peace agreement in Nairobi[93].

A range of mediators have been involved in Uganda at different stages of the conflict. The first mediator worth mentioning is Betty Oyella Bigombe. Being an ethnic Acholi, Bigombe was elected Minister of Parliament in 1986 in

---

[92] Note: Museveni was an old friend of SPLA leader John Garang, who had studied with him in Tanzania.
[93] As indicated by defectors from the LRA (cf. International Crisis Group (2005c): "Africa Briefing #27: Building a Comprehensive Peace Strategy for Northern Uganda", *International Crisis Group*, p.4).

Museveni's government. In 1988, Museveni created a new position in the GoU, the 'Minister of State for Pacification of Northern Uganda, Resident in Gulu', later renamed into 'Minister of State in the Office of the Prime Minister, Resident in Northern Uganda'. Bigombe was appointed to this post and held it until 1997. Throughout this time, Bigombe was first assigned to convince the LRA to surrender and later to initiate peace talks. After Bigombe left the GoU, she immigrated to the US and worked for the Harvard Institute for International Development and the World Bank. Currently, Bigombe is a senior fellow at the U.S. Institute of Peace in Washington, D.C. Being first in a position of an internal mediator to the conflict as official representative of the GoU, she continued her efforts after leaving and became an external mediator to the conflict. Bigombe established a reputation of involving all layers of actors in the conflict such as the main actors, but also representatives from the diaspora, the civil society and powerful individuals (cf. Bigombe 2004, pp.16-17). In addition, she was seen as a kind of "grassroots mobiliser", given her hands-on approach in mediation (O'Kadameri in Accord 2002, p.35).

A second group of mediators are representatives from the wider Northern Ugandan society, mainly including three different branches. First, actively involved is the Ugandan diaspora, mostly based in the UK. Second, there are the religious leaders from Northern Uganda who found the Acholi Religious Leaders' Peace Initiative. Third, other representatives from the civil society were involved such as NGOs like the Catholic organization Community of Sant' Egidio and Acholi chiefs and elders. These actors contributed and organized the KM meetings and thus facilitated one of the peace initiatives.

The third mediator involved in the conflict in Northern Uganda is the semi-autonomous Government of South Sudan (GoSS). Specifically Lt. General Dr. Riek Machar Teny-Dhourgon, the Vice President of the GoSS, is important in this context, since he took over the role as chief mediator in the so-called Juba talks (2006-2008). Machar is a rather 'contentious' figure in Sudan, given that he had split from the SPLA in the 1990s in order to ally with the government of Sudan. However, he reconciled with the SPLA and thus became the GoSS Vice President after the death of John Garang in 2005 (cf. Accord 2010, p.7).

Lastly, I would like to mention the many donors that have been involved in Uganda and specifically Northern Uganda throughout the course of the conflict. Uganda as the 'donors' darling' has uncountable donor partners. Three forms of donors have been active in the region. The first to mention are the multilateral institutions. Be it the World Bank, the IMF, or many of the UN organizations[94],

---

[94] Among others: UNDP, UNFPA, UNHCR, UNICEF, WFP.

they are all active in Uganda and have all paid special attention to Northern Uganda. Also regional multilateral institutions such as the AfDB and the EC have contributed much to Uganda's development. The second group is individual states providing bilateral aid. Donor states include all DAC countries, but also a substantial number of non-DAC countries. Lastly, a vast amount of international NGOs are present in Uganda and in Northern Uganda. In the latter, many focus on humanitarian assistance, providing food, medical services and education to the people in IDP-camps.

The way of support varies. It includes technical and financial assistance and comes in the form of personnel, non-monetary aid, humanitarian/emergency assistance, but also in the form of budget support. Uganda was also one of the countries enjoying the World Bank's Heavily Indebted Poor Countries initiative and the Multilateral Debt Relief Initiative, which resulted in a debt reduction of US$ 3.8 million in 2006[95].

5.1.2   Uganda Analysis

The analysis of the LRA-GoU conflict consists of four sections: firstly, conflict ripeness will be assessed. In order to do so, the course of the conflict will be presented and individual phases are reviewed with respect to their display of conflict ripeness. It will further be assessed whether, when ripeness can be identified, independent variables affected the status of ripeness (5.1.2.1). Secondly, the influx of IDA will be analyzed over the course of the conflict in three categories, which are general IDA targeted at the GoU, humanitarian aid explicitly dedicated to Northern Uganda, and IDA for support of peace negotiations (5.1.2.2). Thirdly, the potential effect of IDA on conflict ripeness as an independent variable is assessed including the interpretation regarding the nature of quality of effect and the conditions accompanying such effect (5.1.2.3). Lastly, a conclusion will be drawn accumulating the results of the case study (5.1.2.4).

---

[95] Cf. http://web.worldbank.org/WBSITE/EXTERNAL/COUNTRIES/AFRICAEXT/UGANDAEXTN/0,,menuPK:374947~pagePK:141132~piPK:141107~theSitePK:374864,00.html., accessed on 12 October 2010.

5.1.2.1 Conflict Ripeness

When looking at the Northern Ugandan conflict from 1986 until today, one observes several phases of the conflict. Ronald R. Atkinson identified five discernable phases up to December 2008, "each with a different duration and with different dynamics, but all with a similar overall rhythm, a strong recurring pattern" (Atkinson 2009, p.6). The pattern Atkinson describes, is "a period of acute insecurity and violence, followed by an interval during which these gradually decline" (Atkinson 2009, p.6). Chris Dolan followed a similar approach, but identified seven phases, which are more or less comparable to Atkinson's system (cf. Dolan 2009, p.41). For the analysis, I follow Dolan and Atkinson, in that I also use a chronological approach, however, I structure the analysis into the four phases (cf. in table below) observed in Northern Uganda that were all marked by individual peace initiatives all ending unsuccessfully[96].

	Phase I	Phase II	Phase III	Phase IV
Conflict Phase	1986-1994	1994-1998	1998-2005	2005-2008
Peace Initiative	1993-1994	1997-1998	2004-2005	2006-2008
Mediator	Betty Bigombe	Diaspora/civil society	Betty Bigombe	GoSS

Table 7: Overview Phases of Conflict in Uganda[97]

After years of small guerrilla warfare by the LRA, the intensity and tactics of the LRA changed in early 1991. As described above, the LRA began terrorizing the Acholi population and abducted children at large scale. The GoU's reaction was a first big military campaign launched in 1991 called Operation North under the leadership of the then Defence Minister Major General David Tinyefuza (cf. Allen 2006, p.47). It had the intent to wipe out the rebel movement. The

---

[96] Many more than four efforts were made to initiate peace talks in Northern Uganda. However, in this thesis, I focus on four that were judged as the most promising with regards to potential success. All other efforts failed at very early stages as for instance the local peace talks in Gulu under auspices of the District Reconciliation and Peace Team in 2001 or the Presidential Peace Team's attempts for negotiations in 2002.
[97] Source: Own illustration.

operation was not successful with regard to defeating the rebels. As a result, the GoU asked Betty Bigombe as Minister of State in the Office of the Prime Minister (OPM) to initiate peace talks. Bigombe established direct contact to the LRA and followed a rather unusual approach by involving not only the two belligerents, but also members of the UPDF, ministers to parliament, religious and traditional leaders from the region and other representatives from the civil society. At first, these peace efforts seemed very promising. It started with a discreet meeting between Bigombe and Okwonga Adek, a trusted advisor of Kony at that time, in the summer of 1993 (cf. O'Kadameri in Accord 2002, p.36). Soon afterwards, the belligerents discussed the arrangements for the first official meeting (O'Kadameri in Accord 2002, p.37). The first face-to-face meeting between the belligerents took place on 25 November 1993 at Pagik. Only middle-ranking officers from the LRA took part who brought a tape-recorded message by Kony (cf. O'Kadameri in Accord 2002, p.37). Several more meetings followed, including one with Kony present. The negotiations resulted in a ceasefire agreement signed by the UPDF and the LRA on 2 February 1994 (cf. published in Accord 2002, pp.81-82). Six days later, Museveni surprisingly issued an ultimatum to the LRA to give up their weapons and surrender within seven days, which proved to be the end of the peace talks. The result was that the LRA started building bases in Southern Sudan. In parallel, violence and the abduction of children escalated, so that the situation deteriorated significantly in the subsequent months and years.

    The question arises whether the conflict was at a ripe phase for this first peace initiative in the conflict in Northern Uganda led by Betty Bigombe in 1993 and early 1994. The first factor to assess is whether the two belligerents faced an MHS or were offered MEOs. Regarding the GoU, one has to look at the development before the peace initiative and their behavior throughout. What has to be noted is that the GoU initiated the step towards negotiations by entitling Betty Bigombe to proceed with peace efforts. After failing in militarily destroying the LRA, the GoU pursued the alternative approach of trying to negotiate. It is noticeable that there was no intense pressure on the government to bring the conflict to an end – neither from external sources nor because of internal reasons. The international community had not started noticing the conflict as a humanitarian catastrophe yet; so no international pressure was put on Museveni to negotiate. Further, even though the UPDF could not destroy the LRA, the LRA did not pose a national threat to the army or the government given that it was solely operating in the rather small area in the North of the country. This parallels with the fact that the main victims of the LRA's atrocities were the Acholi people who did not enjoy the protection or main concern of the government given that it was the traditional opponent. This leads to suggest that the GoU did not perceive a hurting stalemate; particularly, they did not perceive a precipice.

On the other hand, the GoU had just realized that it was not possible to destroy the rebel group militarily, meaning that it became clear that a negotiated solution might have been the only option. This perception would qualify for a 'plateau-situation', where there is no end in sight unless the belligerents find a negotiated solution. However, the circumstances accompanying this plateau-situation were not hurting so much to the GoU that it was unsustainable (cf. O'Kadameri in Accord 2002, p.36). The UPDF was not overly endangered and the overall situation affected the government only peripherally.

The LRA did not face a situation where it perceived to be in a hurting stalemate either. Even though they were attacked heavily by the UPDF throughout Operation North, the LRA's reaction showed their strength and independence from such attacks. The level of violence and the number of abductions increased extensively after Operation North (cf. Allen 2006, p.47). This shows that the LRA is not dependent on large numbers of soldiers, but is able to survive with only few soldiers. By means of abduction and brutal violence, they have the power to both re-enforce their number of soldiers and gain respect by the spreading of fear among the population. For this tactics, only a small amount of combatants are needed as opposed to a classic warfare-strategy where the size of an army might be the decisive factor.

It explains that after Operation North, there was no indication that the LRA perceived a hurting stalemate. Their existence was not endangered and it was easily possible to re-strengthen and re-arm themselves. Thus, the LRA was neither perceiving to be on a plateau nor at a precipice. They simply followed their tactics and continued the guerrilla warfare. Especially the possibility to withdraw into South Sudan, opening up bases there from where it was possible to attack Northern Uganda and receiving arms support from Sudan, was a new chance for them to regain power[98]. The LRA did not face an MHS.

MEOs were not existent either throughout the peace negotiation efforts 1993-1994. As there were no external powerful actors involved, no 'carrots' were offered to the belligerents. Also other potential opportunities did not emerge that would have made a negotiated solution to the conflict at that point in time preferable to continued fighting to any of the belligerents.

Regarding the SWO, it was already mentioned that in a certain way both belligerents did actually see a way out in that situation given that they were both initially willing to negotiate. However, those two ideas of how the process could

---

[98] Cf. *Der Spiegel*, "Uganda: Aufmarsch an der Grenze", 48/1995.

be handled and what the result of a negotiation could be contradicted each other. Museveni was open and clear that a negotiated solution at this point would rather be a form of victory of the GoU, implying surrender by the LRA (cf. O'Kadameri in Accord 2002, p.36). The LRA saw – if at all – the only way out in the form of a truly negotiated solution with compromises of both sides and gains for both. The LRA wanted to be treated as an equal partner and taken seriously in terms of government-formation (cf. O'Kadameri in Accord 2002, p.40). Thus, senses of ways out did exist; but they were not compatible. Therefore, an SWO, implying that both actors sensed a compatible way out, did not exist.

It is therefore possible to state that during peace initiative I, no conflict ripeness existed as the two conditions were not fully given. This means that also the independent variables are not applicable in this context.

The meaning of the issuance of the ultimatum to the LRA and resulting termination of negotiations summarizes best the status of ripeness to this peace initiative. It shows that no conflict ripeness was given. Both the GoU and the LRA were willing to negotiate and even to agree to a ceasefire, but none of them was willing to make compromises for it. Museveni showed by issuing the ultimatum that he wanted the negotiations to be on his terms, implicating that if the LRA agrees, it would rather count as surrender as opposed to a true agreement between the belligerents. And the LRA showed that they were not willing to surrender, but at most be willing to find a commonly acceptable agreement. Both did not go together and thus peace negotiations failed. This final stage of the peace initiative illustrates the status of the situation at the outset of the peace initiative 1993-1994. Betty Bigombe put great effort into the mediation process, however, the support of the two belligerents throughout the process seemed halfheartedly at most.

It is thus possible to state that conflict ripeness was not given at the point of initiating peace efforts in the years of 1993 and 1994 in Uganda.

Despite various attempts to initiate peace talks, only in 1997, some hope for the revival of negotiations arose again (cf. Allen 2006, p.78). This was mainly driven by representatives from the civil society and the diaspora, supported by Betty Bigombe. The trigger for the effort was another round of escalation of brutality and violence. In March 1996, national elections were held. For this event, the LRA declared a unilateral ceasefire to allow the Acholi to take part in the elections and vote for Museveni's opponent, Paul Ssemewogerere, leading the Inter-Political Forces Coalition. The Acholi indeed overwhelmingly voted for the opposition. Nevertheless, Museveni won the elections and announced immediately, that he was determined to defeat the LRA militarily. For this end, he appointed General Salim Saleh, his half-brother, to take charge of the operations. Violence on both sides escalated.

In October 1996, the GoU then began to implement the large scale plan of bringing the people together in the so-called 'protected villages', in order to take away the basis for food and support as well as target from the LRA (cf. Dolan 2009, p.107 and Internal Displacement Monitoring Centre/Norwegian Refugee Council 2009b, p.9). Thus, many Acholi were uprooted and had to move to the IDP-camps. In the same month, the LRA abducted 139 girls from a school in Northern Uganda, the St. Mary's College Aboke. The abductions triggered attention beyond the borders of Uganda. But the violence did not stop. In January 1997, the LRA massacred 400 villagers at once in Kitgum District.

After the mass abductions of girls, international media reacted and brought up the topic for the first time on a broader basis. Thus, actors from NGOs and especially Acholi living in the diaspora started to act. The Kacoke Madit (KM) was held in London in April 1997 and representatives from the belligerent sides were present (cf. James Alfred Obita [spokesman of the LRM] in Accord 2002, p.41). It was the first time that international actors were involved in the peace process. As a consequence from the KM conference, a representative of the LRM wrote to the GoU to ask for peace talks (cf. "Letter from the LRM/A to President Museveni on 6 November 1997", printed in Accord 2002, p.83). The GoU reacted carefully (cf. "Letter from President Museveni to the LRM/A on 22 November 1997", printed in Accord 2002, pp.83-84) and agreed to a meeting in Rome, organized by Sant'Egidio. The Minister of Foreign Affairs thus met with representatives from the LRM in December 1997. Even though the meeting instilled hopes for further negotiations, soon after, the process broke down. The GoU had demanded the involvement of LRA field commanders. In parallel, internal divisions within the LRA arose. A disconnect between the high command of the LRA and the political representatives of the LRM seemed to be the reason. The result was the end of negotiations and an increase in violence; specifically against the civilian population. In September 1998, the GoU reacted with another military campaign: Offensive Operation Zero. Also this military effort could not destroy the LRA and instead led to the old pattern of an escalation of atrocities and abductions.

What was the status of conflict ripeness surrounding this peace effort? Starting with the question of whether an MHS or MEOs were present, one can state that the situation had not significantly changed compared to the 1993-1994 situation. Cycles of violence and escalations thereof shaped the face of the conflict. None of the two parties was substantially endangered in their existence. A precipice was not apparent; the above-described plateau-situation was maintained; but not in a way that it was hurting any of the parties in a threatening way. The GoU felt a mild attention – not to say pressure – from the international community due to the media coverage of the girls' abductions as well as the involvement of the diaspora in London. This explains why the GoU agreed to a meeting in order to signal that they were active and willing to progress in the current situation of conflict; yet, it does not show true commitment or a real interest in peacefully resolving the conflict. It is true that the media started to report on the conflict, but there was no take-up by actors such as states or multi-lateral/non-governmental organizations that would have led to an international outcry to pressure Museveni into a hurting stalemate. Thus, an MHS was not given.

MEOs were equally absent in the situation of 1997-1998. Even though there was international involvement to a certain degree, it was not backed by actors with leverage. Museveni would not have gained anything in agreeing to negotiate sincerely. The same applies to Kony and the LRA. There were neither offers from the GoU nor from external actors that would have induced the rebels to leave the bush.

Regarding the sense of a way out, on a first view, it seems that the two belligerents were open for finding a way out and communicate. The LRA sent representatives from the LRM to the KM who held a speech, outlining their objectives and demands (cf. Government of Uganda 1997, pp.5-6 and p.11). This is a positive sign at first sight – the rebels offer a basis on which it is then possible to negotiate. This would be a sign for an SWO on part of the LRA. However, this would be too fast a judgment. When analyzing the actual objectives and demands, it becomes clear that they were not supposed to serve as a basis for further talks. The demands were rather designed as provocations against the GoU instead of laying common grounds. For instance, the LRA stated as one demand "that Lt. General Yoweri Museveni steps down immediately to allow Uganda to return to civil rule". Such demands signal that the LRA did not perceive an SWO. A second caveat came into play: the internal problems within the LRA. At the KM, the leader of the LRA's delegation was James Obita, Secretary for Foreign Affairs, LRM/A. Obita was a representative from the diaspora. Even though he frequently claimed to be sent by the LRA (cf. Government of Uganda 1997; Obita in Accord 2002, p.44), many signs suggest that the LRA actually did not officially give him procura for the meetings (cf. Obita in Accord 2002, p.44). Instead, it seems that some representatives from the diaspora sympathizing with the LRA came together and claimed to be their political wing. But there are no indications that they were officially asked to represent Kony and his group's idea at any meeting. This analysis is also supported by the later course of events when after the GoU asked to talk to field commanders, the peace process broke down entirely. Thus, the LRA was not involved at all at this peace initiative, so that the stated objectives cannot be taken as signs for the perception of a way out.

When assessing the position of Museveni and the GoU, it becomes clear that an SWO was not given. Two aspects contribute to this conclusion: firstly, Museveni had just been re-elected in Uganda. He enjoyed great support in most of the territory, except for the rebel-affected areas in the North. Furthermore, he was internationally praised for his successes in the development of the country. Thus, he was not in the position to be susceptible for seeing an end to the conflict with the LRA that was on peaceful grounds. Rather he implemented a stronger military position with positioning his half-brother in charge and following the strategy of building IDP-camps. The usage of IDP-camps shows that the GoU was interested in militarily winning against the LRA and not in finding a compromise in a shared agreement. It shows that Museveni did not perceive an SWO. Secondly, after James Obita, as a representative from the LRM, wrote a letter to Museveni asking for peace talks (cf. "Letter from the LRM/A to President Museveni on 6 November 1997", printed in Accord 2002, p.83), Museveni responded in a very clear fashion, mirroring his military stance. He stated, "I personally feel very strongly against these individuals [Kony, Lagony, and Otti]". He proceeded though by stating that, "Uganda is not my personal property" and then stating that he would agree to a meeting (cf. "Letter from President Museveni to the LRM/A on 22 November 1997", printed in Accord 2002, pp.83-84). Nevertheless, the letter demonstrates that Museveni had no real SWO, but instead answered to public demands in negotiating; not committing nor compromising. The GoU did not perceive an SWO.

Given that in this peace initiative neither an MHS/MEOs nor an SWO existed, conflict ripeness was not given during phase II of the Ugandan conflict.

The years thereafter were marked by continued violence and large-scale civil war. Small attempts at initiating peace talks were made in between, but remained unsuccessful (cf. Accord 2010, p.8). For instance in 2001, talks initiated in Gulu Town failed at a very early stage. Government-backed Bigombe had intended to isolate LRA-leader Kony by talking directly to his field commanders. The rebels were apparently not prepared to betray their leader Kony (cf. Kiyaga-Nsubuga in Ali/Matthews 2004, p.93).

A development took place that should prove to be decisive for the following course of events. In August 1999, with the mediation of the Carter Center, the GoU and Sudan started negotiations to normalize relations and end their inter-state conflict. Both rebel groups, the LRA and the SPLA were excluded from these talks. Finally, in December 1999, Sudan's President Bashir and Museveni signed the so-called Nairobi Accords facilitated by the Kenyan President Arap Moi, which concluded an end to supporting the respective rebel groups and allowing the GoU to pursue the LRA militarily even beyond the border to Sudan into the South Sudan territories (cf. Bercovitch/Fretter 2004, p.107 and Haarhaus 2009, p.3).

Furthermore, in November 1999, the Amnesty Act passed into Ugandan law[99]. Already in previous years, Uganda had followed the strategy of offering amnesty to rebels when surrendering, which proved quite successful in cases like the UPDA. The Amnesty Act was expanded to members of the LRA in January 2000.

In March 2001, Museveni won another term in office. He had one opponent, Kizza Besigye, who lost by 28% to 69% of the votes for Museveni. However, again the majority of Acholi voted against Museveni. A change to the overall situation of the conflict occurred in the aftermath of the 9/11-attacks in the US. The US State Department put the LRA on the list of worldwide terrorist organizations. As a consequence, Museveni followed this approach. In March 2002, Uganda passed the Anti-Terrorism Act making LRA-membership a criminal offence (cf. Accord 2010, p.8). This enabled Museveni to build up closer ties to the US government and receive direct support from them. US President Bush gave the UPDF military assistance in sponsoring training of 6,000 soldiers (cf. Accord 2010, p.8).

Another major military attack was launched by the UPDF: Operation Iron Fist in April 2002. During this military campaign, the UPDF operated up to a certain distance inside Sudan to be able to attack the LRA's bases. This operation proved to be more successful than the one in 1991. A rather calm period followed in which slowly a perception of security returned to Northern Uganda. But the LRA was not destroyed. Instead the rebel group had used the time to rearm and re-strengthen. In April 2003, they killed a representative of a Presidential peace team. As a result, the GoU declared everyone a suspect of collaborating with the rebels who was in contact with the LRA (cf. Allen 2006, p.78). Thus, all efforts to establish contact for peace talks were cut off completely. The LRA started a new campaign and conducted major killings and atrocities as well as mass abductions in late 2003 and early 2004[100]. The conflict expanded territorially to the districts of Teso and West Nile, so that the LRA's

---

[99] Cf. The Amnesty Act: http://www.c-r.org/our-work/accord/northern-uganda/documents/2000_Jan _The_Amnesty_Act.doc.
[100] Cf. *Der Spiegel*, "Massaker in Uganda: Rebellen töten 190 Flüchtlinge", 22 February 2004. and *Der Spiegel*, "Uganda: Rebellen töten Dorfbewohner mit Äxten und Macheten", 9 December 2003. For instance, in February 2004, the LRA committed horrific atrocities against the population and massacred about 200 civilians at once.

presence was wide-spread in the entire region of Northern Uganda (cf. Allen 2006, p.73).

In November 2003, the UN Secretary General's Special Representative on Humanitarian Affairs, Jan Egeland, visited Northern Uganda. The conflict enjoyed international attention from then onwards. Egeland labeled it to be "the biggest neglected humanitarian emergency in the world" (Atkinson 2009, p.4). As a consequence, the conflict was put on the agenda of many states, institutions and organizations from the international community.

Museveni referred the case of Northern Uganda to the ICC in January 2004. Investigations started under the leadership of Luis Moreno Ocampo on 29 July 2004 (cf. Bayne 2007, p.7)[101]. In mid-2004, Museveni also faced internal problems. Critique regarding the no-party system in Uganda was heard and the Supreme Court took up the case.

The GoU was ready to agree to another round of talks by late 2004, which proved promising at the onset (cf. Allen 2006, p.72 and Betty Bigombe commenting that there was an interest in ending the rebellion by all in: Bigombe 2004, pp.16-17). It was again Betty Bigombe who initiated contact to the LRA; this time not as an internal but an external mediator. Her involvement was supported by the GoU, but not led by the GoU (cf. Bayne 2007, p.7). She succeeded in arranging a meeting of the top rebel leaders including Kony and representatives of the government in December 2004. Kony, however, did not show up but sent the Second-in-Command, Sam Kolo, who discussed the topic with Interior Minister, Ruhakan Rugunda (cf. International Crisis Group 2005a, p.1). Sam Kolo assured to get Kony to meet government officials with the prospect of signing a peace agreement. On 31 December 2004, the belligerents agreed to a ceasefire and the establishment of safe zones for the period of the negotiations (cf. Accord 2010, p.8). The hopes for a successful resolution at this point were impaired when Sam Kolo surprisingly surrendered in February 2005 under the Amnesty Act[102], which granted him amnesty in Uganda. Bigombe lost her primary contact person and thus the talks stopped, while Sam Kolo enjoyed full protection and amnesty. The peace talks were not destroyed though. By the summer of 2005, Kony signaled that he would be willing to agree to a meeting and sent Vincent Otti as the new Second-in-Command. Otti stressed that the LRA remained committed to the peace efforts (cf. International Crisis Group 2005b, p.4). But then the satellite system broke down, so that the communication between Bigombe and the rebels was cut off (cf. International Crisis Group

---

[101] Cf. http://www.icc-cpi.int.
[102] The Amnesty Act had been introduced by GoU in 2001.

2005c, p.4). Additionally, in October 2005, the ICC issued arrest warrants against five LRA commanders including Kony and Otti under the case *The Prosecutor v. Joseph Kony, Vincent Otti, Okot Odhiambo and Dominic Ongwen (May/July 2005)*[103], which was judged as the final blow to Betty Bigombe's peace initiative (cf. Banfield 2008, p.7 and Mwaniki/Wepundi, et al. 2009, p.11).

In late 2005, the rebels' atrocities intensified again (cf. Allen 2006, p.169) and even affected NGO-workers in the region. However, even that late, Betty Bigombe judged the situation as still "hopeful"[104]. But the process was stalled.

Was the situation ripe for the resolution of the conflict when Betty Bigombe initiated peace talks in 2004-2005? Three aspects speak in favor of the GoU perceiving a hurting stalemate. The first and very convincing factor was international pressure. Betty Bigombe did not intervene as an internal mediator, but as a representative from the international community. Therefore, she brought with her major international attention, substantially supported by Jan Egeland's previous visit to Uganda and subsequent media coverage of the conflict and the conditions in Northern Uganda[105]. Plenty of individual initiatives to support the affected people and to bring peace to the region could be observed during this time (cf. Allen 2006, p.72). Thus, the international community expected from Museveni that he acted. His international reputation was at stake, which put significant pressure on him. The US Congress even passed the 'Northern Uganda Crisis Response Act' in January 2004, pressuring the GoU to take action (US Congress, PL 108-283). And indeed, the GoU felt pressured enough to address the bad humanitarian situation in Northern Uganda. In August 2004, it published the National Policy for Internally Displaced Persons, which was the first national IDP-policy in the world (cf. Government of Uganda 2004). It was a guide to government institutions, humanitarian and development agencies with advice for principles, roles and responsibilities for providing assistance and protection to people in the IDP-camps.

This perceived pressure on the GoU was intensified by the second aspect, being the internal difficulties regarding democratic developments within Uganda. National and international voices were heard complaining about Museveni's no-party system. Challenged by two sides of politics, the pressure put on Museveni was thus even more intense. By acting on one problem (the conflict), Museveni could postpone acting on the other (his government style).

---

[103] Cf. http://www.icc-cpi.int.
[104] Personal Interview by Email with Betty Bigombe, 01 December 2005.
[105] Cf. for example *Der Spiegel*, Thielke, Thilo: "Uganda: Gottes grausame Guerilla", 44/2003.

The third aspect that intensified the GoU's perceived hurting stalemate was the intense campaign conducted by the LRA just before the beginning of the peace talks. Especially given that this brutal and violent attacks occurred after the UPDF had launched another large-scale military offensive against the LRA, Operation Iron Fist, with the support of Sudan and the US, but which had proven to be unsuccessful again (cf. Accord 2010, p.8). Critique arose stating that Museveni might not be interested in winning, and for that matter, ending the conflict, which put substantial additional external pressure on Museveni. But also internally this military failure and prolonged success by the LRA constituted major problems for the government. The fact that after almost 20 years the government was still unable to destroy the rebel army led some people doubt the actual strength of the government.

Taking into account these three aspects, the international attention, the internal problems in connection to the democratization process, and the continued military failure, the GoU did perceive a hurting stalemate. It was not just a sustainable plateau-situation, in which the government found itself, but rather a precipice-situation, where the international and national reputation as well as the financial backing were at stake.

Similarly, it seems that the LRA also perceived a hurting stalemate. Operation Iron Fist had weakened the strength of the rebel group substantially; particularly given that top LRA commanders were killed in 2003[106]. Furthermore, the LRA could not count on the support by Sudan anymore, which significantly affected their strength and tactics (cf. Bercovitch/Fretter 2004, p.107; Haarhaus 2009, p.3; and Schlichte in Bakonyi/Hensell, et al. 2006, p.159). The group was able to recover but was then again substantially hit by two developments. The first was the offering of the Amnesty Act by the GoU. Since it included a reintegration package, it posed a great danger to the LRA's leadership given that it became much more attractive for many of their soldiers to defect (cf. Bayne 2007, p.7). The LRA's strength primarily resulted from abducting children forced to kill their relatives or other people from their villages. Thus, the children had nowhere to return to. The only possible way for most of them to survive seemed to stay with the LRA. However, when the GoU published the Amnesty Act[107], an alternative to continued living in the bush was opened up (cf. Bayne 2007, p.7). It included a potential new beginning and forgiveness through traditional procedures. By mid-2004, more than 5,000 adult

---

[106] Charles Tabuley, Tolbert Nyeko, and Caesar Acellam.
[107] Particularly radio stations in the North publicized the offering of amnesty (cf. Allen Trial Justice: The International Criminal Court and the Lord's Resistance Army, p.75).

combatants from the LRA had surrendered and applied for amnesty (cf. Allen 2006, p.75 and International Crisis Group 2005b, p.3). When finally Sam Kolo defected and leveraged the Amnesty Act late in the negotiation process, this was a major blow to the LRA leadership, given that Sam Kolo was the Second-in-Command (cf. International Crisis Group 2005b, p.4).

The other development hitting the LRA hard were the investigations by the ICC and the subsequent issuance of arrest warrants (cf. Bayne 2007, p.7). Beforehand, the conflict had been an internal matter within Uganda. In a culture where rebel groups had been common for most of the last century, the hope of returning to 'normal' life was always given. The belief system in Northern Uganda provided for traditional rituals with which sins could be forgiven. However, with the ICC involved, Kony and the four other leaders indicted knew that they were internationally searched for and that an internal settling of the conflict was not possible anymore. This contributed significantly to the perception of a hurting stalemate (cf. International Crisis Group 2005b, p.5). The issuance of arrest warrants functioned as a precipice, threatening the LRA.

Tim Allen described the LRA's status at the beginning of 2005 as, "the LRA seemed isolated and under acute pressure" (Allen 2006, p.169; cf. also International Crisis Group 2005b, p.2). This fragile position of the LRA was further aggravated through persistent shortages in the region regarding the food supply. This did not only physically weaken the LRA's combatants, but also had a significant negative impact on the group's morale (cf. International Crisis Group 2005b, p.3).

Thus, it must be assumed that both belligerents perceived a hurting stalemate so that an MHS was apparent in Uganda during the years 2004 and 2005.

Regarding the sense of a way out, the situation was not as clear-cut. Despite the hurting, the GoU did not perceive an SWO. By referring the case to the ICC, Museveni knew that he had destroyed the possibility to settle the conflict internally. Further Museveni repeatedly stressed that "he does not believe in peace talks" and that he saw the only possible solution to the conflict in military victory throughout the negotiation process (cf. International Crisis Group 2004a and Irin News 2005[108]). Museveni quoted George W. Bush's words stating that the LRA rebels were "terrorists with which he does not talk"[109]. When Betty Bigombe announced that "by the end of the week, both sides will have agreed on a date when to sign a ceasefire agreement" in January 2005, Museveni replied a few days later that, "Kony's group has been completely defeated and its

---

[108] Cf. http://www.irinnews.org/print.asp?ReportIT=47568.
[109] Cf. http://www.irinnews.org/S_report.asp?ReportID=47569.

remnants are simply fugitives whom we are capturing day by day"[110]. Publicly announcing such messages made clear that Museveni did not sense a way out (cf. International Crisis Group 2005b, p.4). Kevin Dunn expressed this lack of an SWO by stating that, "Museveni has seemed pointedly uninterested in a peaceful resolution to the conflict" (formulated in 2005, Kevin C. Dunn in Bøås/Dunn 2007, p.148).

The LRA was confronted with the precipice of the ICC arrest warrants, making them internationally searched criminals that were accused of crimes against humanity (cf. Allen 2006, p.1). An SWO meant for them to avoid the final issuance of the arrest warrants. But they did not succeed. The ICC proceeded in their investigations independent from internal developments regarding peace talks. As late as in April 2005, Kony himself expressed his SWO. He reacted to a BBC report stating that he carried hope that the US might support a peace arrangement (cf. International Crisis Group 2005c, p.3). The LRA's SWO was destroyed in October 2005 with the issuance of the ICC arrest warrants, at which time the peace process broke down.

Thus, one of the conditions for ripeness, SWO, was not given. The contradicting strategies put in place by the GoU regarding the Amnesty Act and the ICC referral (cf. Allen 2006, p.72) showed that the GoU did not sense a way out, while the LRA was put under great pressure. Therefore, the SWO did not exist, which means as a consequence that conflict ripeness was not given.

After the breakdown of negotiation efforts in 2005, the level of violence rose again. The LRA even attacked UN peacekeepers in the DRC in January 2006, leaving eight Guatemalan special trained UN soldiers dead. Nevertheless, another attempt was made to pacify Northern Uganda. The Government of South Sudan (GoSS) took the lead this time and asked Dr. Riek Machar, Vice President of the GoSS, to be in charge of the mediation process. This was a change to the previous peace efforts with a mediator in form of a state party. Machar initiated talks between the GoU and the LRA in Juba in July 2006. This peace initiative was judged as exceedingly promising by many observers (cf. Rwot David Onen Acana (Acholi Paramount Chief in Gulu) in an interview with Accord: Accord 2010, p.17; Bayne 2007, p.7; Branch/Team. 2007, p.54; International Crisis Group 2006, p.12; International Crisis Group 2007c, p.2; and Resolve Uganda 2008, p.1)[111]. A Cessation of Hostilities Agreement could be reached and was signed on 26 August 2006. It was renewed in November and after long

---

[110] Cf. *Irin News*, "Uganda: LRA Rebels Should Just Surrender", 27 January 2005.

[111] The hopes for peace were also reflected in international media coverage. See for example *Der Spiegel*, "Uganda: Regierung und Rebellen unterzeichnen Waffenstillstandsabkommen", 26 August 2006.

negotiations, a Comprehensive Final Peace Agreement was formulated by the delegations. After more than a year-and-a-half of difficult, protracted and halting negotiations, the representatives signed the agreement in February 2008 (cf. Atkinson 2009, p.11). Subsequently, the agreement was up for signing by President Museveni and Joseph Kony. As Museveni did not approve it adequate to hold a signing ceremony together with the rebel leader, the negotiators agreed that Kony would sign four days prior to Museveni (cf. International Crisis Group 2008, p.3). When the day of signature was scheduled in April 2008, Kony sent a message of sickness and thus did not show up. The event was rescheduled to November, but also at this date, Kony failed to attend the meeting even though all other ceremony guests were present (cf. Atkinson 2009, p.12).

This marked another end to promising peace negotiations and was followed by the usual pattern: the GoU launched another military offensive against the LRA, Operation Lightning Thunder on 14 December 2008. This time, the UPDF enjoyed significant international support by the US, the UN, the DRC, and the Central African Republic. The attack involved a military incursion of the UPDF into the DRC in pursuit of the LRA. Once again the military offensive was not successful in destroying the LRA despite the grand external support. The UPDF withdrew, leaving the LRA weak, but alive. The result was an increase in violence on part of the LRA with large scale abductions and associated displacements. The LRA responded by conducting the so-called Christmas massacres, in which the rebels killed about 815 people and abducted more than 160 (cf. The Resolve 2010, p.11). This military offensive terminated a 28-month ceasefire.

Again, it must be asked whether this most promising peace initiative in the protracted Northern Ugandan conflict was launched at a time when conflict ripeness was given. Regarding an MHS, the GoU found itself in a strong hurting position. Three aspects contributed to this perception, mirroring mainly the situation from the previous peace initiative but in a more intense fashion. Firstly, the GoU faced immense international pressure. Until 2006, Uganda and the circumstances in the North had moved to the top agenda of many countries from the international communities, supported by civil society lobbying. The GoU feared UN intervention, "posing a risk to Uganda's reputation and sovereignty" (Mwaniki/Wepundi, et al. 2009, p.10). In a United Nations Security Council Update Report in April 2006, it was stated that, "the conflict in Northern Uganda has attracted renewed interest in the Council, largely due to pressure from civil society and UN member states outside the Council such as Canada" (United Nations 2006e, p.1). It shows that the pressure was immense on the GoU to address the topic and try to finally and sustainably resolve the conflict.

Secondly, President Museveni was in a very difficult situation internally. He held general elections in March 2006, which were accompanied by massive internal difficulties. The opposition was oppressed and protests arose in the capital. Even internationally, this was recognized so that Museveni had to compromise on some points of his political agenda in order to maintain his external support and reputation. A negotiated solution to the conflict would have meant a certain kind of MEO with regard to Museveni's political agenda. Calming down critics by sincerely negotiating in the North would distract from political oppression in the capital. As Sarah Bayne formulated it, the GoU increasingly recognized that, "it must address the conflict and chronic poverty and insecurity in the North if it is to restore its international reputation and the confidence of Western donors, which have been seriously damaged by events surrounding the 2006 party elections" (Bayne 2007, p.7).

Thirdly, the failure to militarily destroy the LRA was a permanent obstacle to Museveni's success story and thus had taken its effect. It produced a plateau-situation for the GoU with no exit option apart from negotiating an end to the protracted conflict. It is what the ICG described as "the cost of continued inactivity was becoming too steep" to the GoU (International Crisis Group 2006, p.12). The conflict had accumulated to unbearable costs for the GoU. A study by CSOPNU in 2006 estimated annual costs of war to the GoU of US$ 85 million over a period of 20 years, accumulating to a total of US$ 1.7 billion (CSOPNU 2006, p.9). These three aspects, the international pressure, the internal difficulties and the protracted military failure contributed to a strong perception of a hurting stalemate on part of the GoU.

The LRA also faced a hurting stalemate. Three factors contributed to this perception: firstly, the problems from the previous phase were still flaring and in fact increased. The ICC had issued the arrest warrants, which put significant pressure on Kony and the leadership. Jan Egeland even stated that he believed that "the indictments [from the ICC] had been a factor in pushing the LRA into negotiations" (United Nations 2006b, p.4). The Amnesty Act still endangered the size of the LRA, making it comfortable and easy for combatants to defect.

Secondly, external support to the LRA had mainly ceased to exist. The Sudan, by signing the CPA in January 2005, had committed to refrain from supporting the LRA and instead to chase them. As Bayne expressed it, "the signing of the Comprehensive Peace Agreement (CPA) in January 2005, which requires an end to Sudanese support to the LRA, has shifted this dynamic and placed greater pressure on the LRA" (Bayne 2007, p.6 and cf. also Haarhaus 2009, p.3). This had twofold effects. The LRA faced an even worse food and arms supply issue. Looting was the only way to organize food; however, with the people largely living in camps in Northern Uganda, this became harder and harder and thus the LRA increasingly weaker (cf. Haarhaus 2009, p.4). This meant as a second effect that the LRA had to withdraw even further away from the main territory in Northern Uganda as they were not safe in South Sudan anymore. Therefore, they had to retreat into territories in the DRC and the Central African Republic, which contributed to the pressure on them (cf. Haarhaus 2009, p.3).

This leads to the third factor contributing to the LRA's hurting stalemate. With withdrawing into other states' territories, the Northern Ugandan issue became a regional and even international issue (cf. Mwaniki/Wepundi 2007, p.4). The LRA did not only face the UPDF anymore, but also the UN missions in Sudan and the DRC, the Congolese army as well as the Sudanese army. The UN Security Council repeatedly called for coordinated military action against the LRA throughout the year 2006 (cf. United Nations 2006f and United Nations 2006g) and dedicated several meetings to the topic of how to contain the LRA (cf. United Nations 2006a and United Nations 2006b). It had the effect that the LRA became increasingly nervous and thus perceived additional pressure (cf. Bayne 2007, p.7). One sign for this nervousness was the killing of the Second-in-Command Vincent Otti (cf. Machar 2008, p.5). Thus, the LRA faced a strongly hurting situation with a multi-facetted precipice confronting them. As the ICG observed, "the LRA was fragmented, under military pressure and desperate for food" (International Crisis Group 2007a, p.5) – a formidable description of the perception of a hurting stalemate.

As both belligerents faced hurting stalemates, we can constitute that an MHS was given. It must also be assumed that the belligerents sensed a way out. There are several signs that the GoU saw a way out through negotiations. One such sign was that the GoU realized that they had to act upon the miserable situation in Northern Uganda. One of the LRA's aims had always been that the government addresses the inequality issue. In 2007, the GoU published the Peace, Recovery and Development Plan for Northern Uganda 2007-2010 (PRDP). Strategic objective 4 of the PRDP is concerned with peace building and rehabilitation (cf. Government of Uganda 2007, p.94). The GoU even attributed a budget of about US$ 600 million to it (cf. Government of Uganda 2007, p.112). Thus, this constitutes a sign that the GoU intended to bring peace to this part of the country. It marked an important step "towards addressing the history of neglect and marginalization of the north which lay at the root of the conflict" (Internal Displacement Monitoring Centre/Norwegian Refugee Council 2009a, p.2). Furthermore, the GoU even started to make compromises to the LRA directly in order to reach a settlement. One example was when Museveni announced in October 2007 that Kony would not be extradited to the ICC if he signed the final peace agreement (cf. Heidelberger Institut für Internationale

Konfliktforschung 2008, pp.43-44). Even though Museveni might not have been in the position to make such a promise, compared to his earlier statements, this was a large step into compromising and a great signal for the desire to come to a conclusion (cf. Allen 2006, p.94). The GoU offered that those LRA combatants charged with serious crimes would be tried in a special set up within Uganda's High Court system; and those accused of lesser crimes would be judged according to the traditional justice system Mato Oput[112]. In general, it appears that the GoU did indeed sense a way out and thus took the peace process seriously (cf. the ICG's assessment in April 2007, "the government has finally committed to high-level, sustained involvement at Juba", International Crisis Group 2007c, p.7).

The same is true for the LRA. Given the circumstances, the option to negotiate under the auspices of the GoSS seemed the most promising way to proceed (cf. Atkinson 2009, p.10). The rebel group did not send any half-associated representatives, but instead the top leadership in order to negotiate. Even Joseph Kony himself was perceived as opening up. As Accord noted, "having been largely elusive through decades of warfare, during the Juba talks of 2006-08 he opened up to the international community for the first time. He gave press conferences and met delegations from Northern Uganda, Southern Sudan and the UN" (cf. Accord 2010, p.6).

The process thus started relatively smoothly: the LRA seemed willing to accept many points as seen in the signing of the Cessation of Hostilities Agreement as well as the Comprehensive Final Peace Agreement (cf. International Crisis Group 2007a, p.2). When issues or problems came up, the LRA even agreed to constructively solve these. An example occurred on 5 February 2007, when the LRA released a statement outlining specific concerns from the process (cf. Atkinson 2009, p.11). This was a sign for their willingness to come to conclusions and consensus, providing content for a negotiation basis (cf. Bayne 2007, p.7). Also the statements made by LRA representatives indicated their commitment to an SWO. For example, in June 2007, Vincent Otti gave an interview to Irin News, in which he presented his and the LRA's objective to come to an agreement with the GoU[113].

Thus, we can conclude that both the GoU and the LRA perceived an MHS as well as an SWO. Conflict ripeness was given throughout the years of 2006-2008.

---

[112] Cf. *Sudan Tribune*, "Diplomats Prepare for More Ugandan Peace Talks", 18 April 2008.
[113] Cf. http://irinnews.org/InDepthMain.aspx?InDepthId=58&ReportId=72472.

What impact did the independent variables have on the situation of ripeness? When looking at the tools used by the mediator, two effects become apparent. Firstly, persuasion played a significant role in manifesting conflict ripeness. With Riek Machar as mediator, the two belligerents were confronted with a person that put great effort into the negotiation process offering different channels of communication and a sound mediation process (cf. Bayne 2007, p.6). As Atkinson expressed it, "for the first time, direct talks between the GoU and an official LRA delegation were being held outside Uganda, with an outside mediator that had its own vested interest in successfully helping negotiate an end to the conflict" (Atkinson 2009, p.10). This is a very strong factor in this context given that the peace talks were held in a triadic structure including a structured agenda addressing core issues of the conflict (cf. Mwaniki/Wepundi 2007, p.4). Thus, persuasion positively affected conflict ripeness and strengthened the perception of ripeness for both conflicting parties. The second instrument initiated by the mediator was pressure to a limited extent. The GOSS's effort was supported both financially, but also politically, by many representatives from the international community, particularly the US and the UN. The UN Office for the Coordination of Humanitarian Affairs (UN OCHA) created a US$ 4.8 million support fund for the Juba talks (cf. International Crisis Group 2007c, p.3). Such support helped to build up pressure against the belligerents, so that they knew that the international community might take actions against them in case they do not follow the process. This also positively affected the dependent variable of conflict ripeness and thus intensified the level of ripeness. The third tool, however, inducements were not part of the mediation process. None of the belligerents were promised any benefits for coming to a conclusion. Thus, this independent variable did not have any effect.

Regarding the non-manipulable variables, none of the independent variables significantly affected conflict ripeness. There was no change in the leadership throughout phase IV: both Museveni and Kony had been in their positions for decades. In parallel, these two figures were the central protagonists throughout all processes. This also explains why the assertiveness of the leadership took no effect either. Being strong leaders, their followers were loyal to the policies of their groups. The only relativization in this context might be the killing of Otti by Kony. This was a sign that Kony was being nervous, killing one of his top commanders. The effect of such insecurity was rather negative for conflict ripeness. It showed that the actor was prone to acting intuitively instead of rationally, which endangered the peace process to a limited extent. As constituted in the analysis, none of the conflict parties received external support at that time of the conflict anymore. This situation did not change throughout phase IV, meaning that this independent variable had no effect on conflict ripeness either.

It is thus possible to summarize that peace initiative IV took place when conflict ripeness could be identified. The status of ripeness was positively affected by the independent variables of persuasion and pressure and only mildly compromised because of personal insecurities of Joseph Kony. This finding is supported by Mwaniki and Wepundi who stated that, "the conflict is at its ripest moment for peaceful resolution" in 2007 (Mwaniki/Wepundi 2007, p.4). The following table summarizes the effects of the independent variables on conflict ripeness.

Independent Variable	Effect?	Quality of Effect
Persuasion	Yes	Positive: intensified ripeness
Inducements	No	No impact
Pressure	Yes	Positive: intensified ripeness
Change in leadership	No	No impact
Assertiveness of leadership	Yes	Negative: reduced ripeness mildly
External support to belligerents	No	No impact
IDA	Open	Open

Table 8: Independent Variables Affecting Conflict Ripeness in Uganda[114]

The analysis has shown that the first three peace initiatives were doomed to be unsuccessful given that conflict ripeness could not be established. The fourth peace initiative, however, took place at a time when conflict ripeness could be identified. Additional independent variables positively impacted the status of conflict ripeness so that the initial situation looked very promising.

5.1.2.2   Increase in Development Aid

In this section, it will be analyzed whether IDA can be observed over the course of the conflict. In order to do so, the analysis is split into three parts: firstly, the focus will lie on aid in the form of ODA and debt relief dedicated to the GoU. Secondly, humanitarian aid targeted at Northern Uganda will be analyzed. And

---

[114] Source: Own illustration.

thirdly, the specific type of aid in support of the peace negotiations will be looked at.

The net official development assistance received by the GoU has been formally tracked by the donor community, specifically the OECD (cf. Organization for Economic Cooperation and Development 2010). It includes all state- and institutional actors; however does not cover the contributions by NGOs. ODA seems to be the overarching factor contributing to the GoU's national budget as will be seen below. Since his taking of power in 1986, Museveni was able to increase yearly ODA from US$ 191.56 million to 1,656.76 million in 2008. This refers to total ODA, net disbursements by all donors. It means that the total amount was increased by more than eight times. When looking at the details of this increase, it appears that there was almost a constant increase in ODA over the course of the years (cf. table below).

Year	DAC Countries	Multilateral	Non-DAC Countries	Total
1986	77,26	111,1	3,2	**191,56**
1987	86,75	207,3	4,9	**298,95**
1988	187,99	203,73	-0,13	**391,59**
1989	163,59	255,4	27,51	**446,5**
1990	244,41	376,05	42,64	**663,1**
1991	285,51	326,77	51	**663,28**
1992	255	453,92	14,8	**723,72**
1993	347,98	259,92	1,11	**609,01**
1994	346,93	393,27	10,59	**750,79**
1995	427,72	398,04	7,11	**832,87**
1996	370,56	294,94	8,17	**673,67**
1997	439,13	370,8	2,92	**812,85**
1998	384,09	271,28	-0,22	**655,15**
1999	357,42	246,84	0,72	**604,98**
2000	578,18	269,16	5,67	**853,01**
2001	386,44	432,85	1,86	**821,15**
2002	466,35	257,28	4,97	**728,6**
2003	587,41	408	1,12	**996,53**
2004	684,06	529,3	1,37	**1214,73**
2005	690,75	498,47	1,83	**1191,05**
2006	938,35	611,78	2,74	**1552,87**
2007	1002,73	730,66	2,87	**1736,26**

Year	DAC Countries	Multilateral	Non-DAC Countries	Total
2008	1005,68	647,05	4,03	1656,76

Table 9: Total ODA to Uganda, Net Disbursements in millions of US$[115]

When visualizing this data, it becomes clear, that the total amount of ODA increased significantly – both in absolute numbers, but also relatively. However, there were individual relapses over the time as can be seen in the graph below:

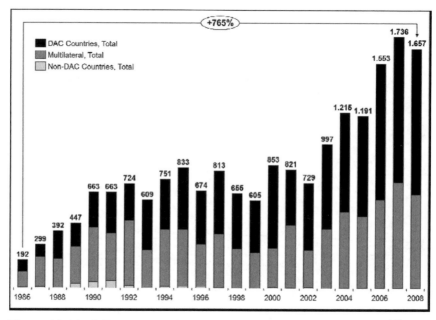

Figure 12: Total ODA to Uganda, Net Disbursements in millions of US$[116]

---

[115] Source: Organization for Economic Cooperation and Development (2010): "World Development Indicators", *Development Assistance Committee of the Organisation for Economic Co-operation and Development, Geographical Distribution of Fianncial Flows to Developing Countries, Development Co-operation Report, and International Development Statistics Database*own illustration.

[116] Source: Organization for Economic Cooperation and Development "World Development Indicators", own illustration.

166

It is to be noted that the overall development shows a significant increase in ODA over the period of time from 1986 to 2008. There is a total increase of 765% comparing the amount of ODA given in 1986 to the amount given in 2008. The main drivers of this increase are both DAC countries as well as multilateral institutions. When looking at the individual donors, interesting donor behavior can be detected. The single largest bilateral donor each year varies. In 1986, 1987 and 1990, this was Italy. In 1994, Denmark gave the most ODA. In all subsequent years until 2001 except for 1993, the United Kingdom took over the role as largest state-donor to Uganda. In 1993 as well as in all the years after 2001, most ODA is provided by the United States (cf. Organization for Economic Cooperation and Development 2010).

The International Development Association is the largest donor during almost the entire period among the multilateral institutions. Only in 1992 and in 2008, the EC gets ahead of the amount provided. But overall, it is the International Development Association who has contributed most. As Datta-Mitra expressed it for the World Bank, "The International Development Association, the largest lender to Uganda, has been a catalyst for other donors and has made a significant contribution to the country's development outcomes" (Datta-Mitra/Dept. 2001, p.xiii). Even though the individual spending by the largest donor of the multilaterals is in general larger per year than the individual spending by the largest donor of the DAC members; the total amount contributed to ODA from the DAC members is in its sum significantly larger than the amount from the multilaterals. Thus, while the multilateral flows had initially dominated the total aid, this changed in 1993, when the bilateral aid flow increased. Since then, the development continued, so that in 2008, bilateral aid almost doubled multilateral aid (cf. Organization for Economic Cooperation and Development 2010).

Therefore, when analyzing the drivers behind the increase in ODA to the GoU over the course of the conflict, it is the individual states, particularly some individual DAC members that make a significant difference in spending. Until 2001, this role was mainly attributed to the United Kingdom; since then, it went over to the US (cf. Organization for Economic Cooperation and Development 2010). Three donors accounted for almost half of the total ODA between 2004 and 2008. The World Bank accounted for 19%, the US for 18%, and the EC for 10% of the total amount. Twelve donors accounted for 90% of the entire

ODA[117]. This shows that the actual disbursement of ODA lies within the hands of only a few donor partners.

Four more details about the type of ODA and aid to the GoU are noteworthy. Firstly, it is to be noted that large parts of the ODA accounted for are grant elements of aid. As Jayati Datta-Mitra and the World Bank point out, in 2001, the grant element constituted 90% of the total ODA (cf. Datta-Mitra/Dept. 2001, p.4). Secondly, the GoU and the donor partners signed a set of Partnership Principles in 2003 in which the GoU emphasized their preference for budget support as an aid modality. Since then, the focus switched more and more away from project support to budget or sector support. "In 2007, 66% of disbursed aid was provided as either general budget support or within program-based approaches"[118]; in 2007, the ICG observed that 41% of the national budget had been financed by external donors (cf. International Crisis Group 2006, p.11). Thirdly, an evaluation by the International Development Department at the School of Public Policy in Birmingham found that until 2006, aid flows averaged 11% of the GDP and 50% of public expenditure (cf. International Development Department (IDD) 2006, (appendix), p.62). The World Bank stated in 2010 that relative to GDP, total ODA stood at 5% in 1986, peaked at 25% in 1992, and averaged 14% in 2004 to 2008[119]. Fourthly, due to the large amounts of ODA provided to the GoU, Uganda depends on foreign aid for 50% of its recurrent expenditures (cf. Rubongoya in Howell/Lind 2010, p.219).

In April 1997, Uganda became eligible for debt relief under the Highly Indebted Poor Countries (HIPC) Initiative, "on the basis of its strong adjustment record" (Datta-Mitra/Dept. 2001, p.4). By that, Uganda qualified as the first benefiter from the program (cf. Furley in Furley/May 2006, p.120). By July 2006, Uganda had received a total of US$ 3.764 billion in debt relief. This consisted of debt relief provided under the Multilateral Debt Relief Initiative (US$ 2.780 billion) and the debt relief committed through the HIPC initiative (US$ 984 million)[120]. Given the large amounts of ODA and other initiatives for Uganda, it is clear that the GoU was and is challenged by a great administrative task. For instance, only during the time between FY1986 and FY1999, IDA

---

[117] Cf. http://web.worldbank.org/WBSITE/EXTERNAL/COUNTRIES/AFRICAEXT/ UGANDAEXTN/0,,menuPK:374947~pagePK:141132~piPK:141107~theSitePK:374864,00.html.
[118] Cf. http://web.worldbank.org/WBSITE/EXTERNAL/COUNTRIES/AFRICAEXT/ UGANDAEXTN/0,,menuPK:374947~pagePK:141132~piPK:141107~theSitePK:374864,00.html.
[119] Cf. http://web.worldbank.org/WBSITE/EXTERNAL/COUNTRIES/AFRICAEXT/UGANDAEXT N/0,,menuPK:374947~pagePK:141132~piPK:141107~theSitePK:374864,00.html.
[120] Cf. http://web.worldbank.org/WBSITE/EXTERNAL/COUNTRIES/AFRICAEXT/UGANDAEXT N/0,,menuPK:374947~pagePK:141132~piPK:141107~theSitePK:374864,00.html.

supported 46 projects (cf. Datta-Mitra/Dept. 2001, p.13). Coupled with the bilateral and non-governmental projects, this demands significant government capacities to handle. As Datta-Mitra expressed it, "the sheer number of projects (more than 250 active projects in January 1999) suggests that government capacity is being unduly stretched to accommodate divergent donor interests" (Datta-Mitra/Dept. 2001, p.38). For that end, however, the GoU took away the coordinating responsibility from five different government units and assembled this task in one unit. The Ministry of Finance, Planning and Economic Development took over the role of coordinating all aid-related topics[121].

In total, two conclusions can be drawn regarding ODA and debt relief given to the GoU. Firstly, a constant increase of assistance to the GoU could be observed. Despite small relapses, the overall IDA constitutes a total of 765% over the time (cf. Organization for Economic Cooperation and Development 2010), which constitutes a significant increase for the GoU's budget. Furthermore, due to debt relief, the overall amount must be even rated higher. Secondly, it became obvious that the GoU and Uganda as a country are highly dependent on aid. About 30% to 40% of Uganda's budget is financed by foreign aid. Therefore, it is evident that external aid given to the GoU plays a significant role in the GoU's policies and behavior.

In parallel to the large amounts of ODA and debt relief for the GoU, many international actors also delivered aid, specifically targeted at Northern Uganda. This is mainly humanitarian aid to support the war-affected population including the many IDPs[122]. This aid is mainly independent from ODA, given that they are largely separate donor-funded projects (cf. Bayne 2007, p.iii). Such assistance (specifically dedicated to Northern Uganda) also increased significantly over the course of the protracted conflict. The triggering event for the increase was Jan Egeland's visit in November 2003. His comments about the conflict (cf. above) were largely covered in the international media. As Chris Dolan observed, this event "sparked a significant increase in levels of external intervention over the next two years" (Dolan 2009, p.56). Similarly, Accord noted that, "in the period 2002 to 2006 the situation in Northern Uganda made a definitive transition from being a 'forgotten conflict' to being highly visible and a centre of attention for the international community" (Accord 2010, p.8). This had the effect that

---

[121] Cf. http://www.finance.go.ug.
[122] The number of IDPs increased significantly over the time. In 1997, the IDP population was estimated to be about 110,000 people; in 1999, the number rose to 400,000. By mid-2002, 522,00 internally displaced persons were counted; and in 2004, it totaled 1.5 million, which represents 80% of the Acholi population (cf. Allen Trial Justice: The International Criminal Court and the Lord's Resistance Army, p.53).

according to Chris Dolan the number of relief-providing organizations active in IDP-camps rose from five in 1996 to more than sixty by 2006 (cf. Dolan 2009, p.239). Also Patrick William Otim observed the increase of relief agencies: "too many Non-Governmental Organizations (NGOs) have emerged over the last two decades. NGO signs are found on every street and they have become an important community 'investment'" (Otim 2009, p.1).

The new attention by the international community and the resulting increase in relief to Northern Uganda had the effect that large parts of the Northern Ugandan population were entirely dependent on the support of international NGOs (cf. Schlichte in Bakonyi/Hensell, et al. 2006, p.159). Further, it also meant that significant responsibility for its people was taken away from the GoU, leaving relief work "very largely in the hands of NGOs and international bodies" (Furley in Furley/May 2006, p.118). The GoU noted the many actors involved in relief delivery. The Chargé d'affaires a.i. of the Permanent Mission of Uganda to the United Nations wrote a letter addressed to the President of the Security Council 2006, stating, "Government in partnership WFP provides 90% of the food needs of the IDPs (Government 15%, WFP 75%). [...] Besides the input of Government and WFP, a number of NGOs are involved in the provision of relief and other services [...]. Such NGOs include MSF, NRC, COOPI, CARE, CONCERN, AVSI, SCIU, ACF etc." (United Nations 2006c, p.8).

Unfortunately, given the widespread types of organizations involved, it is not possible to quantify the amounts of aid delivered. What is possible to determine though is that there are significant amounts of assistance provided to Northern Uganda that cover about 90% of the total living needs of the population. Given the increase in aid dependency over the years and the international media attention in parallel, it is not surprising that there was a steep increase in this development aid. It is possible to conclude, that also for this type of aid, a constant IDA could be observed.

Two main challenges arise in the context of assistance directly dedicated to Northern Uganda. First, given that the projects and humanitarian assistance are largely independent from ODA and thus independently delivered to Northern Uganda without involving the GoU, it is suggested that this might reinforce the people's perception in Northern Uganda that they are neglected by the GoU as the support comes from external sources (cf. Bayne 2007, p.iii). Second, the coordination and accountability of such assistance proves to be very challenging and might be examples for inefficiencies and unintended impacts. For example, Chris Dolan observed that three organizations were active in one IDP-camp (Atiak-Biabia) at the same time, being the World Food Program, the ICRC and World Vision. They all delivered humanitarian assistance (cf. Dolan 2009, p.115).

A third form of external aid should be mentioned in addition to ODA and the relief aid for Northern Uganda. The aid referred to is aid in support of the peace negotiations in Northern Uganda. This constitutes aid that comes into the country as a means to facilitate peace negotiations, provided by external sources.

There is no constant provision of such assistance in this case, but rather an individual spark of aid, however, a relatively significant spark that is defined as IDA. This spark is the establishment of the UN Juba Initiative Fund (JIF) of US$ 4.8 million that was launched on 6 October 2006 to support the Juba Peace Talks (cf. Mwaniki/Wepundi 2007, p.14)[123]. The JIF was put in place in order to fund the facilitation of basic necessities of the peace talks and to support the start-up of the Cessation of Hostilities-monitoring team[124]. The money from the fund was also partly used to incentivize the LRA. It financed supply of food to the LRA (cf. International Crisis Group 2007a, p.5). The ICG reported that the mediator, Riek Machar, handed over US$ 60,000 to the LRA, so they would not loot food. Furthermore, he distributed US$ 50,000 to LRA commanders to convince Kony to take part in the signing ceremony in April 2008 (cf. International Crisis Group 2008, p.17).

Three forms of aid have been identified, analyzed and presented. It could be established that an almost constant IDA existed with regard to ODA. The increase was significant. Second, also aid directly delivered to Northern Uganda, mostly in the form of relief, was assessed, too. Again here, a constant increase could be identified. A peak in the increase occurred in the period of 2002-2004 after a military campaign and the visiting of Jan Egeland and subsequent international media attention. A third form of IDA was identified when looking at the JIF. This is aid particularly dedicated to supporting the Juba Peace Talks. It was a fund limited in time and scale constituting an external influx of aid. It is considered in the further analysis as an increase in development aid. The time of establishment of the JIF was October 2006. With regard to the theoretical model, this means that the case-guiding research question of whether IDA can be observed can be affirmed.

5.1.2.3   Effect of Increase in Development Aid on Ripeness

Having analyzed the individual phases and peace initiatives in the Northern Ugandan conflict considering their individual status of conflict ripeness as well

---

[123] Cf. http://www.un.org/News/Press/docs/2006/afr1439.doc.htm.
[124] Cf. http://www.un.org/News/Press/docs/2006/afr1439.doc.htm.

as having assessed different forms of IDA, the two aspects will now be brought together and assessed with regard to potential correlations and causalities. Specifically, it will be analyzed whether IDA – where identified – had an effect on conflict ripeness – where identified – and of what quality such potential impact was. It is thus to be assessed whether IDA functions as an independent variable in this case and if so, under which conditions IDA takes what kind of effects.

To summarize, four phases have been analyzed with regard to their conflict ripeness. Only in one phase, it was possible to identify conflict ripeness, which was the period of 2006-2008. However, the analysis will also cover phase III in which an MHS could be identified. In this context, it will be assessed whether IDA had an effect on the MHS. Regarding IDA, there were three forms of aid that could be identified as significant effects. Firstly, there was the aid dedicated to Northern Uganda, mainly in the form of humanitarian assistance, which increased significantly in the years 2003, 2004, and 2005. Secondly, there was a spark of aid with the establishment of the so-called Juba Initiative Fund for the support of the Juba Talks in 2006. Thirdly, there was a constant increase in development aid in the form of ODA from 1986 to 2008. Significant IDA was observed. Besides the early years of the conflict in which increases of up to 56% occurred[125], more significant instances were in 2000 when ODA reached US$ 853 million, constituting an increase of 41% to the previous year. Similarly, in 2003 and 2004, ODA increased significantly again by 37% and 22%, accumulating to a total of US$ 1,215 million in 2004. This was again topped in 2006, followed by 2007 with increases of 30% and 12%, totaling US$ 1,736 million in 2007. In 2008, a slight decrease could be observed. The graph below visualizes these observations:

---

[125] These relative increases can be neglected given the small absolute value of numbers.

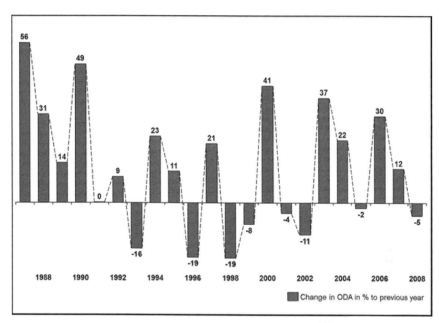

Figure 13: %-Change in ODA in Uganda to Previous Year[126]

There are two incidents to be analyzed with respect to different inputs of IDA. What is relevant to assess is the period of 2002 to 2005 as the preparation period before peace initiative III; and the period between 2005 and 2008 as these two phases were evaluated as 'half-ripe' and ripe. The following graph visualizes these aspects including the three events of IDA.

---

[126] Source: Data from Organization for Economic Cooperation and Development "World Development Indicators", own illustration.

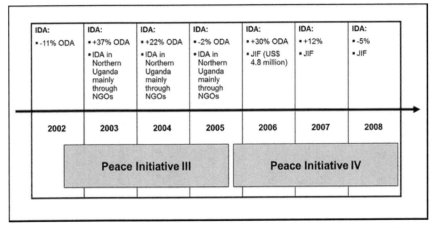

Figure 14: Increase in Development Aid and Peace Initiatives in Uganda[127]

The graph above presents an overview of the increase in development aid and the timely corresponding peace initiatives. Peace Initiative III that covers the phase between 2002 and 2005 witnessed stark increases in ODA in 2003 and 2004 of 37% and 22%. Furthermore, it saw significant increases in the form of mainly humanitarian aid by NGOs dedicated to the people in Northern Uganda. Peace Initiative IV between 2006 and 2008 was equally marked by significant IDA. While ODA was decreased in 2005, in 2006 and 2007, the amount of ODA rose by first 30% and then 12%. Additionally, the Juba peace initiative received funding through a dedicated fund, the JIF between 2006 and 2008 of US$ 4.8 million.

Starting with the Peace Initiative III from 2004 to 2005, it makes sense to also take two years of the previous developments into consideration for the analysis of the dynamics of the conflict. Thus, it is interesting to start in 2002 with the analysis of whether IDA affected the MHS. This case is special given that we have established that no actual full conflict ripeness existed. It is possible though to call the phase half-ripe given that an MHS was apparent.

The MHS was perceived by the GoU largely due to international attention and pressure. The voices became louder asking Museveni to finally conclude the conflict after Jan Egeland's visit. The EU for example referred to "reservations about the military option" and the UK's deputy high commissioner was to have

---

[127] Source: Own illustration.

said the "war effort has failed" (Allen 2006, p.73). Thus, the GoU heard the critique. But the pressure was not credible. What can be observed in this case is a prevention of ripeness through IDA. The GoU felt comfortable in its position. Due to the international developments such as the attacks of 9/11 and the subsequent formulation of lists of terrorist organizations, it was possible for the GoU to "position itself as in the larger 'war on terror'" (Dolan 2009, p.239) and to gain the sympathy of the major international power, the US (cf. Howell/Lind 2010). The strategy worked: a changing attitude of the US could be noted (cf. Allen 2006, p.72). The US became the single largest bilateral donor to Uganda for the first time after Uganda had not been on its priority list as partner country before. Subsequently, Museveni enjoyed large increases of development aid in the form of ODA, so that despite the perception of a hurting stalemate due to civil society and international pressure, he still felt comfortable enough in the situation to not see that a peaceful negotiation would be the best option to solve the conflict with; by that not perceiving an SWO. The sign for this perception was Museveni's referral of the case to the ICC just before Bigombe's initiation of peace talks and repeated statements by him denying a peaceful potential solution. Contributing to this was the fact that large parts of the ODA were direct budget support, leading to substantial contributions to financing the conflict. Even though ODA was not intended to be used for war financing, it had the effect of releasing resources that were allocated differently in the national budget. This in combination with the debt relief made it possible for the GoU to free substantial amounts of money for military expenditure (cf. Prunier in Khadiagala/International Peace Academy 2006, p.112 and Saferworld 2006, p.4).

It is therefore possible to state that Museveni and the GoU directly profited from the increase in ODA, which negatively affected ripeness in that it prevented the situation from becoming ripe on part of the GoU. This is what Gérard Prunier describes when stating that, "what is clear in any case is that foreign aid was an essential factor that kept the war going" (Prunier in Khadiagala/International Peace Academy 2006, p.112).

Apart from the increased ODA, another factor contributed to this development. In this phase, we also observed an increase in aid given in the form of humanitarian assistance to Northern Uganda directly, that is to the affected population, mainly through NGOs, but also through UN organizations and others. The effect was that the government was discharged of its responsibility. John Prendergast described this mechanism when stating, "aid can undermine or even replace the public welfare mandates of local authorities, thus encouraging them to pursue their war agendas unfettered by welfare responsibilities" (Prendergast/Center of Concern 1996, p.35).

This stark increase in relief, mainly triggered by Jan Egeland's visit and subsequent media coverage of the suffering in the North, led to a situation in which the GoU was discharged of the responsibility to take care of its Northern population. The disaster in the North was mainly attended to by international organizations. The IDP-camps received food, medical services, even organizational and administrative support as well as education etc. from large organizations. The government was almost not involved in answering to the man-made disaster from a humanitarian perspective (cf. Dolan 2009, p.231 and Finnström/Atkinson 2008, p.2). As Saferworld put it in a Briefing for the House of Lords in 2006, "in essence, donors tend to treat the North as a different country in need of humanitarian rather than development assistance" (Saferworld 2006, p.1). Furthermore, by supporting the affected people, these organizations indirectly contributed to the system of IDP-camps the GoU had set up (cf. Dolan 2009, p.243 – this case is also made by Matthew Green: cf. Green 2008).

Now, this brings up the question of whether the GoU would have intervened on humanitarian terms in the North if no other support had been provided. This is a hypothetical question and cannot be answered. What is clear though is that the GoU did not perceive to be in a duty to help its people given that the international community took over this responsibility. This helped the GoU to avoid such pressure that most probably would have contributed to the perception of an MHS as well as an SWO.

Regarding the LRA, a similar pattern could be observed. It was not so much the ODA that made a difference for the LRA as the ODA was targeted directly at the GoU in Kampala. However, the significant increase in humanitarian aid to the people in Northern Uganda also helped the LRA to 'not sense' the way out. As mentioned above, the LRA mainly sustained itself by looting and living off the voluntary and non-voluntary support of the Northerners. By providing the people with humanitarian aid, the LRA was able to regain their basic needs. That is why IDP-camps became targets for the LRA. Thus, this type of IDA also contributed to the situation in which the LRA did not sense a way out.

Concluding, it is possible to state that in this case, IDA did have an impact on the quasi conflict ripeness in that the constant supply and even increase of development aid contributed to preventing conflict ripeness to be established. The belligerents were prevented from being able to sense a way out. Thus, we can constitute that IDA negatively impacted potential conflict ripeness.

What were the conditions accompanying these effects? It seems that this case presents a situation in which the belligerents perceive an MHS. However, in parallel despite the MHS, they do not perceive an SWO and are further prevented from perceiving and SWO due to IDA. What is significant here is the unconditional and constant IDA entering the country that is not related to the course of events in the conflict. Independent from the development of the conflict, external parties continue to increase their development aid to the country and the region. Thus, the external pressure built up by other parties on the belligerents makes them perceive and MHS, however, the credibility fades away given the constant monetary assistance that suggests that the threats will not be turned into actions against them. It seems that this effect is highly significant. Arguing counter-factually, one can assume that ODA made conditional in this context, would have set further incentives for the belligerents, particularly the state actor, to perceive conflict ripeness. The large influx of development aid in that sense undermined the previous strategy of conflict resolution efforts. This is related to another condition accompanying the negative effect of IDA on conflict ripeness in this context: the IDA – both ODA as well as the humanitarian aid – were entirely independent and uncontrollable for the mediator. The mediator, Betty Bigombe was not involved in any of the develop-ment aid deliveries. It seemed that development aid and the conflict resolution effort were two completely independent undertakings. Again, connecting the two undertakings would in the hindsight appear to be crucial for a successful effect.

Regarding the developments in the subsequent phase, a similar situation was given at the outset as in the previous phase. However, one crucial difference could be noted: ODA decreased in 2005. This decrease of ODA to the GoU made a significant difference. Suddenly, the pressure on Museveni from the international level to start and take peace talks seriously, was immense, especially due to the fact that the decrease in ODA came along with the donors' and civil society's demand that the GoU attributes the resolution of the Northern Ugandan conflict highest priority (cf. Saferworld 2006, p.1). ODA – and here the decrease of ODA – was used as an indirect instrument to make the GoU perceive an SWO by increasing the pressure and thus the hurting stalemate. International pressure was also given in the previous phase, contributing to the GoU's perception of a hurting stalemate, but the international pressure was not linked to financial support. When in 2005 the influx of ODA was actually smaller than before, Museveni realized that the conflict became an unbearable burden; thus the perception of an SWO and an intensified MHS.

This does not explain though the subsequent development of IDA observed and its impact on the course of events. Wouldn't this mean that Museveni had to lose his interest in peace talks as soon as the ODA was increased again, that is from 2006 onwards? This would be too simplistic a judgment. 2005 served as a warning to the GoU. Museveni had realized that the ODA was not a constant given, but could be leveraged as a tool to pressurize him. With at least one-third of the national budget financed through ODA, this tool was very effective. Thus, in this case, it was not IDA that had an effect on conflict ripeness, but a decrease of development aid.

With regard to the LRA, IDA was indeed decisive. In 2006, as described above, a fund was made available for the financing of the Juba Peace Talks. The fund of US$ 4.8 million was set up as a means to facilitate the mediation process. In parallel, the money was used as a direct support to the LRA, reasoning that it is necessary to supply the LRA with the needs they have in order to convince them to negotiate. This reasoning, though, did not prove to be right. The course of the developments throughout the mediation process shows that through this IDA, the conditions for conflict ripeness were destroyed. While the LRA had felt a significant hurting stalemate, being weak from previous military attacks, pursued internationally due to the ICC arrest warrants, endangered in size because of the amnesty offer, deprived of resources and food due to the cut by Sudan and feeling international pressure due to the regionalization of the conflict (cf. International Crisis Group 2007a, p.5), with the provision of food and needs through the JIF, the LRA was able to re-strengthen itself and become once again a strong rebel group (cf. Haarhaus 2009, p.5 and International Crisis Group 2007a, pp.1-2), capable of committing atrocities such as the Christmas Massacres even after another military attack. The Ugandan newspaper The New Vision even referred to the ICC prosecutor expressing concern that "funds and food aid, supplied to the LRA, was being diverted and used to re-arm"[128]. This renewed strength led to the situation, in which Joseph Kony did not perceive it necessary to bring the peace talks to an end by signing the Comprehensive Peace Agreement. Instead, he did not show up; by that triggering the continuation of the war. Therefore, despite the fact that the amount of money (cf. US$ 4.8 million) was relatively small compared to the increases in ODA, it still had a significant impact on the rebels as it constituted direct assistance to them that was not made conditional on the further progress of the peace process. Even when the LRA did not fulfill its tasks in the negotiation process, the support in form of IDA continued. Thus, the incentive for the LRA to comply with the rules fell away.

Therefore, in this case, it has to be concluded that IDA (here in the form of the JIF) affected conflict ripeness in that it destroyed the perception of an MHS on part of the rebel group. Thus, IDA negatively affected conflict ripeness.

To sum up, two conditions accompanied the varying effects of IDA on conflict ripeness in this case. Firstly, IDA was used as a tool to build up pressure on the belligerents in form of restricting IDA at the initial time of the phase. This

---

[128] Cf. *The New Vision*, Olupot, Milton: "LRA Talks", 28 October 2007.

had a positive effect on ripeness as it contributed to the perception of ripeness. Thus, a conscious use of IDA as an instrument seemed to be decisive for positively manipulating the status. Secondly, however, the use of the tool IDA in a different situation negatively affected conflict ripeness in that it destroyed one of the ingredients, the MHS. The conditions were that IDA was used as a tool by the mediator, the GoSS, in form of a fund financing the peace process. Part of this policy was to provide the rebel group with incentives to join the peace process. Nevertheless, the incentives were offered without conditions. When the rebel group did not comply with the rules of the negotiation process, no sanctions followed. Instead, the IDA was continued to be supplied by the mediator to the rebel group, so that the incentive for the LRA to comply fell away.

5.1.2.4 Conclusion

Different analyses have shed light on the question of why the Ugandan conflict could never be resolved (cf. Dunn in Bøås/Dunn 2007, pp.132-146). This analysis has assessed the question with regard to conflict ripeness. It could be established that conflict ripeness was not given during many peace attempts, including two promising efforts which happened in 1993 to 1994 under the lead of Betty Bigombe (Peace Initiative I) and in 1997 to 1998 under the initiation of the diaspora and civil society representatives (Peace Initiative II).

Later on, conflict ripeness was almost given during Peace Initiative III, which was an effort by Betty Bigombe to mediate the conflict between the GoU and the LRA in the years of 2004 and 2005. While an MHS was perceived, the belligerents were not ready to enter sincere negotiations. In this case, the constant increase of ODA resulted in a situation in which the GoU felt comfortable to continue the conflict and not sense a way out. Thus here, IDA affected ripeness to a certain extent. The quality of the effect was negative.

In 2006 to 2008, a fourth peace initiative was underway under the mediation of the GoSS. In this phase, conflict ripeness was given. Both protagonists to the conflict, the GoU and the LRA perceived an MHS as well as an SWO. Thus, the conditions for ripeness were given. They were even enforced by some independent variables that positively affected ripeness; namely persuasion and pressure. A slight negative influence on ripeness was made by the independent variable of assertiveness of leadership on part of the rebels. This could be found in the case of Joseph Kony as the leader of the LRA who felt significant international pressure. A sign for his nervousness was the killing of his Second-in-Command, Vincent Otti. However overall though, strong conflict ripeness could be identified.

Three findings were made with regard to development aid: Firstly, we could observe that IDA prevented ripeness from being established in phase three of the conflict. Secondly, due to a decrease in ODA, conflict ripeness could be established. The conscious use of IDA as a tool in the conflict resolution effort in form of a decrease of IDA positively affected ripeness. Thirdly, it was found that IDA in the form of a peace fund, facilitating the mediation efforts, destroyed conflict ripeness by destroying the MHS. In this case, the use of IDA as a tool of conflict management led to a situation in which the mediator compromised on his own credibility to the belligerents by not connecting the supply of IDA to the compliance with the peace process. Thus, IDA negatively affected ripeness.

Overall, four conditions could be identified that contributed to the effect IDA took on conflict ripeness: firstly, large amounts of IDA entering the country undermined conflict resolution efforts as the strategy was to put pressure on the belligerents. Secondly, the effect was further strengthened as the mediator was not in control of the development aid entering the country. The two undertakings of development aid and conflict resolution were independent from each other and thus had an antidromic effect on each other. Thirdly, development aid was used as a tool in the mediating effort by way of decreasing the influx of ODA, so that additional financial pressure was put on at least one of the belligerents contributing to both an intensified perception of an MHS and an SWO. Fourthly, the conscious use of IDA in a different setting negatively affected conflict ripeness by destroying the MHS because the provision of aid was not connected to the compliance with the negotiation process. By that, the mediation effort was compromised on and the incentive to comply destroyed. Coming back to the case-guiding research questions, the following table summarizes the findings from the Ugandan case.

#	Question	P I [129]	P II	P III	P IV
1	Is it possible to identify an MHS?	No	No	Yes	Yes
2	If not, is it possible to identify MEOs?	No	No	-	-
3	Is it possible to identify an SWO?	No	No	No	Yes
4	Can conflict ripeness be affirmed?	No	No	No	Yes
5	To what extent does persuasion affect conflict ripeness?	-	-	-	Positively

---

[129] PI stands for Phase I, etc.pp.

#	Question	P I [129]	P II	P III	P IV
6	To what extent do inducements affect conflict ripeness?	-	-	-	No effect
7	To what extent does pressure affect conflict ripeness?	-	-	-	Positively
8	To what extent does a change in leadership affect conflict ripeness?	-	-	-	No effect
9	To what extent does the assertiveness of the leadership affect conflict ripeness?	-	-	-	Negatively
10	To what extent does external support to the belligerents affect conflict ripeness?	-	-	-	No effect
11	Can IDA be observed?	-	-	Yes	Yes
12	Is it possible to identify an effect of IDA on ripeness?	-	-	Yes	Yes
13	Does IDA affect ripeness positively?	-	-	No	Yes
14	Does IDA affect ripeness negatively?	-	-	Yes	Yes
15	Under which conditions does IDA affect conflict ripeness positively and under which conditions does IDA affect conflict ripeness negatively?	-	-	Cf. above	

Table 10: Case-Guiding Research Questions Uganda[130]

5.2 Burundi

The second case to be analyzed examines the conflict in Burundi, beginning in 1993[131]. Specifically, the case study analyzes three phases of the conflict affiliated with three attempts of mediation, making a within-case comparison

---
[130] Source: Own illustration.
[131] 'Beginning' in 1993 might be a confusing term. Large-scale violence and fighting broke out at this time, constituting a civil war. However, violence had been commonplace in Burundi since the gaining of independence in 1962.

181

possible. The first phase was in the period between 1993 and 1995 when UN Special Representative of the Secretary-General, Ahmedou Ould-Abdallah, undertook a peace initiative. The second phase was between the years 1996 and 2000 when Julius Nyerere, followed by Nelson Mandela, mediated the so-called Arusha Process. The third phase is the period between 2000 and 2006, characterized by mediation efforts of South Africa, particularly Jacob Zuma.

The case study mainly follows the same structure as the previous one. First, a general background to the case is provided (5.2.1) including the history and causes to the conflict (5.2.1.1) and the key actors (5.2.1.2). Then, the analysis of the case follows (5.2.2), divided into four parts. Firstly, the question of whether conflict ripeness existed at any point throughout the phases analyzed will be addressed including the potential effects of the independent variables on conflict ripeness (5.2.2.1). Secondly, it will be assessed whether IDA can be identified in the case of Burundi (5.2.2.2). Thirdly, those two analyses will be brought together when looking at the question of whether the IDA (if identified) affected conflict ripeness (if identified). If so, the quality of the impact will also be addressed including the outlining of the conditions accompanying the respective potential effects (5.2.2.3). Lastly, conclusions will be drawn bringing together the findings from this case study (5.2.2.4).

5.2.1   Background

The Republic of Burundi is a landlocked country in Sub-Saharan Central Africa in the Great Lakes region with the main capital Bujumbura. Its neighbors are the DRC in the West, Rwanda in the North, and Tanzania in the East/South. With currently about 9.5 million inhabitants, Burundi is the second most densely populated country in Africa after Rwanda. The population basically consists of two 'ethnic'[132] groups. Approximately 85% Burundians are Hutu, about 14% are Tutsi, and about 1% is Twa[133]. As a republic, Burundi is structured into 17 provinces. The country is currently ruled by the chief of state and head of

---

[132] To speak of 'ethnic' groups in this context does not entirely serve proper analysis. As Filip Reyntjens suggests, "it is paradoxical that the ethnic divide should be so paramount in Burundi's recent history, as Hutu, Tutsi and Twa do not even qualify as 'ethnic groups' in the anthropological sense of the word" (Reyntjens (2000): Burundi: Prospects for Peace, p.5).

[133] Cf. https://www.cia.gov/library/publications/the-world-factbook. These estimates are very vague, given that there has not been any official census on ethnicity in the country. René Lemarchand suggests that the Tutsi population might be as high as 20% (cf. Lemarchand (1994): Burundi: Ethnocide as Discourse and Practice, p.6).

government, President Pierre Nkurunziza, a Hutu, who was elected by popular vote in August 2005. In June 2010, the First Vice President Thérence Sinunguruza, was elected into office and Nkurunziza was re-elected President. After tribe-based communal violence, a protracted civil war that left at least 500,000 people dead since 1962[134] and as a rather resource-poor country, Burundi is one of the ten poorest countries in the world. The Economist even made the observation, "by most indicators Burundi is near the bottom in the world. By some counts it has the world's lowest GDP per person"[135]. In 2009, it was estimated that Burundi had a per capita GDP of about US$ 300 and more than 50% of the population lived below the poverty line (cf. Bentley/Southall, et al. 2005, p.22)[136]. By spending about 5.9% of GDP on military expenditures, Burundi is ranked 11th in the global list of countries. It is after Eritrea the African country spending relatively the most on military expenditures[137] compared to its GDP.

---

[134] Cf. *The Economist*, "Burundi's Election. Pretty Squalid: East Africa's Weakest New Component", 22 July 2010.
[135] Cf. "Burundi's Election. Pretty Squalid: East Africa's Weakest New Component", 22 July 2010.
[136] Cf. https://www.cia.gov/library/publications/the-world-factbook.
[137] Cf. https://www.cia.gov/library/publications/the-world-factbook/rankorder/2034rank.html?countryName=Burundi&countryCode=by&regionCode=af&rank=11#by.

Figure 15: Map of Burundi[138]

---

[138] Source: United Nations, "Burundi, no. 3753 Rev. 6 September 2004, United Nations," (2004a). Published with the courtesy and approval of the United Nations.

184

5.2.1.1   History and Causes

Burundi's history is highly complex with a series of tragic events (cf. Mehler 1995, p.1). It has seen episodes that have been described by many as genocide, has had the highest rate of heads of state to be assassinated and has suffered from continuous internal war for decades (cf. Lemarchand in Khadiagala/International Peace Academy 2006, p.41). It seems that its history is a story of ethnic conflict between Hutus and Tutsis, however, this only covers a shallow part of the causes of violence. It is rather the interplay of colonial rule, manipulation, elite-thinking, inter-communal issues and regional instability that affected the population over the course of its history (cf. Brachet/Wolpe 2005, p.1 and p.5).

Having been colonized under indirect rule by Germany and then Belgium from 1923 onwards, Burundi gained its independence in 1962. The ethnic split between the majority Hutus and the minority Tutsis characterized the colonial period and would later shape future events (cf. Hofmeier 2010, p.3 and Southall in Furley/May 2006, p.202). King Mwambutsa IV, a Tutsi, established a constitutional monarchy in 1962 comprised of equal numbers of Hutus and Tutsis in order to diffuse ethnic tensions. In 1965, the Hutu Prime Minister was assassinated, which resulted in a series of destabilizing revolts initiated by the Hutus. The government reacted with severely repressive measures (cf. Uvin 1999, p.256). One year later, the King's son ascended to the throne, but was removed in the same year by a military coup. The leader was Captain Michel Micombero who abolished the monarchy and declared Burundi a republic. Despite being called a republic, in reality Burundi was led by a military regime that structurally discriminated against the Hutu population, particularly with respect to limiting access to education (cf. Mehler 1995, p.4).

In 1972, Burundi witnessed another cycle of brutal violence and killings. A Hutu insurgency led to violent outbreaks against Tutsis; which was then answered by the government and army with an attack against the Hutus, particularly the educated population (cf. Bundervoet/Verwimp, et al. 2008, p.3 and International Crisis Group 2000b, p.50). More than 100,000 people were estimated to have been killed (cf. International Crisis Group 2000b, p.50; Jos Havermans and Andreas Mehler estimated up to 200,000 victims: Havermans 2002, p.6 and Mehler 1995, p.4). Lemarchand even observed that the killings amounted to genocide, citing the "planned, systematic extermination of Hutu elites and potential elites […], as well as many who would hardly qualify as either" (Lemarchand in Khadiagala/International Peace Academy 2006, p. 41 and p.45 and cf. Reyntjens 1995, p.7).

Until 1987, leadership changed several times. Burundi was basically a Tutsi military dictatorship where human rights were constantly violated and Hutu rebellions oppressed. In 1987, Major Pierre Buyoya, a Tutsi and nephew of Micombero (cf. Uvin 1999, p.257) overthrew the then head of state Jean-Baptiste Bagaza and dissolved the opposition parties, suspended the 1981 constitution, and instituted his ruling Military Committee for National Salvation (CSMN) (cf. Khadiagala 2007, p.108).

During the subsequent four years, increasing tensions emerged between the two ethnic groups. The Tutsis were in control of the government, the bureaucracy, and the army, while the Hutus were mostly prevented from entering these institutions (cf. Reyntjens 1995, p.6 and Uvin 1999, p.257). An estimated 100,000 to 150,000 people were killed during this time and about the same amount of refugees fled into the neighboring countries (cf. Bercovitch/Fretter 2004, p.97 and Uvin 1999, p.258). To address these difficulties and due to intense international pressure (cf. Bundervoet/Verwimp, et al. 2008, p.3 and Mehler 1995, p.11), Buyoya formed a commission to investigate the causes of the unrest and developed a charter for democratic reform, including the opening of the system for democratic institutions as well as the introduction of a public law favoring civil society, which resulted in the founding of numerous local NGOs in Burundi (cf. Herisse 2000, p.296).

Despite his previous reign of military oppression, Buyoya thus opened up "an era of political reform" (Khadiagala 2007, p.108). He approved a constitution on a multi-ethnic government and the establishment of a parliament in 1991; and thus attempted to democratize the country (cf. Reyntjens 2009, p.34). The actual implementation was only started in 1993 though. One of the first steps was to hold presidential elections in a multi-party system[139]. These took place on 1 June 1993. Three candidates ran for the office: the current head of state Pierre Buyoya for the party UPRONA (Unité pour le Progrès National), FRODEBU's candidate Melchior Ndadaye (Front pour la démocratie au Burundi) and the royalist party's candidate Pierre-Claver Sendegeya. The results surprised most observers (cf. Hofmeier 2010, p.3). Buyoya only reached 32.39% of the votes and thus lost the election to Ndadaye who won with 64.75%. The Tutsi-elite's party had lost the presidency to the mostly Hutu party FRODEBU, which indicated that the people had voted along ethnic lines. According to the international community, the elections had been fair and successful (cf. Wohlgemuth in Wallensteen 1998, p.89). This result was further confirmed and reinforced in the National Assembly elections, which took place at the end of the same month, when FRODEBU even reached about seven percentage points more

---

[139] For a detailed account on the course of the elections, please see Reyntjens (1995): Burundi: Breaking the Cycle of Violence, pp.10-11.

coming to 71.4%. The established government had been overthrown and a new administration was put in place that represented the vast majority of Burundians. Melchior Ndadaye was the first Hutu head of state in Burundi (cf. Southall in Furley/May 2006, p.201).

Burundi's elite, mainly consisting of Tutsis, feared losses in power and privileges. Thus, tensions arose all over the country in the aftermath of the elections (cf. Reyntjens 2009, p.34). Open expressions of concern were shown by students – who were mainly Tutsi and privileged – demonstrating in Burundi's capital Bujumbura on 4 June 1993, claiming that the elections had in reality been an 'ethnic inventory of Burundi'; slogans reading "multipartisme oui, multitribalisme non" (Mehler 1995, p.19) or "Oui à la démocratie, Non à l'ethnisation du pouvoir" (Reyntjens 1995, p.12) were shown. An ethnicization of the political sphere in Burundi had manifested.

Subsequently, the new government had to deal with a paradoxical situation within the structures of the state. While FRODEBU had won the elections for the President and the National Assembly, all administrative institutions were still run by the old, Tutsi elites. Thus, the judiciary was for instance mainly controlled by Tutsis, as were the army, the police, the educational system, and the remaining bureaucracy (cf. Southall in Furley/May 2006, p.204). No reforms in these institutions had been undertaken in the period leading up to the elections, which made it almost impossible for the new government to face and tackle the many problems that arose such as the massive return of many, primarily Hutu refugees (cf. Reyntjens 1995, p.12), and the hostility of the public and the private media. The return of the refugees caused major challenges for the judiciary system as the returning Burundians demanded their respective property rights be respected and their land returned (cf. Lemarchand in Khadiagala/International Peace Academy 2006, p.46). As the judiciary was dominated by the old elites, the land disputes could not be settled in a way that was satisfying to the majority of the people. Another example is the problem of the control over internal security. The army and police being mostly Tutsi-ruled, did not support the government in furthering their aims, but instead sabotaged their actions.

In an effort to solve these problems, Ndadaye initiated a policy of "frodebization" (cf. Reyntjens 2000, p.13), referring to a change of ethnic people in civil service, the military, the judiciary etc. This did not only cause significant anger among the Tutsis, but also resulted in a loss of expertise in the relevant institutions. The majority of Hutus had been prevented from attending institutions of higher education and was therefore mostly under-qualified for such positions. The new government also had to deal with a deteriorating economic situation. World coffee prices were falling in the autumn of 1993. As coffee was Burundi's main export product, this caused significant disturbances in the national economy, negatively affecting the principally rural people. Furthermore, the Burundian economic model had been one of state control; structural adjustments required the implementation of a privatization policy. Mainly Tutsis dominated the private sector. Thus, the government had to closely monitor the privatization process in order to avoid that the old elites gained indirect power through the privatization of state owned institutions.

All these factors led to major discontent among the population – both on the Tutsi and on the Hutu side (cf. Bentley/Southall, et al. 2005, p.49). The Tutsis feared and felt their losses and the Hutus could not be satisfied fully. The government initiated many new policies and reforms, but constantly faced strong opposition (cf. Reyntjens 2009, p.34). "On the surface, the democracy drive appeared to be a spectacular success" (Dravis in Gurr 2000, p.190), as Dravis put it, but the actual situation seemed quite different with many problems confronting the new government and a constant increase in tensions and violence amongst the population.

The tensions found their peak on 21 October 1993, when there was a coup d'état in which President Ndadye, the speaker and the deputy speaker of the National Assembly, and a few of Ndadye's closest associates were assassinated four months after the elections (cf. Southall in Furley/May 2006, p.204)[140]. The conflict escalated and thousands of Tutsis were killed, which in turn led to the killing of tens of thousands of Hutus (cf. Bundervoet/Verwimp, et al. 2008, p.4). This marked the beginning of an almost decade-long civil war (cf. Bentley/Southall, et al. 2005, p.21). It was estimated that about 50,000 to 100,000 people in total were killed in the months after the coup (cf. Mehler 1995, p.22 and Uvin 1999, p.262). In fact, the coup was not fully successful and lacked leadership and backing by key sections of the military hierarchy (cf. Bentley/Southall, et al. 2005, p.50).

Thus, in January 1994, Cyprien Ntaryamira, a Hutu, succeeded Ndadye as president; elected as the 'consensus candidate' by the National Assembly (cf. Reyntjens 2009, p.35). He unfortunately died when he was on the plane with his Rwandan counterpart Habyarimana that was shot down in Rwanda only three months later in April 1994. In October, Parliament Speaker Ntibantunganya was appointed President. Both Ntaryamira and Ntibantunganya were members of FRODEBU. Thus, the party elected in 1993 stayed in formal control of the government throughout this time.

---

[140] For a detailed account on Ndadye's assassination, please see Reyntjens Burundi: Breaking the Cycle of Violence.

Until 1996, the government thus officially remained in power, yet, it was basically toothless and unable to control the country. As a result Burundi found itself in a renewed civil war. Violence was commonplace and the rule of law was basically non-existent. From early 1994 onwards, several talks were initiated between the government and the old elites, in which the Hutu government increasingly compromised and shared power with representatives of UPRONA. By December 1995, FRODEBU was left with only 11 out of 26 portfolios. Filip Reyntjens described the situation as, "the President and National Assembly were impotent, the cabinet was divided and unable to formulate and implement coherent policies, and the army effectively controlled what little state power remained in the country" (Reyntjens 2000, p.16), and called this development a "creeping coup" (Reyntjens 1995, p.16 and Reyntjens 2009, p.34). The 'creeping coup' refers to the period from the assassination of Ndadaye until 1996. While the coup d'état against Ndadaye had killed the principal leaders of the country, it was not successful in overthrowing the government completely. However, through constant pressure and with the help of the tools of the military, judiciary and bureaucracy, the old elites succeeded in sabotaging the government until they had basically hobbled the government of Burundi. As Southall put it, "in effect, the creeping coup restored the Tutsi elite to power under a Hutu president" (Southall in Furley/May 2006, p.205). As a result, radical elements of the FRODEBU split, so that the CNDD (Conseil national pour la defences de la democratie) was created including its military wing, the FDD (Force pour la defense de la democratie).

The state of the conflict continuously deteriorated. Massacres from both sides were witnessed as well as targeted assassinations against politicians. For example, in March 1995, the moderate Hutu Ernest Kabushemeye, President of the small Hutu party RPB (Rassemblement pour le peuple du Burundi), was killed in the streets of Bujumbura. Immediately as an act of reprisal, the former mayor of Bujumbura was crucified and killed (cf. Mehler 1995, p.26).

By mid-1996, some 150,000 people had been killed (cf. Bentley/Southall, et al. 2005, p.56 and Southall in Furley/May 2006, p.205). It was at that time that the former Tanzanian President, Julius Nyerere, initiated peace efforts and convened meetings between FRODEBU and UPRONA upon insistence of the OAU. The talks were relatively successful and President Ntibantunganya agreed to a regional peacekeeping force in Burundi (cf. Bentley/Southall, et al. 2005, p.57)[141].

---

[141] A more detailed account on the events in this period will be provided in the analysis-chapter.

The course of events turned again. In July 1996, former President Buyoya was restored to power in a military coup. The 'proto-democratic' order was overturned and the Tutsi elite officially back in the presidential office (cf. Bentley/Southall, et al. 2005, p.52). Even after re-gaining power in 1996, Buyoya was not able to bring peace and normality to Burundi. Grievances were high all over the country and Buyoya's regime was sanctioned with an international embargo instituted on the initiative of the regional powers after the military coup, which resulted in an even stronger deterioration of the economy.

In 1998, Buyoya and the parliament agreed on a transitional constitution and started to take part in a negotiation process. The negotiations finally led to the signing of the Arusha Peace and Reconciliation Agreement on 28 August 2000 (cf. Southall in Furley/May 2006, p.201). A transitional government was put in place in 2001 that included a power-sharing system[142]. Due to two the rebel groups that were predominantly Hutu-aligned (FDD and FNL) who refused to join in the agreement, continued fighting shaped the following years (cf. Bercovitch/Fretter 2004, p.97). In December 2002, the government and the FDD signed a ceasefire agreement in Tanzania. However, this agreement was broken one month later with renewed fighting. As part of the power-sharing government, Domitien Ndayizeye, a Hutu, became Burundian president in April 2003. The fighting still continued and peaked in that year in July when about 200 rebels and 15 government soldiers were killed in an assault on Bujumbura. In November, finally, the FDD agreed to end the civil war and an agreement was signed at the summit of African leaders in Tanzania.

In June 2004, a UN mission took over the task of peacekeeping in Burundi from the previously active African Union troops who had been deployed since November 2001 in an initiative driven mainly by South Africa (cf. Roger Southall in Furley/May 2006, p.209). However, the violence could still not be quenched. In 2005, Burundi held the first parliamentary elections since the start of the civil war. The main former Hutu rebel group conglomerate comprised of CNDD and FDD surprisingly won with 58% of the votes and nominated Pierre Nkurunziza as President (cf. Mottiar/Van Jaarsveld 2009, p.30). The elections had taken place under the auspices of the UN and were judged as generally free and fair (cf. Hofmeier 2010, p.5). Many feared another outbreak of violence but as The Economist expressed it, "that the election which brought him [Nkurunziza] to power – Burundi's first since 1993 – ended peacefully was a surprise to many"[143].

---

[142] A more detailed account on the events in this period will be provided in the analysis-chapter.
[143] Cf. *The Economist*, Burundi and Rwanda.

In September 2006, the last active rebel group, the FNL, signed a ceasefire agreement with the government. The conflict addressed by the ceasefire agreement was judged as non-violent, however as not finally resolved in 2008 (cf. Heidelberger Institut für Internationale Konfliktforschung 2008, p.28). About half a year later, in February 2007, the UN closed its peacekeeping mission, but continued to support the post-conflict reconstruction efforts. Because of positive developments and the achievement of its targets, Burundi was granted total debt relief and thus the Club of Paris of creditor nations cancelled all of Burundi's debt (US$ 134.3 million) in March 2009. In June 2010, presidential elections were held, in which Nkurunziza was re-elected as president with 92% of the vote of registered voters[144]. However, the elections were boycotted by most of the opposition parties (cf. Hofmeier 2010, p.1). Post-election tensions in 2010 renewed fears of violence. At time of writing, the situation had not yet escalated, so that hope remains that the conflict has finally come to an end[145].

5.2.1.2   Key Actors

The complexity of Burundi's history implies that the key actors cannot easily be defined and understood. There are no two clearly definable protagonists and one mediator, but a range of actors that played different roles at different stages of the conflict. I will therefore introduce the actors in two parts. The first part covers the domestic actors from Burundi. This part is comprised of the description of the parties and the individual presidents. The second part covers external, international actors, including organizations, individual persons and states.

Beginning with the parties relevant as actors in the Burundian case, the first party founded in Burundi was UPRONA (Unité pour le Progrès National). UPRONA is a nationalist party that was established upon Burundi's independence to uphold traditional institutions and was initially led by Pierre Louis Rwagasore (cf. Bentley/Southall, et al. 2005, pp.41-42). Until 1992, when the multi-party system was introduced, UPRONA was the only official party, the state party. The party split into two factions in October 1998. One was presided over by Luc Rukingama and one by Charles Mukasi, where Rukingama represented the more moderate side of the party. UPRONA, given that it used to be the state party prior to the democratic elections, was mainly dominated by

---

[144] Cf. "Burundi's Election. Pretty Squalid: East Africa's Weakest New Component", 22 July 2010.
[145] A more detailed account on the events in this period will be provided under the analysis-chapter.

Tutsis, but also had a quarter of Hutu members (cf. International Crisis Group 2000b, Annex 4 and International Crisis Group 2001, p.37).

The primary competition to UPRONA as a political party is FRODEBU (Front pour la Démocratie au Burundi), which is a mainly Hutu dominated party. FRODEBU officially exists since 1992 with the introduction of the Law on Political Parties but was secretly set up as early as 1986. FRODEBU favors non-military means and also includes Tutsis as members (cf. International Crisis Group 1999b, pp.5-6). They won the first democratic elections in 1993 with Melchior Ndadaye as head. Thereafter, Sylvestre Ntibantunganya (1993-1995) and then Jean Minani led the party.

The CNDD-FDD (Conseil National pour la Défense de la Démocratie – Forces pour la Défense de la Démocratie) is the radical and militant political offshoot associated with FRODEBU. While FRODEBU decided against a formal association to the group, it supported the CNDD-FDD financially (cf. International Crisis Group 2002b, p.7). Léonard Nyangoma, one of the founders of FRODEBU and Minister of Interior in the Ntaryamira government, founded the CNDD-FDD in 1994. Since October 2001, it is led by Pierre Nkurunziza (cf. International Crisis Group 2002b, p.8). The mainly Hutu party also has a number of Tutsis in its leadership (cf. Lemarchand in Khadiagala/International Peace Academy 2006, p.46). While the CNDD constitutes the political wing, the FDD is the armed branch, which is led by Jean-Bosco Ndayikengurukiye.

Another major Hutu party is the PALIPEHUTU (Parti pour la Libération du Peuple Hutu) that positions the ethnic issue in a much more prominent position than FRODEBU, promoting the ideology of defending the cause of the Hutu peasants (cf. Vandeginste 2009, p.79). It has thus been the principal vehicle for anti-Tutsi radicalism in Burundi. PALIPEHUTU was founded in 1973 in refugee camps in Tanzania where Hutus sought protection from Tutsi massacres in their home country (cf. Lemarchand in Khadiagala/International Peace Academy 2006, p.46). However, PALIPEHUTU only officially began activities in Burundi in 1992.

In 1989, PALIPEHUTU split into two sub-groups: Frolina (Front pour la Libération Nationale) and PALIPEHUTU-FNL (Forces pour la Défense de la Démocratie). Frolina, led by Joseph Karumba, followed a rather moderate approach. PALIPEHUTU-FNL split again in 1992 into the political wing PALIPEHUTU, led by Etienne Karatasi, and the armed wing FNL, initially founded by Cossan Kabura. In February 2001, Agathon Rwasa took over the leadership. The FNL was supported in its military capabilities by the Rwandan army since its inception (cf. International Crisis Group 2002b, p.7).

A range of additional parties have been and are active in Burundi, dating back to a law introduced by Buyoya in 1993 when he opened the system for political parties. The law stated that a group of at least thirty-two members with a minimum of two originating from each of the fifteen provinces and the capital could form a party. Each party leader was entitled to access to the national radio as well as a four-wheel drive car. This resulted in a sudden 'mushrooming' of political parties in Burundi (cf. Ould-Abdallah 2000, p.33). Among those parties are the Tutsi affiliated ones like PARENA, a radical Tutsi party with the former president Jean-Baptiste Bagaza as its leader, the PRP (Parti pour la Réconciliation du Peuple), the Alliance de Vaillants-Intwari, the Alliance Burundo-Africaine pour le Salut, the Parti pour la Socio-Démocratie, INKINZO, ANADDE (Alliance pour le Droit et le Développement Economique), and the Parti Indépendent pour les Travailleurs; as well as the Hutu affiliated ones such as the PP (Parti du Peuple), the RPB (Rassemblement pour le Peuple du Burundi), and the PL (Parti Libéral) (cf. Havermans 2002, pp.4-5).

Some individual personalities must be mentioned in this context as key actors in the Burundian conflict: the various presidents from 1993 until the present. The first president was Melchior Ndadaye, a Hutu and leader of FRODEBU. Ndadaye was educated as a teacher, but fled from Burundi during the 1972-massacres. He then lived in Rwanda where he also completed his degree in teaching. Furthermore, he completed another degree in banking in France. He returned to Burundi in 1983, becoming politically active as a moderate Hutu in the underground.

After Ndadaye's assassination in October 1993, Cyprien Ntaryamira took over the presidency. Ntaryamira was also a Hutu and member of FRODEBU. Similarly to Ndadaye, Ntaryamira was a refugee in Rwanda where he also completed a university degree in agriculture and returned to Burundi in 1983. Before becoming President, he was the Minister for Agriculture under Ndadaye.

Sylvestre Ntibantunganya of FRODEBU became president in October 1994 after his predecessor died in the plane crash. In the period between Ntaryamira's death and Ntibantunganya's official inauguration, he was interim president of Burundi. His previous positions were foreign minister under Ndadaye and speaker of the National Assembly under Ntaryamira. Originally a member of UPRONA, he became one of the leading thinkers of FRODEBU upon its foundation (cf. Mehler 1995, p.32).

In 1996, Major Pierre Buyoya was reinstalled as president after a military coup. As a Tutsi, he was affiliated with UPRONA and closely connected to the Burundian military. Buyoya had already been president prior to the first democratic elections from 1987 to 1993 and introduced democratic reforms in Burundi leading to the 1993 democratic elections, which he lost to FRODEBU. After regaining power in 1996, Buyoya stayed in office until after the establishment of the power-sharing agreement of 2000 and was thus the first president in the so-called transition government. He remained president until 2003.

In April 2003, as part of the power-sharing agreement, Domitien Ndayizeye, a Hutu from the FRODEBU party, took over the office of president. Ndayizeye's life was also highly impacted by the course of events in Burundi. In 1982, he left his home country and went into exile in Belgium where he completed a degree in engineering. After spending some time in Rwanda, he returned to Burundi in 1993, where he was arrested in 1995 and imprisoned until 1996. After his imprisonment, he became permanent secretary of FRODEBU.

Since 2005, Pierre Nkurunziza, a Hutu, is president. Nkurunziza is thus the first democratically elected Burundian president since the beginning of the civil war. Nkurunziza graduated from the University of Burundi in 1990 with a degree in education and sports. When the civil war broke out in 1993, he was a lecturer at the university. In 1995, Nkurunziza joined the Hutu rebellion in the FDD as an armed rebel. He quickly rose through ranks and became the FDD's chairman in 2001[146]. The table below summarizes the line of Burundian presidents between 1993 and 2006:

President	Party	Time Period	Reason for Ousting
Ndadaye	FRODEBU	06/1993-10/1993	Assassination
Ntaryamira	FRODEBU	01/1994-04/1994	Died in shooting of plane
Ntibantunganya	FRODEBU	10/1994-07/1996	Ousted in coup d'état
Buyoya	UPRONA	07/1996-04/2003	End of term
Ndayizeye	FRODEBU	04/2003-08/2005	End of term
Nkurunziza	CNDD-FDD	08/2005 onwards	Still in office

Table 11: Overview Presidents of Burundi 1993-2006

A range of external, international actors are also significant with respect to the Burundian conflict. In one way or another, they impacted the course of events.

---

[146] Cf. http://news.bbc.co.uk/1/hi/world/africa/country_profiles/1068873.stm.

Until 1993, the international community largely ignored the problems in this small African state. Only with the democratization process underway and the disastrous developments afterwards, Burundi became a center of interest; the international community largely supported this development through projects regarding structural adjustments by the World Bank and the IMF (cf. Mehler 1995, p.11), enforced also through the Rwandan genocide. As a neighboring country, Burundi did not only have to accommodate large numbers of refugees, but also seemed to be at risk of experiencing a similar situation of mass killing given its comparable ethnic structure.

Thus from 1993 onwards, the United Nations started to display a more prominent interest in Burundi. The UN Security Council held numerous sessions on the country and eventually appointed a UN Special Representative of the Secretary-General. The then Secretary-General Boutros Boutros-Ghali offered the position to the Mauritanian diplomat Ahmedou Ould-Abdallah. For the previous six years, Ould-Abdallah had been in charge of African economic affairs at the UN. As a supporting institution, the Secretary-General also established the United Nations Office in Burundi (UNOB), which reported to the UN Department of Political Affairs (cf. Jackson, S. 2006, p.3). Ould-Abdallah took the office in November 1993 und stayed for two years until September 1995, when he submitted his resignation from the position to the Secretary-General, leaving Burundi a few weeks later. Ould-Abdallah's mandate included four objectives: "to restore the democratic institutions overthrown by the abortive coup of October 21 [1993] of that year; to facilitate dialogue between the parties to the crisis; to establish a commission of inquiry into the events of October and the massacres that followed; and to work in close collaboration with the Organization of African Unity (OAU)" (Ould-Abdallah 2000, p.38).

The subsequent engagements of the UN were mainly limited to special envoys, regular monitoring and the support to regional initiatives (cf. United Nations 1994; United Nations 1995a; United Nations 1996; and United Nations 1997, among others). However, in May 2004, the UN decided in Security Council Resolution 1545 to send a peacekeeping mission under Chapter VII of the United Nations Charter for an initial six months (cf. United Nations 2004c). It deployed a force of some 5,650 troops as well as 200 military observers, 125 staff officers and 120 civilian police and additional personnel to Burundi called the United Nations Operation in Burundi (ONUB) (Southall in Furley/May 2006, p.214 and United Nations 2004c, p.3). The peacekeeping force with the mandate to "restore lasting peace and bring about national reconciliation, as provided under the Arusha Agreement" (United Nations 2004c, p.3), was extended several times and finally left Burundi at the end of December 2006 (cf. United Nations 2006h). In October 2006, the UN Security Council decided to establish the UN

Integrated Office in Burundi to be known as BINUB, the Bureau Intégré des Nations Unies au Burundi (cf. United Nations 2006i)[147] in order to, "inter alia, facilitate the implementation of the ceasefire" (Accord 2007, p.32).

Additional to the United Nations, the regional powers also took an interest in the developments in Burundi during the 1990s. The regional powers, comprised of mainly Uganda, Rwanda, the DRC, and Tanzania, affected by the massive amount of Burundian refugees, launched a regional initiative on Burundi in November 1995, when they held their first regional summit under the auspices of former US President Jimmy Carter in Cairo. The meeting was co-presided over by Amadou Toumani Touré from Mali, Julius Nyerere from Tanzania and Desmond Tutu from South Africa (cf. International Crisis Group 2000c, p.1).

Together with the OAU, who supported this regional initiative strongly, the regional powers decided to designate Julius Nyerere as the chief mediator at their second summit in Tunis in March 1996. In total, ten summits of the regional heads of state took place throughout the 1990s (cf. International Crisis Group 2000c, p.1). Julius Nyerere had retired from the Tanzanian Presidency in 1985 and as one of the elder African statesmen, had a reputation of international stature and had close contacts to Burundian politicians from all sides (cf. Southall in Furley/May 2006, p.206). In 1999, Julius Nyerere died at the age of 77 of leukemia during the mediation process.

His successor as mediator in the Burundian conflict was to become former South African President Nelson Mandela. Mandela was chosen because he was "famed as a reconciler of opposites as demonstrated by his key role in negotiating the South African settlement (1990-1994)" (Southall in Furley/May 2006, p.207) and had the advantage of being African, but a regional outsider with great international backing. In his role as a mediator, he worked in a personal capacity, although he was supported by his government (cf. Southall in Furley/May 2006, p.208). Mandela continued Nyerere's work in the so-called Arusha peace process and was able to bring the negotiations to the signing of the Arusha Peace and Reconciliation Agreement for Burundi. With that, his official task was concluded. Even though he remained involved in the further course of events and acted as a "moral guarantor" to the process (cf. Bentley/Southall, et al. 2005, p.89), Mandela passed on the role of facilitator of the Burundian peace process to South African Deputy President Jacob Zuma.

South Africa had positioned itself as one of the main leaders in pushing for peace in Burundi. Together with Tanzania and Uganda, South Africa supported the peace efforts both financially and in terms of personnel. In parallel to this

---

[147] Cf. http://www.un.org/en/peacekeeping/missions/past/onub/index.html.

prominent mediating involvement, South Africa also dominated the peace-keeping role in Burundi. As early as in October 2001, South Africa sent 700 troops to Burundi as the South African Protection Support Detachment (SAPSD) (cf. International Crisis Group 2002a, p.6). These troops built the basis for the African Union's mission to Burundi that arrived in April 2003, the African Mission in Burundi (AMIB), with the mandate to oversee the implementation of the agreements; to support disarmament and demobilization initiatives and advise on the reintegration of combatants; strive towards ensuring favorable conditions for the establishment of a UN peacekeeping mission; and contribute to political and economic stability in Burundi (cf. Svensson 2008, pp.11-12). AMIB had a strength of about 3,000 people, both civilian and military (cf. Svensson 2008, p.12). When the UN took over the mission, South Africa remained the country contributing the largest contingent of troops. Thus, it was not surprising that when the OAU took over the peacekeeping mission in 2007 with the AU special Task Force (AU STF), it was again mainly South African soldiers that were deployed to Burundi (about 1,100 troops) (cf. Accord 2007, p.33).

With regard to development aid, other institutions and states played significant roles in Burundi. To be named here as significant donors are the EU and its institutions, France, Belgium, Germany and the US as individual states as well as the World Bank's International Development Association, the AfDF, the IMF, UNDP, UNHCR and the World Food Program.

Lastly, the numerous international NGOs, institutes, and religious based charity organizations in Burundi should be mentioned. From 1993 onwards, a large inflow of these was observed, with the ICG counting 57 international NGOs operating in Burundi in 2002 (cf. International Crisis Group 2003, p.8). They mainly served two purposes. Either, they were humanitarian organizations (for example Action Aid, CARE, Caritas, Christian Aid, Habitat for Humanity, the ICRC, Oxfam, Save the Children, World Vision, to name a few) or they were organizations dedicated to promoting conflict resolution such as International Alert, International Dialogue, Sant'Egidio, SfCG, the African American Institute, the National Democratic Institute, the Scandinavian Institute of African Studies, among many others (cf. Reyntjens 1995, p.23).

5.2.2   Burundi Analysis

Having contextualized the case of Burundi in its historical development and having introduced the key actors, we will now turn towards the analysis of the case. Given that this case allows for a within-case analysis, similar to the case of

Uganda, the following parts will be structured into the individual sub-phases: conflict ripeness (5.2.2.1), the increase in development aid (5.2.2.2), and the effect of the increase in development aid on ripeness (5.2.2.3). These three parts will deal with each of the phases 1993-1995, 1996-2000, and lastly 2000-2006. The chapter will bring the findings together in an overall conclusion (5.2.2.4).

The three phases to be analyzed all witnessed individual peace efforts. In the first phase between 1993 and 1995, the initiative was mainly driven by UN Special Representative of the Secretary-General, Ahmedou Ould-Abdallah whose main achievement was a power-sharing agreement, the Convention of Government, signed in September 1994 between UPRONA and FRODEBU. The process was further accompanied by Ould-Abdallah until 1995, trying to foster the Convention. The second phase lasted from 1996 until 2000 and was driven by first Julius Nyerere and then Nelson Mandela as chief mediators. It ended with the signing of the Arusha Peace and Reconciliation Agreement for Burundi on 28 August 2000 (cf. Government of Burundi 2000). The third phase started thereafter regarding the implementation of the transition government as well as the mediation of the conflict with the two remaining rebel factions, the CNDD-FDD and the FNL. This initiative was mainly facilitated by Jacob Zuma and is characterized by the milestones of signing a Global Ceasefire Agreement with the CNDD-FDD on 16 November 2003 (cf. Government of Burundi 2003) and a Comprehensive Ceasefire Agreement with the PALIPEHUTU-FNL on 7 September 2006 (cf. Government of Burundi 2006). The following table provides an overview of the three phases with their individual peace initiatives in Burundi, their initiators, the mediators, the achievements and the key internal actors that were involved.

	Phase 1: 1993-1995	Phase 2: 1996-2000	Phase 3: 2000-2006
Initiator	UN Secretary-General	Regional powers	South Africa
Mediator	Ahmedou Ould-Abdallah	Julius Nyerere and Nelson Mandela	Jacob Zuma
Achievement	▪ Convention of Government (power-sharing agreement)	▪ Arusha Peace and Reconciliation Agreement	▪ Global Ceasefire Agreement (with CNDD-FDD) ▪ Comprehensive Ceasefire Agreement (with FNL)

	Phase 1: **1993-1995**	**Phase 2:** **1996-2000**	**Phase 3:** **2000-2006**
Key Internal Actors	▪ Political parties	▪ All factions (both political and armed)	▪ Government and two armed rebel groups

Table 12: Overview Peace Initiatives in Burundi[148]

5.2.2.1 Conflict Ripeness

In order to assess whether conflict ripeness was existent during any of the three phases, each period will be assessed individually. As prescribed through the theoretical model and as used in the previous case studies, the independent variables potentially affecting conflict ripeness will further be looked at as part of the analysis.

Starting with the first phase, the focus lies on the years between 1993 and 1995, which is the time when Ould-Abdallah was appointed as UN Special Representative of the Secretary-General and invested into a peace effort in late 1993. It refers to a period when Burundi found itself in a difficult situation. In June 1993, the first 'democratic' elections had taken place with the result that the government was entirely overturned. FRODEBU had surprisingly won the elections and Ndadaye became president. However, he was killed in October of that year in a coup d'état. Ntaryamira was appointed President in January 1994, but died in April. This resulted in the third president of that legislature, Ntibantunganya, who stayed in office until the end of that phase.

The UN reacted by appointing Ould-Abdallah in an attempt to facilitate negotiations for a power-sharing agreement in order to stabilize the country. Burundi had witnessed a wave of violence after the Ndadaye-assassination, leaving up to an estimated 100,000 people dead, and about 1 million people internally displaced or as refugees by November 1993 (cf. Curtis 2003, p.2). Further, the genocide triggered by the assassination of Habyarimana in Rwanda endangered the weak Burundi with a potential spillover of violence given the vicinity as a neighbor, the similar ethnic distribution in the population and the similar problem in terms of the struggle for power.

---

[148] Source: Own illustration.

The belligerents in this period were mainly two: FRODEBU, as the party officially in power as the state actor and 'mother' party of the Hutu rebel factions, and second, UPRONA, as the opposition party and 'mother' party to the Tutsi rebel factions. Upon arrival in Burundi Ould-Abdallah initiated talks between those two parties, including additional other political parties that were in one way or the other linked to these two main parties.

Finally, on 10 September 1994, almost one year after negotiations had first been initiated, FRODEBU, UPRONA and twelve other political parties signed a power-sharing agreement, the Convention of Government (cf. United Nations 1995a, p.3). The agreement provided for a split of power, so that UPRONA would participate in the government. Thus, even though the position of President continued to be filled by a Hutu representative from FRODEBU, the Prime Ministership was given to the Tutsi-dominated party UPRONA (cf. International Crisis Group 1998b, p.1). The killings, however, continued and the political situation remained as equally disturbed as before (cf. Curtis 2003, p.2). Was this peace effort initiated in a phase when ripeness was existent?

An MHS was not apparent. The democratization process that had been conducted before this period was intended to change the existing form of government and by that moving the country into a peaceful co-existence. Instead, the process triggered large scale violence and massacres on both sides. In the previous setup of Burundi, there had been two groups: the ruling elite, that was mainly Tutsi, and the people, that were mainly Hutu. The main population had been ready for a change in government. This was proven by the large turnout of voters in the 1993 elections. 97.3% of the registered voters participated in the vote. Yet, the ruling elite were not ready to step down from its position of power. The Tutsi politicians in charge enjoyed their privilege to be in control of all spheres of government – the executive in the form of army and police, the legislative in the form of the bureaucracy and administration, and the judiciary. In 1993, there was no significant international pressure, no embargo, no sanctions, and thus no perceived need for change from the Tutsis' perspective.

Therefore, the Tutsis, previously the ruling elite of Burundi, were taken by surprise from the election results. They did not enter the new phase weakened by the results, but instead with anger, ready for revenge and willing and able to fight for it. This was made clear by the assassination of President Ndadaye, through the uncountable number of killings of Hutus and the implementation of the so-called 'creeping coup' throughout the years 1993 to 1995. That is, the Tutsi elite, including UPRONA but also the rebel factions, did not perceive an MHS. They did not find themselves in a hurting position. It is true that they had lost official power in the form of the presidential office; however, they were still in charge of many positions in the state (including the army) and ready to fight back to regain their predominance. The international community greeted the free and fair elections, but did not react to the subsequent acts of violence such as the assassination of Ndadaye, the large scale killings throughout these years or the 'creeping coup' secretly undermining the FRODEBU government (cf. Mehler 1995, p.2). Not only did the international community not react, but it became clear that there was no state or organization willing to take over the responsibility for a conflict intervention if needed. Preoccupied with the events in Rwanda and with the hurting experience of Somalia fresh in their minds (cf. Khadiagala 2007, p.110), no external actor positioned him-/herself as a power putting pressure on the belligerents or willing to intervene militarily if needed (cf. Mehler 1995, p.2 and p.28). Thus neither internal nor external pressure was given that would have created a basis for an MHS.

In parallel, neither MEOs were present that could have lured UPRONA into the peace process for sincere negotiations. No significant incentives were induced and no other opportunities emerged from the context of the situation, so that it would have made sense for UPRONA to take peace efforts seriously.

Similarly, FRODEBU and the armed Hutu groups perceived a comparable strong and not hurting position in 1993 and 1994. From the Hutu perspective, it was revolutionary that they had won national elections. For the first time in the history of Burundian independence, a Hutu became president and was legitimately in charge of ruling the country. The majority of the population felt confirmed and strong. The assassination of Ndadaye and the death of Ntaryamira were strong disappointments; but instead of perceiving a hurting stalemate, the Hutu factions replied with violent attacks and massacres of Tutsis. Neither was a 'plateau-situation' given due to the recent change of the status quo and subsequent developments, nor was a 'precipice-situation' perceived as they legitimately were in charge of the country. Given that the president was not replaced by a Tutsi, the precipice-situation was avoided. The 'creeping coup' was not as visible and perceivable for the population, especially not for the armed rebel groups given that it was implemented in a subtle way on part of the opposition. Thus, the Hutu groups did not perceive an MHS in this phase of the Burundian conflict.

MEOs were not available either to the Hutu factions. They held the highest office in the country, and other incentives were not presented. Thus, it is possible to state that none of the parties perceived an MHS or MEOs. Andreas Mehler summarized this lack of a hurting stalemate and the lack of inducements in 1995 by stating that neither diplomatic negotiations seemed promising, nor a military intervention likely due to lacking interests from external actors, but also due to internal opposition by the belligerents against any form of external intervention – be it diplomatic or the use of force (cf. Mehler 1995, p.2).

Therefore, the ideas of the belligerents on how the further process could potentially develop were rather contradictory instead of presenting a sense of a way out of the civil war. For the Hutu groups, the clear perspective was to expand their power and leverage in the administration beyond the election results and fight for this end. The policy of 'frodebization' was previously mentioned. Finally, after the introduction of democratic results, the Hutu groups, independent of whether political or armed factions, wanted to ferment equal opportunities for Hutus, particularly with respect to access to education. Positions in the bureaucracy, army, administration, etc. were to be filled with Hutus. However, the Tutsi groups had quite a different idea of where the journey should go. They were disappointed by the situation and they asked for the old right back to rule the country. Firstly, they tried it by the means of assassination and an open coup d'état, then, their strategy became more subtle and the instrument of the 'creeping coup' was applied (cf. Reyntjens 1995, p.16), which put them back into the comfortable role of actually running the country and preparing it for the subsequent chain of events. Thus, the two belligerents did not sense a way out of the situation that would have been compatible in any way and they did not show any sense for a peaceful process (cf. Mehler 1995, p.27).

It is therefore possible to conclude that throughout the years of 1993 to 1995, conflict ripeness was not given in Burundi. Neither an MHS or MEOs were apparent, nor did an SWO exist. Both belligerents were in a position to believe they were able to win the conflict through a combination of political and military means. Thus compromising to the other party as part of a peace initiative did not seem a valid option and fighting continued (cf. United Nations 1995a, p.4).

Now, it must be questioned, why the belligerents were nevertheless willing to negotiate with Ould-Abdallah and why they eventually signed the power-sharing agreement in September 1994. In his official position as a representative of the international community, Ould-Abdallah was important to be satisfied – or at least noted – by the belligerent factions. It was feared that without at least hearing Ould-Abdallah's arguments, the international community would become more deeply involved. Neither FRODEBU nor UPRONA were keen on external intervention. UPRONA feared the loss of sovereignty in the army and FRODEBU in its governmental position. The desire for external forces on Burundian territory was not existent on either side. Thus, by agreeing to Ould-Abdallah's process, the belligerents found the least common denominator to avoid such intervention. Further through discussing the power-sharing agreement, both factions hoped for more influence. FRODEBU saw that it could help to get a bit of support to manifest its position in government given that the governmental positions were mainly held by Tutsis; and UPRONA hoped for the legitimatization for holding its positions in office through the agreement as well as gaining more influence through power-sharing, which proved to be a successful strategy given that the Prime Ministership was given to them as an outcome of the negotiations (cf. International Crisis Group 1998b, p.1), manifested also in the election of Sylvestre Ntibantunganya as president on 1 October 1994. He was elected by the Parliament with the support of UPRONA. However, this vote went hand in hand with "a series of concessions that weakened the presidency", as then US Ambassador Robert Krueger noted in his account on his time in Burundi (Krueger/Krueger 2007, p.74). The series of concessions included that all legislation and decrees had to be signed by both the President and (Tutsi) prime minister, that 55% of all major appointments would go to FORDEBU and its allied parties and 45% to UPRONA and its affiliated parties, and that a National Security Council was established with unelected members but so-called 'wise men' to advise on government policy and disputes (cf. Krueger/Krueger 2007, p.74). Thus, the Convention and the political developments actually supported the 'creeping coup' and helped to restore actual leverage to the Tutsi parties. The belligerents took advantage of the peace initiation in order to further their opposing means and not to sincerely negotiate a peaceful co-existence.

As the further course of events showed, the power-sharing agreement facilitated by Ould-Abdallah neither brought an ease to the tensions or even peace to Burundi, nor did it prevent another coup d'état. Thus, it seems it was rather a toothless document that did not make any real change to the distribution of power in Burundi, except for indirectly supporting the 'creeping coup'. It was negotiated and signed by moderate elements from the respective political parties; none of the armed wings signed the Convention. The moderate elements were not in charge of the overall situation. The few moderate politicians, willing to negotiate, were dominated by the extremist parties like the CNDD-FDD or PARENA (cf. Mehler 1995, p.26). As it was formulated in the UN report of the Security Council Mission to Burundi in February 1995, "those extremists have usurped the political initiative, at the expense of the moderate elements who [...] have been silenced through threat and intimidation" (United Nations 1995a, p.4). The Convention was not supported internally or externally. Brachet and Wolpe expressed this as, it was "handicapped by the absence of a power willing to take the lead on either the diplomatic or, with the UN Secretary General's call for a contingent peacekeeping force unanswered, on the security front" (Brachet/ Wolpe 2005, p.2). Conflict ripeness was not given throughout the process and the negotiations were not taken seriously by any of the parties.

This analysis implies that the independent variables were not relevant due to the entire lack of conflict ripeness. As none of the first level variables was fulfilled, the second level variables could not influence the intensity of any of these.

The second phase was marked by the mediation efforts of first Julius Nyerere and then after his death in late 1999 by Nelson Mandela. The approach taken by Nyerere meant a significant change to the overall peace efforts. During phase one, Ould-Abdallah had followed the approach of excluding the extremist factions from the peace process (cf. "My policy during my tenure in Burundi was not to incorporate declared extremists into the peace process" (Ould-Abdallah 2000, p.88)). This was not perceived very well by Secretary-General Boutros Boutros-Ghali who suggested that an inclusive peace process was more promising; leading ultimately to Ould-Abdallah's resignation from office in late 1995 (cf. Ould-Abdallah 2000, p.90). Thus the following attempts that were made tried to be as inclusive as possible and to bring all – both political and armed – factions to the negotiating table. Phase two went through a course of developments with four distinct periods, beginning in March 1996, when Julius Nyerere made the first attempts to approach President Ntibantunganya in the so-called Mwanza process (cf. Southall in Furley/May 2006, p. 206). Ntibantunganya asked for international military assistance to be deployed to Burundi (cf. Reyntjens 2009, p.41). However, upon the return from the negotiations, Ntibantunganya was threatened and sought refuge in the residence of the US Ambassador (cf. International Crisis Group 1998b, p.4). A coup d'état was conducted; it meant that the 'creeping coup' was – as noted by Filip Reyntjens – "made official when the former president Major Pierre Buyoya took over power again" (Reyntjens 2009, p.41). With that, an end was put to the initial peace efforts. The second period lasted from the coup d'état in July 1996 until June 1998. During this period, the peace process was stalled and no progress was made. As a reaction to the coup, the regional heads of state with support from the international community decreed sanctions and thus confronted Burundi with a wide-ranging embargo (cf. Reyntjens 2009, p.42). The situation changed with the third period in June 1998, when Buyoya agreed to peace negotiations. This period lasted until Nyerere's death in October 1999. Then, the last period of this phase began comprising of the negotiations mediated by Nelson Mandela that concluded with the signing of the Arusha Peace and Negotiations Agreement in August 2000.

In 1996, it must be assumed that Ntibantunganya had a strong perception of a hurting stalemate. The consequences of the 'creeping coup' had taken their effect. He realized that his and FRODEBU's actual leverage had almost diminished into nothing. UPRONA dominated most of the administration and had the advantage of controlling the military. The civil war had spread further, now raging in eleven out of fifteen Burundian provinces. As Reyntjens put it, "the government was divided and impotent, and Parliament did not function. Clearly, what was left of the system faced imminent implosion" (Reyntjens 2009, p.41). Ntibantunganya found himself facing a precipice of destruction. Thus, his only hope was to rely on a peace process that would ensure international support and backing for himself and his government (cf. Southall in Furley/May 2006, p.206). But Ntibantunganya and his followers did not represent all Hutu groups. Some parts of FRODEBU and especially other militarized Hutu groups "were alienated by the government's apparent appeasement of Tutsi domination, and increasingly argued that UPRONA, the army and the Tutsi political class would have to be militarily defeated if the Hutu were to enjoy the fruits of democracy" (Bentley/Southall, et al. 2005, p.55). Thus, not all Hutu groups perceived a hurting stalemate. Quite the contrary, some groups were strengthened in their willingness to militarily destroy the belligerent.

Similarly, the opponent, that is UPRONA and the affiliated parties did not perceive a hurting stalemate at that time. Quite the opposite: they were strengthened and had regained almost all power in the Burundian administration. Ntibantunganya's request for international assistance was thus perceived very poorly from their perspective (cf. Bentley/Southall, et al. 2005, p.56) and triggered the initiation of the coup d'état, which made it possible to retake the presidential office and re-install Buyoya as President of Burundi. Therefore, the perception of a hurting stalemate was also lacking throughout the years of 1996 and 1997. They felt strong and successful and not threatened by a precipice or a plateau (cf. Bentley/Southall, et al. 2005, p. 59 and Southall in Furley/May 2006, p.206).

After the military coup in 1996, the international community showed a strong interest in 'saving' Burundi from turning into 'another Rwanda'[149]. In 1998, the situation and perception of Buyoya and his followers changed (cf. Khadiagala 2007, p.137). As Dravis put it, "Burundi's prospects are dim" in 1998 (Dravis in Gurr 2000, p.192). The strict international community's embargo and sanctions left a mark on the Buyoya government (cf. Southall in Furley/May 2006, p.206). The administration started to recognize that their leverage was diminishing and that they needed outside support in order to restore the economy and address the great humanitarian disaster which was more and more unfolding in Burundi. The internal situation in Burundi had deteriorated significantly by 1998. Buyoya was not able to establish stability in the country

---

[149] 'Another Rwanda' in this context refers to the 1994 genocide. It is thus used as an expression stating that the international community was afraid that Burundi was at the risk of massive ethnic violence, amounting to genocide.

and violent conflict was still raging in all parts of the country. Furthermore, due to the embargo on Burundi, the economy had suffered greatly and was basically destroyed. For that reason, Buyoya had difficulty in maintaining his power base – he was increasingly rejected not only by the Hutu groups, but also by the majority of Tutsi groups (cf. Maundi in Sriram/Wermester 2003, p.343). Therefore, he felt a hurting stalemate – a situation, which he seemed not to be able to escape using his own power (cf. Mohammed Maundi in Sriram/ Wermester 2003).

The international community had large stakes in this development. After the first successful developments throughout 1998 with respect to the peace process, they pressured the regional powers to lift the embargo against Burundi, so that the people could feel the move towards peace and in that counter-act unrest in the country: "It must be possible for the people in Burundi to materially distinguish between the destructiveness of the conflict and the benefits of peace" (Nelson Mandela in December 2000, quoted in International Crisis Group 2003, p.ii). A further significant contribution to this development happened when in 1999 Julius Nyerere died and was replaced by Nelson Mandela as chief mediator in Arusha. Mandela was able to convince other statesmen to support this process, as for instance US President Clinton, who was called in to exert pressure (cf. Bentley/Southall, et al. 2005, p.71 and Reyntjens 2000, p.18). He also received continued confirmation from the international community, supporting the process (cf. United Nations 2000a, p.2). Thus, Buyoya had maneuvered Burundi into a largely isolated position where it received nothing but international economic and political pressure (cf. International Crisis Group 1998b, p.i). After two years without the possibility of international trade, two years of regional embargo and two years of a ban on international aid, the economic and social situation was highly critical in Burundi (cf. International Crisis Group 1999a, p.2).

Apart from the external pressure, Buyoya also felt the need for internal development, contributing to the perception of a hurting stalemate. The international pressure and sanctions took their effects upon the Burundian population. On the humanitarian level, the tragic résumé was one million people living as displaced persons or refugees in at least 300 camps in Burundi and more in neighboring countries. From 35% of the population living below the poverty line in 1990, the share of people living below the poverty line in 1997 had risen to 58%. Production levels fell by 5%, inflation was raging (cf. International Crisis Group 1999b, pp.1-3). The situation was disastrous; untenable for the government. The population suffered greatly. A hurting stalemate was perceived by all parties involved: the UPRONA government became more and more isolated from the rest of the country, including its own radical allies. On 25 August 1997 for example, a meeting took place in Arusha under the mediation of Julius Nyerere in which almost all parties, except for the government, took place – even the radical Tutsi parties such as Parena were present (cf. International Crisis Group 1998b, p.6 and Reyntjens 2009, p.179). As Reyntjens noted, "this rather surprising coalition, hardly conceivable six months earlier, declared that it supported the mediation efforts of Julius Nyerere and condemned Major Buyoya for his refusal to participate" (Reyntjens 2009, p.192). Buyoya had to react. He initiated the Internal Partnership for Peace (PIP). It showed that all parties involved acknowledged the need for change in Burundi. It was an initiative towards power-sharing between the main Tutsi and Hutu parties and led to two internal reforms. First, two vice-presidents were put in place rather than one prime minister – one of each party. Second, the twenty-two ministerial portfolios were split, so that the two parties each held eleven. Even though met with some criticism from abroad[150], this internal initiative was welcomed by the Arusha-facilitators as a good approach. It helped that Buyoya could be accepted as formal head of state by all parties involved in the peace process and thus serve as a basis for the further peace negotiation process. Hence, the peace program actually capitalized this move of the Burundian parties rather than bringing it into question in Arusha.

This shows that Buyoya knew he had to change the status quo and thus open up for a peace process. Both because of external and internal pressure, he perceived a hurting stalemate and thus was forced to act in order to find a solution. As a result, the Speaker of the National Assembly announced on 4 December 1997 that the government was ready to enter the peace process (cf. Reyntjens 2009, p.179). As a result, a round of negotiations was initiated in Arusha form 15 to 21 June 1998, where most of the Burundian participants in the conflict were present, in total 17 parties including the government, the National Assembly and 15 further factions (cf. International Crisis Group 1998a, pp.1-2).

Also the belligerent, the Hutu-dominated groups, perceived a hurting stalemate. They had lost all power in the government and had also largely lost the hope of being able to politically regain the power through a democratic process. The attempt in democracy had been undermined and overthrown by the old elites, so that this hope had been destroyed. The length of the conflict contributed to war weariness as did the effects that the international embargo entailed for the population. The Hutu as being the traditional poorer part of society in Burundi were the first to feel the deprivations. This contributed to the hurting

---

[150] Some observers of the process criticized the PIP because they feared that it would work against or in competition to the Arusha Negotiations.

stalemate. Additionally, a significant amount of external pressure was put on the military factions of the Hutu groups. Mandela especially was very outspoken in his criticism of the behavior of the armed groups (cf. Bentley/ Southall, et al. 2005, p.72). Given his international backing, this contributed to an increased feeling of a stalemate.

Regarding the SWO, it was largely Nyerere's achievement to offer the belligerent parties to sense a way out. He ensured that the peace process took careful steps in a controlled process. Nyerere led the negotiations' participants decide what issues should be discussed. Thus, the great achievement in mid-1998 was that the parties signed a joint declaration in which they listed five committees to be set up with themes on which they would further negotiate. These were the nature of the conflict, democracy and good governance, peace and security for all, reconstruction and economic development and finally guarantees for the application of a peace agreement. By setting such a foundation, Nyerere was able to communicate to the belligerents that negotiations do make sense as they had found a basis of topics to negotiate. Thus, Nyerere offered an SWO to all participants in the peace process. Therefore, by mid-1998, with determining the five categories of topics to negotiate, an SWO was given on part of all belligerents.

The perception of an SWO was further intensified with the change in mediator in late 1999. Nelson Mandela took a very determined approach to the conflict in that he was more direct and impatient and insisted on the direct involvement of all rebel factions in the talks. Furthermore, he challenged the Burundian political class on its 'inflexibility'. For instance, in January 2000 Mandela condemned Buyoya's government for the continued detention of hundreds of thousands of civilians in camps as part of a re-groupement policy. He went on in stating that Burundi would not return to peace "if the Tutsi maintained a monopoly in power politics, the military, and the economy" (Reyntjens 2000, p.17). This uncompromising tone brought a new dimension to the Burundian peace process. Buyoya tried to accommodate and announced in the same month that the camps were to be closed down (cf. Bentley/Southall, et al. 2005, p.72). It showed the participants on the belligerent sides that Nelson Mandela was committed and that he did have a master plan for the resolution of conflict in mind. He therefore contributed to a stronger perception of an SWO. His method was offering creative ideas on how to proceed with the actual peace agreement. He came up with the idea of establishing a transitional government for 18 months, which would consist of two terms. The first would be governed by present President Buyoya, and the second by a representative of the Hutu parties. During this transitional period, major reforms should be approached and a ceasefire was supposed to be signed, so that these developments towards full democracy would already be under way prior to the next presidential elections. This was a proposal for an SWO that all parties involved could agree on.

Mandela succeeded in delivering the message that the status quo was not tenable any longer and that a change towards peace had to be found. And he offered the solution of how such a change could be made. He communicated that there was no other way than sensing a way out. The belligerents had to perceive that the only possible way to proceed was to come to a conclusion by way of signing a peace agreement. Thus, Mandela leveraged the MHS in combination with the SWO, intensified the perception and was therefore successful in achieving the objective of a conclusion of a peace agreement – or as summarized by Southall, "Mandela used a mix of international pressure, arm-twisting and argument to propel the talks to a conclusion" (Southall in Furley/May 2006, p.207).

Having asserted that both an MHS and an SWO were apparent in phase two, particularly from 1998 onwards, it is now interesting to turn to the independent variables, evaluating whether they affected the conflict ripeness.

Nyerere and Mandela actively and very successfully used the instrument of persuasion continuously to further strengthen the variable of the SWO. They were able to further develop the SWO to all belligerents by leading a smart mediation process (cf. the focus on the five issue categories at the outset of the negotiations) and by bringing in creative ideas at times of potential deadlocks (cf. the idea of establishing a transitional power-sharing government). Thus persuasion positively affected ripeness.

Besides persuasion, pressure played a significant role in manifesting conflict ripeness. Both belligerents, the Buyoya administration with its affiliated parties and factions as well as the opposition were objectively exhausted. War had raged on for many years, the economy was destroyed through the embargo, an uncountable number of people lived in IDP-camps or as refugees in the neighboring countries, and Burundi was both regionally and internationally isolated (cf. International Crisis Group 1998b, p.i). Therefore, resources were exhausted and war weariness present on all sides. As seen in the analysis, the mediator leveraged this situation by putting additional pressure on the belligerents. While Ould-Abdallah had not enjoyed major leverage or powerful backing in phase one, both Nyerere and Mandela were supported by the regional powers as well as the international community. They were able to coordinate efforts with these countries regarding sanctions and the embargo, which fostered their credibility in the peace process towards the belligerents. Therefore, pressure was used consciously and as a result positively affected conflict ripeness.

Also inducements were used as part of the mediator's strategy. Having built up pressure through the embargo, it was possible for the mediators to offer inducements in terms of lifting the sanctions if compliance with the peace process was ensured. Both belligerents were keen on having the sanctions lifted. The reason was that economically, the country needed external relations in order to be able to return to economic growth – even on a minimum level given that Burundi had been highly dependent on exporting products. On the humanitarian level, Burundi was not able to sustain itself. It was already highly dependent on external aid, however, only a minimum was delivered to the camps. With the lifting of sanctions, the population and the administration hoped for an amelioration of the overall situation. Furthermore, the mediators were clever in sharing the information of an additional inducement that might interest the parties and contribute to their participation in the peace process: the possibility to be included in a future government (cf. Lemarchand in Khadiagala/International Peace Academy 2006, p.50). Therefore, offering inducements positively affected conflict ripeness.

Regarding the non-manipulable independent variables, a different picture is offered. A change in leadership only had an effect at the beginning of the phase. Hutu President Ntibantunganya indicated that he found the peace process very helpful, in fact, it seemed this external diplomatic intervention was the only way for him to be able to handle the 'creeping coup' that had basically left him without leverage in his own country. Thus, he was the only belligerent perceiving a hurting stalemate as was seen by the further course of events with respect to the coup d'état ousting him from the office of President. Thus when Buyoya initially took over leadership, the potential for conflict ripeness was ruined. In 1996, Buyoya had no interest in a peace process. In this context, the change in leadership at the beginning of phase two negatively affected conflict ripeness. In the further course of events though, there was no other change in leadership, so that this independent variable did not affect conflict ripeness at a later stage.

The assertiveness of leadership was not directly relevant in this context as Buyoya and the Tutsi elite as well as their opponents from the Hutu side, particularly FRODEBU, did not show any signs of insecurities that would have led to inconsistencies in their leadership or their groups. However, when looking at the broader context of all Hutu groups, defections could be noticed. Not all groups followed FRODEBU in their directives. During phase two in the Burundian case, the intention was for an inclusive process, meaning that all parties – both political and armed – were supposed to be included in the peace negotiation process (cf. Mottiar/Van Jaarsveld 2009, p.31). But two factions defected from this process, namely the FNL and the FDD. Eventually, those two parties did not sign the peace agreement in 2000. This defection – seen as an involuntary defection by their associated 'mother' party FRODEBU who was hoping to come to an agreement and by that terminate the conflict – negatively affected conflict ripeness. It led to a situation in which the overall process was endangered and in which individuals feared that the defections had the potential to destroy the overall peace efforts. As Southall put it, "unable to break a deadlock within the rebel ranks as to who should represent them, Nyerere ultimately chose to recognize the existing leaderships and to exclude those who had turned against them. This was a crucial moment, for the major elements of the FDD and FNL now remained at war, at odds with the Arusha process" (Southall in Furley/May 2006, p.207). Some observers also stated that the Arusha Peace and Reconciliation Agreement should be judged as not successful exactly for the reason that the FDD and FNL did not sign (cf. Bercovitch/Fretter 2004, p.97; Curtis 2003, p.1 and International Crisis Group 2001, p.ii). Given the later course of events in phase three, thus with the advantage of hindsight, one can state that the peace agreement was crucial as a basis for the further process. The defections by those two groups threatened the overall process in the sense of negatively affecting ripeness, in fact weakening conflict ripeness as the SWO was impacted. However, it did not destroy ripeness and the subsequent development. When looking at changes in the status of external support to the belligerents, it must be noted that the significant changes occurred before. Due to the stop of support, ripeness was created. In that sense, no further changes occurred thereafter. The withdrawal of support lasted; however, no changes could be identified. Therefore, it is possible to assume that this independent variable had no effect on conflict ripeness.

In conclusion, conflict ripeness could be identified in the latter period of phase two. At the outset, the situation seemed favorable, however it was destroyed by the coup d'état in 1996. Then, conflict ripeness was not apparent. Two years later though, the situation in the state had deteriorated significantly. Both because of internal and external pressure, an MHS was given. Also an SWO was apparent that was further intensified through the means of persuasion, pressure and inducements by the mediators. Overall conflict ripeness was thus further positively affected because of a powerful mediator who enjoyed large backing from regional powers as well as the international community, and offering inducements regarding the smart use of sanctions and tactical lifting of sanctions. Slight negative effects were experienced because of the change in leadership in 1996 and the involuntary defections through the FDD and FNL in 2000. But these factors did not destroy ripeness. All in all, "the signing of the Arusha Accord, imperfect and incomplete though it was, constituted a major achievement" (Southall in Furley/May 2006, p.218). The success can be attributed to the fact that the situation was ripe for resolution.

However, with the signing of the Peace Agreement, the conflict was not terminated. As mentioned above, the conflict continued on a different level with the two armed Hutu rebel groups, the FDD and the FNL, who had not signed the peace agreement in August 2000. It does not render the Arusha Peace Agreement meaningless, but implied a further challenge for Burundi to be tackled in parallel – a transformation of the conflict to a different level. The former belligerents FRODEBU and UPRONA were part of a power-sharing agreement, now acting as one actor in the form of the government, and the two rebel groups functioned as two more parties to the conflict.

Thus, it is now to be asked, whether conflict ripeness existed at any point in the third phase (2000-2006), in which a peace effort was made to pacify the last remaining belligerent actors in the Burundian conflict, with the main facilitator being South African Deputy President Jacob Zuma.

Similar to phase two, this phase also underwent a development. As outlined above, neither the FDD nor the FNL were willing to sign the peace agreement in August 2000 and none of the two perceived any kind of conflict ripeness at that point. The two Hutu rebel groups still felt underprivileged and in a position to win the conflict militarily rather than politically. They thus continued their violent insurgency.

The situation changed with the peace agreement in place and the successful implementation thereof. The first party to acknowledge or rather feel this change was the CNDD-FDD. When the transition to the Hutu president was implemented smoothly and they saw that Buyoya stepped back from the office without any problems, the CNDD-FDD started perceiving a hurting stalemate (cf. International Crisis Group 2004b, p.1). They realized that they were losing internal support. The people were generally weary of the war (cf. Brachet/Wolpe 2005, p.3) and felt the amelioration of the living conditions through the slow lifting of the sanctions against Burundi. Therefore, they were not willing to support the armed rebel groups anymore. Also the units of the FDD steadily decreased after the Arusha Peace Agreement because of defections (cf. International Crisis Group 2001, p.5).

The CNDD-FDD, judged as not as extreme and radical as the FNL, therefore felt that their situation had reached a plateau. As a rebel group, they were able to continue fighting, at the same time realizing that it seemed largely impossible for them to overthrow the government or to start a large scale campaign at least. Militarily, the FDD was increasingly weakened by the defections, but also by additional military pressure facing them in battles against the Burundian Armed Forces (cf. International Crisis Group 2002a, p.10) as well as the Tanzanian army who fought the FDD at the border in Kigoma (cf. International Crisis Group 2002a, p.11). The insurgency also made less sense given that the political situation had significantly improved for the Hutu population – thus, the incentive for fighting had disappeared. Furthermore, the current situation was backed not only by regional powers, but by the international community. They did not have to fear another Tutsi overthrow of the government. Therefore, the CNDD-FDD felt a hurting stalemate in their position.

They also saw a way out of the situation. Thus, an SWO existed. Their perception of the situation was twofold. Firstly, there was a mediation team in place, continuously trying to initiate sincere negotiations between them and the government. Thus, the infrastructure for a way out was given. The second ingredient for the SWO was the possibility to achieve more on a political level than through military means as. Free and democratic elections were coming up in 2005, and the CNDD-FDD realized that this was an opportunity for them to enter the government by legitimate means. Furthermore, as part of the peace agreement, the CNDD-FDD was promised to be integrated into the power-sharing agreement, i.e. immediately being able to participate in the government (cf. Southall in Furley/May 2006, pp. 213-214). Thus, it must be assumed that an SWO was perceived.

Similarly, only months later, the situation changed with regard to the FNL's perception. Being more radical, they did not see their chance to enter the government through democratic elections in 2005. They also hung on to their military idea longer than the CNDD-FDD. However, when on 16 November 2003, the CNDD-FDD signed the Global Ceasefire Agreement, they realized that they were the only faction left in Burundi militarily fighting against the government. This not only had a major impact on the FNL with regard to the morale, but also militarily. The FNL being the smaller of the two armed rebel groups with an estimated 3,000 troops in 2002 (cf. International Crisis Group 2002b, p.5) faced a national army that had integrated the fighters of the FDD. The FDD, accustomed to the rebels' tactics, supported the national army significantly, so that militarily, the FNL had also lost most of its comparative power (cf. International Crisis Group 2004b, p.i and International Crisis Group 2007b, p.2).

Facilitator Zuma declared the peace process 'irreversible', and thus put more pressure on the FNL (cf. Southall in Furley/May 2006, p.214). Furthermore, external pressure increased in parallel when in June 2004, the UN military peacekeeping force, ONUB, was deployed to Burundi under Chapter VII of the UN Charter, entitled to use all necessary means to establish peace in Burundi (cf. Issaka/Bushoki 2005, p.5 and United Nations 2004c, p.4). Thus, the FNL suddenly faced an international army fighting against them. This significantly contributed to a perceived hurting stalemate. The final change to their perception happened in 2005 when the FNL witnessed how the CNDD-FDD succeeded in the national elections in August of that year. Not only did the peace process prove successful in that free and fair elections were held in Burundi, but the FNL also saw that a former armed rebel group was able to win the elections and become accepted by the people of Burundi – both the Tutsi and Hutu groups – and the international community as the legitimate incumbent of the presidential office (cf. Jackson, S. 2006, p.19 and United Nations 2005a). This took away the reason for the FNL to continue fighting and thus the support of the population for its insurgency. Vandeginste summarized this situation, "in addition to other important factors like internal divisions and increased military weakness, it was the successful negotiation (and implementation) of the earlier power-sharing agreements (Arusha and the GCA) that forced PALIPEHUTU-FNL to moderate its position and to enter into negotiations from early 2004 onwards. With the agreed ethnic parity in the defense and security forces and the representations of Hutu at all levels of the state, in particularly after the 2005 elections, the movement had lost much of its ideological raison d'être" (Vandeginste 2009, p.80). The FNL thus perceived a hurting stalemate and an SWO, similar to the FDD some two to three years earlier.

It is possible to state that conflict ripeness was apparent for the case of the CNDD-FDD and the government in 2003, facilitating the signing of a peace agreement as well as for the case of the FNL and the government in 2005/2006, also facilitating the signing of a peace agreement, constituting the end to the last armed rebel group in Burundi. The reason is that an MHS and an SWO were not only perceived by the respective armed rebel groups FDD and FNL, but also by the government. The government, first in the transitional constellation and then followed by the Nkurunziza administration from 2005 onwards, perceived hurting stalemates and an SWO with regard to the conflict against the rebel groups. The reasoning for the hurting stalemate was threefold. Firstly, the government depended largely upon the support of the population. The population had become very much tired of the continued warfare, especially coupled with the economic sanctions and embargo that had destroyed the economy and led to a disastrous humanitarian situation. Secondly, the government and the army were very feeble in their new formation after 2000. Thus, they had a great interest in putting an end to the armed rebellion and integrating those two remaining factions into the peace process from Arusha. The continued warfare against the rebel groups not only financially hurt the government, but also demanded significant amounts of resources and energy. Thus, this contributed to the perception of a hurting stalemate. Lastly, enormous pressure was put on the government to try to come to a conclusion of the conflict. The pressure was put in the form of holding back assistance, promising to deliver upon further steps in the peace process. These three reasons combined constituted a strong hurting stalemate on part of the government. It was supported by the sense of a way out offered by the continued facilitation of South Africa, especially Jacob Zuma, who offered a peaceful way out by trying to integrate the two remaining armed factions into the power-sharing agreements. Therefore, conflict ripeness can thus be identified during phase three as both ingredients to ripeness; an MHS and an SWO were established. How were these situations affected by independent variables?

The three manipulable independent variables were all used in a smart strategy put in place by the mediator who connected persuasion with pressure and inducements. The successful implementation of the Arusha Peace Agreement was underway, showing that the transitional government was possible and implemented successfully and showing in the second case that national free and fair elections could be held, bringing the former rebel group CNDD-FDD into the presidential office. This was a possibility for the mediator to persuade the belligerents by showing them that such implementation of peace agreements can indeed work and further, it was sweetened by offering inducements that positively affected conflict ripeness in the two cases: Jacob Zuma proved to be a sensitive mediator who was able to establish contact to the groups offering them an SWO and keeping them involved and informed about all developments. Jacob Zuma also had the advantage of enjoying international and regional support, so that his leverage was significant as seen by the support through peacekeeping troops, which in turn put pressure on the belligerents. Thus, he was able to communicate the offer of inducements. With respect to the CNDD-FDD, he was able to convey that they were allowed and encouraged to take part in the national elections, which offered them a way to gain influence through political instead of military means. Similarly the FNL was offered to become a political party and thus leave the life of a rebel group behind and legitimately enter the political stage. The inducements also comprised of potential financial, humanitarian and development assistance. As Southall expressed it, "South Africa's leadership was encouraged by the international community [...], which although largely sitting on the sidelines, made indications throughout the successive phases of negotiations that financial, humanitarian and development support would be forthcoming if sustainable progress towards peace could be achieved" (Southall in Furley/May 2006, p.218). Thus conflict ripeness was positively affected by this combination of persuasion, inducements and pressure. It was further strengthened by the additional deployment of peacekeeping troops that put significant military pressure on the belligerents. First, the AU mission, then followed by ONUB militarily fought the remaining armed groups.

Thus, the manipulable independent variables were used and leveraged wisely by the mediator significantly strengthening the perception of an MHS and an SWO, so that the level of intensity of conflict ripeness was positively affected. The non-manipulable independent variables, however, did not affect conflict ripeness. No change in leadership occurred and the assertiveness of the leadership in the individual rebel groups as well as the state actor did not allow for illoyalities or defections. Apart from development aid, no other external support was offered to the belligerents. The effect of development aid will be discussed below.

To sum up the analysis of conflict ripeness in the Burundian case, it is possible to state that the first phase lacked any indication of ripeness. Neither an MHS nor MEOs or an SWO were apparent. The belligerents had no interest in a peaceful negotiation process and the few moderate elements opting for peace were not in charge of the situation. The extremists of both parties were in charge and had the perception that they could both win against their opponent by using military means. The second phase, however, went through a course of development. Even though starting on very fragile feet, with the support of external pressure, conflict ripeness could be established. The ripeness was used intelligently to advance the peace process. Independent variables functioned as intensifier of the level of conflict ripeness. Similarly the third phase with a focus on different actors was characterized by further developments. This time, it was rather internal factors contributing to the establishment of ripeness as the progression towards democratic forms of government took away the moral foundation for the insurgencies. Both an MHS and an SWO could be identified in the two cycles of negotiation.

5.2.2.2 Increase in Development Aid

Coming to the second part of the analysis, the focus now lies on the question of whether an increase in development aid can be noted in any of the three phases of peace efforts. In order to grasp the full overview of the aid landscape, this chapter is structured into three sections. Firstly, the provision of official development assistance will be analyzed. Secondly, 'other' development aid will be examined including debt relief, initiatives concerning the peace process, and other contributions. Finally, the findings will be brought together in a conclusion analyzing the overall aid situation in Burundi throughout the three phases. To start with ODA, net disbursements, similarly to the Ugandan case, were formally tracked by the OECD (cf. Organization for Economic Cooperation and Development 2010). All donors taken together contributed total disbursements as summarized in the graph below. All the following charts are based on data provided by the OECD (cf. Organization for Economic Cooperation and Development 2010).

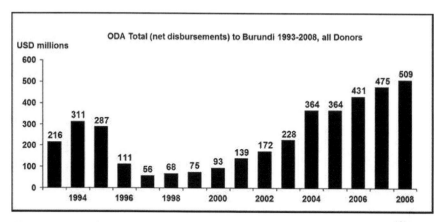

Figure 16: Total ODA to Burundi, Net Disbursements in millions of US$[151]

The graph above shows that while the amount of ODA delivered increased until 1994, it decreased significantly as of 1995, only slowly increasing again after 1997. In 2003, it again reached an amount of over US$ 200 million. It then increased further reaching a level of more than US$ 400 million in 2006.

When looking at the individual contributions of the donor groups, split in bilateral and multilateral assistance, it becomes clear that bilateral and multilateral donors spent about an equal amount of the total disbursement over the period of time under analysis.

---

[151] Source: Data by the OECD: Organization for Economic Cooperation and Development "World Development Indicators", own illustration.

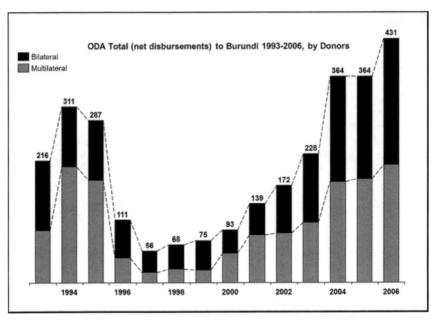

Figure 17: Total ODA to Burundi in millions of US$ by Donor[152]

What is interesting to note about the disbursements to Burundi throughout the years 1993 to 2006 is that the largest individual donors on the bilateral side were France in 1993, Germany in 1994 until 1997, France again in 1998, the US in 1999, Belgium in 2000, the Netherlands in 2001, and the US again from 2002 until 2006. It shows that there was not one individual bilateral donor, dominating the aid provision. When looking at to what extent ODA changed from year to year in percentage points, the graph below helps to visualize the results:

---

[152] Source: Data by the OECD: Organization for Economic Cooperation and Development "World Development Indicators", own illustration.

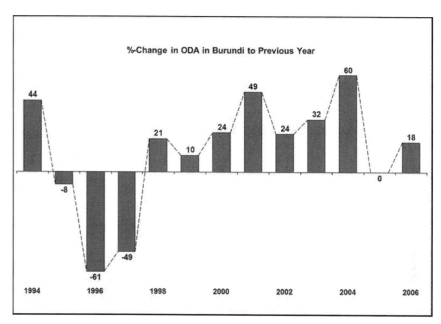

Figure 18: %-Change in ODA in Burundi to Previous Year[153]

The graph demonstrates that a significant loss in ODA was observed in 1996: minus 61%. Significant increases of ODA could be seen in 1998 with 21%, 2001 with 49% and again in 2004 with 60%. Overall from 1993 until 2006, Burundi received an increase of 100% compared to its initial ODA in the timeframe under analysis. The increase from the lowest point onwards, which was in 1997 with US$ 56 million of ODA, to the highest point in 2006 of US$ 431 million, was 666%. This constitutes a significant increase in ODA during the assessed period of time (cf. Organization for Economic Cooperation and Development 2010).

The differences in the provision of ODA can be explained with the historical developments in Burundi. The strong decrease in ODA observed in 1996 and 1997 is explained by the international embargo put on Burundi. Besides the economic sanctions, the embargo also meant that no international aid (or almost none) was provided to Burundi apart from the delivery of basic human needs in the form of relief to IDP- and refugee-camps (cf. International Crisis Group

---

[153] Source: Data by the OECD: Organization for Economic Cooperation and Development "World Development Indicators", own illustration.

1999b, p.4). Even before the embargo was put in place, the international community had decided in 1995 to halt aid given the difficult security situation in Burundi. Only emergency aid was still delivered (cf. Ould-Abdallah 2000, p.83). With the slow lifting of sanctions, ODA increased again over the subsequent years.

Apart from the ODA, other development assistance also entered Burundi. First, debt relief should be mentioned. In August 2005, Burundi qualified for a World Bank debt relief program, lowering Burundi's debt service payments by about US$ 1.5 billion in nominal terms (World Bank 2006 and cf. Issaka/ Bushoki 2005, p.5). Burundi was thus the 28th country to reach the decision point under the enhanced HIPC Initiative[154].

Further, the individual peace initiatives as outlined above received significant support, also qualifying as IDA. The phase two effort led by Nyerere and followed up by Mandela received a total of US$ 15 million from international donors in order to be able to facilitate the negotiation process (cf. Bentley/Southall, et al. 2005, p.65 and International Crisis Group 2000a, p.1).

Linked to the peace initiatives were the four peacekeeping forces deployed to Burundi. They must also be counted into the overall picture of IDA. From November 2001 until 2003, South Africa deployed troops (SAPSD), from 2003 to 2004 this task was taken over by the OAU deploying AMIB, followed by ONUB until 2006. In 2007, the AU Special Task Force took over. The strengths of the deployed forces ranged between 1,000 to almost 4,000 troops. Thus, a considerable amount of personnel, material, and other external influx entered Burundi. The ONUB alone had an estimated amount of expenditures of US$ 678 million[155]. AMIB was financed through a fund that had to cover a budget of about US$ 134 million (cf. Svensson 2008, p.13).

Additionally, many NGOs entered Burundi with two different missions mainly beginning during phase two. As John Prendergast noted, by 1995, almost all aid agencies had withdrawn from Burundi due to security reasons: "Burundi has perhaps become the most dangerous country in the Greater Horn for aid operations. At least ten aid workers were killed in 1995, and dozens of grenade attacks, ambushes along roads, landmine incidents, and armed assaults have occurred. Many agencies have restricted their operations" (Prendergast/Center of Concern 1996, p.19). However, starting in the late 1990s with a promising peace initiation underway, the aid organizations (re-)entered the country. On the one hand, there were the NGOs delivering humanitarian aid. This effort was spurred

---

[154] The completion point was reached four years later in 2009.
[155] Cf. http://www.un.org/en/peacekeeping/missions/past/onub/index.html.

by the international embargo on Burundi. Thus, international NGOs took over increasing responsibility for "providing social services" (International Crisis Group 2003, p.8). The ICG counted 57 international NGOs by 2003 dedicated to humanitarian assistance (cf. International Crisis Group 2003, p.8).

On the other hand, there were multiple conflict resolution NGOs trying to promote peace as part of their individual development assistance to Burundi (cf. Ould-Abdallah 2000, p.85). Lemarchand counted seventeen such international NGOs having entered Burundi between 1994 and 2006 (cf. Lemarchand in Khadiagala/International Peace Academy 2006, p.41). Organizations such as the Carter Center, Sant'Egidio, or SfCG tried to initiate peace-efforts that would revive a democratization process. Also individuals, such as Jan Van Eck as a member of the African National Congress in the South African Parliament tried to initiate what he called "track 2 facilitations" in parallel (cf. Jan Van Eck's account on his experiences from 1996 onwards: Jan Van Eck in Reychler/ Paffenholz 2001, pp.81-90). But until 1998, all of these initiatives proved fruitless (cf. Lemarchand in Khadiagala/International Peace Academy 2006, p.41). Some academics such as Hara even argued that the "profusion of players" in Burundi at the time undermined the coherence of the international community's response and led to competition (Fabienne Hara in Crocker/ Hampson, et al. 1999, p.135). These initiatives were put in place throughout the 1990s and also the following years thereafter. Devon Curtis noted that, "Burundi has sometimes been called a laboratory for conflict resolution approaches", referring to the numerous different initiatives (cf. Curtis 2003, p.1).

Summarizing, this leaves us with the following IDA situations in Burundi: in phase one from 1993 to 1995, no significant IDA could be noted apart from a slight increase in ODA. However, the level of ODA was relatively low in general. Burundi seemed not to be a priority topic for the international community. Therefore, apart from the UN mediation effort through the Special Representative of the Secretary-General, no large influx entered Burundi.

More significant in terms of developments of IDA was phase two from 1996 to 2000. Here, Burundi was first challenged with a significant decrease in ODA and an increase later. ODA went up by about 66% during the period from 1997 to 2000. Furthermore, during phase two the peace initiative of Nyerere and Mandela started. Their efforts were funded with US$ 15 million by the international community. Parallel to the embargo from the early years of that phase, Burundi witnessed a kind of 'mushrooming' of international NGOs entering the country. These NGOs both delivered large amounts of humanitarian aid as well as tried to promote conflict resolution. Despite not being able to clearly quantify these efforts, they do constitute an increase in development aid.

In phase three the increase of overall IDA was even more significant. ODA rose by 210% from 2001 until 2006. Additionally, Burundi was granted acceptance for a debt relief program of about US$ 1.5 billion. Furthermore, four peace-keeping missions entered Burundi, starting in 2001, and provided for further increases in development aid.

All in all, it can thus be stated that phase one and the beginning of phase two witnessed decreases in development aid. However, after the initial decrease, phase two and phase three were characterized by significant increases of development aid. Thus, IDA was given in these latter years of the conflict. The form of IDA included all three types as described above. Financial and technical assistance were provided as well as personnel dedicated to development work.

5.2.2.3 Effect of Increase in Development Aid on Ripeness

Having analyzed individual phases of the Burundian conflict, periods of conflict ripeness could be identified and an increase in development aid was observed at specific times. Now, these findings will be brought together and it will be assessed whether a correlation can be established between the two variables of IDA and conflict ripeness. Further, the quality of correlation – if identified – will be evaluated.

To summarize the findings from above, the conflict was analyzed structured into three phases. The first phase starting with the assassination of the first democratically elected president of Burundi, Ndadaye in October 1993, ended in September 1995 with the resignation of Special Representative of the Secretary-General, Ould-Abdallah, after he tried to initiate a peace process. The second phase followed and was marked by the last months of Ntibantunganya in the presidential office before Pierre Buyoya was reinstalled as president in a coup d'état overthrowing the elected government in July 1996. This phase saw a peace effort by Julius Nyerere, followed up upon his death by Nelson Mandela in 1999, receiving strong international backing. It concluded with the signing of the Arusha Peace and Reconciliation Agreement in August 2000 that provided a blueprint for a power-sharing government and a reform of key institutions, prescribing a 36-month transitional period (cf. Brachet/Wolpe 2005, p.2). But not all conflict parties signed the agreement. Two armed rebel groups, the FNL and the FDD did not take part in the peace process. The conflict with them marked the third phase, starting after the signing of the Arusha Agreement and lasting until 2006. The third phase is characterized by three significant milestones: the signing of the Global Ceasefire Agreement with the FDD in November 2003, the national elections held in 2005, and the signing of the Comprehensive Ceasefire Agreement with the FNL in September 2006.

During the three phases, different levels of conflict ripeness could be identified. In phase one, neither an MHS/MEOs nor an SWO were apparent to the belligerents. Thus in phase one, conflict ripeness did not exist. Phase two saw a development. At the very beginning of that phase – the first months until Ntibantunganya was ousted from the office – at least one of the belligerents felt a hurting stalemate and demonstrated a sense for a way out. The other belligerents though did not perceive hurting stalemates nor were they willing to make any kind of compromises. Instead, they overthrew the government. Thus, the first feeble signs for ripeness were destroyed. Then for the next two years until 1998, no actual changes were observed with respect to the perception of an MHS/MEOs or an SWO on part of any of the belligerents. Yet by 1998, the situation changed. Internal and external pressure had led to a point at which the belligerents perceived a hurting stalemate, constituting an MHS. The threshold for conflict ripeness was passed, when strong mediation skills could also establish an SWO so that ripeness existed in the years between 1998 and 2000. The third phase of the Burundian conflict from 2000 to 2006 witnessed two individual peace processes – one with the FNL, and one with the FDD. Each subsequently experienced conflict ripeness as both groups seemed to perceive a hurting stalemate and an SWO respectively.

With regard to IDA, a similar development could be noted. While phase one saw no significant change in aid, phase two was much more interesting. It began with a significant decrease in overall development aid, followed by an overall significant increase. Phase three was characterized by a steady increase in development aid. These findings are summarized in the following table.

	Phase 1: 1993-1995	Phase 2: 1996-2000	Phase 3: 2000-2006
Conflict Ripeness	No	Yes	Yes
IDA	No	Yes	Yes

Table 13: Overview Conflict Ripeness and IDA in Burundi[156]

---

[156] Source: Own illustration.

The table demonstrates that it is possible to disregard phase one with respect to analyzing the potential effect of IDA as an independent variable on conflict ripeness. More interesting for the analysis are phases two and three.

What happened in phase two was a significant decrease in development aid with a subsequent increase. This happened in parallel to a development towards ripeness. In what sense are these two variables connected? When analyzing the individual mechanisms leading to the perception of ripeness on part of the belligerents in-depth, it becomes clear that they mainly depended upon two factors: the perception of an SWO was triggered through skillful mediation while the perception of an MHS was built up due to external pressure. What happened was that on the initiative of regional powers together with the mediator Julius Nyerere, an embargo was put on Burundi. The embargo included trade, but also general assistance. Furthermore, the embargo was taken up by the international community, so that international development aid was largely cut off. Except for individual humanitarian efforts that provided IDPs and refugees with basic needs, almost all development assistance was stopped as a reaction to the coup d'état in 1996. Thus, Burundi suffered from economic isolation that implied the termination of development aid.

The direct consequence from this policy by the international community was the perception of a hurting stalemate on part of the government as well as also the Burundian people. All parties were affected by the consequences of the embargo. A humanitarian disaster unfolded in Burundi being cut off and isolated from the rest of the world in economic terms. As the ICG described it, "given five years of war, two and a half years of an embargo and no international aid, the state coffers are empty and the socio-economic situation is catastrophic" (International Crisis Group 1999b, p.ii). The situation became untenable and the parties were willing to agree to alternatives other than continued fighting in order to bring change to the country. The government under the leadership of Buyoya realized that they were dependent on external support and economic relations and thus had no other option than to comply with demands from the international donor community. Thus, conflict ripeness in this case was largely created through external actors who established an embargo. When the situation had deteriorated so much that the belligerents showed signs for a willingness to negotiate sincerely, the external powers reacted and started lifting sanctions.

Now, a crucial difference was made compared to other similar situations. Once Buyoya and the opposition parties perceived a hurting stalemate and had a sense for a way out and once they thus came together to negotiate sincerely, the mediators were able to control the influx to Burundi: "At Nyerere's request, donors maintained a de facto embargo on development aid " (International Crisis Group 2000c, p.17). They did not allow for a total lifting of sanctions immediately, nor did they allow for uncoordinated influx of development aid by different actors (cf. Bentley/Southall, et al. 2005, p.77). Instead, Burundi witnessed an outstanding initiative of coordination with regard to donors including NGOs under the leadership of the mediators. Individual donor conferences were held and an initiative was founded called the Consolidated Appeal that included NGOs. Under the auspices of the UN Humanitarian Coordinator, UN agencies, bilateral donors and NGOs came together in August 1998 for the first time to discuss the humanitarian situation and how they could proceed in a coordinated and effective way in order not to destroy the moment of opportunity in Burundi. It was clear to them – on explanation by Julius Nyerere – that they could not simply lift the sanctions and resume all economic relations and development aid, but that they had to proceed carefully, so that the pressure that had been built up beforehand could be used constructively in order to ensure a further successful peace process.

The outcome was the Consolidated Inter-Agency Appeal for Burundi by the Office for the Coordination of Humanitarian Affairs in December 1998 (cf. Bentley/Southall, et al. 2005, p.29). It was an institution that met once a year for the following decade in order to coordinate efforts and determine a common aid strategy. As part of the Appeal, each year a set of requirements was harmonized and formulated that would outline the needed input for the coming year. The table below summarizes the pledges made in the individual appeals (cf. United Nations 1998; United Nations 1999; United Nations 2000b; United Nations 2001; United Nations 2002; United Nations 2003b; United Nations 2004d; United Nations 2005b; United Nations 2006j).

1998	1999	2000	2001	2002	2003	2004	2005	2006
83.6	70.6	102.0	108.0	69.7	70.5	121.4	127.8	131.6

Table 14: Funds Requested by Consolidated Appeal in millions of US$[157]

These individual appeals comprised all intended projects of development aid for the coming year. These efforts were complemented by a range of donor conferences. In December 2000, Nelson Mandela initiated such a conference that

---

[157] Cf. United Nations Consolidated Inter-Agency Appeal 1998-2006.

eventually took place in Paris hosted by French President Jacques Chirac that pledged US$ 440 million for Burundi's reconstruction (cf. Bentley/Southall, et al. 2005, pp.81-82). Another conference took place in January 2004 initiated by Belgium and the UNDP at which the donors pledged a total of US$ 1 billion in support of Burundi (cf. Brachet/Wolpe 2005, p.3). As the UN noted, a whole range of coordination efforts had been put in place with sectoral committees including the UN, NGOs and bilateral donors, meeting on a periodic basis, a weekly Contact Group meeting presided over by the UN Humanitarian Coordinator, and provincial coordination committees (cf. United Nations 1998, p.viii).

What is particularly interesting in this context is that neither the money pledged in the donor conferences nor the projects listed in the inter-agency appeal were simply delivered or implemented. They were restricted on the fulfillment of conditions with respect to the establishment of transitional institutions and the cessation of hostilities (cf. Khadiagala 2007, p.173). Thus, an approach of conditional development aid was followed in Burundi in phase two; an approach that made compliance with the peace process decisive for the provision of assistance. It led to a situation, in which the belligerents realized that progress towards peace was linked to an improvement of the overall situation or as put by Bentley and Southall, "the Burundians needed to be assured that political progress would be matched by material social and economic advance" (Bentley/Southall, et al. 2005, p.81). This way of argument was taken up by the mediators, particularly Nelson Mandela, who realized that "donors therefore needed to make firm commitments to make emergency aid, humanitarian relief and long-term development assistance available in an integrated manner, and to ensure that the advances made were not negated by insistence upon the unreasonable repayment of debt" (Bentley/Southall, et al. 2005, p.81).

In phase three of the Burundian conflict post-2000, this approach of conditioned aid was further implemented. Both the donor conferences and the consolidated inter-agency appeal were tools in order to coordinate all development aid efforts. All different types of actors such as bilateral donors, multilateral institutions, and what is particularly interesting, NGOs were part of this initiative that remained controlled by the mediating team, that is Jacob Zuma and South Africa in the 2000-2006 phase. Also the individual peacekeeping troops were part of the coordination effort, so that the mediator was constantly in control of what influx came into the country.

The consequence of this conscious and controlled approach to development aid was that conflict ripeness was not destroyed despite the change in levels of development aid. A constant increase in development aid could be noted that was used in a carrot and stick approach (cf. International Crisis Group 2000c, p.24

and Southall in Furley/May 2006, p.207). This positively affected conflict ripeness and contributed significantly to the furthering of the peace process. With the careful provision of aid, the population and the government could experience what benefits a peace agreement would entail and in that sense strengthening the sense of the way out. Therefore, the intensity of the hurting stalemate was reduced over the years starting in 1998, however in parallel, the sense for a way out was strengthened. It is a mechanisms that Kristina Bentley and Roger Southall described as, "removal of sanctions indicated to the government the advantages that could follow from a return to peace" (Bentley/Southall, et al. 2005, pp.67-68). The overall level of conflict ripeness remained intact. What is meant by this analysis is that even though the hurting decreased due to the lifting of sanctions, ripeness was not compromised because the alternative was sweetened by inducements.

Therefore, in both instances analyzed from the Burundian case, we could note that IDA did function as an independent variable to conflict ripeness. Here, IDA positively affected conflict ripeness by particularly intensifying the level of an SWO. This positive effect of IDA was facilitated through a truly coordinated effort by the international community including bilateral and multilateral donors as well as NGOs. This prevented the Burundians from being able to "play off some international players against others" (International Crisis Group 2000c, p.24). The mediator, first Julius Nyerere, then Nelson Mandela and later Jacob Zuma, was in charge of coordinating these efforts and could thus use them effectively to advance his individual peace process.

Having established that IDA did indeed function in this case as an independent variable and constituting that the way of causation was positive in that it positively affected conflict ripeness and by that furthered the peace process, now we should focus again specifically on the circumstances and conditions accompanying IDA here. What was specific about this situation, so that IDA had a positive effect? Three conditions seem to have made the difference in the two instances analyzed: Firstly, the development aid delivered and thus the IDA was not simply provided by the donor community in an unreflected way. Instead, it was made part of an overall comprehensive strategy. Thus, IDA was part of a great effort of coordination among the entire donor community – including bilateral, multilateral and non-governmental actors. Secondly, IDA was made conditional. The process was preceded by a stark cutback of external influx, specifically development aid, to the country in the years before 1998. A complete stop of development aid had led to a disastrous internal situation in Burundi. At the same time, this policy contributed to a high degree of credibility for the further process. This led to the situation in which when the embargo was lifted and aid slowly entered the country made conditional, it was very credible to the belligerents that the development aid can be cut off again. Thus, the belligerents believed the threat that if compliance with the peace process was not given, then IDA would be terminated. Thirdly, the IDA entering Burundi throughout the second and third phase of the conflict was controlled by the mediator. The mediator was in charge of the coordination effort of the donor community. By that, a link between the peace efforts and development aid was ensured. The two undertakings went indeed hand in hand and supported one another in their respective effects. Therefore, it is possible to conclude that basically three attributes were decisive for the positive effect of IDA on conflict ripeness: coordination, conditioning paired with credibility and control by the mediator.

5.2.2.4 Conclusion

As Curtis stated, "it is impossible to talk of unmitigated success of the Burundian peace process. Thousands of Burundians have died as a result of conflict since the signing of the Arusha peace agreement" (Curtis 2003, p.3). Thus, even though Burundi is a case of tragedy and protracted civil war, with respect to the use of development aid it is a role model. Development aid was seen by external actors as a tool in the overall process and thus linked to the peace efforts – at least in the second and third phases of the conflict. The first phase was not significant as conflict ripeness was not given. But in the second and third phases, the mediators consciously and carefully used development aid, specifically IDA to their advantage. Decisive was the donor conference in August 1998, making a significant difference to the situation. All donors, including non-governmental organizations, came together and coordinated their efforts. They did not simply increase aid after the lifting of the embargo, but developed a strategy on what conditions must be fulfilled by the local actors, so that IDA did not hurt the process. This process was presided over by the mediator. Thus, this is an example of how IDA can positively affect conflict ripeness and by that the peace process. It shows how IDA can be used positively as an instrument in conflict resolution.

Relating this analysis back to the theoretical model and the case-guiding research questions, the following table shows the results for the Burundian case, whereas it must be noted that the answers to phase two refer only to the time from 1998 until 2000.

#	Question	Phase 1	Phase 2	Phase 3
1	Is it possible to identify an MHS?	No	Yes	Yes
2	If not, is it possible to identify MEOs?	No	-	-
3	Is it possible to identify an SWO?	No	Yes	Yes
4	Can conflict ripeness be affirmed?	No	Yes	Yes
5	To what extent does persuasion affect conflict ripeness?	-	Positively	Positively
6	To what extent do inducements affect conflict ripeness?	-	Positively	Positively
7	To what extent does pressure affect conflict ripeness?	-	Positively	Positively
8	To what extent does a change in leadership affect conflict ripeness?	-	No effect	No effect
9	To what extent does the assertiveness of the leadership affect conflict ripeness?	-	Negatively	No effect
10	To what extent does external support to the belligerents affect conflict ripeness?	-	No effect	No effect
11	Can IDA be observed?	-	Yes	Yes
12	Is it possible to identify an effect of IDA on ripeness?	-	Yes	Yes
13	Does IDA affect ripeness positively?	-	Yes	Yes
14	Does IDA affect ripeness negatively?	-	No	No
15	Under which conditions does IDA affect conflict ripeness positively and under which conditions does IDA affect conflict ripeness negatively?	-	Coordination, conditioning paired with credibility and control by mediator over IDA	

Table 15: Case-Guiding Research Questions Burundi[158]

---

[158] Source: Own illustration.

In conclusion, it is thus possible to state that the case of Burundi shows two instances in which IDA positively affects conflict ripeness. The two instances are two phases that merge to one overall process. Through the smart use of IDA as an instrument in conflict resolution on part of the mediation team, it proved possible that conflict ripeness could be maintained, so that the peace process could advance further. Decisive for the positive effect of IDA on conflict ripeness was a great coordination effort on part of the donor community, the conditioning of IDA in terms of making it dependent upon compliance with the peace process paired with strong credibility, and lastly the established connection between the conflict resolution efforts and development aid by giving the mediator the control over entire strategy of which IDA was made a part.

5.3 Cambodia

The third case study is concerned with a country on the Asian continent, Cambodia. The phase in the Cambodian civil war to be assessed is the mediation process leading up to the Paris Conference in 1991 and the subsequent two years. Two points will be analyzed: firstly, the quality of the peace agreement, and second, whether ripeness existed. Subsequently, the independent variables that might impact the potential conflict ripeness are assessed and evaluated in line with the case-guiding research questions outlined in section 4.3. Special attention will be paid to the potential independent variable of IDA. This section is structured as follows: in order to contextualize the case study properly, the first part will provide a background to the conflict (5.3.1) including the history and causes (5.3.1.1) as well as an outline and description of the actors involved at the moment of interest (5.3.1.2). Subsequently, the actual analysis of the Cambodian case will be conducted (5.3.2). Here, three questions are covered: firstly, whether ripeness existed and to what extent it was affected by independent variables (5.3.2.1), secondly, whether IDA can be identified (5.3.2.2), and thirdly, whether IDA affected ripeness and if so of what quality (5.3.2.3). The case study closes with a conclusion reflecting on the findings with respect to the theory analysis (5.3.3).

5.3.1 Background

The Kingdom of Cambodia[159] in its contemporary form is a multiparty democracy under a constitutional monarchy located in Southeast Asia at the Gulf of Thailand. With its currently ca. 14.5 million inhabitants, Cambodia's neighbors are Thailand, Laos, and Vietnam. The main ethnic group constitutes the so-called Khmer with about 90% of the population. With 96%, the population is mainly Buddhist[160]. Plagued with conflicts and wars since the 1960s, Cambodia held national elections in 2008, which were finally judged as relatively peaceful[161]. Cambodia's economy today heavily depends on international aid with 30 to 40% of the population living on a dollar a day or less (survey year: 2004) (Battaile/ Kayizzi-Mugerwa 2005, p.17). The World Development Report 2010 classifies Cambodia as a 'low income country', which is the lowest category, comprising countries with a GNI (gross national income) per capita of US$ 975 or less (World Bank 2010, p.377).

---

[159] In the following, the conventional short form of the country's name, "Cambodia", will be used. It will also be used in historical context to refer to the country even though the country frequently changed its name: Khmer Republic, Democratic Kampuchea, People's Republic of Kampuchea, State of Cambodia (cf. Hughes (2009): Dependent Communities: Aid and Politics in Cambodia and East Timor, p.ix).
[160] Cf. https://www.cia.gov/library/publications/the-world-factbook.
[161] Cf. https://www.cia.gov/library/publications/the-world-factbook.

Figure 19: Map of Cambodia[162]

5.3.1.1 History and Causes

To present Cambodia's history in context three aspects will be outlined: firstly, the general course of events; secondly, the attempted peace efforts; and third the further development of the country.

In 1953, Cambodia gained independence from France. The country was ruled by Prince Norodom Sihanouk. Ten years later in 1963, a rebel group under the leadership of Pol Pot[163] started insurrections against the government. The

---

[162] Source: United Nations, "Kingdom of Cambodia, no. 3860 Rev.4 January 2004, United Nations," (2004b). Published with the courtesy and approval of the United Nations.
[163] Pol Pot is the commonly known and used pseudonym of Saloth Sar.

rebel group was labeled the Khmer Rouge by Prince Sihanouk (cf. Mayall 1996, p.28). This moment can be described as the beginning of a long and protracted civil war in Cambodia. The political damage to the Sihanouk-government resulting from the insurrections was further aggravated by the 1964 US-intervention in neighboring Vietnam. From 1965 onwards, the US bombed Cambodian villages located at the Vietnamese border. In March 1970, a coup d'état deposed of Prince Sihanouk as head of state. His successor, Lon Nol, began to rule by decree in October 1971 on the grounds that the ongoing civil war could only be managed with such measures (cf. Accord 1998; Bercovitch/Fretter 2004; Brown, F.Z./Timberman 1998; and Talentino in Brown, M.E./Rosecrance 1999).

In 1975, Pol Pot's Khmer Rouge took over the Cambodian capital Phnom Penh and renamed the state into the 'Democratic Kampuchea'. During the following three years, mass executions took place under the Khmer Rouge regime that amounted to genocide (cf. Chong in Milliken 2003, p.213). More than two million people lost their lives during those years[164], which meant a reduction of the country's population by about one-fifth[165]. In 1977, Khmer Rouge forces crossed the border to Vietnam and massacred hundreds of Vietnamese. As a result, Vietnamese forces invaded Cambodia in December 1978 and overthrew the Khmer Rouge government. A Vietnamese 'puppet state' was created. The Khmer Rouge escaped westward from Phnom Penh to the Cambodian jungle and refugee camps on the Thai border from where they organized themselves and carried out attacks against the Vietnamese-backed government. The rebels received significant support by China who channeled their assistance through Thailand. The result was a protracted internationalized civil war throughout the 1980s (cf. Bercovitch/Fretter 2004; Brown, F.Z./ Timberman 1998; Kiernan in Breslauer/Kreisler, et al. 1991; Opitz 1991; Raszelenberg/Schier 1995; Strassner 1991), which is estimated to have cost about 500,000 lives – many of which civilians (cf. Bercovitch/Fretter 2004, p.187).

The Cambodian civil war throughout the 1980s can be described as a proxy war. As it was put by Brown and Timberman, "the Cambodia struggle had become simultaneously a civil war, a regional war, and a great-power proxy war" (Brown, F.Z./Timberman 1998, p.16). The Soviet bloc supported the Vietnamese-backed government, while China, Thailand, and to a certain extent the

---

[164] The exact number of victims is still debated. The reason lies mostly in the different forms of killing. There were plenty of political assassinations, murder and executions, but the main part of the victims died in a so-called auto-genocide, which comprised killing by working to death or by starvation.

[165] Cf. www.cambodia.gov.kh/unisq11/egov/english/country.history.html.

Western Cold War states supported the resistance movements with aid through for example the UN Border Relief Operation, which "fed, housed, and otherwise administered thousands of Cambodian refugees on the Thai border" (Hughes 2009, p.27), and put blanket trade and aid sanctions on the Cambodian government.

The resistance movement consisted of three main factions, which were the Khmer Rouge under the leadership of Pol Pot, the Khmer People's National Liberation Front led by Son Sann (KPNLF), and the National Front for an Independent, Neutral, Prosperous, and Cooperative Cambodia led by Prince Norodom Ranariddh, son of Prince Sihanouk (FUNCINPEC). While the ruling party, the Cambodian People's Party (CPP)[166], and the Khmer Rouge were traditionally rather communist factions, the KPNLF and the FUNCINPEC represented the more conservative and monarchist views.

Several attempts were made to bring the conflict to an end. On the one hand, the ruling regime tried to defeat the Khmer Rouge and the other resistance movements in a number of major offensives throughout the 1980s, but never fully succeeded (Bercovitch/Fretter 2004, p.187). On the other hand, diplomatic efforts were made to facilitate negotiations between the belligerents, such as the JIM I and II, the Bangkok Informal Meeting, the Tokyo Informal Meeting, and intra-Cambodian negotiations. Different external actors tried to mediate in these cases such as ASEAN, Indonesia, Australia, France and finally the five permanent members of the UN Security Council (Perm Five). But none of these attempts resulted in the desired success until 1991 (cf. Hampson 2003, p.7 and Solomon in Crocker/Hampson, et al. 1999, p.275). Only when the Perm Five came together, initiated a series of high-level meetings to discuss the situation in Cambodia, and sent several fact-finding missions to the country to study the administrative, economic and social infrastructure and requirements for the repatriation of refugees, was it possible to agree on a framework that provided the basis for the second Paris Conference, the Framework for a Comprehensive Political Settlement of the Cambodian Conflict (Hazdra 1997, p.75). The framework was announced on 28 August 1990 and marked a milestone in the UN's history, since it was seen as the first time that the five permanent members concluded a common approach to an ideologically stretched issue[167]. It was an attempt to provide the belligerent groups with a basis on which the negotiations could take place.

---

[166] The CPP only took this name in the course of the year of 1991. Before, the party was called Kampuchean People's Revolutionary Party (KPRP).
[167] Cf. *The New York Times*, Prial, Frank J.: "Five U.N. Powers Announce Accord on Cambodia War", 29 August 1990.

The framework contained three main aspects which covered firstly, the proposed mandate for a UN mission including the military arrangements during the transitional period, the proposed election process, a plan for the repatriation of refugees and displaced persons as well as principles for a new Cambodian constitution. Secondly, the framework provided for an agreement covering international guarantees for security; and thirdly, for a declaration regarding the rehabilitation and reconstruction of Cambodia. The framework was the basis for planning the international support and involvement in the Cambodian peace and transition process[168].

The framework functioned as a proposal to the Cambodian belligerent parties for a potential peace agreement. It was discussed frequently over the course of about one year. In September 1990, the four belligerent factions agreed on a ceasefire which took effect in May 1991. But "the ceasefire appeared to fall apart almost as soon as it went into effect May 1, with each faction accusing the other of major violations"[169].

In August 1991, at a Supreme National Council of Cambodia (SNC) meeting in Pattaya/Thailand, the official termination of the Cambodian civil war was proclaimed (cf. Strassner 1991, p.Epilog). Finally in October 1991, the Cambodian belligerent parties concluded a peace agreement in Paris under the supervision of the Perm Five and on the basis of the "Agreements on a Comprehensive Political Settlement of the Cambodia Conflict", also known as the Paris Agreements.[170] As Mark Hong put it, "in part, these [the previous mediation attempts] prepared the way for the Paris Agreement to succeed, because they showed what areas were not possible to agree upon" (Hong 1995, p.93). The Paris Agreements were signed by all four belligerents as well as by eighteen further nations in the presence of the UN Secretary-General on 23rd October 1991[171].

The agreements called for an international peacekeeping force and a provisional government under the auspices of the UN. With the conclusion of the agreements, the UN sent a pre-mission to Cambodia, the United Nations

---

[168] Cf. http://www.cambodia.org/facts/Paris_Peace_Agreement_10231991.php.
[169] Cf. *The New York Times*, Shenon, Philip: "Cambodia Factions Call Truce on Eve of New Talks", 24 June 1991.
[170] Cf. http://www.un.org/en/peacekeeping/missions/past/unamicbackgr.html.
[171] The additional nations signing the agreements were Australia, Brunei Darussalam, Canada, the People's Republic of China, the French Republic, the Republic of India, the Republic of Indonesia, Japan, the Lao People's Democratic Republic, Malaysia, the Republic of the Philippine, the Republic of Singapore, the Kingdom of Thailand, the Union of soviet Socialist Republics, the United Kingdom of Great Britain and Northern Ireland, the United States of America and the Socialist Republic of Vietnam – cf. http://www.cambodia.org/facts/Paris_Peace_Agreement_10231991.php.

Advance Mission in Cambodia (UNAMIC) in October 1991. The actual peacekeeping mission, the United Nations Transitional Authority in Cambodia (UNTAC), started to arrive in March 1992 and kept its mandate until September 1993.

The course of the subsequent events is judged differently by academics. Some argue that the peace agreements and subsequent peacekeeping operation were fully successful (cf. Heininger in Belgrad/Nachmias 1997, p.121 with regard to the repatriation of refugees; Lithgow in Clements/Ward 1994, pp.52-55; Solomon in Crocker/Hampson, et al. 1999, pp.275-276; and head of UNTAC Yasushi Akashi: Akashi 1994, p.210); others emphasized that the violence continued even after the signing of the peace treaty and that thus, the peace process was destroyed. The proponents of this approach claim that only much later, in the late 1990s, the conflict actually found its end (cf. Accord 1998, p.5 and p.20; Berdal/Keen 1997, p.795; Doyle in Brown, F.Z./Timberman 1998, p.79 and 89; Hazdra 1997, p.25; Robert in Kiernan/Hughes 2007, p.40). In fact, even though the second Paris Conference seemed to be successful, one has to acknowledge that soon after, at least one of the parties to the conflict defected from the agreements. Insurrections and widespread violence continued and the first 'free' elections in 1993 were heavily affected by this (cf. Acharya 1994; Mayall 1996; United Nations 1995b; Van der Kroef 1991; and Weiss 1995). As Michael W. Doyle put it, "after the UNTAC period, Cambodia was left with a continuing war and an unreconciled political leadership and bureaucracy. The counter-insurgency war with the remaining 6,000 or so Khmer Rouge, holed up along the western border with Thailand, produced a thousand military and uncounted civilian casualties each year" (Doyle in Brown, F.Z./Timberman 1998, p.89). But not only the Khmer Rouge posed a problem to the peace process in the aftermath of the signing of the Paris Agreements. Even though they officially declared their withdrawal from the agreements and went as far as attacking UN personnel at considerable scale, the other parties also violated their terms. From 1992 onwards, violence and attacks had returned to the country; corruption and political instability were commonplace.

National elections were held in Cambodia in 1993. 4.6 million people, representing about 96% of the estimated eligible population of Cambodia, had been registered for the elections. The UNTAC-supervised elections took place in May 1993. Almost 90% of the registered voters cast their vote, which was counted as a great success for democracy[172]. The FUNCINPEC won the elections with 45% of the vote, followed by the CPP with 38% and the BLDP with 10%.

---

[172] Cf. http://www.un.org/en/peacekeeping/missions/past/untacbackgr2.html.

The BLDP was the political party founded in 1993 as a successor to the KPNLF, led by Son Sann. The Khmer Rouge did not participate in the elections.

After a three month interim provisional government, Cambodia installed a new government in late September 1993 as a parliamentary democracy, adopted a new constitution and Prince Sihanouk was restored to the throne as a constitutional monarch (cf. Darlan 1994, p.1). Further, some 360,000 refugees were repatriated (Acharya 1994, p.300 and Chong in Milliken 2003, p.216). Therefore, UNTAC saw its mission to be completed. The last administrative personnel left Cambodia in May 1994. In UN Resolution 880 (1993) of 4 November 1993, the Security Council noted "with satisfaction the success during the transitional period of the Cambodian people, under the leadership of His Majesty Samdech Preah Norodom Sihanouk, King of Cambodia, in promoting peace, stability and national reconciliation" and "with great satisfaction that, with the successful conclusion of the UNTAC mission following the election of 23-28 May 1993, the goal of the Paris Agreements of restoring to the Cambodian people and their democratically elected leaders their primary responsibility for peace, stability, national reconciliation and reconstruction in their country has been achieved" (United Nations 1993).

However, political instability and violence were still not defeated. Insurrections and attacks continued, also after the elections. In 1994, the Khmer Rouge attempted a coup, which remained unsuccessful, and in 1997, Hun Sen, the leader of the CPP, carried out a coup against the Prime Minister. Eventually, the Khmer Rouge's leader Pol Pot was arrested and put on trial publicly. In 1998, many members of the Khmer Rouge defected and government forces took over their 'traditional stronghold' of Anlong Veng (Talentino in Brown, M.E./ Rosecrance 1999, p.174). The Khmer Rouge's leader, Pol Pot, died in April 1998. This brought the Khmer Rouge insurrections to an end. With the dissolution of the Khmer Rouge and successful negotiations between the remaining Cambodian factions, the conflict was widely seen as terminated in the late 1990s[173].

The Cambodian case of 1990 to late 1993 was selected despite the signing of the peace agreements. It could be argued that with the signing of the agreements, the issue of ripeness would have lost its significance. But following the argument outlined above, the author agrees with the position that the peace agreement actually did not end the conflict. It was thus only an attempt in the peace process – an effort to be evaluated.

---

[173] Cf. Arbeitsgemeinschaft Kriegsursachenforschung, Institut für Politische Wissenschaft, Universität Hamburg: http://www.sozialwiss.uni-hamburg.de/publish/Ipw/Akuf/kriege/132_kambodscha.htm.

5.3.1.2   Key Actors

The period of interest for the subsequent analysis is the phase leading up to the signing of the Paris Agreements in October 1991 and the following two years until the national elections in May 1993. Key actors in this period come both from the domestic and the international level.

On the domestic level, five main actors were important: The party heading the government in Phnom Penh during the years leading up to the peace negotiations was the KPRP, later renamed into CPP, led by Hun Sen. His regime was installed in 1979 with the help of Vietnam. The regime and the party were massively supported by Vietnam throughout their time in government and due to the global political constellation also by the Soviet Union. The CPP controlled about 90% of the country at the time of the Paris Agreements and was in charge of a military force of about 40,000 regular soldiers and 100,000 militias. The CPP signed the Paris Agreements and took part in the subsequent UNTAC-led elections in 1993. They won 38% of the vote and Hun Sen became second prime minister in the coalition government (Doyle 1995, p.17; Strassner 1991). The CPP had been traditionally formed on Marxist-Leninist principles. In the course of the democratic transition period throughout 1991 they abandoned this rather communist outlook.

The second most influential faction were the Khmer Rouge or Party of Democratic Kampuchea. The faction was originally led by Pol Pot, who lived in hiding after being ousted in 1978. Consequently, the official leadership was taken over by Khieu Samphan. The Khmer Rouge earned sad international notoriety through their extreme, Maoist-style regime in Cambodia from 1975 to 1978, when they ruralized the country and inflicted a so-called 'auto-genocide'. Throughout the 1980s and 1990s, the Khmer Rouge constituted a rebel group, principally located at the Thai-Cambodian border with a military force of about 30,000 troops in 1990 and up to 15,000 'disciplined troops' in 1993. The rebels constantly carried out insurrections and attacks against the CPP-government and constituted the strongest military rebel force in Cambodia. The Khmer Rouge primarily received assistance from China and Thailand (cf. Accord 1998, p.17). They signed the Paris Agreements in 1991, but defected in 1992. Their insurrections continued and were even directed against UN peacekeeping personnel. In 1994, the Khmer Rouge controlled almost 10 percent of Cambodian territory (Doyle 1995, p.17; Strassner 1991).

The third and fourth Cambodian factions that are of interest in the context of this analysis are the Khmer People's National Liberation Front led by Son Sann (KPNLF) and the National Front for an Independent, Neutral, Prosperous, and Cooperative Cambodia (FUNCINPEC) under the leadership of Prince Norodom

Ranariddh. These two factions opposed the Vietnamese-backed CPP-government and formed a military opposition. The KPNLF was a 'conservative, middle class movement' and controlled only very small parts in the northwest of Cambodia. The FUNCINPEC also controlled only small parts in the northwest in the early 1990s, however won 45% in the 1993 elections. Thus Ranariddh became the first prime minister of the coalition government (Doyle 1995, p.17; Strassner 1991). The FUNCINPEC was loosely associated with the traditional monarchist movement.

Together with the Khmer Rouge, the KPNLF and the FUNCINPEC established the tripartite Coalition Government of Democratic Kampuchea (CGDK) in June 1982 in order to combat the Vietnamese 'puppet regime'. The US and other Western governments gave considerable financial assistance to the CGDK. Further they supported the CGDK by accepting them as the legitimate government of Cambodia in the sense that it was acknowledged as the *real* representative of the Cambodian state on the international stage even though they did not have effective control over the country. The CGDK was thus allowed to occupy the Cambodian seat in the UN General Assembly until 1990 (cf. Accord 1998, p.17 and Talentino in Brown, M.E./Rosecrance 1999,p.183).

The fifth actor worth mentioning in this context is not a group or faction but an individual: Preah Bat Samdech Preah Norodom Sihanouk Varman (Prince Sihanouk). Prince Sihanouk was King of Cambodia from 1941 until 1955 and from 1993 until 2004. He further acted as Prime Minister from 1960 until 1970, from 1975 until 1976, and from 1991 until 1993. Prince Sihanouk was the founder of the FUNCINEPC. The party was soon taken over by his son. Norodom Sihanouk then acted as an individual from exile and enjoyed great acceptance by the Cambodian people. When he returned to Cambodia in the aftermath of the Paris Agreements, he was welcomed as the savior. Sihanouk took over a crucial role as a facilitator in the negotiation process.

On the international level, three types of actors were involved during the period of interest: individual states, multilateral organizations and other deliverers of aid including a range of international NGOs.

Before the signing of the Paris Agreements in 1991, two major blocs dominated the international dimension of the Cambodian conflict: the classic Cold War blocs. The Soviet Union, together with Vietnam supported the Phnom Penh government; the Western states, China and Thailand supported the rebel groups.

Further significant actors were different multilateral organizations. ASEAN made several attempts to mediate the conflict as the member states had a strategic and tactical interest to bring peace to the region. However, ASEAN remained unsuccessful in its attempts. The UN's Perm Five were crucial once the

Cold War was over, as they were then able to find a consensus on how to handle the Cambodian problems from an international perspective and agreed on a comprehensive framework for the resolution of the conflict, functioning subsequently as the mediator in the peace process. This step proved to be ground breaking in the peace process leading up to the Paris Agreements.

Related to the Perm Five were the United Nations as an organization that was in charge of conducting the peacekeeping operation following the Paris Agreements. The UN first sent an advance mission to Cambodia in November 1991 that acted as a provisional peacekeeping force called UNAMIC. In March 1992, the UN started to deploy the permanent force called UNTAC. In total, the force numbered 22,000 soldiers and civilians to organize and oversee the elections scheduled for 1993. The special representative of UNTAC was the Japanese Yasushi Akashi. Lt. Gen. John Sanderson acted as force commander. UNTAC left Cambodia in early 1994 when the UN considered their mission completed.

The last important group of actors on the international level was the deliverers of aid. Aid came into the country after the Peace Agreements through different sources: firstly, multilateral organizations that supported UNTAC such as UNHCR, UNDP, the World Bank, and the IMF among many others; secondly individual states that provided bilateral aid – directly or through implementing agencies; and finally international NGOs that entered Cambodia en masse in 1992. The individual roles of these actors will be taken up below. It is important to note, however, that each of these three actors was not speaking with one voice or acting with one hand. Rather, the situation could be characterized as a conglomerate of a multitude of individual sub-actors with individual agendas.

5.3.2   Cambodia Analysis

Having put the case of Cambodia into the historical context and described the relevant actors, we will now turn to the actual analysis with regard to conflict ripeness and IDA. Three overall questions will be addressed in the following: firstly, is it possible to identify ripeness among all relevant actors and to what extent was the conflict ripeness affected by independent variables other than IDA (5.3.2.1)? Secondly, can IDA be identified as an independent variable (5.3.2.2)? And thirdly, did IDA impact conflict ripeness and if so, of what quality was the impact (5.3.2.3)?

5.3.2.1 Conflict Ripeness

The analysis of ripeness includes the first level variables of MHS/MEOs and SWO as well as the consideration of whether independent variables affected conflict ripeness and a conclusion bringing the findings together.

As outlined above, in October 1991, the four belligerent factions signed a peace agreement in Paris, with which they officially terminated the decade(s)-long civil war. Subsequently, the Paris Agreements were implemented under the auspices of the United Nations. Cambodians were repatriated and in May 1993, national elections were held. According to some academics who have evaluated this course of events, it was an example of success (cf. Heininger in Belgrad/ Nachmias 1997, p.121 with regard to the repatriation of refugees; Lithgow in Clements/Ward 1994, pp.52-55; Solomon in Crocker/Hampson, et al. 1999, pp.275-276; and head of UNTAC Yasushi Akashi: Akashi 1994, p.210).

To start with the MHS, it is useful to look at the internal actors individually and analyze whether they enough indices can be identified so that an MHS can be established leading up to the peace process in Cambodia.

From the perspective of the Phnom Penh government, the situation indeed appeared disastrous by the beginning of 1991. Certain parallel developments during this period caused a significant destabilization of the government. The major aspect to consider here is the impact of changes at the international level on the regime.

The Hun Sen government had received full backing from Vietnam and the Soviet Union throughout the 1980s. Vietnam did not only station troops in Cambodia, but the Soviet Union also contributed about 80% to Cambodia's budget by June 1989 (cf. Van der Kroef 1991, p.99). The Hun Sen regime thus depended upon both the Soviet Union and Vietnam for the maintenance of its power. However, the end of the Cold War brought about significant changes of interests on the international level. Under Gorbachev's rule from 1985 onwards, the Soviet Union slowly redirected its priorities towards domestic economic reform and thus lost its interest in being involved in proxy wars fought on other states' territories. Furthermore, the Soviet Union tried to improve its relations with China by pursuing the so-called rapprochement policy[174], which created a further incentive to terminate its involvement in the Cambodian conflict due to the fact that the civil war had been a permanent conflict between the two big powers (cf. Doyle 1995, p.23). Therefore, the Soviet Union introduced sharp

---

[174] Cf. February 1989, the Soviet foreign minister, Eduard Shevardnadze visited China. May 1989, Gorbachev himself travelled to China to conclude the Policy of Normalization with Beijing.

cutbacks to the support of Cambodia. The Soviet Deputy Foreign Minister, Igor Rogachev, announced in December 1989 that his government had ceased military shipments to the Phnom Penh government (cf. Van der Kroef 1991, p.99). As Renate Strassner put it, "Cambodia had lost its prominent significance to the Soviet Union" (Strassner 1991, p.305). This unforeseen and radical termination of support affected the regime considerably.

In parallel, the Soviet Union ended its substantial support to Vietnam[175]. As a result, Vietnam's domestic economic situation worsened considerably. Furthermore, due to its military engagement in the Cambodian civil war, Vietnam suffered from international isolation. Many states, in particular in the West, condemned Vietnam's 1978-intervention in Cambodia and the creation of a 'puppet state'. This is demonstrated by the fact that the Cambodian opposition group, the CGDK, was accepted to be the legitimate incumbent of the seat in the UN General Assembly rather than the Phnom Penh government despite the fact that one of the CGDK members was the genocidal Khmer Rouge. Due to this financial and political pressure on Vietnam, it started withdrawing its troops from Cambodia (cf. Talentino in Brown, M.E./Rosecrance 1999, p.184). Encouraged by the Soviet Union, Vietnam announced its military withdrawal from Cambodia in January 1989 and completed it by September 1989, only leaving a few Vietnamese military advisers behind (cf. Kiernan in Breslauer/Kreisler, et al. 1991, p.59). This left the Phnom Penh government without its major source of support and protection and triggered a deadlock for the parties involved (cf. Hazdra 1997, p.58).

Furthermore, smaller states such as Czechoslovakia, Poland, Hungary, and Bulgaria that had previously supported the government withdrew their help (cf. Van der Kroef 1991, p.99). Without the external support from the Soviet Union as its largest donor, but also Vietnam, and the other smaller donors, it seemed impossible for the Phnom Penh government to reach a state at which it would have complete and effective control over the whole territory of Cambodia because of the Khmer Rouge's prevalence and strength (particularly military strength) in some areas of the country – thus, in this respect, it can be assumed that they faced a plateau situation, an unending terrain without relief.

Apart from the pressure put upon the Phnom Penh government that resulted from external actors, the domestic situation also worsened significantly in the following period. Beginning in the early months of 1990, intra-party dissension destabilized the position of the Hun Sen government. A rivalry emerged between the State of Cambodia Premier, Hun Sen, and the National Assembly President

---

[175] Cf. *The New York Times*, "Sighted in Cambodia: Peace", 28 August 1991.

and senior Politburo member, Chea Sin. On 30 May 1990, six senior State of Cambodia officials were arrested by their fellow party members (cf. Van der Kroef 1991, p.95). This expresses the internal difficulties of the regime and indicates a loss of internal and external strength.

Besides, the already bad economic situation of Cambodia[176] fell into decay after the cutbacks of external assistance. The results were high inflation, a quickly growing underground economy, and great hardship for the people in general. Particularly during the year 1990, inflation "raged on" (Van der Kroef 1991, p.98). The bad situation reflected upon the government so that support among the people for the leading elite decreased accordingly. As Van der Kroef expressed it, "in early February [1991] the government granted a nearly 250% increase in rice farmers' subsidies. Notwithstanding, food hoarding and speculation increased, fueling fears of growing shortages" (Van der Kroef 1991, p.98). Cambodia's economic situation was completely destroyed by the end of 1990 (cf. Chong in Milliken 2003, p.215 and Hazdra 1997, pp.59-62).

Summing up all the factors influencing the standing of the Hun Sen government, it is possible to conclude that a hurting stalemate did indeed exist. The relatively sudden termination of external assistance in late 1989 combined with internal difficulties both within the party and at a national economic level in early 1990 constituted both a plateau in terms of the loss of hope for change and a precipice for the regime regarding the looming disasters resulting from political and economic instability. This means that from early 1990 onwards after the Soviet Union had ceased its support, the Vietnamese troops withdrew, additional smaller states cut off their assistance and the political and economic problems arising early 1990, the Hun Sen government must have perceived a hurting stalemate. The government could neither win the war and take over complete control of the country (and by that destroy the opposition parties), nor could they maintain the status quo of continued fighting given the disastrous internal state conditions where salaries could not be paid and soldiers were starving. Therefore, it is assumed that the CPP did perceive a hurting stalemate from early 1990 onwards.

It must be assumed that also the belligerent antagonist, the CGDK, consisting of the Khmer Rouge, the KPNLF, and the FUNCINPEC, faced a hurting stalemate at a similar point in time. The two levels of domestic difficulties and externally provoked problems must be considered. Concerning the latter level, China, Thailand, and the US were the main supporters of the CGDK. China was the principal financial and military patron of the Khmer

---

[176] The Cambodian economy had suffered badly from the decade-long civil war.

Rouge. In the context of the normalization of relations between China and the Soviet Union, China had already supported the idea of national reconciliation under the leadership of Sihanouk in 1987 (cf. Hampson 1996, p.176). However, even throughout 1990, China still sponsored the rebel group. But it cut off its support eventually at the beginning of 1991 because of international pressure.

Thailand terminated its assistance to the CGDK, and the Khmer Rouge in particular, too. Thailand changed its policies in the aftermath of 1987 when Chatichai became elected Prime Minister of Thailand. Under the rule of Chatichai, Thailand started to concentrate its energies on domestic economic reconstruction. One of the preconditions to achieve economic growth was a stable region. This meant that Thailand acquired a strong incentive to actively support an end to the Cambodian conflict. Therefore, Thailand redirected its involvement in the Cambodian conflict from supporting the rebel groups to promoting and pressuring for peace in the period between Chatichai's election and the Paris Peace Agreements (cf. Hampson 1996, p.178). Hence, the support to the rebels from this source also broke away.

The last external resource to the CGDK, the US, terminated its assistance in the summer of 1990. In June, the US Senate Intelligence Committee voted to halt the "annual [US]$ 10 million in covert aid to the resistance"[177]. On 18th July, the US also announced to the press that it was withdrawing its support for the CGDK as the "legitimate incumbent in Cambodia's seat in the UN General Assembly" (Solomon in Crocker/Hampson, et al. 1999, p.297) and that it would open up a dialogue with Vietnam about the facilitation of potential peace talks in Cambodia. According to the former US Assistant Secretary of State for East Asian and Pacific Affairs, Richard Solomon, this decision was mainly taken because of ongoing public revulsion against the US supporting a former genocidal group, the Khmer Rouge (cf. Solomon in Crocker/Hampson, et al. 1999, p.297 and p.307). The US support had become publicly known in April 1990 when ABC News aired a special program hosted by Peter Jennings called, "From the Killing Fields". (cf. Solomon in Crocker/Hampson, et al. 1999, p.307). Thus it was at least partly domestic pressure affecting the US decision. After a meeting with his Soviet colleague, Eduard Shevardnadze, US Secretary of State James Baker stated in June 1990, that the two countries pledged to do anything to stop a return of the Khmer Rouge to power[178]. This indicates the change in policy by the US. The CGDK with its member, the Khmer Rouge, had

---

[177] Cf. *Newsweek*, Manegold, C.S.: "Baker's About-Face On Cambodia - A Turn Toward Hanoi", 30 July 1990.
[178] Cf. *Der Spiegel*, "Kambodscha: Diesmal ums Ganze", 30 July 1990.

lost sympathies from the US. It was estimated that in total, about US$ 24 million in both overt and covert aid were given by the US to the CGDK per year, if, officially, only to the two non-communist factions[179]. Nevertheless, the cooperation between the two non-communist groups and the Khmer Rouge, especially on the battlefield, could not be denied.

The conflicting parties in Cambodia perceived this switching of sides by the US as a "political bombshell" (Solomon in Crocker/Hampson, et al. 1999, p.297). One example of the significance that the external support had for the CGDK is described by Ben Barber. He states that, "during the 1978-91 conflict in Cambodia, the United States and other anticommunist nations funded refugee camps in Thailand that were bases for three Cambodian guerrilla forces fighting the Vietnamese-backed government – one of them Khmer Rouge, whose murderous rule sparked the 1978 Vietnamese invasion" (Barber 1997, p.9). This demonstrates the significance of the termination of US assistance. Without the external support, the bases for the fighting of the rebel group were cut away and thus the CGDK found itself in a non-sustainable situation after the change in policy by the US (cf. Accord 1998, p.17) and thus must have perceived a hurting stalemate, manifest in the loss of hope for victory.

"On several trips between 1982 and 1991 during which I visited all the Cambodian refugee camps along the Thai border, the unholy alliance between refugee aid and the resistance fighting the Vietnamese occupation army was apparent. Relief agencies delivered food, medicine, and other services to the Cambodian refugees by day. But at night, fighters returned to the camps to rest, eat the food and use the medical supplies the agencies had provided, sleep with their wives, visit with their children, and recruit well-fed young refugees. Aid workers would arrive the next day to find more young men vanished to the front lines and refugees who had dared to speak out beaten or intimidated" (Barber 1997, p.9).

The quote above demonstrates the CGDK's dependence on external support for the rebel fighters and the mode in which the support worked. Through external relief and aid, the fighters were able to focus on insurrections while being able to re-strengthen themselves – both structurally as well as physically – in the camps. Having been deprived from such external support, the logistical concept of their strategy broke down and left the fighters without a 'battery charger'.

Observing this change of policy of the three main supporting states, China, Thailand and the US from mid-1990 onwards, it is clear that the CGDK

---

[179] Cf. *The New York Times*, Erlanger, Steven: "Favored Cambodians Lose U.S. Aid", 10 April 1981.

experienced a precipice that seemed unmanageable. Certain domestic developments further strengthened this impression. In mid-July 1990, aerial bombing attacks by Soviet-supplied aircrafts were increased against the Khmer Rouge positions[180]. This naturally caused further difficulties for the Khmer Rouge in their physical and structural strength as well as in their morale. Indirectly, it also affected the other two factions since they both heavily relied upon the leverage, particularly the military strength, of the Khmer Rouge. Without the military, the organizational power, and the strong will of the Khmer Rouge, both the KPNLF and the FUNCINPEC could not carry out major attacks against the Phnom Penh government. Additionally, in particular these three rebel groups were affected by the general war weariness of the Cambodian people. As there were a diminishing number of volunteers to join the ranks of the rebels, the Khmer Rouge even had to use force to prevent people from leaving the refugee camps that served as the basis for Khmer Rouge operations. It demonstrates, that the Khmer Rouge realized they could not establish effective control over their territory or take over the government in Phnom Penh (cf. Hampson 1996, p.191).

Considering all these factors concerning the CGDK, both the externally and domestically caused ones, it can be concluded that this side to the conflict faced a hurting stalemate due to the loss in structural, physical and psychological strength. The hurting stalemate was initiated in mid-1990 when the US started to withdraw its political and financial support and was manifested by early 1991 with China cutting off its assistance. Therefore, it can be established that a mutual hurting stalemated existed by early 1991. The Hun Sen government already faced a hurting stalemate in early 1990, however, the CGDK only experienced the full hurting by early 1991. Thus the mutual character of the stalemate was manifested only in early 1991.

The shifts on the international level thus influenced the domestic power-distributions in Cambodia. The termination of foreign military and financial assistance to all of the Cambodian factions created a situation in which all four conflicting parties faced a mutually hurting stalemate; it established the MHS. Without the extra support, the CGDK seemed to be unable to take over the country and it even seemed that its power diminished immensely as they lost their status as a recognized government-in-exile on the international level by losing its seat in the UN General Assembly. The Phnom Penh government also seemed unable to ever really achieve a situation in which it effectively governed the whole of Cambodia and furthermore, it had to deal with significant pressure

---

[180] As confirmed by Defense Minister General Tea Banh, cf. Van der Kroef (1991): "Cambodia in 1990: The Elusive Peace", *Asian Survey*, p.97.

from international actors. The ongoing violent insurrections created a painful situation and the country was in a bad economic state due to the decades-long civil war and the termination of external inflows of funds. Thus, a precipice threatening the existence of all conflicting parties served as the basis for the mutually hurting stalemate.

This gives evidence to the Theory of Ripeness regarding this variable. However, it could be argued that due to the fact that the precipices were created almost simultaneously to all belligerents and all financial support was cut off more or less equally, the relative power distribution in the conflict did not change and thus a real precipice did not exist. However, as argued in the paragraphs below, this would be a wrong conclusion to draw.

I. William Zartman explicitly points to the significance of the concept of perception in this context. Thus, when external support is terminated to one party, this actor will primarily feel the own limitations and cuts in power. This can trigger precipices that lead to the perception of an MHS – as happened in Cambodia during the years after the end of the Cold War until the signing of the Paris Peace Agreements. The individual perceptions of the parties of their disastrous situations were further enhanced because of the non-transparent processes during the years 1990/1991. For example, the CGDK still suspected the presence of some 3,000 Vietnamese troops supporting the government in 1991. Equally, the Hun Sen government was suspicious that China still continued its support to the Khmer Rouge (Van der Kroef 1991, p.100). Thus, the individual factions could not be sure of what the belligerents' actual positions and powers were. They could primarily judge their own strength, which was diminishing strongly for each individual party.

It has to be noted that third parties played a significant role in creating the MHS in Cambodia. This not only stems from the fact that the Cambodian civil war was characterized by its internationalized form in terms of a proxy war of the great powers, but also from the active involvement of third parties in the course of managing the conflict (cf. the fact that the involved international states agreed on a comprehensive settlement as a basis for a framework for further mediation efforts before confronting the domestic belligerents with the idea). This only became possible after the end of the Cold War when the deadlocked situation of superpower relations ended.

Concluding, it is possible to state that an MHS was apparent in Cambodia throughout a considerable amount of time. It started in early 1991 when the external supporting powers had withdrawn their individual support. As it was expressed in a publication of Accord, "with the end of the Cold War, all four factions had been deprived of external military backing, were weary of war and in need of international legitimacy" (Accord 1998, p.19). Thus, in sum, three factors contributed to the perception of all factions that an MHS existed which are a military stalemate, a weakened political and diplomatic position, and a domestic economic crisis (cf. also Sorpong Peou in Stedman/Rothchild, et al. 2002, p.502).

Was there a sense of a way out prevalent among the conflicting parties at the time of the initiation and processing of negotiations? From the late 1980s onwards, several attempts of bringing peace to Cambodia had been made by international actors, which all failed because of seemingly insurmountable divergences concerning basic outlines for potential solutions between the individual Cambodian factions and also individual interests of key external actors (cf. Hong 1995, p.93; Solomon in Crocker/Hampson, et al. 1999, p.275; Van der Kroef 1991, p.100). Hence, one can say that in those cases, an SWO did not exist. A solution that could have satisfied all parties or at least offer a common ground for further discussions just did not seem feasible.

This deadlocked situation changed after the end of the Cold War when the US announced in July 1990 that it would no longer recognize the CGDK as the Cambodian representative to the UN. At this point, it became possible to first reach an agreement between the Perm Five outlining a framework as a potential basis for negotiations in Cambodia. The US agreed to the idea of other Security Council member states that a Cambodian settlement would have to involve the participation of all four belligerents; meaning that it would also have to accept the involvement of the Khmer Rouge in a potential power-sharing agreement.

Thus in late 1990, the Perm Five presented such a framework for a comprehensive settlement to the Cambodian factions, which was accepted by all as a basis for further peace talks. This framework set up by the external actors has to be seen as a chance for the belligerents, offering an SWO in the form of a potential solution to the conflict in which all parties played a certain role; thus, in which all warring factions had the possibility to gain something. This means the fact that no single faction was excluded from the negotiation process provided the key actors with the 'sense' that a resolution of the conflict was achievable – a solution leaving every party in a better position than in the status quo.

It is worth expanding this aspect even further. The external intervention in the form of mediation in this context was not simply offering help by providing an SWO. The role played by the external actor concerning this issue was much more proactive. By using means of 'muscular mediation' as described above in the context of the MHS, the third party (Perm Five) actually pressured the Cambodian factions into a situation in which there was no alternative for them than 'sensing' a way out. By cutting financial support to all parties and by using means of political pressure, those states succeeded in pressurizing the domestic actors to start negotiations on the grounds of their suggested comprehensive framework, which could offer ways out of the current deadlock and unsustainable situation (cf. Doyle and Suzuki in Weiss 1995, p.140). In particular the two main military antagonists, the Hun Sen government and the Khmer Rouge, were affected by the pressure to negotiate and ultimately also to sign the Peace Agreement due to an apparent lack of other options. The reason for this development lies in the collapse of the Soviet Union and thus the end of the Cold War. The policy of rapprochement emerged more and more between the superpowers. Thus, it was the superpowers that wanted the civil war to be terminated. The incentive behind this proxy war between the great powers lost its validity. As argued above, as soon as the external assistance to the domestic parties was cut off, the individual Cambodian actors did not see themselves anymore in a position, which could lead them to a potential victory, meaning that without the great powers in their backs, any sort of hope was lost to all sides. This is what has been described as an MHS. Further the great powers did not leave the factions to the MHS, but also offered them a way on how to get out of the MHS – to stop the fighting. It means that the SWO must be considered as firstly, brought to the domestic parties from external actors, and secondly, the SWO was not only strengthened by means of persuasion but by means of muscular mediation in the sense that external actors did not leave the domestic parties any choice of not 'sensing' the way out. To look at the four actors individually, it is important to analyze what 'way out' each of them sensed.

To start with the two 'smaller' factions, the KPNLF and the FUNCINPEC, it is relatively obvious what their sense of a way out was. Neither of the two was a strong military faction. They depended upon the military support of the Khmer Rouge, despite the fact that they politically strongly opposed the Khmer Rouge. Thus, a military fight was not in their primary interest. Further, both factions had signaled repeatedly over the course of the previous years that they were willing to find a negotiated solution to the civil war. With the framework offered by the Perm Five, they actually faced an option to not only pacify the country, but also to have realistic chances to become part of the government. As would be proven by the later elections, they were quite successful (particularly the FUNCINPEC who won the elections with 45%). Therefore, their preference for a non-violent political engagement was much more promising to them than the continued military fight, in which their chances were lower. Being supported by the UN and the international community gave them a chance of a very profitable way out of the status quo. Furthermore, it should be mentioned that the associated Prince Sihanouk played a significant role in the perception of an SWO. For Sihanouk, a negotiated settlement was the only option to return to Cambodia from exile and actually return as a pacifying hero. None of the strong military parties would have re-installed him, but a democratically elected government would need the help of the 'father of the Nation'. Therefore, both the FUNCINPEC and the KPNLF did perceive an SWO.

When analyzing the behavior and statements of the Khmer Rouge, there were clear signs displaying their sincere intentions at the time: for example, the Khmer Rouge leader, Khieu Samphan, was quoted with a positive statement regarding the possibility to go forward with a peace treaty. In June 1991, he supported the agreement for a ceasefire "as a token of our willingness and sincerity to proclaim the acceptance of the cessation of hostilities throughout Cambodia and the end of outside military assistance under effective supervision and control of the United Nations"[181]. Samphan's statement is a display of the sincerity with which the Khmer Rouge approached the renewed peace initiative. It demonstrates that they did indeed sense a way out of the situation.

Further internal documents by the Khmer Rouge show that this position was shared even by Pol Pot. In an internal Khmer Rouge document published before their announcement of boycotting the elections in 1993, that is before their official defection from the peace process, Pol Pot is quoted as, "suppose there will be 100 seats in the Kampuchea National Assembly, it would not be bad if we had 20 persons, better if we had 30... if we have a number of popular representatives in the parliament we will inevitably have some representatives in the government and major ministries"[182]. This shows that the Khmer Rouge elite indeed did see a way out by supporting a democratic system. They were willing to accept a power-sharing agreement and did not solely strive for total military victory anymore. They even expressed their willingness to accept their potentially inferior position in the government coalition. Even though the original document of this statement was not seen directly by the author of this thesis, it is still of value that the document of interest is referred to as an internal Khmer Rouge document. Thus, it is neither tailored to impress the other factions nor the international community, but represents a pure positioning and strategy paper of the Khmer Rouge.

One more sign for the sincerity of perceiving a way out, was an event that happened after the signing of the peace treaty in November 1991. When Khieu Samphan came to Phnom Penh for the first time as an official politician, he got attacked. Samphan went to the new Khmer Rouge building. However, in front of the building there were people waiting and demonstrating against the involvement of the Khmer Rouge as a legitimate party. The situation escalated and the

---

[181] Cf. *The New York Times*, "Cambodian Factions Agree to Halt Arms Imports", 25 June 1991.
[182] Cf. *Phnom Penh Post*, Thayer, Nate: "KR Blueprint for the Future Includes Electoral Strategy", 27 August 1992.

people stormed the building, attacking Samphan for about four hours before the Cambodian police rescued him. Samphan was seriously injured and fled immediately back to Thailand[183]. Yet, the Khmer Rouge did not withdraw from their commitments at that point. Instead, only one day later, they announced that they would abide by the peace plan stating that it would "not fall into the trap or maneuvers of the destroyers of the peace agreement"[184]. As a result, Khieu Samphan returned upon recovery to Phnom Penh on 30 December 1991[185] in order to continue supporting the implementation of the Paris Agreements. It is a sign for the sincerity with which the Khmer Rouge pursued the agreement. Even attacks and hurdles did not set them back immediately.

As late as August 1992, there is still evidence that the Khmer Rouge sensed a way out. In an interview with the Phnom Penh Post, Khieu Samphan expressed this very clearly. He stated that they do believe in national reconciliation and in the implementation of the Paris Agreement. But they also felt rejected by UNTAC. He stated, "If we look at the past nine months, we can see that this is the main trend: the western powers' thinking is now to get rid of the forces of the party of Democratic Kampuchea. They try to keep in place the Phnom Penh regime and the Vietnamese forces, to use these forces to try to get rid of the Khmer Rouge"[186]. It is important to note that this interview was an instrument by the Khmer Rouge to gain popularity and further their means. In parallel, it is also a source which shows, that the Khmer Rouge at least were part of the discussion and were trying to bring their messages across – not (only) through military means. Thus, it is fair to state that even here, we find a qualified statement that a certain level of a SWO existed.

Additionally, it can be stated that the Khmer Rouge had a fair chance in the middle and long run to regain popularity and strength in Cambodia through legitimate channels. While it became clear through the stop of external support that a military victory and take-over of power was impossible in 1990 and 1991, they did see the potential to make people forget the atrocities from the past over time and gain political legitimacy – even on the international level – by honoring the ideas put down in the peace treaty. The Khmer Rouge were seen as the only

---

[183] Cf. *The New York Times*, Shenon, Philip: "A Khmer Rouge Suffers Beating By Cambodians", 28 November 1991.
[184] Cf. *The New York Times*, Shenon, Philip: "Khmer Rouge Planning to Stick to Peace Plan", 29 November 1991.
[185] Cf. *The New York Times*, Sanger, David: "Pol Pot Colleague Back in Cambodia", 30 December 1991.
[186] Cf. *Phnom Penh Post*, Thayer, Nate: "An Interview with Khmer Rouge Leader Khieu Samphan", conducted early August 1992, published 27 August 1992.

party in Cambodia that was disciplined and not affected by corruption. The worse the economic situation became the more popular legitimacy they gained[187]. The Phnom Penh Post wrote at the time, "By seizing on issues which improve the lot of the desperately poor and neglected 80 percent of the population who are farmers, their disciplined and non-corrupt organization will look increasingly good in comparison to their opponents"[188].

Furthermore, the Khmer Rouge went through a change in rhetoric in the months from late 1990 until early 1992. Frequently, they expressed their positive outlook for a peaceful Cambodia in the future. One of the favorite channels to do so was the Khmer Rouge radio. As quoted in Newsweek, the radio station broadcasted in December 1991, "all Cambodians should unite and look to the future"[189].

All in all, the potential gains through the participation in the peace process and the subsequent power-sharing government were attractive enough for the Khmer Rouge to sense a way out. By being included as an individual party in the peace process and especially by being treated at par and as a legitimate actor in Cambodia, they could overcome their reputation of genocidaires. Through the Perm Five-offered framework, the Khmer Rouge got the chance to be treated not as war criminals, but as a legal entity. They were able to participate and actually did participate in all the important strategic and political sessions regarding the planning and implementation of the Paris Agreements. This was decisive for them to perceive an SWO in the years of 1990 and 1991.

Also the Hun Sen government signaled that they saw a way out of the status quo. The re-installation of Prince Sihanouk appears to have been crucial for them. Despite being a communist party, the CPP expressed their willingness to find a solution openly. One sign for this was their acceptance of returning to the monarchical system. In that context, the cabinet decided to rename the oldest hotel in Phnom Penh (which had frequently changed the name dependent on the leading system) into "Le Royal"[190] during the summer of 1991. It demonstrates that the government did sense a way out; in fact, they tried to display their SWO openly. Even though the CPP had opposed Prince Sihanouk strongly before, it appeared that they were able to share power in the government. This would be an opportunity on which to base the further peace process. With Prince Sihanouk

---

[187] Cf. *Phnom Penh Post*, Thayer, Nate: "KR Blueprint for the Future Includes Electoral Strategy", 27 August 1992.
[188] Cf. Thayer, Nate: "KR Blueprint for the Future Includes Electoral Strategy", 27 August 1992.
[189] Cf. *Newsweek*, Moreau, Ron: "Roughing Up The Khmer Rouge - For Now, The Cambodian Killers Are Forced To Flee", 09 December 1991.
[190] Cf. *Der Spiegel*, Terzani, Tiziano: "Der Friede hängt an Sihanouk", 19 August 1991.

returning to a representative position (not a political one), the CPP saw that it was possible to gain the support and acceptance of the Cambodian people again.

This was further and significantly supported by the conditions laid out in the framework. With the promised help by the UN regarding the repatriation and the reconstruction of Cambodia, the CPP would be able to solve the country's economic problems and pay the employees' salaries, especially to the military. The CPP was also assured a major role in the power-sharing agreement and in consequence had great chances to win the national elections, once the country received economic aid. Therefore, the perception of an SWO by the CPP was obvious. For them, the alternative of a negotiated solution on the basis of the Perm Five's framework promised a way out of the state of misery.

The government also acted upon their perception of the sense of a way out. After signing the peace agreement, they supported the first steps of implementation rigorously, which again proves their previous sincerity. For instance, in January 1992, they freed 290 political prisoners as a sign for their compliance[191].

It is possible to conclude that an SWO did exist in Cambodia at the moment of interest. The SWO existed from late 1990 onwards, when the Perm Five presented a potential alternative to continued fighting in form of a framework serving as a basis for peace negotiations. All four belligerent factions displayed their willingness to terminate the fighting and to conclude their long-standing civil war.

The analysis of the MHS and SWO shows that in the time leading up to the signing of the peace treaty in 1991, there existed a phase of ripeness in Cambodia. Specifically, ripeness was established in early 1991 when both an MHS and an SWO were given in Cambodia. All belligerents had lost hope of winning the conflict. Furthermore, each of them signaled a sense that there might be a way out; a potential for the resolution of the conflict. This shows that ripeness existed (cf. also Hampson 1996, p.212 and Solomon in Crocker/ Hampson, et al. 1999, p.279). As Brown and Timberman put it, "the collapse of the Soviet Union and the end of the Cold War precipitated a negotiated end to the war in Cambodia" (Brown, F.Z./Timberman 1998, p.16).

The question arises to what extent independent variables then affected the status of conflict ripeness. Some of the variables have already been touched upon in the analysis above, but it is useful to revisit them one by one also with respect to the quality of their effect.

---

[191] Cf. *The New York Times*, "Cambodians to Free 290 Political Prisoners", 15 January 1992.

To begin with, one should look at the independent variables initiated by the mediator, which are persuasion, inducements and pressure. The above made analysis already hinted towards the effect it took on the conflict ripeness. The perception of ripeness was substantially supported by a well-thought through usage of instruments on part of the mediator. Persuasion was combined with the two other tools: inducements and pressure. With the Perm Five as a mediator, the countries with the most leverage and political power came together. It was hugely helpful that they among themselves had agreed upon a basis for the framework of the peace treaty before confronting the belligerents. As Crocker, Hampson and Aall put it, "the Permanent Five's unusual level of cooperation and willingness to act in concert were critical to the Cambodian settlement" (Crocker/Hampson, et al. 1999, p.51).

The mediator supported the notion that there is way out in the form of a readily-written basis. It was also significant that the original plan for the peace treaty included all factions and provided a basis for a kind of power-sharing agreement. By this, all factions were able to profit in one way or the other from the peace treaty and thus find legitimate reasons for why they should stop fighting. This strategy was combined with putting pressure on the belligerents in form of withholding assistance and promising economic support as part of the peace process. Thus, persuasion and inducements combined with pressure supported conflict ripeness.

In support of the MHS, the international powers involved also played upon the possibility to further strengthen the perception of the Cambodian belligerents through inducements. Given the hurting stalemate all factions found themselves in, they were much more susceptible to what is called the strategy of 'carrots and sticks' (cf. Ashley in Brown, F.Z./Timberman 1998, p.50). This refers to significant promises – which functioned as inducements in that context – made as part of the Comprehensive Framework that served as a basis for the peace negotiations (cf. Accord 1998, p.18). The Paris Agreement provided for the following three "carrots", contingent on the factions signing up to the Agreements: firstly, the Agreement made reference to international military involvement. It promised the withdrawal of foreign forces, verified by UNTAC (cf. Paris Agreement, Section IV, Article 8). Furthermore, it outlined that there shall be no individual, outside military assistance to any of the Cambodian parties (cf. Paris Agreement, Section V, Article 10). This was particularly important to the individual factions as they were frightened of continued support to the other parties. The Khmer Rouge suspected continued support by the Vietnamese to Hun Sen and the other way around. With this agreement, all individual factions could feel safe that no such external involvement would occur anymore. The second area serving as a carrot concerned repatriation. The international signatories promised to support the repatriation of all Cambodian refugees and displaced persons through the help of UNTAC (cf. Paris Agreement, Part V: Refugees and displaced persons, Articles 19-20). This was a task of immense scale with more than 350,000 such displaced persons and refugees. None of the factions would have been able to implement such program on their own. The third area of promises concerned the rehabilitation and reconstruction of Cambodia. The Agreement stated, "the Signatories urge the international community to provide economic and financial support for the rehabilitation and reconstruction of Cambodia" (Paris Agreement, Part VII: Rehabilitation and reconstruction, Article 24). This last area is of special interest. It means that parallel to the provision of UNTAC and their mission of repatriation and other tasks, the agreement served as a basis for the promise of large scale international aid. The exact operational steps were even further outlined and detailed in the Annex. Regarding repatriation, in addition to the help of UNTAC, the agreement promised support of UNHCR and the ICRC. In this context, it stated, "the international community should contribute generously to the financial requirements of the repatriation operation" (Paris Agreement, Annex 4, Part III: Operation Factors). Furthermore, the Paris Agreement provided for an individual "Declaration on the Rehabilitation and Reconstruction of Cambodia" as part of the Annex. Among other rules, it referred to the notion that particular attention would be given to food security, health, housing, training, education, the transport network, the infrastructure and public utilities (cf. Paris Agreement, Annex, Declaration on the Rehabilitation and Recon-struction of Cambodia, Article 10). These were the most pressing necessities for all factions involved and thus promised a solid way out of the catastrophic misery the people found themselves in.

The provisions, made in the Paris Agreement, show that by laying out a framework (coordinated and supported by the Perm Five) that served as a discussion basis for the actual agreement, the mediator used the instrument of inducements in order to support the MHS and the consequent willingness of the belligerents to find an agreement. Hence, it can be argued that the Cambodian case provides an excellent example of a sticks and carrots strategy.

This also affected the SWO, which was significantly 'sweetened' by the inclusion of these inducements into the framework (cf. Accord 1998, p.18). All the belligerent parties were able to gain to a certain extent from the implementation of the framework – be it through economic recovery or the repatriation of people. As has been argued by Richard H. Solomon (publicly nominated as US Assistant Secretary of State for East Asian and Pacific Affairs in 1989), "one of the remarkable aspects of the ultimately successful Cambodia settlement was that it substantially reconciled such diverse if not divergent interests" (Solomon in Crocker/Hampson, et al. 1999, p.299)[192]. The offering of a way out as done by the Perm Five through the provision of the framework was thus significantly supported by the outlined "carrots" that were manifested in the agreement. The Perm Five actually did use the strategy of enlarging the pie significantly by promising vital necessities to all belligerents.

The sincerity of the four factions, and by that their will to implement 'the way out', was further underlined through the mediator's active pushing for the realization of the peace plan. For instance, the four Cambodian factions met in late December 1991 writing an appeal to the UN to start deploying the peacekeeping force. The appeal was signed by all of the four belligerents. Chan Youran, the Khmer Rouge envoy to Beijing where the meeting took place, commented that it had been led under "very, very good spirit" and "mutual comprehension" among the factions[193]. The positive inducements offered by the third party with the comprehensive framework serving as a basis for the peace treaty were the final pieces in the puzzle. They ensured that the pie was enlarged and the individual parties could benefit from terminating the civil war. It led to the situation in which all conflicting parties perceived conflict ripeness.

Additionally, the Perm Five also used the instrument of putting pressure on the belligerents to further their aims and by that to manifest ripeness. As outlined above, it seems that it was to a large extent the end of the Cold War and with that the rapprochement of the great powers and their willingness to bring the conflict to an end that enabled ripeness in Cambodia in 1991 (cf. Accord 1998, p.5). Especially with respect to the MHS, pressure significantly supported the perception of ripeness. While the Perm Five were also the main contributors to the belligerents beforehand, during the ripe phase, these countries had ceased all their individual assistance to the conflicting parties. Pressure was thus used in form of continuing the withholding of assistance and at the same time promising economic support if the peace process was to be led sincerely. All four belligerents were heavily affected by this development. While they had profited from previous proxy interests by the Great Powers, the end of the Cold War also ended the proxy war. The continuation of fighting therefore seemed pointless for the individual Cambodian factions given their immense dwindling of resources.

---

[192] It is to be noted here that even though Solomon uses the term 'ultimately successful', he also acknowledged that the fighting did resume soon after the signing of the Peace Agreement (cf. Solomon in Crocker/Hampson, et al. Herding Cats: Multiparty Mediation in a Complex World, pp.275-276).
[193] Cf. *The New York Times*, Sanger, David: "Factions Meeting in Phnom Penh Appeal to U.N. for Peacekeepers", 31 December 1991.

Therefore, it can be concluded that the manipulable independent variables, persuasion, inducements and pressure, were all used consciously as instruments by the mediator in order to further the peace initiative. In that sense, these three variables intensified the level of conflict ripeness.

With regard to the non-manipulable variables, we first look at the effect of those variables that can be initiated by the belligerents' leadership. During the relevant time from early 1991 onwards, there were no significant changes in the leadership of any of the four warring factions. Therefore, it seems that this independent variable can be excluded from the further analysis as it did not affect conflict ripeness. A little more complex is the assessment of the variable assertiveness of leadership. While the leaders of the main belligerents, Hun Sen and Khieu Samphan (and Pol Pot), were very strong protagonists enjoying a strong voice and loyalty within their individual factions, the notion of spoilers or involuntary defections must be examined in more detail. Defections from the Paris Agreements were frequent and came from all sides. They started to happen in the beginning of 1992, which is about three months after the official signing of the peace treaty. In all cases, it must be doubted that these defections were involuntary. In fact, it seems that they were rather planned and used consciously as instruments by the individual factions. Therefore it is possible to conclude that defections did indeed happen, however they were not of an involuntary character. Quite the opposite, the indications speak for a conscious usage of the defections by the belligerents. Consequently, it has to be asked what this implies for the conflict ripeness and why such defections happened. It seems that conflict ripeness was weakened, if not destroyed altogether. The reasons do not lie within the independent variable of assertiveness of leadership but probably in other reasons. This will be covered separately below. What the independent variable of assertiveness of leadership implies is that 'accidents' of violence did occur. Accidents here are considered as incidents in which groups act autonomously and not in accordance with entire factions, or actual accidents in which some kind of violent action is involuntarily triggered. None of those two kinds of defections were witnessed in Cambodia. Therefore, assertiveness of leadership did not affect conflict ripeness.

Before examining the research variable of IDA, the last independent variable to look at is external support to belligerents. As outlined above, the external support significantly changed previous to the ripe phase. However, once ripeness was established, the status quo in this respect did not change. Thus, throughout the months following early 1991, no changes in the external support to the individual belligerents occurred. Therefore, this independent variable had no effect on conflict ripeness.

The analysis has shown that ripeness indeed existed and was relatively intense given the effect of some of the independent variables on the status of ripeness. The independent variables analyzed all enhanced the intensity of conflict ripeness. It seems that from early 1991 onwards, all conflicting parties were sincerely interested in reaching a peace agreement. The Hun Sen government, the KPNLF, and the FUNCINPEC showed a great willingness to find a solution, to compromise, and finally to contribute to the implementation of the agreements. Even the Khmer Rouge displayed a behavior throughout the negotiation process as well as in the immediate time afterwards that allows the observer to conclude that the required sincerity was existent throughout the process. There might be critics claiming that ripeness never actually existed as the Khmer Rouge just 'pretended' to negotiate sincerely and that they actually used the peace process to further their battle: to rearm, re-strengthen the troops or to build up external backing (cf. Solomon in Crocker/Hampson, et al. 1999, p.314 claiming that, "the one element in the coalition that never fully "ripened" was the core of the conflict – the rivalries among the Khmer political factions" or Strassner claiming that the Khmer Rouge were using the status quo to enlarge their military and political basis: Strassner 1991, p.312). However, as outlined above, there are several indications demonstrating that the Khmer Rouge not only changed their policy when they thought it would be right but that they changed their policy due to a change of perception of the process. As David Ashley put it, "beginning of January 1992, the Khmer Rouge grew increasingly skeptical of the peace process" (Ashley in Accord 1998, p.22); which in turn shows that their original intent was sincere.

Also the other three domestic factions, the CPP, the KPNLF and the FUNCINPEC were shown to be sincerely interested in the negotiation process, thus fostering ripeness. The findings from above are supported by a further indication: all three parties had made several attempts throughout the 1980s to negotiate. Even though those previous peace talks failed because of insurmountable differences, it indicates a certain continuous willingness to find solutions. Furthermore, all three factions stopped fighting immediately and demonstrated general determination to a successful implementation of the Paris Peace Agreements by cooperating with UNAMIC and UNTAC. Sincerity is further found in the fact that both former allies of the Khmer Rouge, the KPNLF and the FUNCINPEC, opposed the Khmer's destructive behavior much later in the process. Thus after an attempted coup in July 1994 by the Khmer Rouge to overthrow the government, legislation was passed that officially outlawed the Khmer Rouge, supported by the KPNLF and the FUNCINPEC. This illustrates the sincere commitment of the other factions to foster peace.

To sum up, we can safely assume that all four Cambodian factions were sincere when signing the Peace Agreements on 23 October 1991. Ripeness was significantly supported by some of the independent variables analyzed: "with the decline of the East-West conflict and the Sino-Soviet rapprochement at the end of the 1980s the Cambodia conflict became a political and economic burden for most foreign parties involved, especially for the Soviet Union and Vietnam. Still, it took about two years until a comprehensive international peace agreement and plan had been worked out and signed in Paris on 23 October 1991" (Raszelenberg/Schier 1995, p.18). This analysis is supported by then UN Secretary-General Boutros Boutros-Ghali who stated, "the four Cambodian factions showed great political will in signing the Paris Peace Agreements, but implementation of the peace plan would prove to be an even greater challenge" (United Nations 1995b, p.10). The table below summarizes the effect of the independent variables on conflict ripeness.

Independent Variable	Effect?	Quality of Effect
Persuasion	Yes	Positive: intensified ripeness
Inducements	Yes	Positive: intensified ripeness
Pressure	Yes	Positive: intensified ripeness
Change in leadership	No	No impact
Assertiveness of leadership	No	No impact
External support to belligerents	No	No impact
IDA	Open	Open

Table 16: Independent Variables Affecting Ripeness in Cambodia[194]

5.3.2.2 Increase in Development Aid

Having analyzed the status of conflict ripeness and the effect of independent variables on the status, the question now arises whether IDA serves as an independent variable in this context as well.

With the signing of the peace agreement, the aid-situation in Cambodia immediately changed completely. While the external actors had cut off all support in the previous years to the peace process, contributing to a phase of

---

[194] Source: Own illustration.

ripeness, the Paris Agreements opened up the possibility and duty (as there were significant promises included) to deliver large amounts of aid to the country. Plenty of UN donor agencies, numerous international NGOs and various governments provided assistance of all types (cf. Hendrickson in Accord 1998, p.80). Foreign aid "came to represent more than half the national budget and was potentially an important tool with which to influence government policy" (Hendrickson in Accord 1998, p.80). Cambodia saw a 'new' face of itself: "This week [mid-November 1991], for the first time since Phnom Penh was overrun – and emptied – by the Communist Khmer Rouge 16 years ago, the Cambodian capital is bustling with diplomats and journalists who have come here not to track the battles, but to assess the peace"[195].

Three types of aid for Cambodia will be presented: first, the largest amount provided to Cambodia in the form of the UN missions UNAMIC and UNTAC. Second, and connected to that the multilateral and bilateral assistance; and third, aid provided by international NGOs.

The most significant type of aid was the UN sponsored peacekeeping mission UNTAC that was preceded by its advance mission, UNAMIC. As outlined in the Paris Agreements, UNTAC's task was to plan and coordinate an international effort to rebuild Cambodia (cf. Heininger in Belgrad/Nachmias 1997, p.112). It was the third largest peacekeeping operation in UN history until then (cf. Acharya 1994, p.299 and Robert in Kiernan/Hughes 2007, p.28) with a total of 22,000 personnel. According to Chong, UNTAC can be characterized as an organization displaying many different facets such as being an international aid organization carrying out relief projects and repatriating refugees, as well as a military force providing peacekeeping, and finally a surrogate government directing economic and social policy during the transition period (Chong in Milliken 2003, p.216).

UNTAC was split into five components of which one was the component responsible for aid, the rehabilitation component. This component was in charge of assessing the demand in the country and to coordinate all aid efforts by UN organizations, governments and NGOs. The rehabilitation component only had six staff and hence was much smaller than the other components (cf. Hazdra 1997, p.111), keeping in mind that the overall mission comprised about 22,000 personnel.

Furthermore, the large influx of UNTAC international staff led to an inflow of vast amounts of foreign currency. "During their first eight months, UN staff

---

[195] Cf. *The New York Times*, Shenon, Philip: "Cambodians See the Return of Prince Sihanouk as the Best Hope for Peace", 13 November 1991.

and peacekeepers spent an estimated [US]$ 200 million in Cambodia, fueling a burst of commercial activity that lifted the country's war-shattered economy into the ranks of the world's fastest growing. But with the 21,000-man mission due to begin winding down after the election, Cambodia is likely to witness a changing pattern of investment. [...] When UNTAC pulls out you will see a huge drop in business. I estimate 50%", said Poul Leineweber, the representative for EAC which provides marketing services for Marlboro cigarettes and M&M chocolates in Cambodia"[196].

US$ 2 billion were officially allocated to UNTAC, of which a large amount went into the payment and accommodation of its own employees. Kao Kim Hourn suggested that from 1992 until 1995, an amount of US$ 1.3 billion was actually disbursed as international aid (Hourn in Brown, F.Z./Timberman 1998, p.188).

It is debatable whether one should label the expenses related to UNTAC as development aid. In this case, it makes perfect sense to do so. UNAMIC and UNTAC had the internationally backed task to facilitate national and democratic elections, to repatriate refugees, and to reconstruct the country. All three tasks are part of a classic development aid portfolio. Alan James supports this argument. Referring to UNTAC's mission, he stated, "in a very real sense, any operation which helps to maintain peace has a humanitarian aspect" (James in Belgrad/Nachmias 1997, p.53). Janet E. Heininger agreed and stated, "the Paris Accords gave UNTAC the task of planning and coordinating an international effort to rebuild Cambodia" (Heininger in Belgrad/Nachmias 1997, p.112).

The facts about UNAMIC and UNTAC are as follows. UNAMIC lasted from October 1991 until March 1992. They had an initial strength of 116 military personnel (50 military liaison officers, 20 mine-awareness personnel, and 40 military support personnel) and expanded their mission by 1,090 additional military personnel. UNAMIC suffered no casualties[197]. UNTAC's mission lasted from March 1992 until September 1993 with strength of approximately 22,000 military and civilian personnel. The last staff left Cambodia in early 1994. UNTAC suffered 78 fatalities in total of which 4 were military observers, 41 other military personnel, 14 civilian police, 5 international civilian staff and 14 local staff. According to the UN, the combined expenditures of the two missions totaled US$ 1.62 billion[198].

---

[196] Cf. *Phnom Penh Post*, Burslem, Chris: "UNTAC Bubble Economy Set to Burst", 07 May 1993.
[197] Cf. http://www.un.org/en/peacekeeping/missions/past/unamicfacts.html.
[198] Cf. http://www.un.org/Depts/DPKO/Missions/untac.htm.

Apart from UNTAC, a range of other multilateral organizations were also involved in the reconstruction of Cambodia. UNHCR for instance was in charge of implementing the repatriation of the refugees. They were supported by UNDP conducting so-called quick-impact projects for refugees (cf. Heininger in Belgrad/Nachmias 1997, p.124). According to Janet E. Heininger[199], "by the end of January 1993, [US]$ 3.4 million of the [US]$ 9 million allotted to such projects had been spent. By June UNHCR had funded a total of eighty projects in all twenty-one provinces, including areas controlled by all factions but the Khmer Rouge" (Heininger in Belgrad/Nachmias 1997, p.125).

Furthermore, four trust funds were established by voluntary contributions and administered by the UN, however independent from UNTAC[200]. These trust funds were primarily set in place in order to support projects in the areas of human rights promotion and demining activities. The four trust funds totaled an amount of about US$ 13 million (cf. UNDPI 1994, pp.377-378).

As early as at the end of the year 1991, a group of nations pledged about US$ 90 million worth of development aid in the form of bilateral assistance (cf. Talentino in Brown, M.E./Rosecrance 1999, p.189). This aid-generosity connected to the will to terminate the Cambodian war continued among donor countries. Japan hosted the Ministerial Conference on Rehabilitation and Reconstruction of Cambodia on 20 and 22 June 1992, the so-called Tokyo Conference. The conference was organized in response to an appeal made by the UN Secretary-General Boutros Boutros-Ghali. He had asked for US$ 595 million in the so-called Secretary-General's Consolidated Appeal for Cambodia's Immediate Needs and National Rehabilitation. A large number of donor countries participated and pledged a total of US$ 880 million of aid to Cambodia[201]. The final amount exceeded Boutros-Ghali's expectations by far (cf. Heininger in Belgrad/Nachmias 1997, p.127).

The pledge of US$ 880 million was promised as 'economic assistance' and was supposed to be directed to budget support, training, education, infrastructure repair, and basic social services (cf. Brown, F.Z./Timberman 1998, p.20). In September 1993, the donor community added new pledges of US$ 119 million to the amount (cf. Darlan 1994, p.24). The list of donor countries involved was

---

[199] Source: US Congress, Senate, Committee on Foreign Relations, Reform of United Nations Peace-keeping Operations: A Mandate for Change, 103rd Cong., 1st sess., August 1993, S. Prt. 103-45, p.29.
[200] The four trust funds were the Trust Fund for the Cambodian Peace Process, the Trust Fund for a Human Rights Education Programme in Cambodia, the Cambodia Trust Fund for Rehabilitation Activities, and the Trust Fund for the Demining Programme in Cambodia.
[201] Cf. *The New York Times*, Sanger, David: "880 Million Pledged to Cambodia But Khmer Rouge Pose a Threat", 23 June 1992.

extensive[202]. It was led by Japan with a pledge of US$ 220 million, followed by the US with US$ 135 million, France with US$ 57 million, Australia with US$ 40 million and Sweden with US$ 38 million (Hazdra 1997, p.181).

Actual disbursements, of course, differed from the pledges, or rather, it took time to implement such large scale pledges from the international community. Darlan estimated that in the year 1993, an amount of US$ 155 million was actually disbursed by official donors (Darlan 1994, p.24).

In parallel, even though the Paris Agreements called for foreign countries to only deal with the Cambodian interim administrative body SNC (Supreme National Council), which combined all four belligerent factions until a new government was to be elected, France proceeded to make bilateral arrangements with the authorities in Phnom Penh: "In January [1993], more than 700 municipal officials from Phnom Penh gathered for a conference sponsored by Phnom Penh's sister city, Paris, on urban planning and development. France has had officials giving training and advice to the Phnom Penh authorities' police force since last year. And France has pledged more than 20 million Francs for refurbishing the badly dilapidated Phnom Penh water and electricity system"[203]. Furthermore, as early as in February 1993, the French President Francois Mitterrand visited Phnom Penh with a delegation of 270 people[204].

The US also outlines how they significantly increased development aid to Cambodia. On the USAID website, they state, "US assistance to Cambodia accelerated sharply after the signing of the Paris Peace Accords in 1991, which in turn led to the re-opening of the USAID/Cambodia Mission in 1992"[205]. That means, not only money and goods, but also a significant increase of personnel was dedicated to Cambodia and even stationed locally. In total, they indicate that development assistance in the form of USAID funding of US$ 61 million was paid out in 1993[206].

The net disbursements in the form of ODA have been tracked by the OECD (cf. Organization for Economic Cooperation and Development 2010). As the OECD points out, "ODA consists of disbursements of loans made on

---

[202] Participating countries were Australia, Austria, Belgium, Brunei Darussalam, Cambodia, Canada, China, Denmark, Finland, France, Germany, India, Indonesia, Ireland, Italy, Japan, Laos, Malaysia, Netherlands, New Zealand, Norway, Philippines, Portugal, Republic of Korea, Russian Federation, Singapore, Spain, Sweden, Switzerland, Thailand, United Kingdom, United States and Vietnam (cf. http://www.un.org/en/peacekeeping/missions/past/untacbackgr2.html.).
[203] Cf. *Phnom Penh Post*, *Phnom Penh Post*, Thayer, Nate: "Historical Ties Underpin French Aid", 26 February 1993.
[204] Cf. *Phnom Penh Post*, Thayer, Nate: "Historical Ties Underpin French Aid", 26 February 1993.
[205] Cf. http://www.usaid.gov/kh/history_usaid_cambodia.htm.
[206] Cf. http://www.usaid.gov/kh/history_usaid_cambodia.htm.

concessional terms (net of repayments of principal) and grants by official agencies of the members of the Development Assistance Committee (DAC), by multilateral institutions, and by non-DAC countries to promote economic development and welfare in countries and territories in the DAC list of ODA recipients. It includes loans with a grant elements of at least 25 percent (calculated at a rate of discount of 10 percent)" (cf. Organization for Economic Cooperation and Development 2010).

There was a significant overall increase in the ODA-disbursements to Cambodia from 1991 onwards. From a total of US$ 41 million in 1990, the amount increased to a total of US$ 301 million in 1993, and a further US$ 551 million in 1995 as visualized in the table below (cf. Organization for Economic Cooperation and Development 2010).

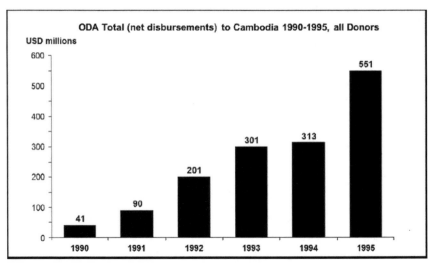

Figure 20: Total ODA to Cambodia in millions of US$[207]

The graph above shows net disbursements of ODA to Cambodia by all donors taken together. This includes bilateral and multilateral institutions (excluding development aid provided to Cambodia by NGOs).

---

[207] Source: Data provided by Organization for Economic Cooperation and Development "World Development Indicators", ; illustration: own source.

When examining the ODA in-depth, it becomes clear that the bilateral share of disbursements was almost always significantly larger than the multilateral share, except for 1992, where the UNHCR made a significant contribution of about US$ 40 million (cf. Organization for Economic Cooperation and Development 2010).

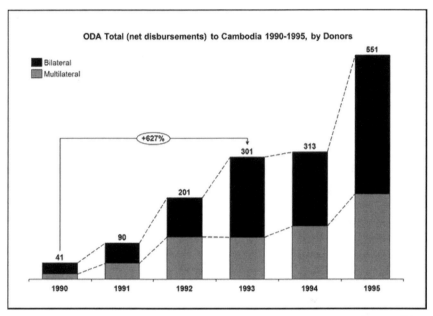

Figure 21: Total ODA to Cambodia, Net Disbursements in millions of US$[208]

What is further interesting about the ODA provided to Cambodia as visualized above is the significant increase in disbursements. Throughout the relevant years, from 1990 to 1993, a total increase of more than 600% can be noted.

Additionally to the significant bilateral and multilateral assistance delivered to Cambodia in the aftermath of the peace treaty, numerous international NGOs came to the country as well (cf. Hourn in Brown, F.Z./Timberman 1998, p.188). By 1993, more than 100 NGOs were officially registered in Cambodia (cf.

---

[208] Source: Data provided by Organization for Economic Cooperation and Development "World Development Indicators", illustration: own source.

Darlan 1994, p.14). By January 1994, Michael Doyle counted 120 NGOs (cf. Doyle 1995, p.62). These organizations covered tasks on a broad scale including projects dedicated to the development of infrastructure, the alleviation of poverty, the promotion of multi-party politics, among others (Cf. Hendrickson in Accord 1998, p.80). The organizations involved were not purely international; especially after 1993, a growing number of local NGOs sprang up. However, most of those active until 1993 were well-known international agencies such as CARE International or Oxfam (cf. Doyle 1995, p.62). In order to be able to deal with the high influx of NGOs, the Cooperation Committee for Cambodia was founded at the end of 1991 as an umbrella organization for NGOs.

What is interesting about this last group of development donors, the international NGOs, is that they were the ones also addressing rural areas – as opposed to bilateral and multilateral efforts. As Guy Darlan expressed it, "employing large numbers of expatriates and working with local counterparts, NGOs offer the assurance that assistance will be implemented and disbursed and that it will reach local target groups" (Darlan 1994, p.v).

All in all, it can be established that significant IDA could be identified in the period of interest in Cambodia. With promises before the signing of the peace agreements, pledges after signing and significant disbursements, large amounts of money, material, and personnel entered Cambodia.

Given that previously, all contributions to Cambodia had been cut off completely, the aid resources facilitated through the Paris Agreement were immense. The UN missions UNAMIC and UNTAC, the significant further bilateral and multilateral disbursements and the explosion of NGOs involved in Cambodia constitute IDA over the years between 1990 and 1995. Each year in fact saw significantly more money, material and people dedicated to development aid coming in.

Therefore, it can be established that large amounts of aid entered Cambodia during the ripe phase. Now it must be asked whether this increase in development aid affected conflict ripeness and thus functions as an independent variable in the theoretical analysis of the situation.

5.3.2.3   Effect of Increase in Development Aid on Ripeness

The analysis so far suggested a successful peace process, in which ripeness existed, and the Cambodian warring factions signed a peace treaty in the end. It seemed that all signature parties were content with the agreement, providing for a power-sharing agreement under the auspices of the UN with a large-scale peacekeeping mission on the way. Moreover, large amounts of foreign aid were promised and delivered. Any casual observer might ask: aren't these the best conditions for a sustainable peace and final end to a decade(s)-long civil war?

The further course of events tells us that this was not the case. Quite the opposite happened. The peace process broke down, none of the belligerent factions honored its commitments made in the Paris Agreement fully and one withdrew altogether (cf. Doyle 1995, p.13). As David Ashley put it, "The 1991 Paris agreements and the resulting UN intervention to implement them reduced and altered, but could not end the Cambodian conflict" (Ashley in Accord 1998, p.20). Other scholars go further and do not even support the idea that the intensity of the conflict was reduced. The dataset COSIMO identifies a new conflict starting in the aftermath of the Paris Agreement, from 1991 to 1999. The COW intrastate war-dataset counts an end to the conflict in 1991, but identifies a new war from 1993 to 1997. AKUF counts the Cambodian conflict without disruption as a continued violent conflict until 1998. Bercovitch and Fretter report, "violence continued into the late 1990s" (Bercovitch/Fretter 2004, p.187).

Throughout the year 1991 (just before and just after the signing), there was potential for peace in Cambodia. As outlined above, conflict ripeness could be identified and the four warring parties to the conflict had negotiated sincerely throughout the process leading up to October 1991. However, by mid-1992, fear, violence and thus conflict had re-emerged (cf. Hong 1995, p.95). Not only did the Cambodian people fear the attacks and insurrections, both in rural and urban areas; but also the peacekeeping personnel was under attack. National elections were held in 1993 – also often judged as successful and peaceful. One must ask though how successful and peaceful they really were. In the beginning of May 1993, then Prime Minister Hun Sen was asked how he felt about the issue of security concerns regarding the upcoming elections. He answered, "I warned UNTAC of an emergency situation, that the Khmer Rouge would disrupt the elections. But my views were not sufficiently taken into consideration. Right now everyone seems to be very scared, too scared from my point of view"[209]. Hun Sen's statement demonstrates the instability and fear in the country at the time.

The course of events seems to confirm Hun Sen's perception of the situation. Even though UNTAC saw its mission completed with the national elections in 1993 (they pulled out the last personnel in early 1994), the civil war raged on until 1998, when the Khmer Rouge leader Pol Pot died.

---

[209] Cf. *Phnom Penh Post*, "Hun Sen Predicts Landslide Victory", 07 May 1993.

So what did exactly happen in Cambodia after the signing of the peace treaty? Why did the originally promising situation break down? And what role did IDA play in this context?

Until the beginning of 1992, almost no defections from the ceasefire were accounted for. The violence started again in the further course of 1992. It became critical in the fall of 1992, peaking in December 1992 (cf. Heininger in Belgrad/Nachmias 1997, p.128). Janet E. Heininger even stated that, "in the early months of 1993, it appeared uncertain whether the May 1993 internationally supervised election for a new government would be held at all" (Heininger in Belgrad/Nachmias 1997, p.128).

The Khmer Rouge were the most active and open opponents to UNTAC throughout 1992. They did not allow UNTAC access to its controlled areas, despite signing this rule in the agreements. Further, they refused to participate in the disarmament process on the grounds of feeling insecure about the strength of the CPP (cf. Hughes 2009, p.91). A kind of vicious circle motivated through a security dilemma followed. The Khmer Rouge used the argument of insecurity and the CPP used it equally as a result. The New York Times reported in November 1992 that, "the [Cambodian] Government wants the United Nations to declare 'an official end' to the disarmament phase of the peace process. Khieu Khanarith, a Government spokesman, said at a news conference today in Phnom Penh. 'We want troops that have been cantoned to go back to their positions', he said, referring to Government soldiers who are now living in United Nations-supervised cantonment sites. 'If the Khmer Rouge continue their attacks, it is necessary that we counter that'"[210]. In the end, the disarmament process broke down altogether (cf. Peou in Stedman/Rothchild, et al. 2002, p.500 and Doyle and Suzuki in Weiss 1995, p.133).

In April 1992, the Khmer Rouge officially withdrew from their commitments made in the Paris Agreements five months earlier. They claimed that they "had abandoned hope of a free and fair election and would continue to put its faith in armed struggle" (Talentino in Brown, M.E./Rosecrance 1999, p.186). After UNTAC established control teams to probe violence and insurrections and to intimidate the warring factions, the Khmer Rouge pulled out of the capital and regrouped in strongholds in April 1993, leaving UNTAC with no official contacts to the Khmer Rouge and no remaining official channels for dialogue. As a demonstration of their strength, the Khmer Rouge killed seven UNTAC officials in April 1993. UNTAC's head of the mission, Akashi, reacted:

---

[210] Cf. *The New York Times*, Shenon, Philip: "Cambodians Ask U.N. to Abandon Its Peace Plan", 4 November 1992.

"the world will not forgive the party of Democratic Kampuchea for disrupting the Cambodian elections. There should be no more sanctuaries for that party, and no more chances"[211]. From this time onwards, the clashes between the Khmer Rouge and Cambodian military as well as peacekeepers escalated (cf. Doyle 1995, p.20). In a range of attacks launched by the Khmer Rouge during the campaigning period between April 7 and May 19 1993, more than 200 people died (Doyle 1995, p.34).

Analyzing the accounts on the years of 1992 and 1993, it appears that also the other factions violated the ceasefire and the Paris Agreements in a significant way. For instance, it was reported that a number of attacks were conducted on people from the FUNCINPEC by government officials. In the period between November 1992 and January 1993, at least 18 assaults were accounted for in which 20 people were killed. Sou Sarith from the FUNCINPEC described an attack on his rural district at which he was abducted and beaten. He witnessed that the attackers were local officials of the Phnom Penh regime[212]. It was even discussed on the official international level whether to cancel or at least postpone the elections. As the UN formulized it in its concluding report: "In light of the situation, the Secretary-General, in a report to the Security Council on 14 July [1992], pointed to two possible courses of action: to suspend the operation until all parties complied with the Paris Agreements, or to pursue the process, thus demonstrating the international community's determination to assist the Cambodian people despite the lack of cooperation from PDK"[213]. The decision was taken in favor of the latter option by the UN Security Council in Resolution 766. They chose to continue the process as started and aim for national elections (cf. United Nations 1992). In November 1992, this decision was again re-confirmed by the Secretary-General in a report to the Security Council[214]. The official withdrawal of the Khmer Rouge from the peace process occurred in December 1992, when they stayed away from an SNC meeting[215]. This was the first such boycott.

In May 1993, the national elections were held despite the boycott by the Khmer Rouge. The reasoning behind the withdrawal of the Khmer Rouge was the perception on their side that the international community did not prove to

---

[211] Cf. *Phnom Penh Post*, Thayer, Nate: "Khmer Rouge: Will They be Back?", 23 April 1993.
[212] Cf. *Phnom Penh Post*, "Sihanouk Slams Political Violence", 15 January 1993.
[213] Cf. http://www.un.org/en/peacekeeping/missions/past/untacbackgr2.html.
[214] Cf. *The New York Times*, Prial, Frank: "Khmer Rouge Should Not Delay Cambodia Vote, U.N. Says", 18 November 1992.
[215] *The New York Times*, "Khmer Rouge Staying Away From High Council Meeting", 9 December 1992.

hold up their promises from the Peace Agreement. The UN's mission did not meet the demobilization timetable (cf. Talentino in Brown, M.E./Rosecrance 1999, p.176). The UNTAC-supervised elections brought up a new government and constitution. They were judged successful by many with a voter turnout of 90% (cf. Talentino in Brown, M.E./Rosecrance 1999, p.174; Solomon in Crocker/Hampson, et al. 1999, p.314). The result of the poll and the subsequent composition of the government were not quite in line though. While the FUNCINPEC won with 45% of the vote, they still had to share power with the CPP, which only won 38% of the vote. As it was assessed by Accord, "Cambodians could only stand by as the international community allowed the ruling Cambodian People's Party to force its way into a power-sharing arrangement with election winners FUNCINPEC, with complete disregard for the spirit of the Paris agreements" (Accord 1998, p.5). What happened was that after the CPP lost the election to the FUNCINPEC, "their leaders mounted an armed secession of the eastern half of the country refusing to hand over power"[216].

The local perception of the outcome was not very positive: "the election is over and it was nobody's success. If someone thought to come here and end the war, it did not happen. The war is not over. You still hear gunshots day and night, and one never knows why"[217]. After the elections and continuous insurrections, the Cambodian Parliament passed a bill outlawing the Khmer Rouge. The Khmer Rouge declared their own government in July 1994 (Hong 1995, p.95). Thus, the fighting against the Khmer Rouge continued – a military solution was to be found by the Royal Cambodian Government. For this end, the government even received support from some foreign governments, which were prepared to offer arms and training to the Phnom Penh armed forces (Hong 1995, p.96). This development represents a reverse policy compared to the original Paris Agreements where all four parties were supposed to work together. By 1994/1995 – despite "massive defections", the strength of the Khmer Rouge was estimated to be 5,000 to 10,000 "dedicated guerrillas who fought regular battles with government troops in Khmer-controlled areas" (Bercovitch/Fretter 2004, p.187). As stated above, violence continued until the late 1990s; the Khmer Rouge kept a significant military force (cf. Bercovitch/Fretter 2004, p.187). Only when Pol Pot died near the Thai border in April 1998, the Khmer Rouge actually resolved. "Two of the three remaining senior leaders of the Khmer Rouge

---

[216] Cf. *Phnom Penh Post*, Thayer, Nate: "New Govt: Who's Really in Control?", 19 November 1993.
[217] Cf. *Phnom Penh Post*, Davies, Robin: "Donors' Cart Must Follow the Cambodian Horse", 27 August 1993.

surrendered in late December 1998, and the last of the rebel fighters formally joined the Cambodian army in February 1999" (Bercovitch/Fretter 2004, p.187).

Plenty of accounts evaluated the UNTAC mission – both positive and negative (cf. Accord 1998; Acharya 1994; Brown, F.Z./Timberman 1998; Doyle 1995; Hazdra 1997; Hughes 1996; Milliken 2003; and United Nations 1995b). Brown and Timberman noted, "scores of Cambodians were killed and hundreds were injured by political violence during the UNTAC period, some by the Khmer Rouge but most as a result of CPP actions" (Brown, F.Z./Timberman 1998, p.18). It demonstrates that ripeness was apparently not maintained throughout the UNTAC-era. Also Hazdra argues that UNTAC was a failure with respect to reconciling the warring factions and that the accounts praising UNTAC were rather examples of communication policy sponsored by the UN (cf. Hazdra 1997, p.25).

The UN themselves formulated that "until January 1992, the ceasefire was generally maintained"[218], implying that afterwards it broke down. Nevertheless, "the international community declared the elections and UNTAC a great success. After all, a principal aim of the peace process had been an internationally recognizable government, and now there was one which not only controlled most of the country but could also claim popular legitimacy. With much relief, the international community declared the Cambodian conflict over" (Ashley in Accord 1998, p.24). Part of this assessment by the international community was also caused by their need to refocus the resources. Other 'pressing' issues came up on the level of international security that demanded both financing and manpower (cf. Solomon in Crocker/Hampson, et al. 1999, p.314). Therefore, they simply could not 'afford' a continued involvement in Cambodia and therefore felt the pressure to evaluate the Cambodian mission as successful. Quite a different assessment was made by the Far Eastern Economic Review in 1992 that "editorialized that UNTAC's presence in Cambodia had left the Khmer Rouge relatively strengthened against the other three Cambodian factions and allowed the faction to expand the territory under its control" (cf. Acharya 1994, p.301). Throughout the following years until the late 1990s, the intensity of violence increased. Doyle called the conflict in these years a "counter-insurgency war" that "produced a thousand military and uncounted civilian casualties each year" (Doyle in Brown, F.Z./Timberman 1998, p.89).

Concluding, one can state that what happened was that the international actors transformed their support away from the pre-Paris Agreements military support to humanitarian assistance. However, they were not successful in ending

---

[218] Cf. http://www.un.org/en/peacekeeping/missions/past/unamicbackgr.html.

the civil war. The disarmament process failed and even though the turnout at elections seemed successful, the government-building and the surrounding events of violence show that also this goal was not achieved. The former Foreign Minister of the State of Cambodia and Senator of the Kingdom of Cambodia, Kong Korm, expressed this in an Open Letter to all Signatory Countries of the Paris Peace Agreement in 2006 very clearly. He stated, "in other words, during 15 years (1991-2006), following the Paris Peace Accord on Cambodia, all events mentioned above [1993 secession event, 1997 coup d'état, bloodshed oppression on 1997 lawful demonstration and 1998 non-violent demonstration] indicate that Cambodia has set one step forward, but two steps backward in strengthening peace and reconstructing Cambodia on the way of democracy and development"[219]. This conclusion by a politician from Cambodia who lived through the years of conflict, negotiations and the post-agreement period, was also supported by academics such as Michael W. Doyle stating, "after an expenditure of more than $ 1.8 billion dollars for UNTAC, the death of 78 UNTAC soldiers and civilians (and many more Cambodians), and more than a billion dollars in foreign aid, Cambodia finds itself in the condition it was in 1990, before the UN peace operation began" (Doyle in Brown, F.Z./Timberman 1998, p.79). Doyle wrote this rather frustrating assessment in 1998. What relation did exist between the influx of aid and the unsatisfying course of events?

The sections above show that all individual factions defected from the commitments made in the Paris Agreements. The Khmer Rouge withdrew altogether and violence returned to the daily life in Cambodia. Political freedom and peace were not existent. In order to see what role IDA played in this context, it is useful to go through the individual actors separately.

Starting with the Hun Sen government, it becomes clear that they became largely dependent on the aid-influx. The government's budget shows that while in 1991, foreign financing accounted for 6.1 billion of riels, the amount grew to 271.4 billion of riels in 1993 (Darlan 1994, p.16). Guy Darlan stated that in 1994, "Cambodia's dependence on the donor community for economic and social rehabilitation is total" (Darlan 1994, p.ii; cf. also Hughes 2009, p.139). It shows that with UNTAC, other multilateral organizations, significant bilateral assistance and numerous NGOs in place, the government was not able to function independently. It also meant that the donor society had immense power over the government. The CPP felt that their individual internal political leverage was decreasing and not increasing over time.

---

[219] Cf. *Cambodian Information Center*, Korm, Kong: "Open letter to All Signatory Countries of Paris Peace Agreement on Cambodia", 24 October 2006.

The dependence on aid went hand in hand though with a strengthening of their troops and government. The CPP was in charge of the Phnom Penh authorities until the elections were to take place in May 1993. Until then, they effectively governed Cambodia – even if they had to report to UNTAC and were bound to the SNC that comprised all four former belligerents. Thus, all assistance that went into governmental authorities strengthened the CPP. In parallel, the CPP benefited strongly from a rather disproportional distribution regarding the coverage of development aid with respect to geography. What happened was that the largest amounts of aid were targeted at mainly urban areas, particularly Phnom Penh as described above. Apart from some NGOs reaching out to the rural population, most aid remained in the capital. The area around the capital was owned and administered by the CPP. Therefore, the CPP received significantly more than the other belligerents from the 'pie of aid'.

In June 1992, the German journal Der Spiegel reported that the prices of many of the goods in Phnom Penh had increased significantly due to the arrival of UNTAC. For example, while twelve bottles of water had cost 1,000 Riel (about one US$) at the end of 1991, six months later, they cost about 2,500 Riel, which constitutes an increase of 150%. The same is true for the development of housing rentals[220]. As Michael W. Doyle explained, "aid channeled through UNTAC did not, however, benefit all areas of Cambodia, especially the disadvantaged, and reach all levels of society" (Doyle in Brown, F.Z./ Timberman 1998, p.88). Doyle further explained why this development had negative effects on both the urban and the rural areas. "Aid flows during the UNTAC period, in fact, were biased in favor of urban areas, returnees, and relief in contrast to the declaration's call for developing rural areas and local capacity building. The urban bias artificially expanded the service sector (including prostitution), fostered high rates of consumer imports, and exacerbated income inequality" (Doyle in Brown, F.Z./Timberman 1998, p.89; cf. also Chong in Milliken 2003, p.217). What was left was a population that was highly unsatisfied and disappointed with regard to previous hopes both in the urban and in the rural areas. Doyle's argument is also supported by others. Most of the aid influx remained in the capital, Phnom Penh, which perpetuated the underdevelopment in rural areas. Other side-effects in the capital also increased inequalities between the urban and rural areas[221]. Judy L. Ledgerwood claims that "most aid money, like most of the million that poured into Cambodia during UNTAC, remains in Phnom Penh. Of the estimated $2 billion in total economic

---

[220] Cf. *Der Spiegel*, Terzani, Tiziano: "UNTAC ist der neue Gott", 01 June 1992.
[221] Cf. *Der Spiegel*, Terzani, Tiziano: "Straße von Furcht und Tod", 26 October 1992.

and financial assistance received from the international community between 1993 and 1996, the majority of funds did not leave the capital" (Ledgerwood in Brown, F.Z./Timberman 1998, p.133). There was a significant tendency of the donors to neglect the rural areas. For example, out of nine Japanese projects, five were targeted at Phnom Penh residents despite the fact that 90% of the Cambodian population lived in rural areas (cf. Heininger in Belgrad/Nachmias 1997, p.128). The focus on the capital had an important impact not only on the perception of the population with regard to aid, but it also had a significant impact on the distribution of political power. Governmental authorities dominated Phnom Penh; hence, all assistance dedicated to the capital primarily supported the Hun Sen party. In that sense, development aid was not neutral, but rather biased – even if unintentionally. The three rebel factions kept their strongholds outside the capital in the rural provinces and thus lacked input of aid and assistance compared to the Hun Sen faction. As Janet E. Heininger put it, "undoubtedly, the preponderance of assistance to urban areas skewed rehabilitation in the Phnom Penh authorities' favor" (Heininger in Belgrad/ Nachmias 1997, p.130).

This led to a perception of regained strength among the CPP. Suddenly, the feeling of a hurting stalemate faded away and the CPP's hopes to fully control Cambodia rose. This is also expressed through the CPP's increasing military attacks against the other factions leading up to the elections. The CPP wanted to win the elections by a large majority in order not to be forced to share power. When the elections showed a different result and the CPP actually lost the elections, they demanded new elections stating that the results were unfair. The conflict intensified and could only eventually be resolved by intense diplomatic efforts and by including the CPP in a power-sharing government. The CPP thus achieved to gain more influence in the new government than what a democratic institution-building would have allowed for. This development proved the previous elections as not democratic and politically absurd given that the results for the government-building did not mirror the results of the elections. It can therefore be established that the CPP felt that they were gaining strength relative to the other factions. The source of this is the biased distribution of IDA towards the capital and the government. This meant that the CPP did not perceive the stalemate anymore and also did not sense that a negotiated solution was necessarily the best outcome they could achieve. Therefore, in this case, it can be concluded that there is a direct line of causation between IDA and the destruction of ripeness and thus a negative impact of IDA on the peace process.

The KPNLF and the FUNCINPEC in comparison were relatively disadvantaged through the aid bias towards the capital and the government. They controlled territories in Cambodia that were located in rather rural areas and thus did not receive as much assistance. Furthermore, as outlined above, both of these two factions were regularly confronted with attacks by the CPP and by the Khmer Rouge. However, both mostly held up their commitments from the Paris Agreements and participated fairly in the elections. Therefore, in this context, no clear relationship between IDA and conflict ripeness can be established. As David Ashley put it, "beginning in January 1992, the Khmer Rouge thus grew increasingly skeptical of the peace process" (Ashley in Accord 1998, p.22). One important drawback for the Khmer Rouge was the French involvement and tight relations to the Hun Sen government before the national elections took place. The Khmer Rouge suspected a "French plot to recolonize Cambodia in conjunction with the Vietnamese"[222] as outlined above. Peter Hazdra even argued that the Khmer Rouge were actively politically isolated after signing the Paris Agreements. They were excluded from the overall political process and significantly disadvantaged in the distribution of aid and external assistance (cf. Hazdra 1997, p.93).

This strongly contributed to the Khmer Rouge's difficulties with the further peace process. It must be assumed that they were sincere in their commitments made in Paris in 1991. However, the situation changed soon. The Khmer Rouge were attacked when returning to the capital to participate in the process and often publicly criticized for their history. While it is understandable when taking into account the 'genocidal time' in this context, such behavior by the international community and UNTAC led to a destructive situation. The Khmer Rouge felt insecure and thus did not comply with the disarmament process. While before the Paris conference, all international actors tried to integrate the Khmer Rouge, the development aid was predominantly dedicated to the other factions. The situation escalated on both sides, so that the international community actively and publicly announced that development aid was only targeted at the factions complying with the commitments made in the Paris Agreements. And even though the Khmer Rouge defected most, the other three factions also did not fully comply, as outlined above. The other three factions were not excluded from the peace process whereas the Khmer Rouge were.

This constellation led to a situation, in which IDA was used politically in order to try to save the peace process. However, by doing so it triggered the opposite reaction – it drove the defecting party even further away and thus the peace process was destroyed altogether. Ripeness was thus destroyed through IDA in this case as the Khmer Rouge had lost its sense of the way out. They

---

[222] Cf. *Phnom Penh Post*, Thayer, Nate: "Historical Ties Underpin French Aid", 26 February 1993.

perceived the situation as hopeless for them and thus returned to their old strategy of military fighting.

After having covered the individual factions, an additional group should be mentioned in this context, which also suffered from the negative effect of IDA: the Cambodian population. Most significantly in this context is the disparity between the expectations that were built up through promises made by the international community and the result that the individual actors (including the people) felt in the aftermath. This is what might be called 'relative deprivation' – one of the core factors identified as a source for conflict in conflict management research as explained above in chapter 2.2.2.4 (cf. Rubin/Pruitt, et al. 1994). Relative deprivation in this case meant high hopes that remained unfulfilled.

After the large promises made in Tokyo, the Cambodian people had hoped for a fast betterment of the situation; instead nothing actually changed in the living status. Peter Hazdra assumed that part of the reason why the development aid did not arrive at the pressing areas was that some donors preferred 'large prestige projects', which needed a longer evaluation and set-up time. Furthermore, most of the early disbursements until December 1992 (about 77%) went solely into the repatriation of refugees and not into reconstruction and development projects (cf. Hazdra 1997, p.181). This gulf between perception and reality was also observed at the time by Roger Lawrence, the UN's chief economist in Cambodia. He stated that "there is a general misconception that the aid package involves millions of dollars that are going to come to Cambodia and will be lying around for people to help themselves to"[223]; not realizing that most of the aid that was pledged was in the form of capital goods and technical expertise that takes significant time to show an effect on the development of a country. Therefore in this case, the promise of IDA and what materialized in reality – or at least perceived reality among the common people – contributed to frustration and disappointment among the population. Their perceived ripeness to move on and hope for a change was therefore negatively impacted.

In conclusion, it can be stated that there were at least four direct causal relationships between IDA and conflict ripeness. The first is a positive one. It was the promise of aid that contributed to the perception of ripeness among the warring factions before the signing of the Paris Agreements. Aid in the form of inducements for the individual parties was a tool used by the international community to lure the factions into perceiving a sense of a way out. Therefore, in this case, IDA positively affected conflict ripeness. However, the second to fourth effects of IDA on conflict ripeness were negative. Firstly, aid towards the

---

[223] Cf. *Phnom Penh Post*, Burslem, Chris: "Donors Set to Meet Over Release of Aid", 16 July 1993.

urban centers created a bias towards the CPP, which thus felt that they were gaining in strength relative to their belligerents. Their hurting stalemate was destroyed and thus the perceived ripeness faded away. Secondly and as a consequence of this first point, the Khmer Rouge felt the relative disadvantage and discrimination through the aid-instruments. Therefore, their feeling of a sense of a way out was destroyed through IDA. Lastly, the promised IDA and large amounts of pledges made by the international community were not felt by the population. Instead, the 'IDA bubble' in Phnom Penh led to inflation and raised the costs of living for the ordinary population. Therefore, the population perceived a strong disparity between the promises and reality and thus had to face relative deprivation, which is one of the main causes for tension and violence. IDA thus negatively affected conflict ripeness in this case, too.

The last aspect to consider when examining whether the above analysis is valid is to consider a counterfactual line of thought. Can we support the findings by arguing that if IDA had not come into the country as it did, conflict ripeness had not been affected and destroyed, so that we can state that IDA really was the independent variable leading to continued violence? As seen above, it seems that some parts of IDA had a very positive effect on conflict ripeness. This was expressed through the analysis of the independent variable of inducements. The 'enlargement-of-the-pie', of which the promise of development aid was part, had the effect that the individual factions were able to sense a way out and thus it helped to establish ripeness in the first place to a certain extent.

However, when looking at the negative effects of IDA as identified in the further course of events after the signing of the peace treaty, it seems that we are facing a paradox. Offering inducements helped, however, then, the disbursement or way of disbursement destroyed ripeness. Counterfactually, two questions have to be analyzed: firstly, would conflict ripeness have been established without offering inducements? And secondly, could IDA have been dispersed in a more intelligent way, so as not to destroy the careful balance of an MHS and an SWO?

Regarding the first question, it seems that indeed IDA – or rather the promise of IDA – was decisive for at least one of the factions to sense a way out: the CPP. All the other factions were attracted to the comprehensive framework due to other reasons, such as the Khmer Rouge having the perspective to become a legitimate and respected political party. The Hun Sen government saw its way out of misery because of IDA. With IDA, they felt that it would be possible to overcome the economic catastrophic situation, to be able to stabilize the government's budget and to stay in power at the same time. Thus, in this case, the counterfactual has to be rejected. IDA was decisive in creating conflict ripeness.

The second question is more complex. What would have happened if the identified IDA had not come into the country? It must be assumed that in this case, the entire process would not have had a chance from the beginning. Without UNTAC and without a controlling force for the government, the factions would have most likely continued fighting immediately. Only through the effort of UNTAC and also other development organizations, a dialogue and continued communication became possible among the belligerents. Further, elections would not have taken place at all without a neutral actor that was able to organize them in all parts of the country. Therefore, this counterfactual also has to be rejected.

Where does this analysis leave us? The answer appears relatively easy: better implementation. If promises are made, then it seems crucial and decisive for the success that they are fulfilled – in the sense of bettering the status quo and in the sense of distributing the aid equally. A negative gap between hopes and reality contributes to a feeling of relative deprivation, which is a trigger point for disappointment and tension. Moreover, it can also be a trigger for the privileged (in this case the CPP) to feel stronger and hopeful of victory again. This analysis leaves us to suggest three conclusions. Firstly, it seems that the continued withholding of development aid would not have furthered the peace process. Instead, it is very likely that any chance for the resolution of the conflict would have died at the beginning of the ripe phase. Secondly, the conscious use of IDA by the mediator in the form of inducements helped to manifest conflict ripeness. It positively affected the peace process. Thus, it seems that if the initiator of the variable becomes the mediator and he uses IDA as one of his tools, it is possible to leverage IDA in order to manipulate the belligerents into perceiving intensified ripeness. Thirdly, however, the way of implementation did not result in the expected success either. Three conditions contributed to the failure of IDA in this context: large amounts of development aid were publicly promised, however the delivery of the aid was perceived by the receivers as slow and not fair. This contributed to a feeling of relative deprivation. Further, the development aid was dispersed independently of the progress in the peace process. If one of the belligerents defected, this had no consequences on the influx of the development aid stream. Lastly, the distribution of the disbursed aid was not implemented in a conflict sensitive way with regard to the fairness between the individual belligerents. Instead, the aid strongly favored one of the conflicting parties by that contributing to an intensification of tensions between the belligerents.

5.3.2.4 Conclusion

Having gone through all the individual aspects of the Cambodian case, it is now important to put the findings into the context of the theory analysis. The case-guiding research questions help to establish the context of how the individual variables function together in the case of Cambodia.

#	Question	Answer
1	Is it possible to identify an MHS?	Yes
2	If not, is it possible to identify MEOs?	-
3	Is it possible to identify an SWO?	Yes
4	Can conflict ripeness be affirmed?	Yes
5	To what extent does persuasion affect conflict ripeness?	Positively
6	To what extent do inducements affect conflict ripeness?	Positively
7	To what extent does pressure affect conflict ripeness?	Positively
8	To what extent does a change in leadership affect conflict ripeness?	No effect
9	To what extent does the assertiveness of the leadership affect conflict ripeness?	No effect
10	To what extent does external support to the belligerents affect conflict ripeness?	No effect
11	Can IDA be observed?	Yes
12	Is it possible to identify an effect of IDA on ripeness?	Yes
13	Does IDA affect ripeness positively?	Yes
14	Does IDA affect ripeness negatively?	Yes
15	Under which conditions does IDA affect conflict ripeness positively and under which conditions does IDA affect conflict ripeness negatively?	Cf. below

Table 17: Case-Guiding Research Questions Cambodia[224]

In conclusion, the case of Cambodia shows that ripeness did indeed exist at the beginning and throughout the mediation process before the signing of the peace agreement. This means, conflict ripeness could be identified in early 1991, lasting until mid-1992. This state of ripeness was created through a cut in

---

[224] Source: Own illustration.

external influx and thus made a mediated agreement between the warring factions possible. The Paris Peace Agreement can be judged as an agreement that was made sincerely by all the involved parties; the evidence from the relevant actors involved proved the sincere intentions from the peace process. The status of conflict ripeness was further intensified through instruments consciously used by the mediator in form of persuasion, inducements and pressure. Fen Osler Hampson assessed the process as follows: "While there may have been enough ripeness to pursue negotiations and reach a political settlement, there was not enough to keep the Khmer Rouge from defecting from the peace process and resuming its armed struggle against the government afterwards" (Hampson 1996, p.213). The beginning of Hampson's assessment can be supported; however, the analysis showed that it is not the case that there was not enough ripeness for the further process. Indeed, by the beginning of 1991 until early 1992, conflict ripeness could not only be identified, but it could also be established that the status of ripeness was significantly intensified through the effect of independent variables. It was mainly the mediator, the Perm Five, who leveraged his tools in order to enlarge the perception of conflict ripeness on part of all belligerents. Thus, it was not the case that there was not 'enough' ripeness, but rather a further independent variable destroyed the existing conflict ripeness.

First, IDA was promised and used before the signing of the peace agreement as a tool to make the treaty more attractive. In this regard, IDA affected conflict ripeness positively. But then, IDA started to come into the country upon the signing of the peace agreement in 1991. The further analysis helped to establish the notion that IDA was the decisive variable destroying conflict ripeness. In the end, the way of distribution of IDA led to the defection of one of the belligerent parties, to renewed violence and thus to the continuation of the civil war. Therefore, the case of Cambodia is an example where it must be concluded that IDA functioned as an independent variable to conflict ripeness as the dependent variable in that it significantly affected conflict ripeness to the extent that the dependent variable was destroyed.

The further analysis showed that it was mainly four conditions accompanying IDA that led to an effect of IDA on ripeness. The first condition was that the mediator consciously used IDA as a tool in his peace efforts. The mediator included IDA into the overall carrots and sticks strategy and thus was able to positively manipulate the situation, so that conflict ripeness was intensified. The other three conditions contributed to the situation in which IDA negatively affected conflict ripeness. Firstly, the discrepancy between the large amounts of IDA publicly promised and the lack of perceiving the positive effects of IDA thereafter among the domestic actors turned IDA into a negative impact. Secondly, the lack of interconnecting the influx of IDA and the progress of the peace efforts seemed to undermine the previous strategy of the mediator of carrots and sticks. Thirdly, the relative favoring of one party to the other in the distribution of the aid seemed to increase and renew the tensions between the belligerents. Drawing a conclusion, it is possible to see that indeed ripeness was affected by IDA as an independent variable. It was both a positive and a negative effect that it took. The overall effect was negative though given that the peace process broke down.

5.4 Synthesis of Findings

In the previous sections of this chapter, three case studies have been conducted: Uganda, Burundi and Cambodia. The remaining of the chapter will bring the findings of all case studies together by providing synthesized results (5.4.1). Further contingent generalizations will be drawn on the basis of the comparative findings (5.4.2).

5.4.1   Comparative Findings

Three cases were analyzed with respect to the research objective of whether IDA functions as an independent variable to the dependent variable of conflict ripeness. Concretely, this meant that it was analyzed whether conflict ripeness existed in the cases at hand and whether such ripeness was affected by independent variables. Then, IDA was brought in as an additional independent variable and it was tested whether IDA affected ripeness and if so, in what way. Lastly, the analysis was concerned with the conditions accompanying effects of IDA on ripeness. Thus, it was examined under which conditions IDA intensifies the level of conflict ripeness and under which conditions IDA reduces the level of conflict ripeness.

5.4.1.1   Background to the Cases

All three countries in which the case studies were located had been colonized. All three countries had experienced major conflict, brutality and large scale violence in the subsequent years and decades after gaining independence. Even though the colonizers differed (France in Cambodia, Belgium in Burundi and the United Kingdom in Uganda), colonial times left similar marks on the setup of all three countries. While the Burundian history was a story of ethnic identities and power struggle, the Cambodian history was marked by political ideology. Uganda's history is shaped by tribal tensions, or rather a 'classic' North-South divide of the country.

The conflicts analyzed in the three case studies started at different times, but all in the second half of the 20th century. While the conflict in Cambodia started as early as 1978, Uganda's conflict broke out in 1986, and Burundi's in 1993. None of the conflicts was a sudden outbreak. Instead they all resulted from a long history of insurgencies and power struggles. They all started with a regime change as in the case of Cambodia with the installation of the Vietnamese 'puppet state', in the case of Uganda with Museveni's gaining of power, and in the case of Burundi with the first democratic elections resulting in a change in government.

The individual phases of the conflicts analyzed differ. While the Cambodian case focused on a rather late period in the life-cycle of the conflict, the Ugandan and Burundian cases looked at the conflicts in their entirety. This allowed for within-case comparison in the two latter cases in addition to the cross-case comparison between the three countries' conflicts. The three cases fundamentally differ in their individual type of conflict. Cambodia is a conflict of ideology. It had become a classic example of what is called a proxy war with support of the super powers to the respective belligerent sides. Basically, four different factions fought against each other with the objective of ruling the country. Uganda is a conflict of tribal history. A long and traditional feeling of deprivation led to a North-South divide of the country. With the gaining of power of a representative of the one side, a rebel group established itself and fought against the government. What is distinct about the Ugandan case is that the conflict mainly affects only one part of the country and not the entire territory (as in the cases of Cambodia and Burundi). Burundi is a conflict of ethnicity. Two ethnic groups fight each other due to a long history of discrimination and manipulation. Old elites and the majority of the people are facing each other competing for influence and power.

All three conflicts are examples of protraction. Cambodia's conflict lasted for two decades, Uganda's conflict as well for at least two decades (it is still ongoing) and Burundi's conflict for slightly more than one decade. What they have in common as a result is a large scale humanitarian disaster. Displacement and refugee are inherent parts of the story in each of the conflicts. In all cases, it was the civilian population that predominantly suffered. This is a characteristic that all three cases share: the insurgencies are led by the instrument of involving the population. Innocent civilians are terrorized and killed.

The types of belligerents differ. Cambodia mainly has four factions fighting each other with one faction being in the government. Similarly, in the case of Burundi two groups are fighting for the power in government. The distinct difference is that the holder of the government is not in charge of the military. Uganda's case differs. Here, there is the clear state-actor that is fighting a local rebel group that is generally limited to one part of the country.

Also the mediators differ in the three cases. In Cambodia, the United Nations' Permanent Five led the mediation efforts. In Uganda, an individual, Betty Bigombe, the civil society and then the GoSS were in charge. In Burundi, first a UN representative (Ould-Abdallah) mediated; then individuals that had been designated by regional powers (Julius Nyerere and Nelson Mandela), and finally a country not from the region, but from the continent: South Africa. Thus, all different types of actors are represented in the case studies.

5.4.1.2 Conflict Ripeness

We constituted that conflict ripeness is given when two ingredients are given: an MHS/MEOs and an SWO. A detailed definition on ripeness and the threshold that must be passed so that ripeness is established are provided in chapter 4.2.1. It was also defined that the intensity of any of the two ingredients can be increased or decreased by independent variables. As mentioned above, conflicts rarely follow a general path. Each conflict is unique and displays unique instances or phases throughout its life cycle. In the analysis, three cases have been assessed of which two of the cases comprised of more than one incident. In order not to confuse the findings, it is helpful to recall the individual instances that are analyzed by way of cross-case comparison as well as within-case comparison. The table below summarizes the individual eight instances of which four were located in Uganda (phase 1: 1986-1994; phase 2: 1994-1998; phase 3: 1998-2005; and phase 4: 2005-2008), three in Burundi (phase 1: 1993-1995; phase 2: 1996-2000; and phase 3: 2000-2006), and one in Cambodia from 1990 to 1993.

Case	Time	Phase
Uganda	1986 – 1994	Phase 1
Uganda	1994 – 1998	Phase 2
Uganda	1998 – 2005	Phase 3
Uganda	2005 – 2008	Phase 4
Burundi	1993 – 1995	Phase 1

Case	Time	Phase
Burundi	1996 – 2000	Phase 2
Burundi	2000 – 2006	Phase 3
Cambodia	1990 – 1993	Phase 1

Table 18: Case Studies and Phases Analyzed[225]

In order to be able to compare the individual situations of conflict ripeness, the ingredients as well as the independent variables will be looked at individually and compared. With regard to the first phase in the Ugandan case (1986-1994), we have seen that neither the GoU nor the LRA perceived an MHS. The GoU felt no international or internal pressure. The conflict did not constitute a national threat. The LRA had just 'survived' a military offensive and perceived itself as a strong resistant to the situation.

The second phase in the Ugandan case (1994-1998) saw almost no change to the first phase. Neither the GoU nor the rebels perceived a hurting stalemate as no external or internal pressure was put on them. Both belligerents felt strong and able to maintain the situation with the hope to win the war.

In the third phase in the Ugandan case (1998-2005), the situation changed. Both belligerents, the GoU and the LRA perceived a hurting stalemate. The GoU's hurting originated from three aspects: firstly, the conflict had come to international attention. The government's great international reputation was thus at stake. Secondly, internal difficulties accompanied the external pressure with regard to needed democratic reforms. Thirdly, the constant military failure against the rebel group took its effect. The military was criticized and accusations were heard stating that the President might want to prolong the conflict consciously. The LRA perceived hurting due to two reasons: firstly, it struggled militarily. The group had lost major commanders in the battle, the Second-in-Command had defected and the government had started a policy, which granted amnesty to rebels defecting. Secondly, external pressure was put on the LRA as the ICC started investigating against the rebel groups on grounds of crimes against humanity. Thus, both belligerents found themselves in a precipice-situation, constituting an MHS.

Phase four in the Ugandan case (2005-2008) is an example for a strong MHS. The GoU perceived both a precipice and a plateau-situation. Immense international pressure including the threat of a UN intervention and internal difficulties through a strong opposition threatening the state-setup contributed to

---

[225] Source: Own illustration.

the precipice. The constant failure of not being able to militarily win against a small rebel group constituted the plateau-situation, which suggested that there is no alternative than agreeing to negotiations. The LRA faced a steep precipice. The ICC had issued arrest warrants against the leaders of the group, which put great international pressure on the rebels. Further, the only external source of support to the group, the Sudan, ceased its assistance, and additionally, the group had to retreat into the territories of neighboring countries, so that the conflict suddenly became internationalized – or at least regionalized. This contributed to a strong perception of nervousness and fear on part of the leadership. Therefore, it is possible to conclude that phase four saw a strong MHS in Uganda.

In the first phase in the Burundian conflict (1993-1995) none of the belligerents perceived an MHS. The conflict had 'just' started and faced a situation of ever-increasing violence. Both main parties tried to expand their political positions and believed they were able to win the conflict.

The second phase in the Burundian case from 1996 to 2000 ended with a strong perception of a hurting stalemate by all belligerents. In the first situation in early 1996, the President perceived a hurting stalemate due to internal developments. His effective power had ceased to exist; the opposition was basically in charge of the country. That implies that the belligerent did not perceive a hurting stalemate, but instead was on a rather successful track. The second situation from mid-1996 until 1998 was characterized by a continuation and intensification of these perceptions. Only in the third situation from 1998 to 2000, an MHS was perceived. On part of the government, international pressure had taken its effect. An international embargo had led to a disastrous situation in Burundi that was not sustainable. Thus, the government faced a precipice. The belligerent perceived a hurting stalemate due to a continued plateau-situation. Their attempt at establishing power through democratic elections had not worked and they found themselves in protracted suffering constantly losing their means of fighting. Thus, an MHS was given with a precipice-situation on part of the government and a plateau-situation on part of the belligerent.

In the third phase of the Burundian case (2000-2006), the belligerents all perceived hurting stalemates as well. The government, being transitional and relatively fragile in character, realized that it could not win against the rebels militarily. Their existence was threatened by the rebel attacks, which could have easily escalated into a full blown renewed national conflict. The two other belligerents, one after the other, faced hurting stalemates because of the developments in the country. Given that their political wing was able to increasingly manifest its position in the Burundian government, the armed wings' motivation to continue fighting diminished. Thus internally, the groups were significantly weakened. The CNDD-FDD reached a plateau-situation realizing that they could continue fighting as a rebel insurgency, but the hopes of overthrowing the government and gaining full power had ceased. The FNL faced a similar situation; however was additionally pressured by a sort of precipice given international military presence and a stronger national military army fighting them. Thus they perceived both a plateau and a precipice. An MHS was given.

In the case of Cambodia all belligerents perceived an MHS in 1991. The Hun Sen government's hurting stalemate was triggered through three factors. First, external support was stopped, meaning that both the Soviet Union and Vietnam, who had substantially supported the government financially and militarily, terminated their support due to international developments. In parallel, also smaller states, such as Czechoslovakia, Poland, Hungary, and Bulgaria withdrew from their assistance to Cambodia. Second, intra-party dissension led to a destabilization of the faction, so that it was substantially weakened, and third, the government faced a significantly deteriorating economic situation in the country. These three factors combined to both a plateau-situation given that a change to the situation was not to be hoped for anymore, and also to a precipice-situation given a looming disaster on the political and economic level. The belligerent, the CGDK consisting of the Khmer Rouge, the KPNL, and the FUNCINPEC, also perceived a hurting stalemate. In this case, it was mainly externally driven. International actors such as the US, China, and Thailand, that had supported the CGDK financially, militarily and politically, withdrew their support. This cut in external support led to a significant worsening of the situation internally. The factions lost their military strength, their organizational power, and the strong will to fight. These developments resulted in the perception of a steep precipice.

It is thus possible to conclude that mainly international developments – in this case the end of the Cold War that led to the policy of normalization and thus to the termination of proxy wars – resulted in a situation in which the supporters to the individual factions terminated their assistance. This led to internal difficulties and ultimately to a precipice-situation perceived by all sides, constituting an MHS.

In conclusion, out of the eight instances analyzed, five displayed situations, in which all belligerents involved perceived hurting stalemates. The main drivers for the perception of an MHS were cessation of external support, international pressure, internal difficulties, military pressure and protracted failure in acquiring power[226]. The following table summarizes the results:

	MHS?	Form of MHS	Main Drivers for MHS
Uganda P 1	No	-	-
Uganda P 2	No	-	-
Uganda P 3	Yes	Precipice	▪ International pressure ▪ Internal difficulties
Uganda P 4	Yes	Precipice and plateau	▪ International pressure ▪ Internal difficulties ▪ Cessation of external support
Burundi P 1	No	-	-
Burundi P 2	Yes	Precipice and plateau	▪ Int. pressure through embargo ▪ Protracted failure at trying to get to and/or maintain power
Burundi P 3	Yes	Precipice and plateau	▪ National/political pressure ▪ Internal difficulties losing motivation to fight ▪ Military pressure (both national and international)
Cambodia	Yes	Precipice	▪ Cessation of external support to all belligerents

Table 19: Comparison Mutually Hurting Stalemate[227]

During the first peace initiative analyzed in the Ugandan conflict from 1993 to 1994, none of the Ugandan belligerents sensed a way out of the conflict through means of negotiation. Instead, both still believed in their potential to win. Thus, an SWO was not given. Also in the subsequent phase between 1997 and 1998, there was no SWO given in Uganda. Similarly, phase three in the Ugandan case, 2004-2005, did not display an SWO. The situation was not as clear-cut as in the

---

[226] The term driver in this context is not to be confused with the independent variables discussed below. The independent variables affect conflict ripeness. Drivers are the main reasons why conflict ripeness was established. These drivers refer to the reasons for creating ripeness and not affecting ripeness.
[227] Source: Own illustration.

previous instances though. Both parties somehow indicated that they were willing to negotiate. Yet, the actions and parallel statements made clear that they both found themselves in states of mind in which they could not imagine the end to the conflict through a negotiated, peaceful settlement. However, in phase four between 2006 and 2008, the Ugandan belligerents both displayed a sense of a way out. The GoU showed its commitment through offering compromises to the belligerents beforehand and through addressing the humanitarian catastrophe in the affected region. The LRA demonstrated its sense for a way out through the involvement of the high leadership in the process. The main drivers for the generation of an SWO differed with respect to the two parties. The GoU felt intense international pressure to finally address the humanitarian challenges in Northern Uganda and to sustainably resolve the conflict. The LRA sensed a way out due to the choice of mediator. Having a truly external party as a mediator in the process enabled the LRA to enter the negotiations without prejudices.

Burundi's first phase, 1993-1995, did not see an SWO. The belligerents did not display any sign of serious commitment or an imagination of how a potential peace process could lead to a peaceful, negotiated end of the conflict.

The second phase from 1996 to 2000, however, displayed an SWO in Burundi. It was the mediator facilitating the sense of a way out for the belligerents. The main way of doing so was to convene early meetings in which the opposing parties could agree on which issues should be part of the discussion process. As a result, they were able to agree on five committees. This process enabled the belligerents to see that a potential solution could be found. Further, the SWO was enforced through the attitude of the mediator. By pushing for results, he displayed the feeling that a solution to the conflict is actually reachable by that intensifying the sense for a way out.

The third phase in the Burundian case, 2000-2006, was also characterized by an SWO on part of the belligerents. The government established the SWO because of experience. They saw the positive developments in the country and saw that it was indeed possible to integrate rebel groups peacefully. Similarly, the rebel groups could not close their eyes facing the positive developments. Their SWO comprised of two main ingredients: a powerful mediation team constantly reaching out to them and thus giving the feeling of security and the acknowledgement that indeed it seemed possible to gain power through political instead of military means. Thus an SWO was perceived.

An SWO was identified for all four belligerent factions in the Cambodian case. In different ways of communication and through actions, it became clear that the factions all sensed that it was possible to actually find and come to an agreement as part of a peace process. What is interesting in this context is the question of why the SWO existed. In the Cambodian conflict, the SWO emerged through international diplomatic intervention. The UN Perm Five agreed on a framework that was suggested to serve as a basis for a comprehensive settlement. They offered this framework to the belligerents. By doing so, the belligerents were able to read what the agreement potentially had to offer and thus, they were able to sense a way out of the protracted status quo.

To sum up, in four of the eight instances analyzed, an SWO could be identified. The main drivers[228] for the generation of the SWOs were rather diverse. They reached from external diplomatic intervention in the form of offering a basis for the talks, over international pressure, the choice of the mediator, and positive developments as experiences. In general, it can be stated though that it seems that an SWO can be significantly influenced by the mediation team and/or other external involvement – be it through skillful mediation, inducements offered, or pressure. The table below visualizes the results.

	SWO?	Main Drivers for SWO
Uganda 1993-1994	No	-
Uganda 1997-1998	No	-
Uganda 2004-2005	No	-
Uganda 2006-2008	Yes	▪ International pressure ▪ Choice of mediator
Burundi 1993-1995	No	-
Burundi 1996-2000	Yes	▪ Facilitation of early discussions where issues to be discussed are defined by belligerents ▪ Providing belligerents with feeling that solution is possible on part of mediator
Burundi 2000-2006	Yes	▪ Positive developments raising hope ▪ Guarantees through powerful mediation team

---

[228] Cf. definition of drivers above.

	SWO?	Main Drivers for SWO
Cambodia 1991-1993	Yes	• External diplomatic intervention in the form of offering a framework serving as a basis for the peace process

Table 20: Comparison Sense of a Way Out[229]

The tables above show that in five instances, it was possible to identify an MHS and in four instances, it was possible to identify an SWO. MEOs were not identified as ingredients for conflict ripeness in the analyzed cases. Therefore, we can conclude that in four instances the dependent variable of conflict ripeness was given: Uganda 2006-2008, Burundi 1998-2000, Burundi 2000-2006, and Cambodia 1991-1993. These are the interesting ones for the further analysis. Thus, it was tested to what extent independent variables and specifically IDA as a potential independent variable affected the status of conflict ripeness that was constituted in the four instances outlined above.

Recalling the theoretical model, a range of independent variables was identified that potentially affect the dependent variable of conflict ripeness. The way of affecting conflict ripeness was by either increasing or reducing the level of intensity of the two ingredients to conflict ripeness: MHS/MEOs and/or SWO. Two categories of variables were looked at, which were manipulable and non-manipulable variables from the perspective of the mediator. The manipulable independent variables were persuasion, inducements and pressure – instruments that the mediator can use in order to manipulate a given situation. The non-manipulable variables were structured into those ones that were initiated by the belligerents' leadership (change in leadership and assertiveness of leadership) and into those ones that were initiated by other parties (external support to belligerents and IDA). IDA was included into this framework as an additional independent variable and the objective was to test whether IDA also functions as an independent variable and if so, in what way. In order to be able to analyze the effect of IDA, it is crucial to isolate the variable. That means all other independent variables have to be examined carefully, so that wrong conclusions and mistakes in the process-tracing could be avoided. The following results were found when assessing the effect of the other independent variables (except from IDA) on conflict ripeness.

---

[229] Source: Own illustration.

During the last phase in the Ugandan conflict from 2006 to 2008, conflict ripeness could be identified. The level of conflict ripeness was further intensified through two independent variables that took an effect by way of increasing the level of intensity of ripeness. The two variables were persuasion and pressure. The mediator used these two tools as part of his strategy in order to positively affect ripeness and by that the peace process. However, one independent variable negatively affected conflict ripeness, which was the assertiveness of the leadership. Here, we could observe that the rebel group's leader became nervous and thus temporarily showed signs of nervousness, which resulted in irrational behavior. This effect, however, only mildly impacted the conflict ripeness negatively as outlined above. It did not destroy the ripe phase. Phase two in the Burundian case, 1996 to 2000, was also affected by independent variables. Similarly to the Ugandan example, this case showed that conflict ripeness was strengthened through instruments of the mediator. Here, all three instruments were used of persuasion, inducements and pressure; meaning that all manipulable independent variables had a positive effect on conflict ripeness. Also in this case, the independent variable of assertiveness of the leadership compromised on the level of intensity of conflict ripeness. While most people followed their leadership team loyally, two groups separated from the overall process and continued resistance to the peace process. This led to the situation, in which the conflict was transformed to a different level and then continued to a next phase.

Conflict ripeness throughout the third phase in the Burundian case 2000-2006 was also affected by the independent variables; however, only by the manipulable ones. These all positively affected the dependent variable, by that intensifying the level of conflict ripeness and thus contributing to the furthering of the peace process. The recent experiences in Burundi had shown that an integrated process was indeed possible and would lead out of the hurting stalemate. By constantly reaching out to the belligerents and offering ideas of how the conflict could be solved, the mediator thus played an important role. It was thus a combination of persuasion with inducements that was decisive in this respect. But also the involvement of pressure by engaging peacekeeping troops further affected the situation. By that, the mediator was able to implement an intelligent carrot-and-stick strategy and by that contribute to both the intensity of the SWO and the MHS. Similarly, Cambodia's case showed that the manipulable independent variables played a significant role in further manifesting the status of conflict ripeness. All three independent variables went hand in hand and affected the dependent variable. Persuasion on part of the mediator, as well as inducements offered as part of a framework serving as the basis for the peace process were essential for the belligerents to sense a way out of the deadlocked situation. Further, the MHS was intensified through additional pressure. The non-manipulable variables did not affect the situation, so that the overall effect was purely positive on conflict ripeness.

Comparing all four incidents in which conflict ripeness existed, we can observe that in all cases the manipulable independent variables were decisive. In two cases, a negative effect of an independent variable on conflict ripeness could be noted. The assertiveness of the leadership affected the ripeness both in the fourth phase of the Ugandan conflict and the second phase of the Burundian conflict. The leadership in these two instances was not able to fully control the situation and be in charge of their rational decisions. While in Uganda, the rebel leader showed signs of nervousness and as a result acted irrationally, in Burundi, two groups separated themselves and continued the conflict despite the progressing peace process. What is interesting when comparing these four instances of conflict ripeness and their individual experiences with independent variables affecting conflict ripeness, it seems that once ripeness was established, the status remained relatively stagnant. Most effects that independent variables took were positive and consciously triggered by the mediator in place. The following table summarizes the effects of the independent variables on conflict ripeness in the four instances analyzed.

Independent Variable	Uganda P 4	Burundi P 2	Burundi P 3	Cambodia
Persuasion	Positive	Positive	Positive	Positive
Inducements	No effect	Positive	Positive	Positive
Pressure	Positive	Positive	Positive	Positive
Change in leadership	No effect	No effect	No effect	No effect
Assertiveness of leadership	Negative	Negative	No effect	No effect
External support to belligerents	No effect	No effect	No effect	No effect

Table 21: Summary: Effect of Independent Variables[230]

It can be stated that the three case studies in total analyzed eight phases in conflicts and assessed their conflict ripeness. It was found that in four of these instances, conflict ripeness was identified with both first level variables fulfilled.

---

[230] Source: Own illustration.

In three of these four instances, the conflict ripeness was further intensified through all three manipulable independent variables: persuasion, inducements and pressure. In one case, two of the three manipulable independent variables positively affect conflict ripeness (persuasion and pressure). In two cases, the assertiveness of leadership negatively affected the dependent variable and thus decreased the level of intensity of conflict ripeness, however did not destroy it. It seems that the mediator takes over a significant role in the manifestation of ripeness. He has the tools of persuasion, inducements and pressure. These three tools can be leveraged, so that conflict ripeness is further intensified. If this is the case, potential negative effects on the status, might be absorbed, so that overall ripeness is not destroyed. The following table summarizes all results so far from the case studies.

	Uganda				Burundi			Cambodia
Phase	1993-1994	1997-1998	2004-2005	2006-2008	1993-1995	1996-2000	2000-2006	1990-1993
MHS	No	No	Yes	Yes	No	Yes	Yes	Yes
MEOs	No	No	-	-	No	-	-	-
SWO	No	No	No	Yes	No	Yes	Yes	Yes
Conflict Ripeness	No	No	No	Yes	No	Yes	Yes	Yes
Persuasion	↔	↔	↔	↑	↔	↑	↑	↑
Inducements	↔	↔	↔	↔	↔	↑	↑	↑
Pressure	↔	↔	↔	↑	↔	↑	↑	↑
Change in leadership	↔	↔	↔	↔	↔	↔	↔	↔
Assertiveness of leadership	↔	↔	↔	↓	↔	↓	↔	↔

	Uganda				Burundi			Cambodia
External support to belligerents	↔	↔	↔	↔	↔	↔	↔	↔

Legend: ↑ *Positive effect;* ↓ *Negative effect;* ↔ *No effect/not applicable.*

Table 22: Summary Conflict Ripeness[231]

5.4.1.3 Increase in Development Aid

After conflict ripeness, the next step of the analysis was to assess whether an increase in development aid could be identified in the individual instances of the case studies. To recall, development aid had been defined as including financial and technical assistance as well as personnel dedicated to development work. Furthermore, humanitarian aid had been defined as a sub-category of development aid. Benefiters of aid (for example the government, the people, individual organizations, or groups) are as diverse as the potential donors, which range from bilateral donors, over multilateral donors, to private institutions, individuals or companies, to non-governmental organizations. An increase of aid constitutes one of two options. Either it refers to an actual increase in the value of an ongoing development effort or to the initiation of entirely new efforts. Measuring IDA is rather a qualitative task by way of analyzing whether an increase resulted in the receiver's perception of more aid.

The three cases found themselves in different situations at the outset of the analyzed periods. Uganda in 1987 had experienced a period of minimal external support given its recent history of tyrannical regimes. The international community had not provided significant assistance throughout these times. Burundi in 1993 faced a situation, in which the support was neither extensively large nor insignificant. During the previous years, the level was held relatively constant. Thus, we can label it 'average'. It was not on a high priority list of the donor countries and institutions, but was supported moderately. Cambodia had previously experienced two years of no external support. All international donors and supporters, who had mainly contributed to one or more of the factions'

---

[231] Source: Own illustration.

budgets, had all ceased their involvement after a coordinated effort of the international community. What must be noted for the further developments in terms of the individual instances analyzed in Uganda and Burundi, the situations changed. For Uganda, constant IDA was to be noted so that each phase started at a point where an ever increasing amount of development aid was provided to the country. Burundi's second phase started at a point when an international embargo was put on the country so that development aid actually decreased significantly. The question was to what extent these situations from previous periods changed at the phases of interest, which will be addressed below.

Looking at bilateral and multilateral aid, Uganda and Cambodia faced similar situations. They both experienced a constant and significant increase of assistance. This can be observed by looking at the development of ODA in these countries. Cambodia started out in 1990 with annual net disbursements of ODA of US$ 41 million. Until 1993, ODA had increased by 627% to US$ 301 million. This trend was further continued in the subsequent years reaching a level of US$ 551 million by 1995.

Uganda similarly enjoyed a constant increase in ODA. In 1986, Uganda received US$ 192 million. By 2008, the annual disbursements lay at US$ 1,657 million, which constituted an overall increase of 765% over the entire period of time. While there was some degree of variance in the provision of ODA with small decreases between individual years, the overall development was an increase – and a very steep increase. Phase one, 1987 to 1994, displayed an increase of 292%. Phase two, ending in 1998, actually saw a slight decrease of 13%. Phase three until 2005, was marked by an increase again of 82%. In the last phase, ODA also increased by 39%. Furthermore, Uganda enjoyed high debt relief. Uganda had received a total of US$ 3.764 billion in debt relief by 2006.

Burundi witnessed a rather different and more complicated development with regard to the provision of bilateral and multilateral aid. Starting out in 1993 with net disbursements of ODA of US$ 216 million, Burundi first experienced an increase in development aid. But with the following international embargo, Burundi reached its lowest level of development aid in 1997 with US$ 56 million. Afterwards, annual disbursements increased again very slowly. In 2000 with the beginning of phase three, Burundi received US$ 93 million. ODA constantly increased, reaching a level of US$ 509 million in 2008. From 1993 to 2008, this constituted an overall increase in development aid of 138%. Similarly to Uganda, also Burundi enjoyed high debt relief. Burundi qualified for the program in 2005, lowering its debt service payments by about US$ 1.5 billion in nominal terms. However only in 2009, Burundi reached its completion point.

The IDA provided to the three countries in the form of peacekeeping missions and support of peace initiatives differed from case to case. The largest benefiter was Cambodia with the deployment of UNAMIC and UNTAC. With up to 22,000 personnel and individual components for repatriation and rehabilitation and reconstruction of the country, the peacekeeping missions constituted a significant increase. Combined, it was estimated that a total of US$ 1.62 billion was disbursed.

The second highest benefiter of the three cases in this respect was Burundi. Although Burundi did not receive any significant assistance throughout phase one, phase two was marked by the external support of the peace initiative. In total, US$ 15 million sponsored the peace process. In phase three, IDA was also given in this context through the deployment of different peacekeeping missions. The UN mission, ONUB, alone meant disbursements of US$ 678 million within two years (2004-2006).

Uganda was in comparison disadvantaged, given that no peacekeeping mission was deployed throughout the conflict. Further no significant support was given for the peace initiatives in the first three phases. Only the fourth peace initiative enjoyed the support through a dedicated fund (JIF) of US$ 4.8 million in 2006. Compared to Burundi's US$ 15 million, the disbursements for Uganda's peace initiative were rather small, however proving to have an important impact (cf. below).

With regard to IDA through international NGOs, all three cases saw significant increases. Upon the beginning of peace talks in Cambodia, the number of NGOs active in the country 'mushroomed'. It had reached a level of more than 100 registered NGOs by 1993.

Also Uganda witnessed a significant increase in NGOs, specifically in Northern Uganda, where the conflict was set. Starting in 2003, international attention and media coverage of the humanitarian suffering had motivated multiple new NGOs to come to the region. It is estimated that about 90% of the total living needs were sponsored by NGOs in Northern Uganda during the phases three and four.

Burundi went through a kind of development. While at the end of phase one, most international NGOs terminated their engagement in Burundi due to security reasons, from 1998 onwards, they returned on large scale.

Thus overall, a significant IDA can be constituted in all three countries through international NGOs. Specifically humanitarian needs are answered through this type of development aid, largely disburdening the governments.

Comparing the developments of the provision of bilateral and multilateral aid, especially through ODA, it becomes clear that Cambodia and Uganda enjoyed significant increases that constantly rose. Disbursements to Burundi also increased overall, however, also saw a stark cutback in between. Furthermore, the increase in Burundi was not as large as in the other two countries. Analyzing the IDA in the three cases with respect to peacekeeping missions and the support of peace initiatives, one can see that Cambodia experienced the highest level of IDA, followed by Burundi. To Uganda only small disbursements were made. NGOs were increasingly present and engaged in all three countries, constituting IDA. But Burundi experienced a development with a termination of support and then strong increase throughout the second phase. To sum up, it can be stated that in all cases an overall IDA could be identified. The following table summarizes the results.

	Uganda	Burundi	Cambodia
Preceding Situations	▪ No significant external assistance	▪ Average ▪ At beginning of P2: int. embargo	▪ All external assistance cut off
Bilateral/ Multilateral Aid; ODA	▪ Significant increase ▪ ODA: From US$ 192 mill. in 1986 to US$ 1,656 mill. in 2008 ▪ Increase in ODA 1986-2008: 765% ▪ High debt relief	▪ Increase, decrease and then increase ▪ ODA: From US$ 216 mill. in 1993 to US$ 56 mill. in 1997, to US$ 93 mill. in 2000, to US$ 431 mill. in 2006 ▪ Increase in ODA 1993-2006: 100% ▪ Debt relief	▪ Significant increase ▪ ODA: From US$ 41 mill. in 1990 to US$ 301 mill. 1993 and US$ 551 mill. in 1995 ▪ Increase in ODA 1990-1993: 627%
Peace-keeping Missions/ Support of Peace Initiatives	▪ No peacekeeping force ▪ No significant support for peace initiatives I, II, and III ▪ Support for peace initiative IV in 2006: US$ 4.8 mill.	▪ No significant support in P1 ▪ Support of peace initiative II: US$ 15 mill. ▪ Peacekeeping forces in phase three (ONUB 2004-2006: US$ 678 mill.)	▪ Significant increase through peacekeeping missions ▪ Total disbursement 1992-1995: US$ 1.62 billion

	Uganda	**Burundi**	**Cambodia**
International NGOs	• No significant support in P1, P2 • Significant increase in humanitarian aid to Northern Uganda in phases three and four, covering 90% of total living needs	• Decrease in P1 • Significant increase in P2 and P3	• Significant increase (by 1993 more than 100 registered NGOs)

Table 23: Summary Increase in Development Aid[232]

5.4.1.4 Effect of Increase in Development Aid on Ripeness

The analysis of the theoretical model resulted in the question of whether IDA affects conflict ripeness. Specifically, it was found that countries at civil war are predominantly developing countries. Therefore, in most cases, large amounts of development aid enter these countries, particularly at times when peace efforts are initiated. It was thus asked whether such influx of development aid influences conflict ripeness by that furthering or compromising on the peace process. It was chosen to focus on an increase in development aid in order to be able to isolate the independent variable of development aid and thus to be able to analyze its effect on the overall situation. The final step in the analysis was to examine which conditions accompanied the effects of IDA on ripeness in order to be able to identify what conditions have to be given so that IDA functions as an intensifier of conflict ripeness or to the contrary, which conditions favor a negative effect of IDA on conflict ripeness, reducing or destroying ripeness.

Concretely, what has been analyzed in the individual case studies was the question of whether IDA functions as an independent variable to conflict ripeness as the dependent variable in the theoretical model of the Theory of

---

[232] Source: Own illustration.

Ripeness. Thus, the first step was to constitute whether IDA did have an effect on conflict ripeness; the second step to analyze of which quality the effect was and which conditions accompanied it. Was the effect positive or negative and why?

In the Ugandan case, it was possible to identify two instances, in which IDA affected conflict ripeness. At an early time in the period between 2006 and 2008 when conflict ripeness was given, IDA was consciously used in Uganda as a tool by way of restricting IDA. Through restricting IDA, pressure was built up against the belligerents, so that the perception of an MHS was intensified. Therefore, conflict ripeness was positively affected. The second instance, however, was a negative effect of IDA on ripeness. IDA was provided to the belligerents in form of a peace fund. The peace fund, used also as a conscious tool by the mediator to bring the belligerents to the negotiating table, ultimately destroyed ripeness here. The analysis showed that the reason was that IDA was provided in an unconditioned and uncontrolled way to the belligerents, particularly to the rebel group. Increases in aid and assistance were not made dependent upon compliance with the peace process. Therefore, the credibility of the mediator was lost and thus conflict ripeness destroyed. The rebel group could profit from the gains of the increased aid, however did not have to comply with any of the processes of the peace initiative. Therefore, the incentive for the rebels to comply faded away.

Furthermore, the Ugandan case also offered additional interesting findings. In phase three of the Ugandan conflict, ripeness could not be identified. However, the analysis did find a correlation between IDA and the MHS. The GoU used the strategy of aligning to the US 'war on terror' by that securing high levels of IDA in the form of increases in ODA, specifically provided by the US. The international community's pressure on the GoU to bring the conflict to an end was thus not credible as financially, the GoU experienced ever higher levels of development aid. Thus, the GoU did not perceive an MHS. IDA had a negative effect on the creation of ripeness by way of preventing an MHS. Furthermore, IDA in the form of humanitarian assistance entered Uganda. The IDA was targeted at Northern Uganda, provided for by NGOs and UN agencies. The external provision of aid to this region disburdened the GoU from taking over this responsibility and by that freed up resources to continue the warfare. Therefore, also this kind of IDA prevented an MHS from being established and thus negatively impacted conflict ripeness.

In the case of Burundi, in both relevant phases (phases 2 and 3), a positive effect of IDA on conflict ripeness could be observed. IDA constantly entered the country from 1998 onwards and ultimately led to an increase in the level of the sense of the way out, while the level of the hurting stalemate was constantly, but slowly, reduced. Three conditions were the reason for this positive effect of IDA on ripeness: a great effort of coordination among the donor community, the conditioning of the IDA on compliance with the peace process and the link between the conflict resolution effort and the development aid by way of putting the mediator in charge of controlling the IDA.

In the case of Cambodia, four relationships between IDA and conflict ripeness could be established: firstly, the promise of aid in the form of pledges (counted here as an indirect form of IDA) contributed to the perception of an SWO, especially on part of the CPP. The international community was thus able to led the parties perceive an SWO more intensely through inducements, thereby contributing to conflict ripeness. A positive impact of IDA on conflict ripeness could be observed. Secondly, the CPP was relatively favored by the way of the IDA's distribution. The reasons were the positive bias for urban areas and the intense support of governmental institutions. Both – urban areas and the governmental institutions – were controlled by the CPP. The CPP was thus relatively advantaged compared to the other factions. The result was that the CPP felt relatively stronger and therefore perceived itself as more powerful. By that the MHS and SWO that had been perceived by the CPP were destroyed through IDA. IDA negatively affected conflict ripeness in this case. Thirdly, the Khmer Rouge felt relatively disadvantaged by the distribution of IDA and thus perceived a relative discrimination and isolation. This had the effect that the Khmer Rouge's perception of an SWO was destroyed. Here, IDA had a negative effect on conflict ripeness. Fourthly, the population was increasingly dissatisfied as they could not 'feel' the promises made beforehand that IDA would improve their living conditions. Thus, a great level of disappointment led to the destruction of sensing a way out through the peace process and the associated IDA. The population felt that the donors were rather interested in 'large prestige projects' instead of directly improving the people's lives. Therefore, IDA had a negative effect on conflict ripeness. Thus, one instance could be observed in the Cambodian case in which IDA positively affected conflict ripeness by supporting the establishment of ripeness and three instances in which IDA negatively affected conflict ripeness by destroying either the MHS or SWO or both.

Overall, it is possible to conclude that the four instances analyzed showed that IDA indeed functions as an independent variable to the dependent variable of conflict ripeness in the Theory of Ripeness. In total, ten instances were observed, in which IDA directly affected one or both of the ingredients to conflict ripeness. The effect varied – in some instances a positive, in others a negative effect could be identified. The table below summarizes these findings.

Case	Causal Relationship	Quality of Effect
Uganda, P3	Significant IDA in form of ODA after alignment with war on terror prevented MHS – state actor did not perceive hurting stalemate due to constant influx of ODA	Negative
Uganda, P3	Significant IDA in form of humanitarian aid freed up resources from state actor – prevented perception of hurting stalemate	Negative
Uganda, P4	Restricting IDA in form of ODA to state actor put pressure on belligerent and increased credibility of international community – intensified perception of MHS	Positive
Uganda, P4	IDA in form of peace fund destroyed MHS as aid was provided to rebels independent from compliance with peace process. Hurting was stopped through assistance	Negative
Burundi, P2	IDA increased level of SWO and reduced level of intensity of MHS. Overall level of conflict ripeness held constant	Positive
Burundi, P3	IDA increased level of SWO and reduced level of intensity of MHS. Overall level of conflict ripeness held constant	Positive
Cambodia	Promise of IDA supported perception of SWO	Positive
Cambodia	Relative favoring of one belligerent destroyed his perception of MHS. Belligerent felt strengthened and regained belief in possibility to militarily win conflict	Negative
Cambodia	Relative favoring of one belligerent destroyed other belligerent's perception of SWO	Negative
Cambodia	Dispatch between promises of IDA and perceived provision destroyed SWO	Negative

Table 24: Summary Effect of IDA on Conflict Ripeness[233]

---

[233] Source: Own illustration.

The table above illustrates that the quality of effect between IDA and conflict ripeness varies in the individual cases. Therefore, it is further interesting to look at the observed conditions that accompanied the individual causal relationships in order to be able to assess the findings for potential generalizations and/or patterns.

In the Ugandan case, the following four observations could be made. Firstly, it seemed that IDA would have a negative effect on conflict ripeness if large amounts of IDA enter the country in an unreflected way with respect to the status of the peace efforts, preventing hurting stalemates. Secondly, if the two undertakings of IDA and mediating are not connected and separately pursue their aims, it seemed that this negatively affects conflict ripeness. Thirdly, if IDA is used as a conscious tool by the mediator and he leverages for example the restriction of IDA, he can positively affect the status of ripeness. Fourthly, if IDA is used as a tool in conflict management, but then is provided without conditions on the progress of the peace process, this takes a negative effect on conflict ripeness.

The analysis of the Burundian case has revealed three effects of IDA on conflict ripeness. Firstly, if IDA is accompanied by a coordinated approach of the entire donor community, this has a positive effect on ripeness. Secondly, such effect is strengthened if the IDA is also made conditional on the progress in the peace process and on the compliance with certain rules as part of the peace process. Such conditionality seems to be particularly promising if the credibility of sanctions upon non-compliance is given. Thirdly, the level of conflict ripeness is increased in its intensity if such approach of IDA that is coordinated and conditioned is put in charge of the mediator. By this way, the Burundian case showed that the two undertakings of development aid and conflict resolution could be interlinked making them both more powerful in their respective effectiveness.

Cambodia has offered three accompanying conditions that led to the individual effect of IDA on ripeness. Firstly, it showed that if IDA is promoted publicly, expectations rise among the population. There is then a high risk of disappointment, which might destroy conflict ripeness. Thus, even if public announcements might lead to an increased perception of an SWO, a non-fulfillment of the promises leads to disappointed expectations and thus results in relative deprivation and a destruction of conflict ripeness. Secondly, the distribution of IDA among the conflict parties seemed crucial. When favoring one party, this carries high risks in strengthening the favored party so that this party loses the perception of a hurting stalemate and it might also lead to a situation in which the other conflicting party loses its sense for a way out, feeling relatively disadvantaged. Thus, a biased distribution of IDA carries strong implications.

Thirdly, if IDA is accompanied by a strategy and thus consciously used, the result seems to be favorable for increased levels of ripeness.

5.4.2 Contingent Generalizations

The comparison of the three case studies seems to suggest that certain patterns can be identified. It is important to recall how the cases were selected. While presenting three in-depth case studies that comprised for the possibility of within-case comparison, the three cases were selected as representing a universe of cases of 31 potential cases in total. By selecting two cases that were set in one region and one case that took place on a different continent, by looking at cases with varying motivations for conflict, and by selecting cases that displayed different types of mediators, it was aimed for a case selection that embraced most of the potential characteristics of such conflicts. Therefore, it is possible to draw generalizations if careful analysis and interpretation are taken into account.

The comparative case studies allowed observing certain patterns that occur when increases of development aid are provided to a country at a ripe phase in a conflict situation. Again, it is important to note that the contingency of the generalizations drawn are limited to the universe of cases presented above. The following eight generalizations can be drawn:
- IDA provided at a phase of ripeness affects the conflict ripeness by way of affecting one or both of the ingredients to conflict ripeness.
- The effect of IDA can vary: it might be positive or negative.
- Whether IDA functions as an intensifier or destroyer of conflict ripeness depends on the accompanying conditions.
- IDA reduces the level of conflict ripeness or even destroys conflict ripeness if it is given to one or more of the belligerents without connecting the IDA to the peace process. This means, if IDA is provided without respect to conflict sensitivity, it has a negative effect on conflict ripeness.
- IDA negatively affects conflict ripeness, if it is distributed in a way significantly favoring and by that strengthening one of the belligerents.
- IDA negatively affects conflict ripeness, if there is a significant discrepancy between amounts promised and amounts delivered or perceived to be delivered. This disappoints the previously established expectations and thus results in perceptions of deprivation, reducing the level of the SWO.
- IDA destroys conflict ripeness, if it is provided without being made conditional upon the compliance with the peace process. If violations of

the peace process are not answered by restrictions in IDA, IDA functions as a simple 're-energizer' to the respective belligerent by that destroying the perception of a hurting stalemate.
- IDA only functions positively by way of intensifying conflict ripeness if three conditions are fulfilled: all development aid must be coordinated, the provision of IDA must be made conditional in a credible way upon the compliance with the peace process, and finally, the undertakings of development aid and conflict resolution must be interlinked – ideally by way of putting the mediator in charge of the provision and control of IDA. In that sense, IDA must be seen as a manipulable independent variable to the Theory of Ripeness.

6 Implications for the Theory of Ripeness

Having conducted the comparative case studies and summarized the results with regard to the effect of IDA on conflict ripeness and having drawn contingent generalizations, it must be asked, how these findings relate to the Theory of Ripeness as outlined above. Which implications result from the comparative case studies? In order to address this question, the chapter is structured into two sections. Firstly, the findings of the case studies will be related back to the hypotheses as outlined in chapter 3.5. To what extent can the hypotheses be validated (6.1)? Secondly, the theoretical model will be taken up and refined through integrating the findings (6.2).

6.1 Comparison of Findings with Hypotheses

Prior to the conduction of the case studies, four hypotheses had been formulated in chapter 3.5. The first hypothesis stated:

H_1: *If a mediator consciously uses his instruments of persuasion, inducements and pressure, then he is able to positively affect conflict ripeness. Thus, through leveraging the manipulable independent variables, the intensity of the dependent variable, conflict ripeness, is increased.*

The empirical analysis of the cases showed that indeed, the mediator can consciously leverage the tools of persuasion, inducements and pressure. If doing so, the cases indicated that those tools positively affect the intensity of conflict ripeness. Therefore, hypothesis one has been validated. The second hypothesis said:

H_2: *If changes to the conflict situation occur that are not manipulable or controllable by the mediator, they carry the potential to negatively affect conflict ripeness. Thus, because of non-manipulable independent variables, the intensity of the dependent variable, conflict ripeness, might be reduced or destroyed.*

Also hypothesis two has been validated in the empirical analysis. Especially the variable of increase in development aid as a non-manipulable independent variable was observed as negatively affecting conflict ripeness. In fact, IDA that was not controlled and/or manipulated by the mediator showed disastrous effects on the status of ripeness and thus reduced the chances for a peaceful resolution of the respective conflicts. This line of thought also applies to hypothesis three (cf. below) that was thus validated as well. In each instance, in which IDA was provided to the country of interest at a ripe phase and when it was not manipulated by the mediator, it reduced the level of intensity of ripeness.

H_3: If an increase in development aid occurs at a ripe phase and the mediator is not in charge of this influx into the country of interest, then the intensity of the dependent variable, conflict ripeness, is generally reduced or even destroyed.

Lastly, hypothesis four stated:

H_4: Only if the mediator becomes the initiator of an increase in development aid and by that transforms IDA into a mediator's tool, then he can leverage the influx and thus positively affect conflict ripeness, strengthening the intensity of the independent variable.

The empirical analysis has demonstrated that indeed, IDA can function as a tool for the mediator during a ripe phase of an internal conflict. If the mediator leverages IDA as a tool, he has the power to positively affect conflict ripeness and by that furthering the peace process. In that sense, IDA transforms in this context from being a non-manipulable variable into a manipulable variable. Thus, hypothesis four was validated in the analysis.

6.2 Expansion of the Theoretical Model

In chapter three, an analysis of the Theory of Ripeness was provided. The theory was outlined as established by I. William Zartman including the description of first level variables and second level variables. Further, a closer definition of ripeness was provided as well as academic challenges to the Theory of Ripeness. The author then introduced independent variables affecting conflict ripeness as the dependent variable. These factors constitute second level variables to the Theory of Ripeness. They were structured into manipulable and non-manipulable independent variables from the perspective of the mediator. IDA was identified as an additional independent variable that was non-manipulable in its character. IDA was then analyzed by way of comparative case studies including the questions whether IDA affects conflict ripeness and whether the effect is of positive, negative or ambivalent nature. It could be established that IDA serves as a significant independent variable to the Theory of Ripeness and constitutes an ambivalent effect on conflict ripeness: either positively or negatively depending on the accompanying conditions under which IDA is provided. With respect to the overall Theory of Ripeness, it was found that it makes sense to integrate IDA as an additional independent variable into the construct of the Theory of

Ripeness. IDA serves as a second level variable impacting the first level variables of MHS and SWO and by that having an effect on the intensity of overall conflict ripeness. The quality of effect is ambivalent depending on the circumstances of the situation. Thus, the expanded visualization of the Theory of Ripeness as introduced in Chapter 3 of this analysis could be confirmed.

The further analysis with respect to normative implications showed that IDA only affects conflict ripeness positively if it is part of a comprehensive strategy initiated by the mediator. In order to fulfill that three conditions were decisive: coordination of the IDA among the donor community, conditionality of the IDA in form of making the provision to the belligerents dependent upon the compliance of rules of the peace process, and thirdly the linking of the two undertakings of development aid and conflict resolution by putting the mediator in charge of the distribution and control of IDA. Therefore, the adopted Theory of Ripeness including the normative implications should provide for IDA as a manipulable variable that is thus under the auspices of initiation of the mediator and not of another external party to the conflict. Then, IDA does not function as an uncontrollable independent variable anymore that carries the potential to reduce or destroy the level of conflict ripeness, but instead becomes an instrument in the toolbox of the mediator that he can leverage to positively manipulate conflict ripeness. In that constellation, the visualization of the Theory of Ripeness looks as follows:

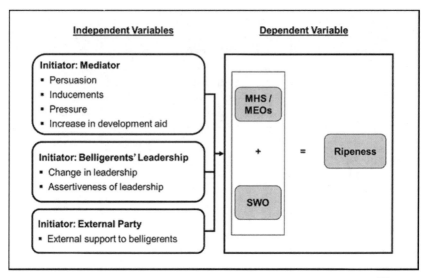

Figure 22: Expanded Theory of Ripeness with Normative Implications[234]

Concluding, the comparative case studies have helped to analyze the operationability of the Theory of Ripeness and to concretize it by evaluating the effect of the additional independent variable, IDA. Thus, the overall research objective could be obtained.

This refers back to the value of Stedman's statement, "the possible fruitfulness of ripeness as a concept is twofold: as indicator or signal of an objective situation and as a malleable process that can be affected by the acts of individuals within or outside the conflict" (Stedman 1991, p.235). With introducing IDA into the analysis, an additional lever of how the process can be affected by 'the acts of individuals within or outside the conflict' has been identified. We found that IDA has the potential to destroy the peace process, however, also displays the potential to strengthen it.

---

[234] Source: Own illustration.

7 Conclusions

This final chapter recapitulates the findings on the overall research question: does development aid affect conflict ripeness? In order to do so, a short summary of findings will be provided (7.1). This is followed by outlining the lessons learned and an attempt to bring the analysis onto a normative level formulating implications for policy-makers (7.2). Lastly, a critical look at the theory and analysis will be provided including addressing unresolved issues and valid objections (7.3).

7.1 Summary of Findings

This doctoral thesis started out by describing the current shift in international relations from less and less international wars (often also described as traditional wars) towards more and more internal conflicts, civil wars, or what is often described as so-called "new wars" in political sciences (cf. Tetzlaff/Jakobeit 2005, p.107). These wars – that are by no means new phenomena – display specific challenges to addressing them, i.e. to conflict managers. One of the challenges is associated to the fact that the prevalence of civil wars is mainly given in developing countries. These generally receive large amounts of aid – development, humanitarian/emergency aid of all types and of a large range of donors. These two phenomena were brought together by way of analyzing the concept of conflict ripeness and the effect of an increase in development aid on the status of conflict ripeness.

The following results could be found: the Theory of Ripeness is a useful concept in the realm of conflict management. It helps defining variables that need to be given so that a conflict has the potential to be resolved through a mediation effort, i.e. peacefully. Further, the intensity of conflict ripeness can be affected by a range of independent variables. These have an effect – either positive or negative – on the ingredients constituting conflict ripeness. One of these independent variables is the increase in development aid (IDA). IDA is ambivalent in character, meaning that it might have a positive or a negative effect on conflict ripeness depending on the accompanying conditions under which IDA is provided.

When expressing the findings in mathematical terms, it is possible to see ripeness as a sum, consisting of two ingredients: a mutually hurting stalemate (MHS) and a sense of a way out (SWO). Together, these two ingredients add up to conflict ripeness. When analyzing the increase in development aid, it becomes clear that generally additional aid entering a country – independent of who the benefiter is – decreases the value of an MHS (sometimes also of an SWO). Thus, it is crucial to leverage the potential of the instrument of IDA as the mediator to increase the SWO, so that the overall value is held constant. Then it is possible that IDA has a positive impact on conflict ripeness.

IDA is a challenge but also an opportunity for the resolution of conflicts. What makes the difference is the conscious usage of IDA as an instrument in conflict management. By that IDA becomes part of an overall conflict management strategy – or mediation strategy – and does not remain isolated from peace efforts.

Coming back to the example of a fruit, in which a conflict was compared to an avocado that has to be 'ripe' in order to be of use. An unripe or rotten avocado does not taste good. It ruins a salad and makes further efforts useless. When taking IDA into this fruit-example, one can compare IDA to a sort of fertilizer, being put at the avocado tree. It has the potential to ruin the fruit if it is provided in an uncontrolled and unchecked way. However, if used in a smart approach, then, it actually helps the avocado to become even tastier or riper. IDA has an effect on the situation of conflict ripeness – as has the fertilizer on the development of the fruit. The effect might either be positive or negative – dependent on the way of provision.

Concluding, the claims of Anderson, Galama and Tongeren, Klingebiel and others were right: aid given during conflict can have unintended consequences and do more harm than good (cf. Anderson 1999, p.1; Galama/Tongeren 2002, p.28; Klingebiel/Eberle, et al. 2000, p.1). The analysis showed that this is not only true for the phase during conflict, but that aid has a direct effect on conflict resolution efforts and might display unintended consequences in this realm. It is to be noted that it seems that the typical conflict cycle actually does not only exist of the three stages of pre-, in-, and post-conflict, but of four stages. The additional stage is the conflict resolution phase – a phase that ideally can be described as being ripe. It is important to single out this stage from the in- and post-conflict phases, as it requires special attention and thus policies in order not to destroy the process of conflict resolution. This is particularly the case as we have seen due to the fact that different actors involved at this stage of conflict resolution pursue varying aims and interests that might work against each other – as often in the case of development aid and conflict mediation. If this is the case, then the conflict mediation efforts are counter-acted by providers of development aid. This – as seen in the cases above – might have disastrous consequences for the further course of the conflict and thus spoil peace efforts. Such consequences cannot be the aim of development workers that originally wanted to help the country to progress. Therefore, it is of crucial importance that actors from the development community and actors involved in mediation efforts come together and coordinate their efforts.

Concluding, it was found that IDA only functions positively by way of intensifying conflict ripeness if three conditions are fulfilled: all development aid must be coordinated, the provision of IDA must be made conditional in a credible way upon the compliance with the peace process, and finally, the undertakings of development aid and conflict resolution must be interlinked – ideally by way of putting the mediator in charge of the provision and control of IDA. In that sense, IDA must become an instrument in the mediator's toolbox instead of being a non-manipulable variable that is not controllable.

7.2 Lessons Learned and Implications for Policy-Making

"When decision makers at any level organize interventions to prevent, mitigate, or resolve international conflicts, they are attempting to change the course of history. They therefore need to learn lessons from history about why past interventions had the results they did – that is, they need to have the interventions evaluated in a relatively systematic way" (Stern/Druckman 2000, p.38). What Stern and Druckman express in this statement for international conflicts, equally applies to internal conflicts.

This doctoral thesis aimed at evaluating certain diplomatic and aid interventions under a specific aspect – the effect of IDA on conflict ripeness. The aim was to improve conflict resolution strategies and to improve aid – as also claimed by Mary Anderson when stating "Our purpose is to improve aid" (Anderson 1999, p.3). Now the question arises what lessons can be learned from the analysis and what are the implications for the relevant policy-makers?

Development aid is a complex topic. There are many actors involved, such as donors, receivers, and sometimes also distributors. And all actors involved pursue their very own agendas varying from humanitarian over economic to self-preservation goals. What is clear is that, "aid cannot be viewed in isolation from the wider foreign policy objectives of donor governments" (Atmar/Goodhand 2002, p.26). I would like to add that aid cannot be viewed in isolation from wider policy constellations in the receiving country – specifically at a point, when constellations are changing, as happens at a point when peace efforts are taken up in situations of civil war.

Also conflict resolution is a complex topic. Specifically, policy-makers deciding whether to intervene, to move into a conflict and to initiate peace talks have to choose the moment carefully. We have learned that if such peace talks are initiated at a wrong timing, the consequences might be very harmful. We have also learned that the right point in time is a phase of ripeness.

A certain kind of "crowdedness" of external actors at sites of internal conflicts can be observed – and it does not help. A plentitude of external actors are involved ranging from mediators to representatives from the development aid community (cf. Khadiagala 2007, pp.11-12).

That is why this analysis tried to uncover three main lessons for policy-makers: first, the provision of aid is a complex task and specifically in contexts of violent conflict, the situation has to be analyzed carefully and put into context so that the development aid delivered in fact is effective and does not contribute to even more harm. Second, if a policy-maker wants to intervene diplomatically into a conflict and take over the role as a third party mediator, it is worth analyzing the situation carefully, so that it can be ensured that a ripe moment indeed exists. Third, the two first aspects must be intertwined: at the moment of conflict resolution, changes, especially increases in development aid, might carry a significant effect on the overall political situation of the country of interest. In fact, an increase in development aid either has the potential to negatively affect conflict ripeness by that destroying the potential for peace or it has the potential to positively affect conflict ripeness by that enhancing opportunities for a peaceful resolution of the conflict. The conditions accompanying the provision of IDA are decisive on whether conflict ripeness is affected negatively or positively.

One would think that compared to the overall conflict and war economy, aid is such a small amount that the impact is insignificant. But we have seen that this is not true. Aid in itself but also as a carrier of messages in the political system has a great impact on a certain constellation of power in a conflict situation. This is also stressed by Mary Anderson stating that, "even small amounts of aid have power. Although aid may be marginal when compared with the total resources devoted to wars, there is sufficient evidence showing its influence on the course of warfare that aid providers must take responsibility for its impacts" (Anderson 1999, p.68). In that sense, "aid, far from being politically neutral, is a political and economic resource" (Macrae/Zwi 1994, p.27). What concrete implications for policy-makers can be drawn from the analysis? Three lessons to learn can be identified:

Firstly, when a third party decides to intervene into a conflict by way of mediating the conflict, the third party must ensure that conflict ripeness is given. This implies two potential ways of action. Either the third party carefully analyzes the situation and finds that conflict ripeness is given, then a mediation effort makes sense and carries the potential for success. Or the third party carefully analyzes the situation and finds that conflict ripeness is not given. Then, the third party can use a range of means in order to 'ripen' the situation. This can be done by creating the ingredients serving as the basis for conflict ripeness: a mutually hurting stalemate and a sense of a way out. The creation of these ingredients can be undertaken by means of diplomacy, sanctions and/or force (muscular mediation).

Secondly, the mediator then has to pay attention to potential effects on conflict ripeness that can either reduce/destroy the level of ripeness or enhance it. The potential effects that could reduce/destroy the level of ripeness are non-manipulable events such as changes in the leadership of the belligerents, the assertiveness of the belligerents' leadership, external support to the belligerents and increases in development aid. If any of these events takes an effect, the mediator must counterbalance the effect by enhancing ripeness. The tools to do so are persuasion of the belligerents, the offering of inducements, putting pressure on the belligerents and taking control over increases in development aid.

Thirdly, it is decisive of how increases in development aid are provided to the belligerents and/or the country of interest. Three implications could be identified in this context. If increases in development aid are provided during a ripe phase in which a mediator conducts a conflict resolution effort, the development aid entering the country at stake must be coordinated in its entirety. All donors including bilateral, multilateral and non-governmental actors must adopt a common approach and coordinate how much and to whom the development aid is given. Further, the provision of the development aid must be made conditional to the belligerents upon compliance with the peace process. If one or more of the belligerents does not comply with the process, this must imply sanctions to the belligerent in form of restricting the IDA. This strategy must be a credible threat to the belligerents, so that compliance with the overall peace process is not endangered through increases in development aid. It must be taken into account that increases in development aid reduce the level of hurting to one or more of the conflicting parties. Given that the hurting is one of the ingredients to conflict ripeness, the second ingredient must thus counterbalance such reductions in intensity. Thus, the sense of a way out must be strengthened in parallel. This can only be done if the belligerents know that non-compliance will result in cuts of the development aid. It also means that compliance will be answered with positive incentives: further and constant increases in development aid. Lastly, such approach towards IDA should be controlled by the mediator. By putting the mediator in charge of distributing and controlling IDA, the two undertakings of development aid and conflict resolution are interlinked. This strategy ensures that development aid becomes part of the conflict resolution approach. In that sense, IDA must become an instrument in the mediator's toolbox that he can leverage to further strengthen the peace process.

"Until recently, superpower rivalries made an international policy toward civil war unrealistic. Developing country governments lined up on one side or the other, and many rebel movements could count on some degree of cover from the opposing superpower" (Collier, P. 2003, p.6). This is how Paul Collier described the dynamics of the so-called proxy wars that were common during the period of the Cold War when the superpowers used regional conflicts for implementation of their very own agendas. Given that the Cold War is history, this reasoning has lost its validity. One of the primary aims of the community of states should be to contribute to peaceful conflict resolution. Therefore, international cooperation on all levels in case of engagement in developing countries undergoing war is not only absolutely necessary, but also possible.

7.3 Critical Look at the Theory: Unresolved Issues/Valid Objections

"Let's imagine a time two decades from now. Seen from there, the present debate on crisis prevention and conflict management in TC [technical cooperation] will be considered one of the most significant debates in development cooperation" (Mehler/Ribaux 2000, p.153). Mehler and Ribaux stated this in the year of 2000, about 10 years ago. As seen in the literature review, it is true that the topic of conflict management in technical cooperation and development aid in general has been increasingly addressed in academia, but also in the world of practitioners. This analysis has taken up this claim and has put a special focus on the impact of an increase in development aid on conflict resolution – by that turning Mehler and Ribaux' around and looking at it from the other perspective.

This analysis has tried to contribute to academia and practice in three ways. Firstly, it has developed tools in order to better operationalize the Theory of Ripeness and by that help policy-makers to improve their strategies with regard to conflict resolution approaches and methods. Secondly, the analysis has refined the Theory of Ripeness by analyzing variables that potentially destroy a ripe phase and by that act counter-productively to the resolution of the conflict. A special focus was put on IDA at the time of ripeness. The theoretical analysis predicted and the empirical cases showed that IDA at ripeness might either function positively or negatively depending on how it is provided. What is undebated is that IDA affects conflict ripeness. Thirdly, a range of implications for policy-making were concluded, which were generated from the previous analyses of the interplay between conflict resolution and development aid.

Now, let me put the question of analysis into the broader context of the debate regarding unresolved issues and valid objections. To begin with the latter, it is useful to shed a light on the analysis and the findings from the doctoral thesis. Specifically, the question of humanitarian implications comes up. The topic has been touched upon in chapter 3.3.3. The Theory of Ripeness has been criticized in the past for depending on high levels of violence. The claim was that the variable of a mutually hurting stalemate leads to a situation, in which enormous suffering seems to be the condition for a potential peaceful negotiation process. The objection has been answered by referring to mutually enticing opportunities and by stating that instead of making the suffering painful to the belligerents, it might also work to induce them.

The comparative case studies – especially the cases of Burundi and Cambodia – have shown that there might be some validity to the point that the suffering has to be increased and that it helps that the situation deteriorates greatly before initiating peace efforts. In Cambodia, the hurting situation was addressed immediately and large amounts of aid were delivered. This sudden and large inflow of aid led to continued conflict. The situation was resolved differently in Burundi. Aid was given, however, restricted on the fulfillment of conditions and in a very slow and controlled pattern. This strategy proved more successful. What is the implication from this analysis? Does that mean the less aid the better? The more hurting the better? Does that mean that the international community should contribute to worsening the situation significantly, so that in the long run a chance to promote peace comes up? Do the civilians have to experience a humanitarian catastrophe before the situation can be resolved?

This objection cannot be rejected by the author. As Daniel Chong put it, "international aid agencies may be faced with the dilemma that their aid is used to prolong the conflict, but that without aid thousands of vulnerable non-combatants may die, while the withdrawal of aid may cause impoverished warriors to plunder civilian populations even more violently. Aid agencies are in an unenviable ethical position" (Chong in Milliken 2003, p.204). This argument has even been expanded by the findings of the doctoral thesis. Not only is there the risk of prolonged conflict through the emergence of a kind of war economy and warriors that re-strengthen themselves through aid, but also it has been shown that aid might change the entire constellation of perceptions. Less aid seems to lead to an increased perception of hurting and thus to an enhanced and more promising starting position for the initiation of peace efforts.

This refers to an objection to the Theory of Ripeness that is absolutely valid. It seems that with the help of sanctions, an embargo, the cut in assistance, the concept of creating ripeness for potential peace negotiations, is more effective. It implies great humanitarian challenges and moral trade-offs. It implies what I.

William Zartman and Avaro DeSoto stated, "ripeness is a characteristic of conflict, and heightened conflict and attempts at escalation may be necessary to set up the conditions for ripeness" (Zartman/DeSoto 2010, p.45). The question of peace versus justice comes back to mind. What is the task of the international community in this context? What is the responsibility? This topic reaches into the realm of philosophy and must be addressed. It constitutes a valid objection to the usage of ripeness as a tool – at least in the context of a situation where 'ripening' is considered. However, due to a lack of alternatives from the current state of the art, it seems the only and best solution for creating sustainable peace.

Furthermore, the analysis touched upon a range of other topics that would have surmounted the scope of the analysis but should be taken up by other students of conflict management or development studies. Apart from the philosophical debate and implications of peace and justice in the context at least sixth other unresolved issues emerge. Firstly, the aspect of over-ripening should be addressed. The open questions in this context are as follows. How is it possible to identify a situation where the phase of ripeness has passed and the phenomenon of 'over-ripening' has occurred? If happened, how is it possible to influence the situation, so that ripeness can be re-constituted? In what relation can IDA help in this context (or to what extent does IDA function as a threat to a potentially successful process)?

Secondly, and similar to the first aspect, the potential lack of recognition of ripeness should be analyzed in more detail. This challenge goes back to the core question of how to identify ripeness. While this doctoral thesis, as well as many accounts by I. William Zartman and others, have already addressed this question, it is an infinite task. Individual situations must be analyzed so that lessons can be learned for policy-makers when considering a mediation attempt. Every case displays a different set of causal mechanisms and unique experiences. It is not possible to create a blueprint in this context. Nevertheless, an increasing number of analyses will contribute to a rich portfolio of indications. These are needed for policymakers to identify patterns and try to best analyze a given situation.

Thirdly, the doctoral thesis has extracted a range of independent variables affecting conflict ripeness from the academic literature. Then, one independent variable was looked at in more detail because it appeared relevant in the context. The question arises whether the list of independent variables is exhaustive. By no means could this be confirmed. The list of potential independent variables affecting conflict ripeness might be infinite. It is important though to focus on the variables that significantly affect ripeness such as increase in development aid as seen in the above analysis. Thus, it would be of great value if students of conflict management invest in trying to discover more variables that have the potential to destroy, but also to enhance conflict ripeness. By way of doing so, a great contribution would be made to conflict management as it enables mediators to better identify risks and threats to the peace process that have to be addressed. Further, mediators would be able to integrate more instruments into their conflict resolution toolbox to foster ripeness.

Fourthly, the doctoral thesis analyzed the effect of an increase in development aid. By way of side-findings of the analysis, it was possible to identify at least two instances in which a decrease in development aid intensified the level of ripeness. To a certain extent, this consideration relates back to the peace versus justice-debate and moral implications as a decrease in development aid resulted in large scale humanitarian suffering. Thus, it would be a great contribution to academia and policy implications to further research on the effects of decreases in development aid.

The fifth aspect that carries further potential for research concerns the way of implementation – thus covers a rather practical approach towards development studies. The question is what the best strategy for donor institutions is. How can they maximize the effectiveness of their contributions and how exactly would coordination with mediators work? This issue relates back to the debate on coordination mechanisms among the development society, starting with coordination within one donor country. A positive example is the current effort in German development cooperation trying to consolidate a range of actors, so that German development work can be implemented in a coordinated way. If this trend could also be carried forward beyond national donor country boundaries, a more comprehensive and coherent strategy might be possible.

Lastly, the sixth aspect builds on the fifth one discussing the best way of coordination of development aid efforts. Recently, a tendency of empowerment is observed in the context of development aid. An increasing number of actors claim that empowerment of the receiving states is important and that aid should not be conditioned. Developing states' governments should decide for themselves on how to use aid provided to them. However, in the specific context of analysis, the research has shown (cf. Uganda's preference in budget support that led to further protraction of the conflict) that an approach of conditional aid might be the best option for improving the country's situation; particularly a country at war. An in-depth analysis in this context seems very interesting and might shed more light on the advantages and disadvantages of the strategy of empowerment. Particularly the specific challenges resulting from a conflict situation and/or a peace process-situation should be taken into account. It seems questionable whether empowerment always serves the objective or whether conditioned aid might also carry substantial value.

Thus, a range of issues have remained unresolved – both from the field of conflict management and the field of development studies. What has become clear is that a relationship exists between the two fields and that they affect each other. It would be helpful for academia and practitioners if the links between the two fields were to be deepened and leveraged. Alexander George demanded to "bridge the gap" between scholarship and practice (George 1993, p.265). By communicating, reaching out to each other, and following a coordinated, coherent and comprehensive approach, it will be possible to ameliorate efforts to further society and address humanitarian catastrophes in a more effective way. This asks for a coordinator guiding all external efforts to a developing country at war – both from the development aid perspective as well as from the conflict resolution perspective; and potentially from other perspectives such as private investments etc. It is a claim for an all-embracing institution (be it an individual or a group of people, states or agencies). The task to agree on such a common representative might be very challenging given individual agendas and interests by third parties involved, but it seems pivotal for terminating protracted conflicts.

Bibliography

Accord (1998): *Safeguarding Peace: Cambodia's Constitutional Challenge*. An International Review of Peace Initiatives. London: Conciliation Resources.
—— (2002): *Protracted Conflict, Elusive Peace: Initiatives to End the Violence in Northern Uganda*. Edited by Lucima, Okello. London: Conciliation Resources.
—— (2007): South Africa's Peacekeeping Role in Burundi: Challenges and Opportunities for Future Peace Missions. *The African Centre for the Constructive Resolution of Disputes (ACCORD), Occasional Paper Series* 2, no. 2 (2007).
—— (2010): *Initiatives to End the Violence in Northern Uganda: 2002-2009 and the Juba Peace Process*. Edited by Ramsbotham, Alexander. London: Conciliation Resources.
Acharya, Amitav (1994): Cambodia, the United Nations and the Problems of Peace. *The Pacific Review* 7, no. 3 (1994): 297-308.
Adams, Robert (2001): The So-Called 'Right' of Humanitarian Intervention. *Yearbook of International Humanitarian Law* 3 (2001): 3-51.
Akashi, Yasushi (1994): The Challenge of Peacekeeping in Cambodia. *International Peacekeeping* 1, no. 2 (1994).
Ali, Taisier Mohamed Ahmed, and Robert O. Matthews (2004): *Durable Peace: Challenges for Peacebuilding in Africa*. Toronto; London: University of Toronto Press.
Allen, Tim (2006): *Trial Justice: The International Criminal Court and the Lord's Resistance Army*. London: Zed.
Amaza, Ondoga (1998): *Museveni's Long March: From Guerrilla to Statesman*. Kampala, Uganda: Fountain Publishers.
Anderson, Mary B. (1999): *Do No Harm: How Aid Can Support Peace - Or War*. Boulder, Colo.; London: Lynne Rienner Publishers.
Arnson, Cynthia, and I. William Zartman (2005): *Rethinking the Economics of War: The Intersection of Need, Creed, and Greed*. Washington, D.C., Baltimore: Woodrow Wilson Center Press and Johns Hopkins University Press.
Assefa, Hizkias (1992): The Challenge of Mediation of Internal Wars: Reflections on the INN Experience in the Ethiopian/Eritrean Conflict. *Security Dialogue* 23, no. 3 (1992).
Atkinson, Ronald R. (2009): *From Uganda to the Congo and Beyond: Pursuing the Lord's Resistance Army*. Edited by Lupel, Adam. New York: International Peace Institute.
Atmar, Haneef, and Jonathan Goodhand (2002): *Aid, Conflict and Peacebuilding in Afghanistan: What Lessons can be Learned?* London: International Alert Organisation.
Bakonyi, Jutta, Stephan Hensell, and Jens Siegelberg (2006): *Gewaltordnungen bewaffneter Gruppen: Ökonomie und Herrschaft nichtstaatlicher Akteure in den Kriegen der Gegenwart*. 1. Aufl. ed. Baden-Baden: Nomos.
Banerjee, Abhijit V. (2007): *Making Aid Work*. Boston Review Book. Cambridge, Mass.: MIT Press.
Banfield, Jessica (2008): Building a Peace Economy in Northern Uganda: Conflict-Sensitive Appraoches to Recovery and Growth. *Investing in Peace by International Alert* No. 1, no. September 2008 (2008).
Barber, Ben (1997): Feeding Refugees, or War? The Dilemma of Humanitarian Aid. *Foreign Affairs (U.S.)* 76 (1997): 8-14.

Battaile, William G., and Steve Kayizzi-Mugerwa (2005): *The Poverty Reduction Strategy Initiative: Findings from 10 Country Case Studies of World Bank and IMF Support*. Washington, D.C.: World Bank [London: Eurospan distributor].
Bayne, Sarah (2007): *Aid and Conflict in Uganda: Conflict, Security and Development in the Horn of Africa*. London: Saferworld.
Belgrad, Eric A., and Nitza Nachmias (1997): *The Politics of International Humanitarian Aid Operations*. Westport, Conn.; London: Praeger.
Bentley, Kristina A., Roger Southall, Nelson Mandela Foundation., and Human Sciences Research Council. Democracy and Governance Research Programme. (2005): *An African Peace Process: Mandela, South Africa, and Burundi*. Cape Town, South Africa: HSRC Press.
Bercovitch, Jacob, Paul F. Diehl, and Gary Goertz (1997): The Management and Termination of Protracted Interstate Conflicts: Conceptual and Empirical Considerations. *Millennium - Journal of International Studies* 26, no. 3 (1997): 751-769.
Bercovitch, Jacob, and Judith Fretter (2004): *Regional Guide to International Conflict and Management from 1945 to 2003*. Washington, D.C.: CQ Press.
Bercovitch, Jacob, and Scott Sigmund Gartner (2009): *International Conflict Mediation: New Approaches and Findings*. London: Routledge.
Bercovitch, Jacob, and Allison Houston (1993): Influence of Mediator Characteristics and Behavior on the Success of Mediation in International Relations. *International Journal of Conflict Management* 4, no. October (1993): 297-321.
Bercovitch, Jacob, Viktor Aleksandrovich Kremenyuk, and I. William Zartman (2009): *The SAGE Handbook of Conflict Resolution*. Los Angeles; London: SAGE.
Bercovitch, Jacob, and Jeffrey Z. Rubin (1992): *Meditation in International Relations: Multiple Approaches to Conflict Management*. Macmillan P.
Bercovitch, Jacob, and G. Schneider (2000): Who Mediates? Political Economy of International Conflict Management. *Journal of Peace Research* 37, no. 2 (2000): 145-165.
Berdal, Mats, and David Keen (1997): Violence and Economic Agendas in Civil Wars: Some Policy Implications. *Millennium - Journal of International Studies* 26, no. 3 (1997): 795-818.
Betts, Richard K. (1994): The Delusion of Impartial Intervention. *Foreign Affairs* 73, no. 6 (1994): 20-33.
Bigdon, Christine, and Benedikt Korf (2004): The Role of Development Aid in Conflict Transformation: Facilitating Empowerment Processes and Community Building. *Berghof Research Center for Constructive Conflict Management* (2004).
Bigombe, Betty. "Peace Process in Northern Uganda." In *Reconciliation: The Way Forward*, edited by Affairs, Ministry of Internal. Gusco Peace Centre, Gulu, 2004.
Blaker, Michael, Paul Giarra, and Ezra F. Vogel (2001): *Case Studies in Japanese Negotiating Behavior*. Herndon, Va.: USIP; St Albans.
BMZ (2005): Krisenprävention, Konfliktbearbeitung und Friedensförderung in der deutschen Entwicklungszusammenarbeit. *Bundesministerium für wirtschaftliche Zusammenarbeit und Entwicklung, Referat: "Entwicklungspolitische Informations- und Bildungsarbeit"* (2005).
Bøås, Morten, and Kevin C. Dunn (2007): *African Guerrillas: Raging Against the Machine*. Boulder: Lynne Rienner Publishers, Inc.
Böge, Volker, and Tobias Debiel (2003): Kriege und Kriegsbewältigung. *Stiftung Entwicklung und Frieden, Frankfurt am Main* Globale Trends 2004/2005 (2003): 309-330.
Bohm, David (2004): *On Dialogue*. [New ed.] / with an introduction by Peter Senge; edited by Lee Nichol. ed. London: Routledge.
Bonacker, Thorsten (Hrsg.) (2005): *Sozialwissenschaftliche Konflikttheorien. Eine Einführung*. 3rd ed. Wiesbaden: VS Verlag für Sozialwissenschaften.
Bowden, Mark (1999): *Black Hawk Down: A Story of Modern War*. 1st ed. New York: Atlantic Monthly Press.

Brachet, Juana, and Howard Wolpe (2005): Conflict-Sensitive Development Assistance: The Case of Burundi. *Conflict Prevention & Reconstruction: Social Development Papers, The World Bank* 27, no. June 2005 (2005).

Branch, Adam, and Human Rights Focus Project Team. (2007): Fostering the Transition in Acholiland: From War to Peace, from Camps to Home. *Human Rights Focus Gulu, Uganda* September 2007 (2007).

Breslauer, George W., Harry Kreisler, and Benjamin Ward (1991): *Beyond the Cold War: Conflict and Cooperation in the Third World*. Research Series. [Berkeley, Calif.]: International and Area Studies MacArthur Interdisciplinary Group on International Security Studies, University of California at Berkeley.

Bricmont, J. (2006): *Humanitarian Imperialism: Using Human Rights to Sell War*. New York: Monthly Review Press.

Brown, Frederick Z., and David G. Timberman (1998): *Cambodia and the International Community: The Quest for Peace, Development, and Democracy*. Singapore: Institute of Southeast Asian Studies.

Brown, Michael E., and Richard N. Rosecrance (1999): *The Costs of Conflict: Prevention and Cure in the Global Arena*. Lanham, Md.; Oxford: Rowman & Littlefield Publishers.

Brunnengräber, Achim, Ansgar Klein, and Heike Walk (2005): *NGOs im Prozess der Globalisierung: Mächtige Zwerge - umstrittene Riesen*. Bonn: BpB.

Buckley-Zistel, Susanne (2008): *Conflict Transformation and Social Change in Uganda: Remembering After Violence*. Basingstoke: Palgrave Macmillan.

Bull, Hedley (1984): *Intervention in World Politics*. Oxford [Oxfordshire]; New York: Clarendon Press; Oxford University Press.

Bundervoet, Tom, Philip Verwimp, and Richard Akresh (2008): Health and Civil War in Rural Burundi. *World Bank, Development Research Group, Post-Conflict Transitions Working No. 18* Policy Research Working Paper 4500 (2008).

Bundesregierung (2004): *Aktionsplan "Zivile Krisenprävention, Konfliktlösung und Friedenskonsolidierung"*. Berlin: Die Bundesregierung, Deutschland.

Burall, Simon, Simon Maxwell, and Alina Rocha Menocal (2006): *Reforming the International Aid Architecture: Options and Ways Forward*. London: Overseas Development Institute.

Burke, Edmund, Ira M. Lapidus, and Ervand Abrahamian (1988): *Islam, Politics, and Social Movements*. Berkeley; London: University of California Press.

Bush, Kenneth (1998): A Measure of Peace: Peace and Conflict Impact Assessment (PCIA) of Development Projects in Conflict Zones. *International Development Research Centre (IDRC): The Peacebuilding and Reconstruction Program Initiative & Evaluation Unit* Working Paper No. 1 (1998).

Carlson, Khristopher, and Dyan Mazurana (2008): *Forced Marriage within the Lord's Resistance Army, Uganda*. Medford, Massachusetts: Feinstein International Center, Tufts University, Gerald J. and Dorothy R. Friedman School of Nutrition Science and Policy.

Carment, David, and Albrecht Schnabel (2003): *Conflict Prevention: Path to Peace or Grand Illusion?* Edited by Foundations of Peace. Tokyo; New York: United Nations University Press.

―――― (2004): *Conflict Prevention from Rhetoric to Reality*. Lanham, Md.; Oxford: Lexington Books.

Clausewitz, Carl von, James John Graham, and Anatol Rapoport (1968): *On war, edited with an introduction by Anatol Rapoport*. (Pelican classics.): Harmondsworth: Penguin.

Clements, Kevin P., and Robin Ward (1994): *Building International Community: Cooperating for Peace: Case Studies*. Canberra: Allen & Unwin in Association with the Peace Research Centre, RPSAS, ANU.

Cogan, Charles (2003): *French Negotiating Behavior: Dealing with La Grande Nation*. Washington, D.C.: United States Institute of Peace Press.

Collier, David, and James Mahoney (1996): Insights and Pitfalls: Selection Bias in Qualitative Research. *World Politics* 49, no. 1 (1996): 56-91.
Collier, Paul (2003): *Breaking the Conflict Trap: Civil War and Development Policy*. A World Bank Policy Research Report. Washington, D.C., New York: World Bank; Oxford University Press.
Collier, Paul, and Anke Hoeffler (2004a): The Challenge of Reducing the Global Incidence of Civil War. *Copenhagen Consensus Challenge Paper, Centre for the Study of African Economies, Department of Economics, Oxford University, Oxford* (2004a).
────── (2004b): Greed and Grievance in Civil War. *Oxford Economic Papers (U.K.)* 56, No. 4 (2004b): 563-595.
Cortright, David, and George A. Lopez (2000): *The Sanctions Decade: Assessing UN Strategies in the 1990s*. Boulder, Colo.: Lynne Rienner Publishers.
Coser, Lewis A. (1967): *Continuities in the Study of Social Conflict*. New York: Free Press.
Cracknell, Basil E. (2000): *Evaluating Development Aid: Issues, Problems and Solutions*. New Delhi; London: SAGE.
Crocker, Chester A. (1992): *High Noon in Southern Africa: Making Peace in a Rough Neighborhood*. New York; London: W.W. Norton.
Crocker, Chester A., Fen Osler Hampson, and Pamela R. Aall (1996): *Managing Global Chaos: Sources of and Responses to International Conflict*. Washington, D.C.: United States Institute of Peace Press.
────── (1999): *Herding Cats: Multiparty Mediation in a Complex World*. Washington, D.C.: United States Institute of Peace Press.
────── (2001): *Turbulent Peace: The Challenges of Managing International Conflict*. Washington, D.C.: United States Institute of Peace Press.
CSOPNU (2006): Counting the Cost: Twenty Years of War in Northern Uganda. *Civil Society Organisations for Peace in Northern Uganda* (2006).
Curtis, Devon (2003): The Peace Process in Burundi: Successful African Intervention? *Global Insight, Institute for Global Dialouge*, no. 24 (September 2003) (2003).
Danesh, H.B. (2006): Towards an Integrative Theory of Peace Education. *Journal of Peace Education* 3, no. 1 (2006): 55-78.
Daniel, Donald C., Bradd C. Hayes, and Chantal de Jonge Oudraat (1999): *Coercive Inducement and the Containment of International Crises*. Washington, D.C.: United States Institute of Peace Press.
Darlan, Guy (1994): *Cambodia from Rehabilitation to Reconstruction*. [Washington, D.C.]: Country Operations Division, Country Dept. I, East Asia and Pacific Region.
Datta-Mitra, Jayati, and World Bank. Operations Evaluation Dept. (2001): *Uganda: Policy, Participation, People*. Washington, D.C.: World Bank.
Davies, John L., and Ted Robert Gurr (1998): *Preventive Measures: Building Risk Assessment and Crisis Early Warning Systems*. Lanham, Md.; Oxford: Rowman & Littlefield.
Debiel, Tobias, and Martina Fischer (2000): Krisenprävention und zivile Konfliktbearbeitung durch die EU. Konzepte, Kapazitäten und Kohärenzprobleme. *Berghof Report* 4 (2000).
Debiel, Tobias, Martina Fischer, Volker Matthies, and Norbert Ropers (1999): Effektive Krisenprävention: Herausforderungen für die deutsche Außen- und Entwicklungspolitik. *Stiftung Entwicklung und Frieden* Policy Paper 12 (1999).
Deininger, Klaus W., and World Bank. "Causes and Consequences of Civil Strife: Micro-Level Evidence from Uganda." In *Policy Research Working Paper 3045*. Place Published: World Bank, 2003.
DeMars, William E. (2005): *NGOs and Transnational Networks: Wild Cards in World Politics*. London: Pluto.

Destradi, Sandra, and Andreas Mehler (2010): Wann, wie und warum enden Kriege? *German Institute of Global and Area Studies, Leibniz-Institut für Globale und Regionale Studien (GIGA) Focus* 4 (2010).
Diamond, Louise, and John W. McDonald (1996): *Multi-Track Diplomacy: A Systems Approach to Peace*. 3rd ed, Kumarian Press Books for a World That Works. West Hartford, Conn.: Kumarian Press.
Dolan, Chris (2009): *Social Torture: The Case of Northern Uganda, 1986-2006*. Human Rights in Context. New York: Berghahn Books.
Doyle, Michael W. (1995): *UN Peacekeeping in Cambodia: UNTAC's Civil Mandate*. International Peace Academy Occasional Paper Series. Boulder, Colo.; London: Lynne Rienner Publishers.
Duffield, Mark (1997): NGO Relief in War Zones: Towards an Analysis of the New Aid Paradigm. *Third World Quarterly* 18, no. 3 (1997): 527-542.
Duffy, Terence (2000): Peace Education in a Divided Society: Creating a Culture of Peace in Northern Ireland. *Prospects* 30, no. 1 (2000): 15-29.
Easterly, William Russell (2006): *The White Man's Burden: Why the West's Efforts to aid the Rest have done so much Ill and so little Good*. Oxford: Oxford University Press.
Eck, Kristine (2005): A Beginner's Guide to Conflict Data: Finding and Using the Right Dataset. *UCDP Papers (Uppsala Conflict Data Program, Department of Peace and Conflict Research)* 1 (2005).
Eckstein, Susan (1989): *Power and Popular Protest: Latin American Social Movements*. Berkeley; London: University of California Press.
Engel, Ulf, Cord Jakobeit, and Heribert Weiland (2002): *Das "Afrika-Memorandum" und seine Kritiker: Eine Dokumentation*. Hamburg: Institut für Afrika-Kunde.
Esposito, John L. (1983): *Voices of Resurgent Islam*. New York; Oxford: Oxford University Press.
Europa Publications. (1978): *Africa South of the Sahara 1978-79*. London: Europa Publications Limited.
Fahrenhorst, Brigitte (1999): Die Rolle der Entwicklungszusammenarbeit in gewalttätigen Konflikten: Dokumentation einer Fachtagung in der TU Berlin vom 3.-5.12.1999. *Society for International Development - Berlin Chapter* (1999).
Fassin, Didier, and Mariella Pandolfi (2010): *Contemporary States of Emergency: The Politics of Military and Humanitarian Interventions*. New York: Zone.
Faust, Jörg, and Dirk Messner (2007): *Organizational Challenges for an Effective Aid Architecture - Traditional Deficits, the Paris Agenda and Beyond*. Bonn: Deutsches Institut für Entwicklungspolitik.
Fearon, James D., and David D. Laitin (2003a): Additional Tables for 'Ethnicity, Insurgency, and Civil War'. *http://www.stanford.edu/group/ethnic* (2003a).
——— (2003b): Ethnicity, Insurgency, and Civil War. *American Political Science Review* 97, no. 1 (2003b): 75-90.
Finnemore, Martha (1996): *National Interests in International Society*. Ithaca, N.Y.; London: Cornell University Press.
Finnström, Sverker (2008): *Living with Bad Surroundings: War, History, and Everyday Moments in Northern Uganda*. Durham, N.C.; London: Duke University Press.
Finnström, Sverker, and Ronald R. Atkinson (2008): Building Sustainable Peace in Northern Uganda. *Horn of Africa Bulletin: Analysis - Context - Connections* 20, no. 4 (April 2008) (2008).
Fischer, David Hackett (1971): *Historians' Fallacies: Toward a Logic of Historical Thought*. London: Routledge and Kegan Paul.
Fischer, Martina (2006): Civil Society in Conflict Transformation: Ambivalence, Potentials and Challenges. *Berghof Research Center for Constructive Conflict Management* (2006).
Fisher, Roger, Elizabeth Kopelman, and Andrea Kupfer Schneider (1994): *Beyond Machiavelli: Tools for Coping with Conflict*. Cambridge, Mass.; London: Harvard University Press.

Fisher, Roger, and William Ury (1981): *Getting to Yes: Negotiating Agreement without Giving In*. Boston: Houghton Mifflin.
Fisher, Ronald J. (1997): *Interactive Conflict Resolution*. 1st ed, Syracuse Studies on Peace and Conflict Resolution. Syracuse, N.Y.: Syracuse University Press.
—— (2001): Methods of Third-Party Intervention. *Berghof Handbook for Conflict Transformation* (2001).
—— (2005): *Paving the Way: Contributions of Interactive Conflict Resolution to Peacemaking*. Lanham, Md.; Oxford: Lexington Books.
Fitzduff, Mari, and Cheyanne Church (2004): *NGOs at the Table: Strategies for Influencing Policies in Areas of Conflict*. Lanham, Md.; Oxford: Rowman and Littlefield.
Forbes, Ian, and Mark Hoffman (1993): *Political Theory, International Relations, and the Ethics of Intervention*. Southampton Studies in International Policy. New York, N.Y.: St. Martin's Press in association with the Mountbatten Centre for International Studies, University of Southampton.
Fortna, Virginia Page (2004): *Peace Time: Cease-Fire Agreements and the Durability of Peace*. Princeton, N.J. ; [Great Britain]: Princeton University Press.
Fukuyama, Francis (2004): *State-Building: Governance and World Order in the 21st Century*. Ithaca, N.Y.: Cornell University Press.
Furley, Oliver, and Roy May (2006): *Ending Africa's Wars: Progressing to Peace*. Aldershot: Ashgate.
Galama, Anneke, and Paul van Tongeren (2002): *Towards Better Peacebuilding Practice: On Lessons Learned, Evaluation Practices and Aid & Conflict*. Utrecht; [Great Britain]: European Centre for Conflict Prevention.
George, Alexander L. (1993): *Bridging the Gap: Theory and Practice in Foreign Policy*. Washington, D.C.: United States Institute of Peace Press.
George, Alexander L., and Andrew Bennett (2005): *Case Studies and Theory Development in the Social Sciences*. BCSIA Studies in International Security. Cambridge, Mass.: MIT Press.
German Development Institute (2001): *Approaches to Crisis-Preventing and Conflict-Sensitive Development Cooperation*. Vol. (4/2001), Briefing Paper. Bonn: German Development Institute.
—— (2002): *Improving Coherence between Development Policy and Other Policies - The Case of Germany*. Vol. (1/2002), Briefing Paper. Bonn: German Development Institute.
—— (2004): *The Development-Military Relationship: the Start of a New Alliance*. Vol. (1/2004), Briefing Paper. Bonn: German Development Institute.
Giddens, Anthony (1984): *The Constitution of Society: Introduction of the Theory of Structuration*. Berkeley: University of California Press.
Gingyera-Pinycwa, A. G. G. (1992): *Northern Uganda in National Politics*. 1st ed. Kampala: Fountain Publishers.
Gleditsch, Nils Petter; Harbom, Lotta; et al. "UCDP/PRIO Armed Conflict Dataset ": Uppsala Conflict Data Program (UCDP), www.ucdp.uu.se and Centre for the Study of Civil Wars, International Peace Research Institute, Oslo (PRIO), www.prio.no/cscw 2008a.
—— (2008b): UCDP/PRIO Armed Conflict Dataset Codebook. *Uppsala Conflict Data Program (UCDP), www.ucdp.uu.se and Centre for the Study of Civil Wars, International Peace Research Institute, Oslo (PRIO), www.prio.no/cscw* 4 (2008b).
—— (2009a): *UCDP/PRIO Armed Conflict Dataset*. 2008 ed. Vol. 4: Uppsala Conflict Data Program (UCDP), www.ucdp.uu.se and Centre for the Study of Civil Wars, International Peace Research Institute, Oslo (PRIO), www.prio.no/cscw.
—— (2009b): UCDP/PRIO Armed Conflict Dataset Codebook. *Uppsala Conflict Data Program (UCDP), www.ucdp.uu.se and Centre for the Study of Civil Wars, International Peace Research Institute, Oslo (PRIO), www.prio.no/cscw* 4 (2009b).
Goodhand, Jonathan (2006): *Aiding Peace? The Role of NGOs in Armed Conflict*. Boulder, Colo.; London: Lynne Rienner Publishers.

Götze, Catherine (2004): "Humanitäre Hilfe - Das Dilemma der Hilfsorganisationen". *Der Bürger im Staat* 54, no. 4 (2004): 210-216.
Government of Burundi (2000): Arusha Peace and Reconciliation Agreement for Burundi. *http://www.ucdp.uu.se/gpdatabase/peace/Bur%2020000828a.pdf* (2000).
―――― (2003): Global Ceasefire Agreement between the Transitional Government of Burundi and the National Council for the Defence of the Democracy-Forces for the Defence of Democracy (CNDD-FDD). *http://www.ucdp.uu.se/gpdatabase/peace/Bur%2020031116.pdf* (2003).
―――― (2006): Comprehensive Ceasefire Agreement Between the Government of the Republic of Burundi and the PALIPEHUTU-FNL. *http://www.ucdp.uu.se/gpdatabase/peace/Bur%20200609 07.pdf* (2006).
Government of Uganda. "A Case for National Reconciliation, Peace, Democracy and Economic Prosperity for All Ugandans: The Official Presentation of the Lord's Resistance Movement/Army (LRA/M) by Dr. James Alfred obita, Secretary for External Affairs and Mobilisation, and Leader of Delegation ", edited by (KM1997), Kacoke Madit 1997. Nairobi, 1997.
――――. "The National Policy for Internally Displaced Persons." edited by Office of the Prime Minister, Department of Disaster Management and Refugees. Kampala: The Republic of Uganda, 2004.
――――. "Peace, Recovery and Development Plan for Northern Uganda (PRDP) 2007-2010." edited by Uganda, Republic of. Kampala: Government of Uganda, 2007.
Grävingholt, Jörn (2004): *Crisis Potentials and Crisis Prevention in Central Asia: Entry Points for German Development Cooperation.* Bonn: Deutsches Institut für Entwicklungspolitik.
Green, Matthew (2008): *The Wizard of the Nile: The Hunt for Africa's Most Wanted.* London: Portobello.
Greig, J. Michael (2005): Stepping into the Fray: When do Mediators Mediate? *American Journal of Political Science* 49, no. 2 (2005): 249-266.
Gugel, Günther (2006): *Gewalt und Gewaltprävention: Grundfragen, Grundlagen, Ansätze und Handlungsfelder von Gewaltprävention und ihre Bedeutung für Entwicklungszusammenarbeit.* Tübingen: Institut für Friedenspädagogik Tübingen e.V.
Gurr, Ted Robert (1970): *Why Men Rebel.* [S.l.]: Princeton U.P.
―――― (2000): *Peoples versus States: Minorities at Risk in the New Century.* Washington, D.C.: United States Institute of Peace Press.
Haarhaus, Sophie (2009): Offensive gegen die Lord's Resistance Army im Kongo: Hintergründe und Perspektiven der militärischen Kooperation von Uganda, Kongo und Südsudan. *AKUF Analysen, Universität Hamburg, Institut für Politikwissenschaft, Arbeitsgemeinschaft Kriegsursachenforschung (AKUF)* Nr. 5, Februar 2009 (2009).
Haass, Richard (1992): *Conflicts Unending: United States and Regional Disputes.* New ed. ed: Yale U.P.
―――― (1999): *Intervention: The Use of American Military Force in the Post-Cold War World.* Rev. ed. Washington, D.C.: Brookings Institution Press.
Haass, Richard, and Council on Foreign Relations (1998): *Economic sanctions and American diplomacy.* New York: Council on Foreign Relations.
Hamburg, David A. (2002): *No More Killing Fields: Preventing Deadly Conflict.* Lanham, Md.: Rowman & Littlefield.
Hampson, Fen Osler (1996): *Nurturing Peace: Why Peace Settlements Succeed or Fail.* Washington, D.C.: United States Institute of Peace Press.
―――― (2003): Can the UN Still Mediate? *Revised Draft - 1/11/2003* (2003).
Hampson, Fen Osler, and David Malone (2002): *From Reaction to Conflict Prevention: Opportunities for the UN System.* Boulder, Colo.: Lynne Rienner Publishers.
Hansohm, Dirk, and Robert Kappel (1993): *Schwarz-weisse Mythen: Afrika und der entwicklungspolitische Diskurs.* Bremer Afrika-Studien Bd. 5. Münster: Lit.

Harmsen, Richard, and Alexei Kireyev (2008): *Global Monitoring Report 2008 - MDG and the Environment*. Publication.
Hauswedell, C. (2006): *Deeskalation von Gewaltkonflikten seit 1945*. 1. Aufl. ed, Frieden und Krieg, Beiträge zur historischen Friedensforschung. Essen: Klartext.
Havermans, Jos (2002): Burundi: The Peace Accords - Impact and Prospects. *UNHCR Emergency & Security Service, WriteNet* 15/2001 (2002).
Hayner, Priscilla B. (2002): *Unspeakable Truths: Facing the Challenge of Truth Commissions*. New York: Routledge.
Hazdra, Peter (1997): *Die UNO-Friedensoperation in Kambodscha: Vorgeschichte, Konzept, Verlauf und kritische Evaluierung des Internationalen Engagements*. Europäische Hochschulschriften. Reihe XXXI, Politikwissenschaft. Frankfurt am Main; New York: P. Lang.
Heidelberger Institut für Internationale Konfliktforschung (2008): *Conflict Barometer 2008: Crises - Wars - Coups d'État - Negotiations - Mediations - Peace Settlements*. 17th Annual Conflict Analysis. Heidelberg: Heidelberg Institute for International Conflict Research at the Department of Political Science, University of Heidelberg.
Hellmann, Gunther (1993): *Weltmachtrivalität und Kooperation in regionalen Konflikten: die USA und die Sowjetunion in den Kriegen des Nahen und Mittleren Ostens, 1973-1991*. Baden-Baden: Nomos.
——— (2006): *Deutsche Außenpolitik; Eine Einführung*. Vol. 39, Grundwissen Politik. Wiesbaden: VS Verlag für Sozialwissenschaften.
Hellmann, Gunther, Siegmar Schmidt, and Reinhard Wolf (2007): *Handbuch zur deutschen Außenpolitik*. 1. Aufl. ed. Wiesbaden: VS Verlag für Sozialwissenschaften.
Hellmann, Gunther, Klaus Dieter Wolf, and Michael Zürn (2003): *Die neuen internationalen Beziehungen: Forschungsstand und Perspektiven in Deutschland*. 1. Aufl. ed, Weltpolitik im 21. Jahrhundert Bd. 10. Baden-Baden: Nomos.
Heraclides, Alexis (1997): The Ending of Unending Conflicts: Separatist Wars. *Millennium - Journal of International Studies* 26, no. 3 (1997): 679-707.
Herisse, Rockfelder P. (2000): Development on a Theater: Democracy, Governance, and the Socio-Political Conflict in Burundi. *Agriculture and Human Values* 18 (2000): 295-304.
Hinzen, Eckhard, and Robert Kappel (1980): *Dependence, Underdevelopment, and Persistent Conflict: On the Political Economy of Liberia*. Veröffentlichungen aus dem Übersee-Museum Bremen. Series F, Bremen Africa Archives. Bremen: Übersee-Museum.
Hoffman, Mark (2004): *Peace and Conflict Impact Assessment Methodology. Berghof Research Center for Constructive Conflict Management* (2004).
Hofmeier, Rolf (2010): Wahlen in Burundi: Rückschlag für die Demokratie. *German Institute of Global and Area Studies, Leibniz-Institut für Globale und Regionale Studien (GIGA) Focus* 6 (2010).
Holzgrefe, J. L., and Robert O. Keohane (2003): *Humanitarian Intervention: Ethical, Legal, and Political Dilemmas*. Cambridge; New York: Cambridge University Press.
Hong, Mark (1995): The Paris Agreement on Cambodia: In Retrospect. *International Peacekeeping* 2, no. 1 (1995): 93-98.
Howell, Jude, and Jeremy Lind (2010): *Civil Society Under Strain: Counter-Terrorism Policy, Civil Society, and Aid Post-9/11*. Sterling, VA: Kumarian Press.
Hufbauer, Gary Clyde (2007): *Economic Sanctions Reconsidered*. 3rd ed. Washington, DC: Peterson Institute for International Economics.
Hughes, Caroline (1996): *UNTAC in Cambodia: The Impact on Human Rights*. Occasional Paper. Singapore: Indochina Programme, Institute of Southeast Asian Studies.
——— (2009): *Dependent Communities: Aid and Politics in Cambodia and East Timor*. Studies on Southeast Asia. Ithaca, N.Y.: Southeast Asia Program Publications, Cornell University.

Human Rights Watch (1997): *The Scars of Death: Children Abducted by the Lord's Resistance Army in Uganda*. London: Human Rights Watch.
Humphrey, Michael (2002): *The Politics of Atrocity and Reconciliation: From Terror to Trauma*. Routledge Studies in Social and Political Thought 34. London; New York: Routledge.
Iklé, Fred Charles (1991): *Every War Must End*. Rev. ed. New York: Columbia University Press.
Internal Displacement Monitoring Centre, and Norwegian Refugee Council (2009a): Peace, Recovery and Development: Challenges in Northern Uganda. *Internal Displacement Monitoring Centre (IDMC) and the Norwegian Refugee Council (NRC)* February 2009 (2009a).
────── (2009b): *Uganda: Returns Outpace Recovery Planning*. Geneva: Internal Displacement Monitoring Centre (IDMC) and Norwegian Refugee Council (NRC).
International Crisis Group (1998a): Burundi's Peace Process: The Road from Arusha. *International Crisis Group: Report* 2, no. 20 July 1998 (1998a).
────── (1998b): Burundi under Siege: Lift the Sanctions; Re-Launch the Peace Process. *International Crisis Group: Report* 1, no. 27 April 1998 (1998b).
────── (1999a): Burundi: Internal and Regional Implications of the Suspension of Sanctions. *International Crisis Group: Report* 3, no. 4 May 1999 (1999a).
────── (1999b): Burundi: Proposals for the Resumption of Bilateral and Multilateral Co-operation. *International Crisis Group: Report* 4, no. 4 May 1999 (1999b).
────── (2000a): Burundi: Neither War nor Peace. *International Crisis Group Africa Report* 25, no. 1 December 2000 (2000a).
────── (2000b): Burundi: The Issues at Stake. Political Parties, Freedom of the Press and Political Prisoners. *International Crisis Group Africa Report* 23, no. 12 July 2000 (2000b).
────── (2000c): The Mandela Effect: Prospects for Peace in Burundi. *International Crisis Group Central Africa Report* 13, no. 18 April 2000 (2000c).
────── (2001): Burundi: Breaking the Deadlock: The Urgent Need for a New Negotiating Framework. *International Crisis Group Africa Report* 29, no. 14 May 2001 (2001).
────── (2002a): Burundi after Six Months of Transition: Continuing the War or Winning Peace? *International Crisis Group Africa Report* 46, no. 24 May 2002 (2002a).
────── (2002b): The Burundi Rebellion and the Ceasefire Negotiations. *International Crisis Group Africa Briefing* 6 August 2002 (2002b).
────── (2003): A Framework for Responsible Aid to Burundi. *International Crisis Group Africa Report* 57, no. 21 February 2003 (2003).
────── (2004a): Africa Briefing #77: Northern Uganda: Understanding and Solving the Conflict. *International Crisis Group* April (2004a).
────── (2004b): End of Transition in Burundi: The Home Stretch. *International Crisis Group Africa Report* 81, no. 5 July 2004 (2004b).
────── (2004c): *Northern Uganda: Understanding and Solving the Conflict*. Africa Report n°77 - 14 April 2004. Nairobi: International Crisis Group.
────── (2005a): Africa Briefing #22: Peace in Northern Uganda: Decisive Weeks Ahean. *International Crisis Group* 21 February 2005 (2005a).
────── (2005b): Africa Briefing #23: Shock Therapy for Northern Uganda's Peace Process. *International Crisis Group* 11 April 2005 (2005b).
────── (2005c): Africa Briefing #27: Building a Comprehensive Peace Strategy for Northern Uganda. *International Crisis Group* (2005c).
────── (2006): Africa Briefing #41: Peace in Northern Uganda? *International Crisis Group* 13 September 2006 (2006).
────── (2007a): Africa Briefing #46: Northern Uganda Peace Process: The Need to Maintain Momentum. *International Crisis Group* Kampala, no. 14 September 2007 (2007a).
────── (2007b): Burundi: Finalising Peace with the FNL. *International Crisis Group Africa Report* 131, no. 28 August 2007 (2007b).

―――― (2007c): *Northern Uganda: Seizing the Opportunity for Peace.* Africa Report n°124 - 26 April 2007: International Crisis Group.

―――― (2008): *Northern Uganda: The Road to Peace, with or without Kony.* Africa Report n°146 - 10 December 2008: International Crisis Group.

International Development Department (IDD), University of Birmingham. (2006): *Evaluation of General Budget Support: Synthesis Report.* A Joint Evaluation of General Budget Support 1994-2004. Birmingham: International Development Department (IDD), School of Public Policy, University of Birmingham.

Issaka, Mashood, and Batabiha Bushoki (2005): Civil Society and Democratic Transitions in the DRC, Burundi and Rwanda. *International Peace Academy* April 2005 (2005).

Jackson, Richard (2000): Dangers of Regionalizing International Conflict Management: The African Experience. *Political Science* 52, no. 1 (2000): 41-60.

Jackson, Stephen (2006): The United Nations Operation in Burundi (ONUB) - Political and Strategic Lessons Learned. *Conflict Prevention and Peace Forum, New York, Independent External Study, United Nations Peacekeeping* July 2006 (2006).

Jagielski, Wojciech (2010): *Wanderer der Nacht. Eine literarische Reportage.* Berlin: Transit Verlag.

Kapoor, Kapil (1995): *Restructuring Uganda's Debt: The Commercial Debt Buy-Back Operation.* Policy Research Working Paper. Washington, DC: World Bank.

Kappel, Robert (1999): *Afrikas Wirtschaftsperspektiven: Strukturen, Reformen und Tendenzen.* Hamburger Beiträge zur Afrika-Kunde. Hamburg: Institut für Afrika-Kunde.

Kasozi, A. B. K., Nakanyike Musisi, and James Mukooza Sejjengo (1994): *The Social Origins of Violence in Uganda, 1964-1985.* Montreal; London: McGill-Queen's University Press.

Kern, Alexander (2009): *Economic Sanctions: Law and Public Policy.* Basingstoke: Palgrave Macmillan.

Khadiagala, Gilbert M. (2007): *Meddlers or Mediators? African Interveners in Civil Conflicts in Eastern Africa.* International negotiation series. Leiden; Boston: Martinus Nijhoff.

Khadiagala, Gilbert M., and International Peace Academy (2006): *Security Dynamics in Africa's Great Lakes Region.* Boulder, Colo.: Lynne Rienner Publishers, Inc.

Khadiagala, Gilbert M., and Terrence Lyons (2001): *African Foreign Policies: Power and Process.* SAIS African Studies Library. Boulder, Co.; London: Lynne Rienner Publishers.

Kiernan, Ben, and Caroline Hughes (2007): *Conflict and Change in Cambodia.* London: Routledge.

King, Charles H. (2001): The Benefits of Ethnic War: Understanding Eurasia's Unrecognized States. *World Politics* 53, no. 4 (2001): 524-552.

Kleiboer, Marieke (1994): Ripeness of Conflict: A Fruitful Notion? *Journal of Peace Research, Sage Journals* 31 (1994): 109-116.

―――― (1996): Understanding Success and Failure of International Mediation. *Journal of Conflict Resolution* 40, no. 2 (1996): 360-389.

Klein, Ansgar, and Silke Roth (2007): *NGOs im Spannungsfeld von Krisenprävention und Sicherheitspolitik.* 1. Aufl. ed, Bürgergesellschaft und Demokratie. Wiesbaden: VS Verlag für Sozialwissenschaften.

Klingebiel, Stephan (1999): *Wirkungen der Entwicklungszusammenarbeit in Konfliktsituationen.* Bonn: Deutsches Institut für Entwicklungspolitik / German Development Institute.

―――― (2006): *New Interfaces between Security and Development: Changing Concepts and Approaches.* Studies (Deutsches Institut für Entwicklungspolitik). Bonn: German Development Institute.

―――― (2008): *Donor Contributions to the Strengthening of the African Peace and Security Architecture.* Bonn: German Development Institute.

Klingebiel, Stephan, Bettina Eberle, Susanne Kühn, Jochen Möller, Stefan Nöthen, Katja Roehder, and Axel Ulmer (2000): *Socio-Political Impact of Development Cooperation Measures in*

Tanzania: *Analysing Impacts on Local Tensions and Conflicts*. Bonn: German Development Institute, GDI.
Klingebiel, Stephan, and Katja Roehder (2004): Development-Military Interfaces: New Challenges in Crises and Post-conflict Situations. *German Development Institute, GDI, Reports and Working Papers* 5 (2004).
Krueger, Robert, and Kathleen Tobin Krueger (2007): *From Bloodshed to Hope in Burundi: Our Embassy Years During Genocide*. 1st ed, Focus on American History Series. Austin: University of Texas Press.
Kuperman, Alan J. (2001): *The Limits of Humanitarian Intervention: Genocide in Rwanda*. Washington, D.C.: Brookings Institution Press.
Kurtenbach, Sabine, and Matthias Seifert (2010): *Development Cooperation after War and Violent Conflict - Debates and Challenges*. Duisburg: Institute for Development and Peace, University of Duisburg-Essen (INEF-Report 100/2010).
Kutesa, Pecos (2006): *Uganda's Revolution, 1979-1986: How I saw it*. Kampala, Uganda: Fountain Publishers.
Lange, Maria, and Mick Quinn (2003): *Conflict, Humanitarian Assistance and Peacebuilding: Meeting the Challenges*. London: International Alert.
Leatherman, Janie (1999): *Breaking Cycles of Violence: Conflict Prevention in Intrastate Crises*. West Hartford, CT: Kumarian Press.
Lederach, John Paul (1997): *Building Peace: Sustainable Reconciliation in Divided Societies*. Washington, D.C.: United States Institute of Peace Press.
Leggett, Ian (2001): *Uganda*. Oxford: Oxfam.
Lemarchand, René (1994): *Burundi: Ethnocide as Discourse and Practice*. Washington: Woodrow Wilson Center Press; Cambridge: Cambridge University Press.
Lieberfeld, Daniel (1999a): Conflict "Ripeness" Revisited: The South African and Israeli/Palestinian Cases. *Negotiation Journal* 15, no. 1 (1999a): 63-82.
――― (1999b): *Talking with the Enemy: Negotiation and Threat Perception in South Africa and Israel/Palestine*. Westport, Conn.: Praeger.
Lipsky, Michael (1968): Protest as a Political Resource. *American Political Science Review* 62, no. 4 (1968): 1144-1158.
Loane, Geoff, and Céline Moyroud (2001): *Tracing Unintended Consequences of Humanitarian Assistance: The Case of Sudan: Field Study and Recommendations for the European Community Humanitarian Office*. Edited by Network., SWP-Conflict Prevention. 1. Aufl. ed, Aktuelle Materialien zur internationalen Politik Bd. 60/9. Baden-Baden: Nomos.
Lomo, Zachary, Lucy Hovil, and Refugee Law Project (Uganda) (2004): *Behind the Violence: Causes, Consequences, and the Search for Solutions to the War in Northern Uganda*. Refugee Law Project Working Paper. Kampala: Refugee Law Project.
Lund, Michael S. (1996): *Preventing Violent Conflicts: A Strategy for Preventive Diplomacy*. Washington, D.C.: United States Institute of Peace Press.
Lyons, Gene, and Michael Mastanduno (1995): *Beyond Westphalia? State Sovereignty and International Intervention*. Baltimore; London: Johns Hopkins University Press.
Lyons, Terrence, and Gilbert M. Khadiagala (2008): *Conflict Management and African Politics: Ripeness, Bargaining, and Mediation*. London: Routledge.
Machar, Riek. "Report of the Chief Mediator of the Peace Process Between the Government of the Republic of Uganda and the Lord's Resistance Army, 16 June 2008." Juba: Government of Southern Sudan (GoSS), 2008.
Macrae, Joanna, and Anthony B. Zwi (1994): *War and Hunger: Rethinking International Responses to Complex Emergencies*. London; Atlantic Highlands, N.J.: Zed Books in association with Save the Children Fund (UK).

Mayall, James (1996): *The New Interventionism, 1991-1994: United Nations experience in Cambodia, former Yugoslavia, and Somalia.* LSE monographs in international studies. New York: Cambridge University Press.
McCarthy, John D. (1977): Resource Mobilization and Social Movements. *American Journal of Sociology* 82 (1977): 1212-1241.
Mehler, Andreas (1995): *Burundi vor einem weiteren Genozid? Zum Hintergrund der politischen Krise.* Focus Afrika, IAK-Diskussionsbeiträge. Hamburg: Institut für Afrika-Kunde im Verbund der Stiftung Deutsches Übersee-Institut.
Mehler, Andreas, and Claude Ribaux (2000): *Crisis Prevention and Conflict Management in Technical Cooperation: An Overview of the National and International Debate.* Schriftenreihe der GTZ. Wiesbaden: Deutsche Gesellschaft für Technische Zusammenarbeit, Universum Verlagsanstalt.
Menck, Karl Wolfgang (2005): *Gewaltsame Konflikte in Entwicklungsländern: Ursachen und Maßnahmen zur Vermeidung.* HWWA-Report, 0179-2253. Hamburg: Hamburgisches Welt-Wirtschafts-Archiv (HWWA).
Milliken, Jennifer (2003): *State Failure, Collapse and Reconstruction.* Development and Change Book Series. Malden, MA: Blackwell Pub.
Montville, Joseph V. (1991): *Conflict and Peacemaking in Multiethnic Societies.* Lexington, Mass.: Center for the Study of Foreign Affairs, Lexington Books.
Mooradian, Moorad; Druckman, Daniel (1999): Hurting Stalemate or Mediation? The Conflict over Nagorno-Karabakh, 1990-1995. *Journal of Peace Research, Sage Journals* 36, no. 6 (1999): 18.
Mottiar, Shauna, and Salomé Van Jaarsveld (2009): Mediating Peace in Africa: Securing Conflict Prevention. *The African Centre for the Constructive Resolution of Disputes (ACCORD), Ministry of Foreign Affairs of Finland* March 2009 (2009).
Moyo, Dambisa (2009): *Dead Aid: Why Aid is not Working and How There is Another Way for Africa.* London: Allen Lane.
Mueller, John E. (2004): *The Remnants of War.* Cornell Studies in Security Affairs. Ithaca; London: Cornell University Press.
Muscat, Robert J. (2002): *Investing in Peace: How Development Aid can Prevent or Promote Conflict.* Armonk, N.Y.: M.E. Sharpe.
Museveni, Yoweri, Elizabeth Kanyogonya, and Kevin Shillington (1997): *Sowing the Mustard Seed: The Struggle for Freedom and Democracy in Uganda.* London: Macmillan.
Mutibwa, Phares (1992): *Uganda Since Independence: A Story of Unfulfilled Hopes.* London: Hurst.
Mwaniki, David, and Manasseh Wepundi (2007): The Juba Peace Talks: The Chequered Road to Peace for Northern Uganda. *Global Crisis Solutions, Promoting Rights through Practice and Policy: Situation Report* (2007).
Mwaniki, David, Manasseh Wepundi, and Harriet Morolong (2009): The (Northern) Uganda Peace Process: An Update on Recent Developments. *Institute for Security Studies* 2 February 2009 (2009).
Neuberger, Ralph Benyamin (1986): *National Self-Determination in Postcolonial Africa.* Boulder, Colo.: L. Rienner Publishers.
O'Kane, Eamonn (2006): When Can Conflicts be Resolved? A Critique of Ripeness in Civil Wars. *Civil Wars, Routledge* 8, no. 3&4 (2006): 268-284.
Ohlson, Thomas, Stephen John Stedman, and Robert H. Davies (1994): *The New is Not Yet Born: Conflict Resolution in Southern Africa.* Washington, D.C.: The Brookings Institution.
Omara-Otunnu, Amii (1987): *Politics and the Military in Uganda, 1890-1985.* Basingstoke: Macmillan in association with St. Antony's College, Oxford.
Opitz, Peter-Joachim (1991): *Frieden für Kambodscha? Entwicklungen im Indochina-Konflikt seit 1975.* Frankfurt am Main: Lang.

Organization for Economic Cooperation and Development (2010): World Development Indicators. *Development Assistance Committee of the Organisation for Economic Co-operation and Development, Geographical Distribution of Fianncial Flows to Developing Countries, Development Co-operation Report, and International Development Statistics Database* http://stats.oecd.org/Index.aspx?DatasetCode=ODA_RECIP (2010).

Otim, Patrick William (2009): The Role of the Acholi Religious Leaders Peace Initiative in Uganda's Peacebuilding. *Beyond Intractability* March 2009 (2009).

Ottaway, Marina (2003): Promoting Democracy after Conflict: The Difficult Choices. *International Studies Perspectives* 4, no. 3 (2003): 314-322.

Ould-Abdallah, Ahmedou (2000): *Burundi on the Brink, 1993-95: A UN Special Envoy Reflects on Preventive Diplomacy*. Washington, D.C.: United States Institute of Peace Press.

Paffenholz, Thania (2001): Designing Transformation and Intervention Processes. *Berghof Handbook for Conflict Transformation* (2001).

Paine, S. C. M. (2009): *Nation Building, State Building, and Economic Development: Case Studies and Comparisons*. New York: M.E. Sharpe.

Peck, Connie (1996): *The United Nations as a Dispute Settlement System: Improving Mechanisms for the Prevention and Resolution of Conflict*. Boston, MA: Kluwer Law International.

——— (1998): *Sustainable Peace: The Role of the UN and Regional Organizations in Preventing Conflict*. Lanham; Oxford: Rowman & Littlefield Publishers.

Picciotto, Robert (2006): *Development Effectiveness at the Country Level*. Bonn: German Development Institute.

Power, Samantha (2003): *A Problem from Hell: America and the Age of Genocide*. London: Flamingo.

Prendergast, John, and Center of Concern (1996): *Frontline Diplomacy: Humanitarian Aid and Conflict in Africa*. Boulder, Colo.: L. Rienner.

Prendergast, John, and Julia Spiegel (2008): A New Peace Strategy for Northern Uganda and the LRA. *ENOUGH Strategy Paper* 19, no. May 2008 (2008).

Pruitt, Dean G. (1997): Ripeness Theory and the Oslo Talks. *International Negotiation, Kluwer Law International* 2 (1997): 237-250.

Prunier, Gérard (2009): *From Genocide to Continental War: The 'Congolese' Conflict and the Crisis of Contemporary Africa*. London: Hurst.

Raszelenberg, Patrick, and Peter Schier (1995): *The Cambodia Conflict: Search for a Settlement, 1979-1991: An Analytical Chronology*. Hamburg: Institute of Asian Affairs.

Reimann, Cordula (2004): Assessing the State-of-the-Art in Conflict Transformation. *Berghof Handbook for Conflict Transformation* (2004).

Resolve Uganda (2008): A Strategy for Sustainable Peace in Northern Uganda. *Resolve Uganda Policy Brief* February (2008).

Reychler, Luc, and Thania Paffenholz (2001): *Peacebuilding: A Field Guide*. Boulder; London: Lynne Rienner Publishers.

Reyntjens, Filip (1995): *Burundi: Breaking the Cycle of Violence*. Minority Rights Group International.

——— (2000): *Burundi: Prospects for Peace*. Minority Rights Group International.

——— (2009): *The Great African War: Congo and Regional Geopolitics, 1996-2006*. Cambridge: Cambridge University Press.

Rieff, David (1998): Humanitarian Illusion. *The New Republic* March 16 (1998).

Rittberger, Volker (1990): *International Regimes in East-West Politics*. London: Pinter.

Roberts, Nancy Charlotte (2002): *The Transformative Power of Dialogue*. 1st ed, Research in Public Policy Analysis and Management v. 12. Amsterdam; Boston: JAI.

Ropers, Norbert (1997): Roles and Functions of Third Parties in the Constructive Management of Ethnopolitical Conflicts. *Berghof Occasional Paper* 14 (1997).

Rosenberg, Marshall B. (1999): *Nonviolent Communication: A Language of Compassion.* Del Mar, CA: PuddleDancer Press.
Rubin, Jeffrey Z., Dean G. Pruitt, and Sung Hee Kim (1994): *Social Conflict: Escalation, Stalemate, and Settlement.* 2nd ed, McGraw-Hill Series in Social Psychology. New York: McGraw-Hill.
Sachs, Jeffrey (2005): *The End of Poverty: Economic Possibilities for Our Time.* New York: Penguin Press.
Saferworld (2006): Saferworld Briefing for House of Lords Starred Question on Uganda on 28 February 2006. *Saferworld London* (2006).
——— (2008): Conflict-Sensitive Development - Briefing. *Saferworld London* (2008).
Samarasinghe, S. W. R. de A., and K. M. De Silva (1993): *Peace Accords and Ethnic Conflict.* London: Pinter.
Sambanis, Nicholas (2004): What Is Civil War? Conceptual and Empirical Complexities of an Operational Definition. *Journal of Conflict Resolution* 48, no. 6 (2004): 814-858.
Seitz, Volker (2009): *Afrika wird armregiert oder Wie man Afrika wirklich helfen kann.* München: Deutscher Taschenbuch Verlag GmbH & Co. KG (dtv).
Seybolt, Taylor B., and SIPRI (2007): *Humanitarian Military Intervention: The Conditions for Success and Failure.* Oxford, England; New York: Oxford University Press.
Sisk, Timothy D. (1995): *Democratization in South Africa: The Elusive Social Contract.* Princeton, N.J.: Princeton University Press.
Skaar, Elin, Siri Gloppen, and Astri Suhrke (2005): *Roads to Reconciliation.* Lanham, Md.: Lexington Books.
Skocpol, Theda (1994): *Social Revolutions in the Modern World.* Cambridge [England]; New York: Cambridge University Press.
Smock, David R. (1996): *Humanitarian Assistance and Conflict in Africa.* Peaceworks no. 6. Washington, DC: U.S. Institute of Peace.
Spelten, Annika, Tanja Hausmann, and Miriam Shabafrouz (2006): *State and Non-State Cooperation for Crisis Prevention and Peace-Building Policy.* International Expert Workshop: Working Group on Development and Peace (FriEnt) and Institute for Development and Peace (INEF), Bonn.
Sriram, Chandra Lekha, and Karin Wermester (2003): *From Promise to Practice: Strengthening UN Capacities for the Prevention of Violent Conflict.* Boulder, Colo.: Lynne Rienner; London: Eurospan.
Stedman, Stephen John (1991): *Peacemaking in Civil War: International Mediation in Zimbabwe, 1974-1980.* Boulder: L. Rienner Publishers.
——— (1997): Spoiler Problems in Peace Processes. *International Security* 22, no. 2 (1997): 5-53.
Stedman, Stephen John, Donald Rothchild, and Elizabeth M. Cousens (2002): *Ending Civil Wars: The Implementation of Peace Agreements.* Boulder, Colo.; London: Lynne Rienner.
Stern, Paul C., and Daniel Druckman (2000): *International Conflict Resolution after the Cold War.* Washington, D.C.: National Academy Press.
Stockholm International Peace Research Institute (2009): *Armaments, Disarmament and International Security: SIPRI Yearbook 2009.* Oxford; New York: Stockholm International Peace Research Institute (SIPRI); Oxford University Press.
Stokes, Susan Carol (1995): *Cultures in Conflict: Social Movements and the State in Peru.* Berkeley: University of California Press.
Stott, Noel (2007): *Negotiating in Practice what is Non-Negotiable in Principle: Development Policy and Armed Non-State Actors.* Discussion Paper (Deutsches Institut für Entwicklungspolitik). Bonn: DIE.
Strassner, Renate (1991): *Der Kambodscha-Konflikt von 1986-1990 unter besonderer Berücksichtigung der Rolle Vietnams.* Münster: Lit.

Svensson, Emma (2008): The African Mission in Burundi: Lessons Learned from the African Union's First Peace Operation. *FOI, Swedish Defence Research Agency, Division of Defence Analysis, Stockhol* (2008).
Tarrow, Sidney G. (1998): *Power in Movement: Social Movements and Contentious Politics*. 2nd ed, Cambridge Studies in Comparative Politics. Cambridge [England]; New York: Cambridge University Press.
Tetzlaff, Rainer, and Cord Jakobeit (2005): *Das nachkoloniale Afrika: Politik - Wirtschaft - Gesellschaft*. Lehrbuch - Grundwissen Politik. Wiesbaden: VS Verlag für Sozialwissenschaften.
The Resolve (2010): From Promise to Peace: A Blueprint for President Obama's LRA Strategy. *The Resolve* September 2010 (2010).
Touval, Saadia (1982): *The Peace Brokers: Mediators in the Arab-Israeli Conflict, 1948-1979*. Princeton, N.J.: Princeton University Press.
Umozurike, U.O. (1982): Tanzania's Intervention in Uganda. *Archiv des Völkerrechts* 20 (1982).
UNDPI (1994): *Yearbook of the United Nations 1993*. New York: United Nations.
United Nations (1992): UN Resolution 766 (1992) of 21 July 1992. *United Nations Security Council*, no. S/RES/766 (1992).
——— (1993): UN Resolution 880 (1993) of 4 November 1993. *United Nations Security Council*, no. S/RES/880 (1993).
——— (1994): Report of the Security Council Mission to Burundi on 13 and 14 August 1994. *United Nations Security Council* 9 September 1994, no. S/1994/1039 (1994).
——— (1995a): Report of the Security Council Mission to Burundi on 10 and 11 February 1995. *United Nations Security Council* 28 February 1995, no. S/1995/163 (1995a).
——— (1995b): *The United Nations and Cambodia, 1991-1995*. The United Nations Blue Books Series v. 2. New York, NY: United Nations, Dept. of Public Information.
——— (1996): Report of the Secretary-General on the Situation in Burundi. *United Nations Security Council* S/1996/660, no. 15 August 1996 (1996).
——— (1997): Report of the Secretary-General on the Situation in Burundi. *United Nations Security Council* S/1997/547, no. 17 July 1997 (1997).
——— (1998): *United Nations Consolidated Inter-Agency Appeal for Burundi January - December 1999*. New York and Geneva: United Nations, UN Office for the Coordination of Humanitarian Affairs (OCHA), Complex Emergency Response Branch (CERB).
——— (1999): *United Nations Consolidated Inter-Agency Appeal for Burundi January - December 2000*. New York and Geneva: United Nations, UN Office for the Coordination of Humanitarian Affairs (OCHA), Complex Emergency Response Branch (CERB).
——— (2000a): UN Resolution 1286 (2000). *United Nations Security Council* S/RES/1286 (2000), no. 19 January 2000 (2000a).
——— (2000b): *United Nations Consolidated Inter-Agency Appeal for Burundi January - December 2001*. New York and Geneva: United Nations, UN Office for the Coordination of Humanitarian Affairs (OCHA), Complex Emergency Response Branch (CERB).
——— (2001): *United Nations Consolidated Inter-Agency Appeal for Burundi January - December 2002*. New York and Geneva: United Nations, UN Office for the Coordination of Humanitarian Affairs (OCHA), Complex Emergency Response Branch (CERB).
——— (2002): *United Nations Consolidated Inter-Agency Appeal for Burundi January - December 2003*. New York and Geneva: United Nations, UN Office for the Coordination of Humanitarian Affairs (OCHA), Complex Emergency Response Branch (CERB).
———. "Uganda, no. 3862 Rev.4 May 2003, United Nations." 2003a.
——— (2003b): *United Nations Consolidated Inter-Agency Appeal for Burundi January - December 2003*. New York and Geneva: United Nations, UN Office for the Coordination of Humanitarian Affairs (OCHA), Complex Emergency Response Branch (CERB).
———. "Burundi, no. 3753 Rev. 6 September 2004, United Nations." 2004a.

———. "Kingdom of Cambodia, no. 3860 Rev.4 January 2004, United Nations." 2004b.
——— (2004c): UN Resolution 1545 (2004). *United Nations Security Council* S/RES/1545, no. 21 May 2004 (2004c).
——— (2004d): *United Nations Consolidated Inter-Agency Appeal for Burundi January - December 2005*. New York and Geneva: United Nations, UN Office for the Coordination of Humanitarian Affairs (OCHA), Complex Emergency Response Branch (CERB).
——— (2005a): Special Report of the Secretary-General on the United Nations Operation in Burundi. *United Nations Security Council* S/2005/586, no. 14 September 2005 (2005a).
——— (2005b): *United Nations Consolidated Inter-Agency Appeal for Burundi January - December 2006*. New York and Geneva: United Nations, UN Office for the Coordination of Humanitarian Affairs (OCHA), Complex Emergency Response Branch (CERB).
——— (2006a): 5415th Meeting, Wednesday, 19 April 2006. *United Nations Security Council*, no. S/PV.5415 (2006a).
——— (2006b): 5525th Meeting, Friday, 15 September 2006. *United Nations Security Council*, no. S/PV.5525 (2006b).
——— (2006c): Letter Dated 16 Janauray from the Chargé d'affaires a.i. of the Permanent Mission of Uganda to the United Nations addressed to the President of the Security Council incl. Annex. *United Nations Security Council*, no. S/2006/29 (2006c).
——— (2006d): Report of the Secretary-General Pursuant to Resolutions 1653 (2006) and 1663 (2006) of 29 June 1006. *United Nations Security Council*, no. S/2006/478 (2006d).
——— (2006e): Uganda, 18 April 2006. *United Nations Security Council* Update Report No. 5, 2006 (2006e).
——— (2006f): UN Resolution 1653 (2006) of 27 January 2006. *United Nations Security Council*, no. S/RES/1653 (2006f).
——— (2006g): UN Resolution 1663 (2006) of 24 March 2006. *United Nations Security Council*, no. S/RES/1663 (2006g).
——— (2006h): UN Resolution 1692 (2006). *United Nations Security Council* S/RES/1692, no. June 2006 (2006h).
——— (2006i): UN Resolution 1719 (2006). *United Nations Security Council* S/RES/1719, no. October 2006 (2006i).
——— (2006j): *United Nations Consolidated Inter-Agency Appeal for Burundi January - December 2007*. New York and Geneva: United Nations, UN Office for the Coordination of Humanitarian Affairs (OCHA), Complex Emergency Response Branch (CERB).
Uvin, Peter (1998): *Aiding Violence: The Development Enterprise in Rwanda*. West Hartford: Kumarian Press.
——— (1999): Ethnicity and Power in Burundi and Rwanda: Different Paths to Mass Violence. *Comparative Politics* 31, no. 3 (April) (1999): 253-271.
Van der Kroef, Justus M. (1991): Cambodia in 1990: The Elusive Peace. *Asian Survey* 31, no. 1, January 1991 (1991): Part I.
Van Evera, Stephen (1997): *Guide to Methods for Students of Political Science*. Ithaca, N.Y; London: Cornell University Press.
Vandeginste, Stef (2009): Power-Sharing, Conflict and Transition in Burundi: Twenty Years of Trial and Error. *Africa Spectrum* 44, no. 3 (2009): 63-86.
VENRO (2003): Armutsbekämpfung und Krisenprävention: Wie lässt sich Armutsbekämpfung konfliktsensitiv gestalten? *Verband Entwicklungspolitik Deutscher Nichtregierungsorganisationen e.V.* (2003).
Vincent, R. J. (1974): *Nonintervention and International Order*. Princeton, N.J.: Princeton University Press.

Vüllers, Johannes, and Sandra Destradi (2010): Mehr Engagierte, weniger Engagement? Die wachsende Komplexität internationaler Mediation. *German Institute of Global and Area Studies, Leibniz-Institut für Globale und Regionale Studien (GIGA) Focus* 9 (2010).

Wallensteen, Peter (1998): *Preventing Violent Conflicts: Past Record and Future Challenges.* Uppsala, Sweden: Dept. of Peace and Conflict Research, Uppsala University.

Walter, Barbara F. (1997): The Critical Barrier to Civil War Settlement. *International Organization* 51, no. 3 (1997): 335-364.

——— (1999): Designing Transitions from Civil War: Demobilization, Democratization, and Commitments to Peace. *International Security* 24, no. 1 (1999): 127-155.

Walzer, Michael (1997): *On Toleration.* The Castle Lectures in Ethics, Politics, and Economics. New Haven: Yale University Press.

Wasmuht, Ulrike C. (1992): Friedensforschung als Konfliktforschung. Zur Notwendigkeit einer Rückbesinnung auf den Konflikt als zentrale Kategorie. *AFB-Texte* 1/1992 (1992).

Weber, Max, and Johannes Winckelmann (1976): *Wirtschaft und Gesellschaft: Grundriss der verstehenden Soziologie.* 5., revid. Aufl. ed. Tübingen: Mohr.

Wehr, Paul, and John Paul Lederach (1991): Mediating Conflict in Central America. *Journal of Peace Research, Sage Journals* 28, no. 1 (1991).

Weiss, Thomas George (1995): *The United Nations and Civil Wars.* Emerging Global Issues. Boulder, Colo.: L. Rienner Publishers.

Weller, Christoph (2007): *Zivile Konfliktbearbeitung. Aktuelle Forschungsergebnisse.* Duisburg: Institute for Development and Peace, University of Duisburg-Essen (INEF-Report 85/2007).

Wendt, Alexander (1999): *Social Theory of International Politics.* Cambridge: Cambridge University Press.

Wheeler, Nicholas J. (2000): *Saving Strangers: Humanitarian Intervention in International Society.* Oxford; New York: Oxford University Press.

Wilkenfeld, Jonathan, Kathleen J. Young, David M. Quinn, and Victor Asal (2005): *Mediating International Crises.* Routledge Advances in International Relations and Global Politics. London; New York: Routledge.

World Bank (2006): World Bank Press Release No: 2006/047/PREM. *World Bank* (2006).

——— (2010): *World Development Report: Development and Climate Change.* Washington D.C.: The International Bank for Reconstruction and Development/The World Bank.

Wulf, Herbert, and Sebastian Esser (2000): *Disarmament and Conflict Prevention in Development Cooperation: Proceedings of an International Conference, 30-31 August 1999.* Edited by Conversion, Bonn International Center for, Report / Bonn International Center for Conversion. Bonn: Bonn International Center for Conversion.

Zartman, I. William (1978): *The Negotiation Process: Theories and Applications.* Beverly Hills, Calif.: Sage Publications.

——— (1985): *Ripe for Resolution: Conflict and Intervention in Africa.* New York: Oxford University Press.

——— (1989): *Ripe for Resolution: Conflict and Intervention in Africa.* Edited by Relations, Council on Foreign. Updated ed. New York: Oxford University Press.

——— (1995): *Elusive Peace: Negotiating an End to Civil Wars.* Washington, D.C.: Brookings Institution.

——— (2001a): Preventing Deadly Conflict. *Security Dialogue* 32, no. 2 (2001a): 137-154.

——— (2001b): *Preventive Negotiation: Avoiding Conflict Escalation.* Carnegie Commission on Preventing Deadly Conflict. Lanham, Md.: Rowman & Littlefield Publishers.

——— (2001c): The Timing of Peace Initiatives: Hurting Stalemates and Ripe Moments. *The Global Review of Ethnopolitics* 1, no. 1 (2001c): 8-18.

——— (2007): *Peacemaking in International Conflict: Methods and Techniques.* Rev. ed. Washington, D.C.: United States Institute of Peace.

Zartman, I. William, and Avaro DeSoto (2010): *Timing Mediation Initiatives*. Peacemaker's Toolkit. Washington D.C.: United States Institute of Peace; Conflict Management Program, The Paul H. Nitze School of Advanced International Studies, The Johns Hopkins University.

Zartman, I. William, Guy Faure, and International Institute for Applied Systems Analysis. (2005): *Escalation and negotiation in international conflicts*. Cambridge ; New York: Cambridge University Press.

Zartman, I. William, and J. Lewis Rasmussen (1997): *Peacemaking in International Conflict: Methods & Techniques*. Washington, D.C.: United States Institute of Peace Press.

Newspapers

Cambodian Information Center, Korm, Kong: "Open letter to All Signatory Countries of Paris Peace Agreement on Cambodia", 24 October 2006. http://editorials.cambodia.org/2006/10/open-letter-to-all-signatory-countries.html.

Phnom Penh Post, Thayer, Nate: "An Interview with Khmer Rouge Leader Khieu Samphan", conducted early August 1992, published 27 August 1992.

Der Spiegel, "Kambodscha: Diesmal ums Ganze", 30 July 1990.

Der Spiegel, Terzani, Tiziano: "Der Friede hängt an Sihanouk", 19 August 1991.

Der Spiegel, Terzani, Tiziano: "Straße von Furcht und Tod", 26 October 1992.

Der Spiegel, Terzani, Tiziano: "UNTAC ist der neue Gott", 01 June 1992.

Der Spiegel, "Uganda: Land ohne Hoffnung", Nr. 16/1987.

Der Spiegel, "Uganda: Nach Hause", 2/1994.

Der Spiegel, "Uganda: Aufmarsch an der Grenze", 48/1995.

Der Spiegel, Thielke, Thilo: "Uganda: Gottes grausame Guerilla", 44/2003.

Der Spiegel, "Uganda: Rebellen töten Dorfbewohner mit Äxten und Macheten", 9 December 2003.

Der Spiegel, "Massaker in Uganda: Rebellen töten 190 Flüchtlinge", 22 February 2004.

Der Spiegel, "Uganda: Regierung und Rebellen unterzeichnen Waffenstillstandsabkommen", 26 August 2006.

Der Spiegel, "Uganda: Schlappe für den Autokraten", 6/2006.

The Guardian, http://www.guardian.co.uk/world/2004/oct/22/2.

Irin News, "Uganda: LRA Rebels Should Just Surrender", 27 January 2005.

Newsweek, Manegold, C.S.: "Baker's About-Face On Cambodia - A Turn Toward Hanoi", 30 July 1990. www.newsweek.com/id/127906.

Newsweek, Moreau, Ron: "Roughing Up The Khmer Rouge - For Now, The Cambodian Killers Are Forced To Flee", 09 December 1991. www.newsweek.com/id/123886.

The New Vision, Olupot, Milton: "LRA Talks", 28 October 2007.

New York Times, Kissinger, Henry: 12 October 1974.

The New York Times, "Cambodian Factions Agree to Halt Arms Imports", 25 June 1991.

The New York Times, "Cambodians to Free 290 Political Prisoners", 15 January 1992.

The New York Times, Erlanger, Steven: "Favored Cambodians Lose U.S. Aid", 10 April 1981.

The New York Times, "Khmer Rouge Staying Away From High Council Meeting", 9 December 1992.

The New York Times, Prial, Frank J.: "Five U.N. Powers Announce Accord on Cambodia War", 29 August 1990.

The New York Times, Prial, Frank: "Khmer Rouge Should Not Delay Cambodia Vote, U.N. Says", 18 November 1992.

The New York Times, Sanger, David: "880 Million Pledged to Cambodia But Khmer Rouge Pose a Threat", 23 June 1992.

The New York Times, Sanger, David: "Factions Meeting in Phnom Penh Appeal to U.N. for Peacekeepers", 31 December 1991.

The New York Times, Sanger, David: "Pol Pot Colleague Back in Cambodia", 30 December 1991.

The New York Times, Shenon, Philip: "A Khmer Rouge Suffers Beating By Cambodians", 28 November 1991.
The New York Times, Shenon, Philip: "Cambodia Factions Call Truce on Eve of New Talks", 24 June 1991.
The New York Times, Shenon, Philip: "Cambodians Ask U.N. to Abandon Its Peace Plan", 4 November 1992.
The New York Times, Shenon, Philip: "Cambodians See the Return of Prince Sihanouk as the Best Hope for Peace", 13 November 1991.
The New York Times, Shenon, Philip: "Khmer Rouge Planning to Stick to Peace Plan", 29 November 1991.
The New York Times, "Sighted in Cambodia: Peace", 28 August 1991.
Phnom Penh Post, Burslem, Chris: "Donors Set to Meet Over Release of Aid", 16 July 1993.
Phnom Penh Post, Burslem, Chris: "UNTAC Bubble Economy Set to Burst", 07 May 1993.
Phnom Penh Post, Davies, Robin: "Donors' Cart Must Follow the Cambodian Horse", 27 August 1993.
Phnom Penh Post, "Hun Sen Predicts Landslide Victory", 07 May 1993.
Phnom Penh Post, *Phnom Penh Post*, Thayer, Nate: "Historical Ties Underpin French Aid", 26 February 1993.
Phnom Penh Post, "Sihanouk Slams Political Violence", 15 January 1993.
Phnom Penh Post, Thayer, Nate: "Khmer Rouge: Will They be Back?", 23 April 1993.
Phnom Penh Post, Thayer, Nate: "KR Blueprint for the Future Includes Electoral Strategy", 27 August 1992.
Phnom Penh Post, Thayer, Nate: "KR Blueprint for the Future Includes Electoral Strategy", 27 August 1992.
Phnom Penh Post, Thayer, Nate: "New Govt: Who's Really in Control?", 19 November 1993.
Sudan Tribune, "Diplomats Prepare for More Ugandan Peace Talks", 18 April 2008.
The Economist, "Burundi's Election. Pretty Squalid: East Africa's Weakest New Component", 22 July 2010.
The Economist, Burundi and Rwanda.
The Wall Street Journal, Kuperman, Alan J.: Rambouillet Requiem: Why the Talks Failed.

Interviews

Personal Interview with Andrew Bennett on 05 May 2009 in Washington D.C.
Personal Interview by Email with Betty Bigombe, 01 December 2005.
Personal Interview with Kirsten Garacochea on 20 July 2010 in Berlin, Germany.
Personal Interview by Email with Natalie Hoffmann, HIIK, 14 September 2010.
Personal Interview with Samuele Tognetti (Administrator of St. Mary's Lacor Hospital) in August 2005 in Gulu Town, Uganda.
Personal Interview with I. William Zartman on 07 May 2009 in Washington, D.C.
Personal Interview with I. William Zartman on 18 June 2009 in Munich, Germany.

Webpages

http://www.sozialwiss.uni-hamburg.de/publish/Ipw/Akuf/kriege/132_kambodscha.htm.
http://www.sozialwiss.uni-hamburg.de/publish/Ipw/Akuf/kriege_aktuell.htm#Def.
http://www.c-r.org/our-work/accord/northern-uganda/documents/2000_Jan_The_Amnesty_Act.doc.
http://www.avert.org/aids-uganda.htm.
http://news.bbc.co.uk/1/hi/world/africa/country_profiles/1068873.stm.
http://www.bmz.de/de/was_wir_machen/laender_regionen/subsahara/uganda/index.html.
https://www.cia.gov/library/publications/the-world-factbook.

https://www.cia.gov/library/publications/the-worldfactbook/rankorder/2034rank.html?countryName=
    Burundi&countryCode=by&regionCode=af&rank=11#by.
http://www.cambodia.org/facts/Paris_Peace_Agreement_10231991.php.
http://www.oecd.org/glossary/0,2586,en_2649_33721_1965693_1_1_1_1,00.html.
http://www.akuf.de.
http://www.correlatesofwar.org.
http://hiik.de/en/kosimo/index.html.
http://www.icc-cpi.int.
http://www.internal-displacement.org.
http://irinnews.org/InDepthMain.aspx?InDepthId=58&ReportId=72472.
http://www.irinnews.org/print.asp?ReportIT=47568.
http://www.irinnews.org/S_report.asp?ReportID=47569.
http://www.povertyactionlab.org.
http://www.un.org/News/Press/docs/2006/afr1439.doc.htm.
http://www.finance.go.ug.
http://www.un.org/en/peacekeeping/missions/past/onub/index.html.
http://pantheon.yale.edu/~ns237/index/research.html#.
http://www.prio.no/CSCW/Datasets/Armed-Conflict.
http://www.statehouse.go.ug.
http://www.un.org/ecosocdev/geninfo/afrec/vol14no2/uganda.htm.
http://www.un.org/ecosocdev/geninfo/afrec/vol14no4/htm/uganda_box.htm.
http://www.un.org/en/peacekeeping/missions/past/unamicfacts.html.
http://www.un.org/en/peacekeeping/missions/past/unamicbackgr.html.
http://www.undp.org.ug/hivaids.htm.
http://www.un.org/Depts/DPKO/Missions/untac.htm.
http://www.un.org/en/peacekeeping/missions/past/untacbackgr2.html.
http://www.usaid.gov/kh/history_usaid_cambodia.htm.
http://web.worldbank.org/WBSITE/EXTERNAL/COUNTRIES/AFRICAEXT/UGANDAEXTN/0,,
    menuPK:374947~pagePK:141132~piPK:141107~theSitePK:374864,00.html.

VS Forschung | VS Research
Neu im Programm Politik

Michaela Allgeier (Hrsg.)
Solidarität, Flexibilität, Selbsthilfe
Zur Modernität der Genossenschaftsidee
2011. 138 S. Br. EUR 39,95
ISBN 978-3-531-17598-0

Susanne von Hehl
Bildung, Betreuung und Erziehung als neue Aufgabe der Politik
Steuerungsaktivitäten in drei Bundesländern
2011. 406 S. (Familie und Familienwissenschaft) Br. EUR 49,95
ISBN 978-3-531-17850-9

Isabel Kneisler
Das italienische Parteiensystem im Wandel
2011. 289 S. Br. EUR 39,95
ISBN 978-3-531-17991-9

Frank Meerkamp
Die Quorenfrage im Volksgesetzgebungsverfahren
Bedeutung und Entwicklung
2011. 596 S. (Bürgergesellschaft und Demokratie Bd. 36) Br. EUR 39,95
ISBN 978-3-531-18064-9

Martin Schröder
Die Macht moralischer Argumente
Produktionsverlagerungen zwischen wirtschaftlichen Interessen und gesellschaftlicher Verantwortung
2011. 237 S. (Bürgergesellschaft und Demokratie Bd. 35) Br. EUR 39,95
ISBN 978-3-531-18058-8

Lilian Schwalb
Kreative Governance?
Public Private Partnerships in der lokalpolitischen Steuerung
2011. 301 S. (Bürgergesellschaft und Demokratie Bd. 37) Br. EUR 39,95
ISBN 978-3-531-18151-6

Kurt Beck / Jan Ziekow (Hrsg.)
Mehr Bürgerbeteiligung wagen
Wege zur Vitalisierung der Demokratie
2011. 214 S. Br. EUR 29,95
ISBN 978-3-531-17861-5

Erhältlich im Buchhandel oder beim Verlag.
Änderungen vorbehalten. Stand: Juli 2011.

www.vs-verlag.de

Abraham-Lincoln-Straße 46
65189 Wiesbaden
tel +49 (0)6221.345 - 4301
fax +49 (0)6221.345 - 4229